The Feminist Companion to the Bible

10

Editor
Athalya Brenner

Sheffield Academic Press

a Feminist Companion to

the Hebrew Bible
in the
New Testament

edited by Athalya Brenner

Copyright © 1996 Sheffield Academic Press

Published by Sheffield Academic Press Ltd
Mansion House
19 Kingfield Road
Sheffield, S11 9AS
England

Printed on acid-free paper in Great Britain
by The Cromwell Press
Melksham, Wiltshire

British Library Cataloguing in Publication Data

A catalogue record for this book is available
from the British Library

ISBN 1-85075-754-2

To the memory of

Fokkelien van Dijk-Hemmes

ת.נ.צ.ב.ה.

CONTENTS

Part IV
ANTI-JUDAISM IN THE NEW TESTAMENT AND ITS
FEMINIST INTERPRETATIONS?

ABBREVIATIONS

AB	Anchor Bible
ABD	D.N. Freedman (ed.), *Anchor Bible Dictionary*
ANET	J.B. Pritchard (ed.), *Ancient Near Eastern Texts*
Bib	*Biblica*
BJRL	*Bulletin of the John Rylands University Library of Manchester*
BJS	Brown Judaic Studies
BK	*Bibel und Kirche*
BR	*Biblical Research*
BSac	*Bibliotheca Sacra*
BTB	*Biblical Theology Bulletin*
CAD	*The Assyrian Dictionary of the Oriental Institute of the University of Chicago*
CBQ	*Catholic Biblical Quarterly*
CRINT	Compendia rerum iudaicarum ad Novum Testamentum
CurTM	*Currents in Theology and Mission*
EBib	Etudes bibliques
EKKNT	Evangelisch-Katholischer Kommentar zum Neuen Testament
EncJud	*Encyclopaedia Judaica*
EvT	*Evangelische Theologie*
ExpTim	*Expository Times*
FRLANT	Forschungen zur Religion und Literatur des Alten und Neuen Testaments
GCS	Griechische christliche Schriftsteller
HBT	*Horizons in Biblical Theology*
HNT	Handbuch zum Neuen Testament
HTR	*Harvard Theological Review*
ICC	International Critical Commentary
IDB	G.A. Buttrick (ed.), *Interpreter's Dictionary of the Bible*
Int	*Interpretation*
JAAR	*Journal of the American Academy of Religion*
JBL	*Journal of Biblical Literature*
JFSR	*Journal of Feminist Studies in Religion*
JSNT	*Journal for the Study of the New Testament*
JSNTSup	*Journal for the Study of the New Testament, Supplement Series*

JSOTSup	*Journal for the Study of the Old Testament,* Supplement Series
JTS	*Journal of Theological Studies*
LCL	Loeb Classical Library
LD	Lectio divina
Neot	*Neotestamentica*
NICNT	New International Commentary on the New Testament
NovT	*Novum Testamentum*
NTD	Das Neue Testament Deutsch
NTS	*New Testament Studies*
NTTS	New Testament Tools and Studies
OTL	Old Testament Library
PG	J. Migne (ed.), *Patrologia graeca*
PW	Pauly–Wissowa, *Real-Encyclopädie der classischen Altertumswissenschaft*
PWSup	Supplement to PW
RevExp	*Review and Expositor*
SB	Sources bibliques
SBLMS	SBL Monograph Series
SBLSP	SBL Seminar Papers
SBT	Studies in Biblical Theology
SC	Sources chrétiennes
SNTSMS	Society for New Testament Studies Monograph Series
SPAW	Sitzungsberichte der preussischen Akademie der Wissenschaften
TDNT	G. Kittel and G. Friedrich (eds.), *Theological Dictionary of the New Testament*
THKNT	Theologischer Handkommentar zum Neuen Testament
TS	*Theological Studies*
TU	Texte und Untersuchungen
TWNT	G. Kittel and G. Friedrich (eds.), *Theologisches Wörterbuch zum Neuen Testament*
VT	*Vetus Testamentum*
WW	*Word and World*
ZAW	*Zeitschrift für die alttestamentliche Wissenschaft*
ZNW	*Zeitschrift für die neutestamentliche Wissenschaft*
ZTK	*Zeitschrift für Theologie und Kirche*
ZWT	*Zeitschrift für wissenschaftliche Theologie*

A Personal Note

This is the tenth volume of the Feminist Companion to the Bible: a good opportunity for me to thank at least some of the people who have been involved in this project. First, of course, come the contributors to all the volumes, especially those who consented to participate in more than one. David Clines and Philip Davies of Sheffield Academic Press have supported the project throughout. The patient editors of the Press, especially Helen Tookey, made it materialize.

I have met many people through working on the series, and learnt much from their helpful comments. Some became friends whose valuable advice accompanied my editorial efforts and, without any doubt, continue to enrich my life. I would particularly like to thank these friends and colleagues: Alice Bach, Margaret Barker, Adrien Bledstein, Carole Fontaine, Lillian Klein, Amy-Jill Levine and Carol Meyers.

Some of the volumes were edited in Israel; others while I was working in The Netherlands. I am grateful to the Faculty and administration staff at the Universities of Utrecht, Nijmegen and Amsterdam for help extended to me.

Athalya Brenner
Amsterdam, March 1995.

INTRODUCTION

Athalya Brenner

The programme of this volume is to make a contribution to the understanding of the relationship between the Hebrew Bible and the New Testament, and between Judaism and Christianity, from the perspectives of the gender relations reflected in both groups of texts and their interpretations. The results of the analyses provided illustrate that there is a strong link between sexist and anti-Semitic/Judaic ideologies. The struggle with the former is therefore inseparably related to and bound up with the latter. Four clusters of issues are addressed: the recycling of Hebrew Bible characters in the New Testament; the utilization of Hebrew Bible models of femininity for the portrayal of New Testament female characters; the gendering of the female body in the New Testament and its links to Hebrew Bible representations; and the potential anti-Judaism in the New Testament and its feminist interpretations. As in other volumes of the Feminist Companion series, the following collection is just a sample of feminist-critical materials now available.

This collection is, to a large extent, addressed to the New Testament afterlife or—if we wish—consecutive life of Hebrew Bible literary items that are affiliated with femaleness, femininity and gender relations. The perspectives which inform the discussions are various feminist perspectives: this the authors of the articles collected here have in common. But the authors differ in their coincidental membership of other social and religious groups: some are Jewish, others Christian; some are females, others males. Multiple group membership informs the reader's location in time and space and concurrent ideological commitments; hence this multiple membership is a determinant that generates, even engenders, interpretation and meaning—

in reading the Hebrew Bible as well as the New Testament and their interpretations.

The Feminist Companion series has focused on the Hebrew Bible. In so far as non-Hebrew texts were discussed,[1] the discussion centred on the Hebrew text. In accordance with this specified tendency, in this volume too the Hebrew text is considered the primary text and the New Testament text an interpretation. This by no means constitutes a value judgment: it reflects historical sequentiality. And, although the translations of the Hebrew Bible, especially the LXX, have had a crucial mediating function for the New Testament, that fact is hardly reflected in this volume because of its necessarily limited scope.

Part I: Hebrew Bible Characters Recycled: Some Principles

Hebrew Bible characters have, so to speak, an infinitely long afterlife beyond their original location in the biblical text. 'Their' stories are retold again and again, through various lenses and—as far as we can judge—for various purposes; they also serve as prooftexts for creating and narrating new characters. The same holds for numerous Hebrew Bible motifs, models, paradigms and configurations.

This process of amplification, augmentation, elaboration and re-creation is evident already within the Hebrew Bible. For instance, the three wife/sister narratives (Gen. 12.10–13.2; 20; 26.1, 6-11) and the two stories about women called Tamar (Gen. 38; 2 Sam. 13.1-22) may be *read* as internal biblical midrash; it is even conceivable that they were initially *written* as such.[2] The book of Deuteronomy is certainly an ideological re-write, a re-presentation of 'history' and characters from a time/space location different to that of other parts of the Pentateuch. Other Hebrew Bible examples can easily be adduced.[3] Postbiblical

---

1.   Such as the Greek versions of Esther, Judith and Susanna. Cf. vol. 7 of this series: A. Brenner (ed.), *A Feminist Companion to Esther, Judith and Susanna* (Sheffield: Sheffield Academic Press, 1995).

2.   I shall not discuss the question of which is the primary text and which is/are the derivatives in each of the instances cited. A quick glance at commentaries will show that the answers vary.

3.   Cf. the material on Jacob in Hos. 12, which differs at points from

Jewish literature of course continues the practices of Torah updating and adaptation to changing needs and circumstances. These updates are perforce tendentious: the ideologies that underscore them have to be uncovered. Paradoxically, such practices moor the primary traditions in a spatio-temporal framework while, coincidentally, giving them a continuous quality of timelessness.

The existence of ideological re-tellings and new utilization of models in the New Testament is thus neither surprising nor extraordinary. However, it remains to be seen whether a phenomenology or phenomenologies of re-telling can be defined here as well and anchored in chronological and cultural contexts, especially since the re-tellings have had a continuing prominence in Western culture—that is, have been converted into timelessness.

In her two articles, '"Only a Remnant of them Shall Be Saved": Women from the Hebrew Bible in New Testament Narratives' and '"Old Wine in New Wineskins": The Refashioning of Male Hebrew Bible Characters in New Testament Texts', Heather McKay sketches some of the principles that underscore the transformations Hebrew Bible characters undergo in the New Testament. Surveying the list of Hebrew Bible female and male figures who reappear in the New Testament, McKay demonstrates how the recycled figures are used as a rhetorical device, since the audience's knowledge of the 'original' characters is to be assumed. Female and male Hebrew Bible characters undergo different (mis)handlings in the New Testament. Women characters are demeaned by truncated accounts of their words, thoughts and deeds; they lose powerful character traits and are used by New Testament writers as scenery, props or rhetorical decoration. Male figures become objectified by their use as donors of character traits to Jesus or other New Testament figures, or are transformed into negative role models. They are used as raw materials for instruction, reformation or rejection. McKay concludes that any description

Jacob/Israel traditions in Gen. 25–35, be the presumed source origins of the latter as they may. Again, whether the texts may simply be *read* as comments on each other, or were deliberately *composed* as such is a moot point.

or use of such New Testament texts for commentary or preaching which does not incorporate a critique of the techniques deployed for the literary abuse of women or men (especially young men), is complicit in perpetuating discriminatory ideas. Such ideas are both 'present' in the New Testament texts and have been supported by a long tradition of New Testament reception history.

McKay emphasizes that Hebrew Bible male figures are utilized for religious propaganda. Thus, although the literary shifts are motivated by ideology in both gender categories, the ideology is different in each case. The literary treatment accorded to Hebrew Bible female figures is primarily and perceptibly motivated by gender ideology, even more so (according to McKay) than in the Hebrew Bible itself; whereas the treatment meted out to male characters is informed primarily by religious ideology. The two ideologies of supremacy —New Testament/Christianity over Hebrew Bible/Judaism, masculinity over femininity—are seen as parallel. This claim has important implications and will re-surface in most of the essays.

To move from the general to the particular, Mark Bredin discusses in his 'Gentiles and the Davidic Tradition in Matthew' some hows and whys for the incorporation of female figures into Jesus' genealogy. Bredin places the Matthean community in 'Palestine' of the first century CE, from where it was forced to flee to Syria following political events. He argues that the inclusion of the four female figures—Tamar, Rahab, Ruth and 'the wife of Uriah'—as well as the designation of Jesus as 'son of Abraham' and the story of the Canaanite women, are the result of the ensuing debate within the community. The issue implicitly addressed is the debate against or for a mission to the Gentiles: 'The mention of the three women would recall righteous Gentiles, and more specifically the mention of Uriah would recall his righteousness against David's wickedness'. This, together with recalling Elijah's healing of the Sidonite woman's son and the promise to Abraham, links the David and Abraham traditions in a favourable attitude towards Gentiles. It would therefore appear, from Bredin's analysis, that the recycling of the Hebrew Bible characters—be they female or male—has little in common with their Hebrew Bible setting; it is directed by a well-defined, specific ideology.

In his essay, 'Sarah's Seminal Emission: Hebrews 11.11 in the Light of Ancient Embryology', Pieter van der Horst examines a rather peculiar text. Can Sarah, Abraham's wife, have 'seed'—like males? This verse constitutes a departure from Hebrew Bible traditions about Sarah to which it is related. Most translations and commentaries offer solutions that sidestep the problem, proceeding from the assumption that Sarah could not have discharged semen. Van der Horst conducts us through a review of ancient Near Eastern, Greek, Hellenistic and early Christian theories of genetics and hereditary traits, from 500 BCE to 500 CE. He shows that 'many philosophers, physicians, poets, and others held that the contributions of men and women to the formation of a fetus were strictly equal'. A short discussion of rabbinic literature and exegeses of certain Hebrew Bible passages shows that the rabbis were familiar (through Greek influence) with a dual-gender seed theory, making it plausible for the author of Hebrews to be acquainted with it as well. The abundant information on the genetic responsibility of both parents is enlightening: it is gratifying that not all the ancients believed that a father provided the sole genetic pool for his children. This might prove a consolation for feminists, with significant implications. If van der Horst's conclusions are accepted then, in this instance at least, the Hebrew Bible's Sarah acquires a new dimension in the New Testament.

Part II: Women and the Feminine: New Testament Women Characters

Even if we do not agree with McKay's conclusions to her survey studies, her presentations clearly illustrate that Hebrew Bible figures indeed undergo radical changes in character and meaning when they are re-utilized in New Testament texts. What happens to Hebrew Bible models when applied anew in the New Testament? The next six articles are case studies of narratives about particular New Testament women and New Testament concepts of the feminine which, at times, draw on Hebrew Bible portrayals and configurations.

In 'Mary's Call', Bea Wyler applies the Hebrew Bible

paradigm of a leader/prophet's call to office[1] first to Hebrew
Bible women and then to Mary. The fully developed structure,
as apparent in Gideon's case (Judg. 6), has six features: divine
confrontation, introductory phrase, commission, objection,
reassurance and sign. The pattern is applicable to narratives
about Abraham, Isaiah, Ezekiel and other prophets but also to
women, like Sarah (Gen. 18) and Samson's mother (Judg. 13).
Having established how women too can be 'called', by recourse
to the pattern, Wyler now turns to an analysis of the annunciation to Mary in Lk. 1.26-38. The pattern in Mary's case is
complete: all six features are present; however, the call is
imparted not to the future leader Jesus but to his mother! This
adoption of a Hebrew Bible pattern as a New Testament configuration raises questions concerning the provenance of the New
Testament text, authorial intention, ideo-social background,
knowledge of biblical and rabbinic sources and, especially, the
status of women in the author's place and time. It also shows
that even though the call pattern is similar in the cases of men
and women, its gender application differs—in the Hebrew Bible
as well as in the New Testament.

Jane Schaberg reads the New Testament infancy narratives in
Luke and Matthew as a suspicious, resisting womanly reader.
She therefore suggests, in her article 'The Foremothers and the
Mother of Jesus', that those narratives were originally about an
illegitimate conception which, already in pre-Gospel stage,
acquired a theological significance and became connected with
divine power. The concept of an illegitimate messiah is,
potentially, both liberating and dangerous: its presentations in
the two gospels were subsequently obscured by androcentric
interpretations. Illegitimacy was forgotten and supplanted by
virginal conception. Reading Matthew 1 in terms of illegitimate
conception explains four important features: the inclusion of
four Hebrew Bible female characters in Jesus' genealogy,[2] the
marital and legal situation of young women at the time and
place narrated, the role of the holy spirit, and the allusion to

---

1. After N. Habel, 'The Form and Significance of the Call
Narratives', *ZAW* 77 (1965), pp. 297-323.
2. Cf. Mark Bredin's article, 'Gentiles and the Davidic Tradition in
Matthew'.

Isa. 7.14. In Schaberg's interpretation, in the Lukan version Mary symbolizes the liberation of the oppressed; the Matthean version, however, is androcentric and fails to confront the causes for oppression. But, Schaberg continues, 'By linking her [Mary's] story, however, with those of the four women listed in the genealogy, Matthew implies that salvation history is not essentially a male enterprise'.

Schaberg emphasizes the immportance of her own readerly location for her interpretation. And the next article, Arie Troost's 'Elisabeth and Mary—Naomi and Ruth: Gender-Response Criticism in Luke 1–2', takes this issue further while, at a certain point, offering a reading of Schaberg's reading. Neither texts nor authors and readers are gender-neutral. In traditional interpretations of Luke 1–2 Elisabeth and Mary are configured as unequal mothers of exceptional but unequal sons. Troost finds that, narratologically, there obtains a reciprocity rather than an opposition between the two figures. A discussion of what 'gender-response' criticism implies is followed by examples of three (female) reader-located interpretations by Fuchs, Gilman and Schaberg; and two author-oriented interpretations by Resch and Harnack, German (male) scholars from the beginning of this century. Finally, Troost reads the New Testament story about Elisabeth and Mary together with the Hebrew Bible model, or parallel, of Naomi and Ruth. A paradigm of cooperation between women and its potential for social change is clearly present in both texts. Whether that is helpful for uncovering women's voices in the Lukan text or, for that matter, in the Hebrew Bible Ruth scroll remains motivated by the reader's location in the ideological communities she or he inhabits.

In 'From Narrative to History: The Resurrection of Mary and Martha', Adele Reinhartz attempts to flesh out the two sister-characters from the three passages in which they feature (Lk. 10.38-42; Jn 11.1-44; 12.1-7). Clearly, the writers were not interested in the women characters for their own sake but, rather, used them to enhance Jesus' significance. Even if 'they' are not historical they suggest that, historically, women did function as disciples in the time of Jesus and early Christianity. The re-reading of the relevant passages results in multiple images that 'are due primarily to the varying perspectives of the scholars who created them'. Reinhartz then moves to reconstruct a tentative historical image of the sisters' household from the narrative material. In this portrait, the sisters are independent of father or husband, a potential role model of community integration for early-church women. They are able to combine their lives and their faith even if their mode of life is different from the enveloping patriarchy. Tracing the figures of Martha and Mary may, in Reinhartz's view, 'lead to new insights, not only about the history of the early church but also about the narratives—their implied authors, their theological and social agendas, and their literary ploys—from which we try to recreate that history'.

Women characters play prominent roles in John. The possibility of using 'their' stories as role models, and the Hebrew Bible traditions drawn on for their portrayals, are the concerns of Judith Lieu in 'Scripture and the Feminine in John'. The Hebrew Bible feminine Wisdom, or *Sophia*, is transformed in the prologue of John into a masculine *logos*: the focus on Jesus supersedes the earlier feminine image. The meeting with the Samaritan woman (Jn 4) recalls Hebrew Bible images of women as foreigners and 'others', although the foreign woman is allowed a voice here. The figure of Jesus' mother echoes Hebrew Bible themes; but the significance of these themes is not easy to interpret. Birth and rebirth images and women as mediators of divine intervention are much in evidence; Hebrew Bible parallels are again not infrequent. The beginning of Genesis is especially important: in John, a return to the creation is necessary for understanding Jesus, whose status as source of salvation supersedes that of Hebrew Bible patriarchs.[1] The Johannine refashioning of Hebrew Bible themes may be experienced as liberating by feminists. It may also be experienced and interpreted as anti-Hebrew Bible and anti-Judaic.[2] Lieu warns that we should pay heed to the dangers the Johannine text poses for interpreters, especially feminist ones.

Lieu resists a precise reading for the mother-of-Jesus figure, while acknowledging Hebrew Bible references in 'her'

1. Cf. McKay, '"Old Wine in New Wineskins"'.
2. And see below, Part IV.

characterization. Lyn Bechtel, in 'A Symbolic Level of Meaning: John 2.1-11 (The Marriage in Cana)', calls for a metaphoric/ symbolic interpretation of that same figure while, simultaneously, not excluding the explicitly literal/historical in favour of the implicitly symbolic. For Bechtel, interpretation must proceed from historical location: the Johannine community feels like rejected orphans (Jn 14.18) and has to reformulate its identity. The mother figure, vaguely addressed as 'woman', symbolizes Judaism, the 'mother' of the new community. Jesus is presented as breaking away from his matrix, but not totally: at the end, 'she' is at the foot of the cross. Distancing is followed by reaffirmation of the relationship. A see-saw dynamics of recognition and negation of the mother (community) is embodied in Jesus' narrated attitudes. This ambivalence informs the Johannine text; ultimately, a mother—even a seemingly rejected mother—is always a mother.

Part III: On the Gendering of the Female Body

Some views of the female body and female sexuality in the Hebrew Bible are disturbing, to use an understatement. This is especially pronounced in the case of so-called prophetic literature, where the sexual metaphor of the divine/male faithful husband and the human/female faithless wife is used as religious propaganda that betrays negative attitudes with far-reaching ideo-social consequences for Bible-inspired gender relations.[1] Similar disapproval of the (erotic, bodily) feminine is discernible in some New Testament texts. This section contains three articles about the depreciation of corporeal femininity which is sustained by both scriptural sources.

In 'Eve through Several Lenses: Truth in 1 Timothy 2.8-15', Beverly Stratton analyses the damaging potential of the 1 Timothy passage for gender relations in modern Western society in general and for women's physical welfare in particular. The text, including its midrashic claim on Adam and

---

1. A representative cluster of articles related to this issue is to be found in A. Brenner (ed.), *A Feminist Companion to the Latter Prophets* (*The Feminist Companion to the Bible*, 8; Sheffield: Sheffield Academic Press, 1995), pp. 243-352.

Eve (Gen. 3), has been interpreted as a mandate for male dominion over female subordinates. Stratton calls for a distinction to be made between what the texts originally 'meant' and what they may 'mean' for readers now, in order to neutralize their effects. A starting point for her reading of 1 Timothy is therefore tracing the history of interpretation of Genesis 3 and the implied gender relations from the Hebrew Bible to extra-biblical sources: from ancient (targumic, intertestamental, rabbinic, gnostic, Greek, patristic) texts to modern and feminist readings. Stratton then moves to her own reinterpretation of the 1 Timothy passage: in her view, it advocates a godly household order of gender hierarchy whereby woman is a subordinate but *neither* (unlike some other interpretations of the Genesis story) represented as a beautiful sexual seductress *nor* associated with the serpent. Stratton admits that the weight of interpretation makes this text 'irredeemable'. Nevertheless, she writes, 'we need to shift our interpretations of this passage and perform a more imaginative reading of the text', away from male domination of female bodies and toward an appreciation by both genders of women's corporeality, mind and emotions.

In the book of Revelation there are scenes which 'portray women either being sadistically brutalized or violently coerced through language that uses their body/sexuality as a metaphor'—as in Hosea, Ezekiel and Jeremiah. Marla Selvidge discusses the Revelation promotion of violence against women in her 'Reflections on Violence and Pornography: Misogyny in the Apocalypse and Ancient Hebrew Prophecy'. Selvidge outlines female portraits in Revelation—Jezebel, and Babylon as harlot, queen and widow—against the background of these images' counterparts in the Hebrew Bible. She establishes that both sources objectify woman pornographically as an 'other', an adversary of God and the 'projection of the writers' own inabilities to cope with present political circumstances'; and concludes that these violent anti-woman images are propaganda designed to invoke horror in their target audience.

If women are literally and physically considered as 'others' in the cultures reflected in the Bible, what will be the status of the blemished, ill or disabled female body? Carole Fontaine attempts to answer this question in 'Disabilities and Illness in the Bible: A Feminist Perspective'. She shows how physically handicapped people suffer from their disabilities as well as from the theological ambivalence these evoke. Illness and disability are viewed as undesirable conditions in both the Hebrew Bible and the New Testament. This is particularly relevant to specific female conditions of disability or illness—again in both sources. Such conditions may be seen as forms of impurity, or as an objectified lesson in divine action. Fontaine admits that such portrayals reflect certain religio-social milieux; nevertheless, they also affect our thinking today and marginalize disabled or ill women even further than 'normal' women (that is, able-bodied women) are marginalized. As an antidote, she suggests feminist appropriation of biblical features that might work for disabled women, such as New Testament emphasis on spirituality and healing by faith, or ancient Near Eastern and Hebrew Bible traditions of women as wise, healers and carers. In view of the facts that female corporeality—especially when associated with specifically female sexual organs or behaviour—is downgraded in the Bible, and that some female illnesses today are still not taken as seriously as male-specific ones,[1] Fontaine's strategies may be used with profit by abled as well as disabled women.

Part IV: Anti-Judaism in the New Testament and its Feminist Interpretations?

One of the issues which recurs in discussions of the New Testament in the light of the Hebrew Bible, and has been in evidence in some of the articles of this volume, is the relationship of the former not only to the latter but also to the Judaism or, rather, Judaisms that emerged concurrently with Christianity. This issue is important for understanding the history of Christian anti-Semitism, nowadays quaintly called

---

1. For instance attention, facilities and funds have been poured into research of treatments for cardiac disorders (statistically male-related in the contemporary Western world), with dramatic reduction in mortality rates. Treatments for breast cancer and cancer of the uterus, obviously female ailments, are far less funded and less advanced—although, in recent years, women's awareness has facilitated a change.

anti-Judaism. It is particularly important within a feminist context. While feminists are ostensibly committed to fight discrimination on any grounds, anti-Jewish (and anti-Israeli) sentiments have been expressed within feminist theory and exegesis. As an Israeli Jewish woman who spends part of her working time in Europe every year, the anchoring of such sentiments in Scripture—the New Testament or the Hebrew Bible, or both—causes me sorrow, concern and even amazement, especially when such anti-Judaism masquerades as feminist theology; especially when it calls itself, is called, liberation theology; especially when it originates in Germany. To my delight, Christian colleagues are also very concerned about this phenomenon—as evidenced, for instance, in the Fall 1991 issue of the *Journal of Feminist Studies in Religion*.[1] Therefore, the final section of this volume is, appropriately, addressed to this issue by Jewish and Christian feminist scholars, including prominent German women theologians.

In 'Second Temple Judaism, Jesus, and Women: *Yeast of Eden*', Amy-Jill Levine posits the problem as follows. Reconstructions of first-century Judaism frequently depict a systemic patriarchy that oppressed and repressed Jewish women. They also argue that the messages attributed to Jesus liberated women from their hierarchical and misogynistic social context and located them within a new egalitarian community. Levine explores the Gospels for materials that might reflect the Jesus movement and summarizes as follows. The sayings material does not reflect gender equality. Women of the Q community did not escape gendered patriarchy into a new society. The words might be words of liberation; the praxis—in the name of stability and social order—remains that of oppression for women. While the words can still be explored for liberation potential, the claim that the Jesus movement improved on Judaic

---

1. Cf. M.-Th. Wacker, 'Feminist Theology and Anti-Judaism: The Status of the Discussion and the Context of the Problem in the Federal Republic of Germany', *JFSR* 7 (1991), pp. 109-16; F. van Dijk-Hemmes, 'Feminist Theology and Anti-Judaism in The Netherlands', *JFSR* 7 (1991), pp. 117-23; L. Siegele-Wenschkewitz, 'The Discussion of Anti-Judaism in Feminist Theology—A New Area of Jewish-Christian Dialogue', *JFSR* 7 (1991), pp. 95-98.

attitudes to women is groundless. The implications of this analysis for anti-Judaic feminist interpretations that are grounded in this type of argument are clear.

In 'Through German and Feminist Eyes: A Liberationist Reading of Luke 7.36-50', Luise Schottroff demonstrates how anti-Judaism and sexism operate in New Testament interpretation in traditional German scholarship. A prostitute, a Pharisee and Jesus are the characters narrated. Schottroff interprets the woman as a loving woman whose occupation reflects her circumstances, with no value judgment attached; Simon the Pharisee as a representative of false attitudes, not necessarily of Judaism *per se*; and Jesus as a Jewish prophet of God, the Torah and love. She then discusses two mainstream German interpretations in which sexism (the woman is a sinner) and anti-Judaism are central, whether admitted or not. Schottroff goes on to admit that German feminist theologians have adopted Christian anti-Judaic attitudes from their male colleagues. She states that being a (German) feminist must entail the combat of anti-Judaism and, likewise, any prejudice against any type of female sexual behaviour. To come back to the 'prostitute' of the Lukan passage, Schottroff suggests that her non-patronizing treatment by the story's Jesus implies hope for a new, non-discriminatory feminist theology of sexuality and sensuality.

Like Schottroff, Leonore Siegele-Wenschkowitz has been involved in recent years in the fight against anti-Judaism in feminist theology and in inter-faith dialogues with Jewish colleagues.[1] In her article, 'In the Dangerous Currents of Old Prejudices: How Predominant Thoughts Have Disastrous Effects and What Could Be Done to Counter Them', she defines anti-Judaism as 'religiously and theologically constituted hatred which incorporates points of view and modes of thought developed predominantly within the Christian tradition'. Siegele-Wenschkowitz describes anti-Judaic feminist claims in Germany as involving two clusters of themes: accusations of Hebrew Bible religion and, by metonymy, Judaism of murdering the figure of the goddess (central to some feminist trends) in

---

1. Cf. Siegele-Wenschkewitz, 'The Discussion of Anti-Judaism in Feminist Theology'.

favour of a monotheistic god; and attributions to Jesus of a liberating power whose 'Christian' character removes him from his Jewish origins into a new and improved land, vastly contrasted with the 'old' one. Like Schottroff, Siegele-Wenschkowitz maintains that a dichotomy between Judaism and Christianity is typical of mainstream German thought: it has tied Christianity with Nazism, with the consent of scholars and theologians. In her view, 'a hermeneutic of suspicion must—at least in view of German history—equate anti-Judaism with anti-Semitism'. Therefore, German feminist theology should make two moves: away from androcentric/sexist theology to a feminist theology; and away from anti-Judaic/anti-Semitic theology in the direction of a Christian theology that affirms its links to Judaism via an inter-faith dialogue.

Is Siegele-Wenschkowitz's project viable, given the ideo-social climate of modern Germany? Edna Brocke, in 'Do the Origins Already Contain the Malady?', has her doubts. She makes the following points. Negative Christian attitudes are so pervasive that an escape from their fundamental weight seems almost impossible; Christian identity depends on that, as continuous interpretations of New Testament texts show. Inner-Jewish controversies that appear in the New Testament are no longer understood as such, but as Jewish–Christian controversies. Hebrew Bible and New Testament models are not updated into modern contexts. And the question of the nature of the links, in Christian tradition, between the Hebrew Bible and the New Testament is not reopened. Christianity has, for centuries, felt superior to Judaism, with well-known historical results. If, in spite of all these Scripture-related and other obstacles, feminists will combat the 'masculine theology' of the Western world, that will be a great step forward.

Lillian Klein's 'On "Anti-Judaism" in German Feminist Thought: Some Reflections By Way of a Response' counters claims reported in the previous three articles. Klein reminds us that the inferior social position of women reflected in the Bible is broadly attested in other ancient cultural groups of the Mediterranean. Suppression of goddess-worship occurred all over the ancient Near East, inclusive of so-called Aryan cultures, hence can hardly be traced exclusively to the Bible. The Christian church in its turn contributed to that suppression, Mariolatry notwithstanding. The link between anti-Judaism and anti-femaleness or anti-erotics in Christianity is, and should be, a target for feminist Christian theologians. Finally, the issues of New Testament attitudes to women and their interpretations call for investigations by themselves, apart from their comparison to texts and cultures of the Bible and ancient and modern Judaisms. Jewish and Christian feminists share the task of uncovering new 'truth' from underneath the patriarchal culture: this is certainly more important than 'passively to buy into the patriarchal system of scape-goating'. Hatred of the 'other' cannot, in the long run, function as an efficient substitute for reflection on the divided self.

Part I

HEBREW BIBLE CHARACTERS RECYCLED: SOME PRINCIPLES

'ONLY A REMNANT OF THEM SHALL BE SAVED':[*]
WOMEN FROM THE HEBREW BIBLE IN
NEW TESTAMENT NARRATIVES

Heather A. McKay

The Aim of this Study

This study sets out to distinguish the textual strategies by which androcentric control of female characters[1] is achieved and underpinned in New Testament texts. The phenomenon has already been clearly pointed out by many scholars for Hebrew Bible texts, but this article will show that in the New Testament the suppression of women—by means of suppression of women characters—is pursued even more ruthlessly.

The modes of reading recommended by this study will not necessarily involve blaming or replacing the texts. Rather readers of the Bible will be invited to observe for themselves the selective concentration of the New Testament authors and asked to disown it and compensate for it by widening their gaze when reconstructing the narrative world for themselves. The author or narrator is a selective spectator and reporter; but the reader is nonetheless at liberty to envisage the whole field of view.[2]

---

[*]   Rom. 9.27; cf. 11.5. Hebrew Bible women characters have suffered a similar (minimal) degree of preservation, by the 'grace' of the New Testament authors/narrators.

1.   I have adopted the understanding of 'characters' as readerly constructs and of the characterization process as occurring in the nexus of author, narrator and active reader, as set forth in the discussions of these matters in *Semeia* 63. References to particular papers will occur at appropriate points in my discussion.

2.   Cf. A. Bach, 'Signs of the Flesh: Observations on Characterization in the Bible', *Semeia* 63 (1993), pp. 61-80.

The Effects of Male Authorship of Texts

The Hebrew Bible and the New Testament are literary artefacts from the ancient world. They reflect the worldviews of their time. They can do no other.

But ancient texts have justly been described as the 'literature of men for men',[1] and often reveal the jealousy with which male writers guarded their exclusive control over the literary medium.[2] Both as a consequence of this partiality and as evidence of it, most texts depict a narrative world from the perspective of male readers. Such a construction of the narrative world has recently been admirably illustrated by Susan Durber in Luke's parables of losing and finding—often previously perceived as being pro-women.[3]

The images of women as presented in biblical texts interest and delight a male audience; likewise the issues the texts address are those important to males, issues such as the rearing of sons and heirs,[4] and control over the sexuality of the women in the family so as to avoid the shaming of male honour by their wives' or daughters' (mis)deeds.[5] Even the fantasies about the

---

1. H.A. Musurillo, *Symbol and Myth in Ancient Poetry* (New York: Fordham University Press, 1961), p. 53.

2. J.M. Snyder, *The Woman and the Lyre: Women Writers in Classical Greece and Rome* (Bristol: Bristol Classical Press, 1989), pp. 103-21.

3. S. Durber, 'The Female Reader of the Parables of the Lost', in G.J. Brooke (ed.), *Women in the Biblical Tradition* (Lampeter: Edwin Mellen, 1992), pp. 187-207.

4. J.C. Exum, '"Mother in Israel": A Familiar Story Reconsidered', in L.M. Russell (ed.), *Feminist Interpretation of the Bible* (Oxford: Basil Blackwell, 1985), pp. 73-85; E. Fuchs, 'The Literary Characterization of Mothers and Sexual Politics in the Hebrew Bible', in A.Y. Collins (ed.), *Feminist Perspectives on Biblical Scholarship* (Atlanta: Scholars Press, 1985), pp. 117-36; *idem*, 'Who Is Hiding the Truth? Deceptive Women and Biblical Androcentrism', in Collins (ed.), *Feminist Perspectives on Biblical Scholarship*, pp. 137-44.

5. P.A. Bird, 'Images of Women in the Old Testament', in R.R. Ruether (ed.), *Religion and Sexism* (New York: Simon & Schuster, 1974), pp. 41-88 (p. 51); C.V. Camp, 'Understanding a Patriarchy: Women in Second Century Jerusalem through the Eyes of Ben Sira', in A.-J.

lovers in the Song of Songs may be construed as male fantasies.[1]

Re-Readings of Biblical Texts

Current studies of the place of women in biblical texts, however, do not reveal a whole-hearted acceptance of this critical position. Many writers indeed display unease with traditional androcentric interpretations and try to offer more woman-friendly exegeses. Others feel wrong-footed before they begin because they feel intellectually trapped within the discourse of the male-dominated education they have received.[2] They experience dissonance between its assumptions and their own ideas but continue using its mode of discourse—although uncomfortably or reluctantly. The inconsistencies in their presentations reveal their unease.

Such commentators try to speak highly of the women of the Bible, giving them their full place as equal members of the society portrayed in the narrative world, but give themselves away in the chapter and section headings of their work, where they identify women as objects rather than subjects. Such writers attempt what Carolyn Osiek calls a 'loyalist' approach to the text but cannot sustain it throughout.[3]

So, for example, Thierry Maertens's book affirming woman in biblical society as 'man's equal' deconstructs in its title and section headings its own avowed message.[4] For, in his title—*The Advancing Dignity of Woman*—he makes it plain that women had to advance from their (disadvantaged) starting

Levine (ed.), *'Women Like This': New Perspectives on Jewish Women in the Greco-Roman World* (Atlanta: Scholars Press, 1991), pp. 1-40 (pp. 13, 36-39).

1.   D.J.A. Clines, 'Why is there a Song of Songs? And What Does it Do to You if You Read It?', *Jian Dao* 1 (1993), pp. 3-27 (pp. 10-14).

2.   G. Lerner, *The Creation of Patriarchy* (Oxford: Oxford University Press, 1986), pp. 224-29.

3.   C. Osiek ('The Feminist and the Bible', in Collins [ed.], *Feminist Perspectives on Biblical Scholarship*, pp. 93-106 [p. 103]) classifies feminist hermeneutical styles into five main approaches: loyalist, rejectionist, revisionist, sublimationist and liberationist.

4.   T. Maertens, *The Advancing Dignity of Woman in the Bible* (trans. S. Dibbs; De Père, WN: St Norbert Abbey Press, 1969).

point in order to 'attain' equality with men, and in his chapter titles women are referred to by means of passive past participles: woman is the possessed, woman is the excommunicated, woman is the 'well-named' (named by whom?), woman is derived from man.[1] Only—in his view—in the New Testament is woman finally equal with man.[2] My study will, however, undermine that conclusion.

In similar tone and with nearly identical grammatical forms, Ann Brown denotes the women of the Bible by the terms 'abused', 'overlooked', 'devalued', 'excluded', 'property', 'unclean' and only worthy of respect when 'clothed with strength and dignity'.[3] But 'clothed' does not here imply an active designer, spinner and weaver of Israelite 'power dressing'; rather it implies a passive woman being wrapped in 'suitable' clothes by another—probably her husband, brother or father.

Similarly Sharon Pace Jeansonne, in her chapter on Sarah, makes Sarah the subject of only one of her ten headings, treating her as secondary to Abraham in two headings and as an object in four.[4] So, for example, the section on Sarah's experience of childbirth is titled 'The Long-Awaited Birth of Isaac'. So is it Sarah to whom this event is important? How can we tell? She is invisible! The male writers' perspective characterized by Gale Yee as portraying Sarah as 'the legitimate or "correct" wife and mother of the male successor' has been internalized by Jeansonne.[5] She writes about Sarah reactively, rather than proactively—sympathetically as if speaking of a fellow 'object' trapped in a typical female role as sidekick to male characters, rather than affirmingly as an equal, in the shared role of active, principal subject.

Some authors adopt an idealized view of the Bible's concern

1. Maertens, *The Advancing Dignity of Woman*, Contents and *passim*.

2. Maertens, *The Advancing Dignity of Woman*, p. 149.

3. A. Brown, *Apology to Women: Christian Images of the Female Sex* (Leicester: IVP, 1991), pp. 119-36.

4. S.P. Jeansonne, *The Women of Genesis: From Sarah to Potiphar's Wife* (Minneapolis: Fortress Press, 1990), pp. 14-30.

5. G.A. Yee, 'Sarah', in *ABD*, V (Garden City, NY: Doubleday, 1992), pp. 981-82.

with widows and orphans, equating it with what they discern in the text as an incipient realization of a soon-to-be-accomplished-equality for women, and so place themselves in Osiek's 'sublimationist' category. I evaluate this mental manoeuvre as largely self-deception in the face of unpalatable realizations about a sacred text.

Typical of purveyors of these views is Bonnie Bowman Thurston. She interprets the New Testament texts as turning 'the widow' into 'an exemplary figure', and finds in the New Testament writers' 'relatively open attitude toward women' reasons for what she calls the 'dramatic change' in the status of women in the world of the New Testament narrative—although she accepts that 'the New Testament evidence is not sufficient to suggest full equality'.[1] So saying, Thurston accepts that there is some doubt about women's equality in the minds of the early Christian authors, yet does not enter into debate with the ideology of the text. She allows the judgments of the text—and its writers—to stand unchallenged, for example, Paul's view that widows are 'happier' remaining widows. She also writes of Jesus' elevation of widows 'to a position of spiritual prominence', which she understands as an instance of God's exalting the humble.[2]

It is hard to be convinced that widows were in any real sense in 'a position of spiritual prominence', either at the time of Jesus or in the early church. I am sure that the Temple priests, and the preachers and apostles of the new community, remained more spiritually prominent than widows. The only 'prominence' widows received was, if anything, an elevation from their original position at the very bottom of society—but that made them no more 'prominent' than, for example, the average tradesman or craftsman, at best. Thurston accepts without critique that the interpretation of women's value to society may be pronounced by male voices and remain unchallenged by differently conceived female evaluations. She is willing to allow that giving widows something less than or equal to the status of

---

1.   B.B. Thurston, *The Widows: A Women's Ministry in the Early Church* (Minneapolis: Fortress Press, 1989), pp. 17-18.

2.   Thurston, *The Widows*, pp. 21, 28.

the average male can acceptably be described as giving them 'prominence'.

Other writers either condone, or are unaware of, the fact that women are patronized by the texts—continuing in that mode in their own writings, claiming or implying that it is only through the generosity of God or Jesus that women *become* equal with men. Thus Ben Witherington, for example, claims that Jesus, contrary to the practice of other rabbis, '*allowed* them to follow him',[1] implying that Jesus made liberal changes to current practice. He also argues that Jesus' attitude to women— including foreign women, whom he regarded as 'lost sheep of Israel'—led to his treating them as 'God's creatures, even daughters of Abraham'.[2] Presumably he is implying that women were more on a par with Gentiles—or perhaps animals— before, or apart from, Jesus' ministry. Elsewhere he concludes that the parable of the wise and foolish virgins contains 'perhaps a hint of a woman's right to participate in the messianic banquet'.[3] Did he otherwise envisage an all-male dinner in the kingdom of heaven? And all this marginalizing of women with faint praise is written in spite of his earlier claim that 'patriarchy need not always lead to misogyny'.[4]

In similar vein the anthropologist Alan Aycock, using a structuralist method to study gender relations in the Genesis narratives, introduces Sarah in the guise of a possession— 'Abraham's wife'—but does not similarly and equitably introduce Abraham by the phrase 'Sarah's husband'.[5] And Ruth, as an example of a feminine figure, is described by James Williams as a 'Reversal of the Patriarchal Mode'—language that nevertheless prioritizes the male role and names Ruth a disrupter of norms, rather than an active subject or role-maker in her own right.[6]

1. B. Witherington, *Women and the Genesis of Christianity* (Cambridge: Cambridge University Press, 1990), p. 119, my emphasis.
2. Witherington, *Women and the Genesis of Christianity*, pp. 86-87.
3. Witherington, *Women and the Genesis of Christianity*, p. 63.
4. Witherington, *Women and the Genesis of Christianity*, p. 63.
5. A. Aycock, 'Potiphar's Wife: Prelude to a Structural Exegesis', *Man* NS 27 (1992), pp. 479-94 (pp. 488, 489).
6. J.G. Williams, *Women Recounted: Narrative Thinking and the*

Other writers defend women against the charge of inequality with men and seek to prove in what ways women complement men without either outstripping or mimicking them. Kathryn Pfisterer Darr displays something of this perspective in her book, *Far More Precious than Jewels*, when she describes women as 'more than' various epithets they have been given by men.[1] She thus places herself within Osiek's category of 'loyalist' in her response to the biblical texts by making much of those few occasions when women are credited with powers or qualities exceeding those of men. Nonetheless, in adopting this comparative approach, she reveals her unease with the usual representation of women in the biblical texts, for drawing attention to those few places where women are 'more than' men can only highlight the prevailing, in this case androcentric, stance where men are patently 'more than' women on most counts.

No commentator, feminist or otherwise, has, to my knowledge, taken the position that the claim—or rather the unexamined assumption—that little of importance in society has been said or done by women and that everything of importance has been said or done by men should never have come to court. No one has said that the unexamined assumption is a trumped-up charge—no less dangerous in not having been voiced as a charge—and should be dismissed forthwith as not deserving of being taken seriously. There has been no authoritative rejection of the original, false, premise that women have never been, and had to struggle to catch up in order to be, equal in the qualities and powers that men possess *a priori*. Writers who argue against the 'charges' give credibility to mere prejudice; they make its unargued assumptions real, respectable, powerful.

But, then, perhaps they know that not to present the case for women allows the nonsense to remain unchallenged, holding the field—to use a military metaphor. So, in response to the continued repetition of unexamined assertions, many excellent

God of Israel (Bible and Literature Series, 6; Sheffield: Almond Press, 1982), Contents.

1. K.P. Darr, *Far More Precious than Jewels* (Louisville, KY: Westminster/John Knox, 1991), Contents and *passim*.

works of feminist biblical scholarship have shown how risible, indefensible and unjustifiable the marginalization, ghettoization and objectification of women, both textual and societal, has been.[1]

In order to read the biblical text 'against the grain' and to identify what is going on in the text, I have adopted the approach of Gerda Lerner, applying scepticism as a means of stepping outside patriarchy—being sceptical towards the systems of thought favoured by the text, being critical of its assumptions and reassessing its judgments and system of values.[2]

It is also necessary to demote historical tradition from its dominance as the definitive means of validating a methodology to being merely one approach among others,[3] thus relativizing the current mode of scholarly writing as a time-conditioned 'fashion' of thought. The androcentric perspective may represent reality but it is not timeless truth. In the language of Andrea Dworkin, it is real, but it is not true.[4]

We may, as readers and interpreters of texts, perceive 'sexual structure' as no more than another means of understanding and describing reality—parallel, in its validity as a key to understanding, to political structure, economic structure and social

1.   Bird, 'Images of Women', and 'The Harlot as Heroine: Narrative Art and Social Presupposition in Three Old Testament Texts', *Semeia* 46 (1989), pp. 119-39; Exum, 'Mother in Israel'; Fuchs, 'The Literary Characterization of Mothers' and 'Who Is Hiding the Truth?'; N. Furman, 'His Story Versus Her Story: Male Genealogy and Female Strategy in the Jacob Cycle', in Collins (ed.), *Feminist Perspectives on Biblical Scholarship*, pp. 107-16; and L.C.A. Alexander, 'Sisters in Adversity: Retelling Martha's Story', in Brooke (ed.), *Women in the Biblical Tradition*, pp. 167-86.

2.   Lerner, *The Creation of Patriarchy*, p. 228.

3.   E. Schüssler Fiorenza, 'Remembering the Past and Creating the Future', in Collins (ed.), *Feminist Perspectives on Biblical Scholarship*, pp. 43-64 (pp. 48-55); R.R. Ruether, 'Feminist Interpretation: A Method of Correlation', in Russell (ed.), *Feminist Interpretation of the Bible*, pp. 111-24 (pp. 112-13); T.D. Setel, 'Feminine Insights and the Question of Method', in Collins (ed.), *Feminist Perspectives on Biblical Scholarship*, pp. 35-42 (pp. 36-38); Lerner, *The Creation of Patriarchy*, pp. 15-35.

4.   A. Dworkin, *Our Blood: Prophecies and Discourses on Sexual Politics* (London: The Women's Press, 1982), pp. 109-10.

structure. We may, equally, bring the controlling effects of sexual structure into focus so that they may be seen as accretions on the human condition, rather than *a priori* norms; and as a result we may demand 'an integrative means of description' of reality.[1] The popularist H.V. Morton, however, evaluated such an increase in range of perception as a criticism of women when he noted that women 'do not look directly at a thing, but all the way round it!'[2]

Theories of Characterization

Critical approaches to narrative have, in the past, been focused on plot or story, but more recently interest has focused on characterization—both in current literature and in the literature of the ancient world—and particularly on the question of whether characters in texts, of whatever sort, are more properly to be thought of as *words* or as *people*.

When dealing with self-avowed fiction it is relatively easy to understand that the entity called the Big Bad Wolf is a fictive character created by a collection of images, traits, actions and attitudes attributed to that character by the author/narrator of the tale. The proper name is patently a convenient peg in the reader's mind on which to gather the bits of information the text offers.

More tricky to be clear about in one's mind are characters such as Macbeth and Julius Caesar, who were living persons, and who had their lives recorded with varying degrees of convincing verisimilitude—accuracy is not an appropriate word here—by different writers. We ask: What relation does the 'real' Macbeth have to Shakespeare's character of the same name? Or more complex still: What relation do the 'real' Julius Caesar, the narrator of *de Bello Gallico* and Shakespeare's Caesar bear to each other *in our consciousness of history, drama and culture?*— that being the only place where all three may coexist, after all.

One critical view—that of 'purists'—is that characters are no more than a function of the text and its plot, created out of

1.   Setel, 'Feminine Insights', pp. 38-40.
2.   H.V. Morton, *Women of the Bible* (London: Methuen, 1940), p. 22.

words solely for the purposes of the author, as voiced in Robert Scholes's claim that 'No character in a book is a real person'.[1] On the other hand, 'realists', as typified by psychoanalytic critics, claim that (at least some) characters in fiction attain an individuality or personality that 'transcends' the text and acquire an independent existence in the reader's mind—in much the same way that the personalities of family and friends are understood by that individual, built up from their words, actions, reactions and attitudes over a period of time.[2] The same items in fiction as in real life create images of pomposity, generosity, etc. associated with a specific person or character.

Seymour Chatman attempts to combine the two approaches, envisaging a spectrum of possibilities between the purist and realist extremes, but nonetheless accepting that any 'character' is produced by reading the text, is an effect of the reading process.[3] The reader will 'create' the character depending on the reading skills that each reader brings to the process. And here we come to the problem of wondering if there are sufficient similarities between the reading milieu of the biblical authors and our reading strategies. (Though in the final analysis we can read texts only by means of our own present-day reading strategies.)

For many years, classical readers have been thought to have viewed individual characters in story or drama as if they were 'types' of a somehow 'representative' nature, rather than fully individuated persons. Recent critics, however, discern an element of character development through the course of ancient dramas and believe that the ancient readers/audience were able to appreciate that type of growth in the 'characters' they construed from the speeches, chorus and action. Also, the very different characterizations of named personages in different

1.   R. Scholes and R. Kellogg, *Elements of Fiction* (New York: Oxford University Press, 1968), p. 17; cf. S. Rimmon-Kenan, *Narrative Fiction: Contemporary Poetics* (New York: Methuen, 1983), pp. 31-32.

2.   J. Weinsheimer, 'Theory of Character: Emma', *Poetics Today* 1 (1979), pp. 185-211.

3.   S. Chatman, *Story and Discourse: Narrative Structure in Fiction and Film* (Ithaca, NY: Cornell University Press, 1978), pp. 96-146 (pp. 113, 138).

works of Greek drama suggest that ancient audiences were as sophisticated as modern audiences in understanding 'characters' —although reading by means of different codes.

The approach followed here is to conceive of a spectrum of degrees of characterization:[1] as an agent—a mere functionary of the plot or part of the setting; as a type—a stereotype portraying the traits of a class of characters; as a character— about whom we know more than the plot demands. The reader gives different amounts of notice to these differently characterized members of the *dramatis personae* and invests different amounts of attention in their expected future roles in the plot.

Anonymous characters—including the narrator—can similarly be given different degrees of characterization. The reader envisions the anonymous character through the same reading process, though with a less clearly labelled—and so less recognized—location for assembling the accumulation of descriptions, actions and traits.

I accept these views of the characterization process but also believe that we may, for ease of communication, temporarily suspend the theoretical distinction between real people and characters, and deal with the characters in the texts more or less as if they were 'real' people.[2] My study shows that—for women characters—this approach, though not completely possible for the Hebrew Bible texts, is less feasible still in the New Testament where women characters have much less than their full share of 'real life'. However, by assuming 'real' status for the women characters in the narratives we can more easily observe the loss, or lack, of that 'real' status.

The (Mal)Treatment of Women Characters from the Hebrew Bible in the New Testament

Hebrew Bible women are used to support or illustrate arguments in New Testament texts, but in many cases the original characterizations are radically altered, usually by restriction of the women characters' already limited status or

---

1. A. Berlin, *Poetics and Interpretation of Biblical Narrative* (Sheffield: Almond Press, 1983), p. 32.
2. Weinsheimer, 'Emma', pp. 202, 208.

role (in the Hebrew Bible). The female characters are damaged again in this secondary usage; their degree of characterization is diminished.

Typically, the shrinkage or fading of women characters is achieved in three ways: by reducing the specificity of designating women characters ;[1] by curtailing and restricting the accounts of women characters; and by writing out of the text powerful female character traits.

Within the Hebrew Bible itself, intertextual reference to women characters does not damage them further than they have already been damaged in their original portrayals. So, for example, Sarah is named in Isa. 51.2 in parallel with Abraham—and seemingly not of lesser importance there—in notable contrast with the handling of her story and character in the New Testament, as we shall see.

Similarly, the characters Rachel, Leah and Tamar, for example, gain only respect from their inclusion in the genealogy cited in the celebration of Obed's birth in Ruth 4.11-12 (Tamar also in 1 Chron. 2.4), for they are named as the mothers of ancestors. This restatement of their continuing importance does, however, depend on their role as mothers of important males, the mothering of daughters not attracting such approbation. Only the mothering of unconventional daughters—and sons—attracts comment.[2]

---

1.   For a discussion of the role and importance of names and designations in the readerly construction of 'characters', see F.W. Burnett, 'Characterization and Reader Construction of Characters in the Gospels', *Semeia* 63 (1993), pp. 3-28(17-18), and A. Reinhartz, 'Anonymity and Character in the Books of Samuel', *Semeia* 63 (1993), pp. 117-42.

2.   Leah's mothering of Dinah is mentioned (Gen. 30.21; 34.1), Abigail has her ancestry supplied by means of her mother's name (2 Sam. 17.25.), Aiah is named as mother of the recalcitrant Rizpah (2 Sam. 3.7; 21.8-11), and an unnamed Israelite of mixed parentage is identified through his mother (Lev. 24.11), as are some of Esau's descendants. There are two definite and two uncertain references to 'son of N, daughter of N' in Gen. 36.2, 14, 18, 39 (parallel in 1 Chron. 1.50). But, surprisingly, even where the questions of incest and consanguinity depend on the existence of different mothers—as for Amnon and Tamar—the mothers of the principal characters are not necessarily named (2 Sam. 13). Generally, it is the ancestry of important males that includes mothers' names, for

Alterations in Designations of Women Characters

Some Hebrew Bible women are both named and feature in stories about important events in their lives—for example, Sarah. Others, such as Pharaoh's daughter in Exodus,[1] have designations rather than names but, still, have a powerful part to play in the narrative. Yet others have no name but are designated by their social role and importance in someone else's story, for example the Queen of Sheba.[2] Finally some women (such as maidservants) are alluded to only as background characters, for example, the maidservant in Naaman's household.[3] This range of nomenclature, indicating the perceived importance of the characters in the narrative world/s created by the authors of the text, is an authorial device employed to control the readers' ability to envisage and sustain a transcendent 'personality' for these characters.

Bathsheba

Although some female characters appear in New Testament narratives in the same terms as in the Hebrew Bible—for example, Sarah, Hagar, Rebekah and Jezebel—others are referred to in less specific and personal ways. Bathsheba, for example, is authorially demoted—she loses her name.[4] She appears in the New Testament (Mt. 1.6) exclusively as 'the wife of Uriah', an appellation that is only one among many in the unfolding of her story in the Hebrew Bible. Surely she earns her place in Jesus' genealogy because she was David's wife, and mother of the great king, Solomon? But neither of these roles is indicated in the way she is named. She is not described even as

example, in the identification data of various kings. Thirteen kings are identified by means of their mothers (2 Kgs 15.33; 18.2; 21.19; 22.1; 23.31, 36; 24.8, 18; 2 Chron. 13.2; 20.31; 27.1; 29.1). Uniquely, Zelophehad has his daughters listed following the intimation of, and presumably as a result of, the fact that he had no sons (Num. 26.33, cf. 1 Chron. 7.15).

1.   Exod. 2.5-10.
2.   1 Kgs 10.1-13; 2 Chron. 9.1-12; see also the woman of Shunem in 2 Kgs 4.8-37.
3.   2 Kgs 5.2-3.
4.   See also Bredin, in this volume.

the incubator of the 'seed of David'; she is rather named as the possession of her previous owner/husband. She is present in the genealogy as a dead soldier-courtier's widow or ex-wife; she is indicated by means of a circumlocution. None of the more familiar ways of naming a royal female such as Bathsheba, for example, as David's wife or Solomon's mother, is used; the phrase chosen by Matthew is one that does Bathsheba no honour and which, it can be argued, reminds readers—of both genders—of what males could regard as her dishonour.[1]

Curtailment in Accounts of Women Characters

Those female characters designated in the Hebrew Bible by their relationship to a man, for example, Lot's wife[2] and Pharaoh's daughter,[3] have their appellation preserved in the New Testament, but there they appear as symbols rather than real characters in the plot, their characters or stories being conjured up merely to provide one key feature for the New Testament author's purpose. And I argue that this process diminishes those women characters by objectifying them.

Lot's Wife

Lot's wife has a definite role in the Hebrew Bible narrative: as an inquisitive and also sceptical character in the story of the destruction of Sodom and Gomorrah. But in Lk. 17.32 she serves only as symbol of loss through hesitation, dallying when it is time to be clear about where one is going. Her sharp desire for evidence and explanations is reduced to indecision—a trait the Hebrew Bible character did not suffer from or else she would have remained in Sodom.

Pharaoh's Daughter

Pharaoh's daughter briefly replays her vital role in the story of Moses in Acts 7.21. In Luke's retelling of Israel's past in Stephen's speech, she is the only woman, listed with eight

---

1. 2 Sam. 11–12; for an extensive treatment of the characterization of Bathsheba, see Bach, 'Signs of the Flesh'.
2. Gen. 19.26; Lk. 17.32.
3. Exod. 3.5-10; Acts 7.21; Heb. 11.24.

famous men.[1] But in Heb. 11.24, although she features as a third woman along with Sarah and Rahab in a list with fifteen men, she is not—as the men are—presented as a hero of the faith.[2] Perhaps her inclusion in Stephen's speech represents a high honour *for a woman*, but the reason for her inclusion in the Hebrews text is not her intervention to effect the saving of Moses' life—she is not included because of any action she initiated; she is included to remind readers that Moses rejected the Egyptian power and status that she symbolizes. Sarah and Rahab are included as heroes of the faith but she, Pharaoh's daughter, in her role as adoptive mother, is rejected as another sign of Moses' great faith. She was useful, even vital, but expendable, whether from the point of view of Moses or the author of Hebrews.

The Widow of Zarephath and the Queen of Sheba
Those women indicated not by name but by social role, such as the widow of Zarephath and the Queen of Sheba, have their designations preserved unaltered in the New Testament—but their portrayal is truncated and they function, in the main, symbolically.

In the book of Kings the widow of Zarephath has a family life, which is interrupted and disrupted by the activities of both God and Elijah; and in the Hebrew Bible narrative she has the power to call both to account and demand redress (1 Kgs 17). But in Lk. 4.25 the widow of Zarephath has no real identity, her degree of characterization is minimal, she merely stands for the ordinariness of widows and the particularity of God in choosing far-flung venues for displays of divine power by his favoured agents. Her function in Luke is to set Jesus in parallel with Elijah and to provide a way of excusing Jesus' performance of miracles in parts of the country far from his home in Nazareth.

Similarly, the Queen of Sheba, who has a Hebrew Bible narrative in her own right as a powerful and independent ruler who can travel widely in the ancient Near East,[3] features in Mt.

1.   Abraham, Isaac, Jacob, Joseph, Moses, Aaron, David, Solomon.
2.   Like Abel, Cain, Enoch, Noah, Abraham, Isaac, Jacob, Joseph, Moses, Gideon, Barak, Samson, Jephthah, David, Samuel.
3.   1 Kgs 10; parallel in 2 Chron. 9.

12.42 simply to give glory to Solomon and even greater glory to Jesus by extrapolation.[1]

Unnamed Women

The Hebrew Bible texts include many totally unnamed women, women whom I resist calling *nameless* for I believe they had, or should have had, names. The designation 'unnamed' indicates that the biblical author, via the narrator—for whatever reason—chose not to name these characters. The lack of a proper name represents a severe deprivation in the formation of a character from textual indicators.[2] In an alternative, but to my mind not fully validated, perception, the lack of a proper name allows closer identification of the readers' interests and stances with those of the anonymous characters in question.[3] Beck claims that the reader can more readily identify with the narrative stances of anonymous characters than of named persons.[4]

The unnamed women of the Hebrew Bible have their counterparts in the New Testament: mothers, wives, sisters, daughters, widows, mistresses, prostitutes—all designated by their relations to males; and maidens, maidservants and wise women—designated by their employment. For them it is enough to fulfil a service role without an identity. They do not merit, or require, a name. Surely the most unnamed of all, unnamed to a greater degree than even Bathsheba when she is referred to as Uriah's wife, is the woman known longwindedly as Simon's wife's

1. Parallel in Lk. 11.31.
2. Burnett, 'Characterization', p. 17.
3. D.R. Beck, 'The Narrative Function of Anonymity in Fourth Gospel Characterization', *Semeia* 63 (1993), pp. 143-58 (pp. 147-49); although Beck, in my view somewhat inappropriately, applies observations on characters with fluid identities directly to anonymous characters. Only the notion of increased empathetic identification could be used to illumine the functioning of anonymous characters in the reader's mind. It is relevant also to state that in the same volume, the response of R. Polzin, 'Divine and Anonymous Characterization in Biblical Narrative', pp. 205-14 (p. 209), quite properly points out that Beck uncritically applies to mimetic literature insights into named and anonymous characters produced by work on postmodern fiction.
4. Beck, 'Anonymity', p. 147.

mother—an appendage or servitor accompanying Peter's wife in her role as male possession transferred to the patrilocal home.[1]

But most pathetic of all the unnamed women in the New Testament is the woman described merely in terms of an illness, a persistent discharge of blood, a woman character whose misery supplies no more than a narrative device. In the Hebrew Bible, the problem of gynaecological disorder in a sexually active woman is treated, in Leviticus 15, with measured severity, in the same way that genital discharge in an adult male is treated—because such matters are of serious concern to all the community. But in the New Testament story such a woman is used to show, at worst, the healing power of Jesus' clothes, and, at best, the pacific way in which the erstwhile founder of a formerly timid but now blossoming and maturing Christian church treated the formerly ailing but now healed, though no longer fecund, Judaism.[2]

Among the unnamed women, only the widow who gave the two small coins to the Temple, alone of all the women in the New Testament, is presented as an ideal for males to follow— for sister Mary is held up as a foil only to sister Martha. Is this unnamed widow a successor to other notable widows from the Hebrew Bible: Naomi, Ruth, the wise woman of Tekoa, the widow of Zarephath, or the 'widow' Jerusalem? There are no clues identifying her with them. She is a shadowy creation. Even her enormous power in the story is dwarfed by her low profile.

More easily identifiable with the wise women of the Hebrew Bible—the wise woman of Tekoa, the wise woman of Abel, and the medium of Endor[3]—is the Syro-Phoenician woman who jousts verbally with Jesus, staking her wits against his to gain healing for her child, and, by implication, for others who might

1.   Mk 1.30; parallels in Mt. 8.14 and Lk. 4.38.

2.   Jesus tells the healed older woman to 'Go in Shalom'. For my reading of the two women, older and younger, as symbolic representations of the two communities with which Jesus was associated see McKay, *Sabbath and Synagogue: The Question of Sabbath Worship in Ancient Judaism* (Religions in the Graeco-Roman World, 122; Leiden: Brill, 1994), pp. 158-59.

3.   Reinhartz ('Anonymity and Character', p. 117) eschews the term 'witch' on the grounds that it is hostile to women.

also be classed as dogs.[1] In order to win crumbs—no more—she must represent herself and her family as despised canines, more inimical creatures than 'lost sheep'. She has the better of the argument, but may not class herself as an equal—not even with Jesus, the supposed friend of outcasts.

Rachel

There is a possibility that Rachel is referred to in Mt. 2.18, but as the original Jeremiah reference (31.15) leaves matters unclear as to whether it is Rachel who is referred to or a bereaved ewe, it is hard to know to what aspect of Rachel's story or personality this text could be referring. Rachel's story, as we have it in the Hebrew Bible, could only admit of weeping over as yet unconceived children, not of weeping over live children whether lost or dead.

Hannah

Is Hannah in the New Testament or not? Because of the common features of false attribution of drunkenness and the activity of prophesying or praying,[2] it is possible that the character Hannah is being used by the writer of Acts to provide a religious, and non-alcoholic, precedent for the behaviour of the apostles on the day of Pentecost.[3] But as Hannah is not mentioned explicitly it is hard to decide whether she is 'there' or not. However, if she is 'there' she serves only as a religiously acceptable means of reinstating the apparently drunken apostles with Jewish readers.

Non-Accompanying Persons

Some women—Noah's wife, Asenath, Miriam, Zipporah, Deborah, Delilah, Abigail, Michal and Abishag—are absent from the New Testament texts although their menfolk are

1.   Mk 7.26.
2.   1 Sam. 1. 9-18.
3.   Acts 2.1-17. I have found no reference to this possibility in commentaries.

present.[1] Noah appears in the New Testament six times,[2] Joseph twice,[3] Barak and Samson once each,[4] and David and Moses on various occasions.[5] It is hard to believe that the stories, lives and characters of their wives are passed over so consistently by accident rather than design. The familiar image of these women shut up at home and gazing at the world through a lattice must surely be reversed. The authorial gaze through the androcentric lattice is selective by design rather than restricted by circumstance—as theirs would be.

Removal of Powerful Character Traits

Various strategies are used to place women securely into secondary narrative status in the New Testament. These are: absence from key stages of the narratives, silent narrative presence, lack of direct speech, lack of name and lack of development in their characterization. Women characters often acquire less than the status of 'agents', and can be presented as part of the backdrop instead of being placed centre stage and sharing in the limelight alongside their male counterparts.

Women as Scenery

Sarah,[6] Hagar, Rebekah and other women characters are both named in the Hebrew Bible and have powerful roles in stories about themselves and about other main characters in the narrative. But in the New Testament they play smaller roles or function as mere props. To serve this end, the totality of a woman's life is often reduced to one of two summarizing adjectives: she is good or bad. 'Good' women, such as Sarah and Rebekah, are characterized by successful childbearing and 'bad' women by sexual depravity and/or wrong-headedness—

1. Also not referred to in the New Testament are Esther, Huldah and Jael, but neither are their male counterparts.
2. Mt. 24.37-38; Lk. 3.36; 17.26; Heb. 11.7; 1 Pet. 3.20; 2 Pet. 2.5.
3. Acts 7.8-18; Heb. 11.21-22.
4. Heb. 11.32.
5. Heb. 11.
6. Morton, (*Women of the Bible*, p. 19) notes that 'Brief though the account of Sarah is, it is a full-length portrait of a real woman'; we might add the rider, 'constructed for male gaze'.

like Jezebel, Eve, Hagar and Lot's wife. Women with a 'past'—by which the reader understands sexual irregularity as defined by father or husband or brother—may be 'reinstated' if they bear the 'right' offspring, as happens to Rahab and Tamar in Matthew's genealogy of Jesus.[1]

Sarah

As far as Sarah is concerned, the narrator of Genesis 18 gives the elderly Sarah both a certain knowledge of her body and the self-confidence to express that knowledge in laughter when she hears males speak of her as a future producer of progeny (Gen. 21). Sarah resists patriarchy, whether human—at the hand of the narrator—or divine. But in Rom. 4.19 Sarah's barrenness is seen as a problem only for Abraham, a testing of the strength of *his* faith in God's promise.

In Galatians Sarah is implied—though not named—as the free counterpart of the slave woman Hagar.[2] Here an implied Sarah functions to promote the cause of the Christian side in the debate with the Jews. In contrast with Hagar, whose child is born of the flesh, and whose descendants are children in slavery, i.e. the Jews, Sarah's child is born of the promise and is the ancestor of the Christians. Interestingly, this is also an example of literary sleight of hand since Isaac's descendants were allegedly the Jews and Ishmael's the Arab races. Thus the annexing of Sarah as ancestress of the Christians is illogical, since Hagar is most definitely not the ancestress of the Jews.

In Hebrews Sarah's faith is said to be the reason for her conception following her long period of barrenness.[3] By presenting her as an exemplar of faith, not scepticism or resistance, the writer of Hebrews silences her sceptical laughter —she trusted in God all along—and Sarah becomes a meek creature of faith, completely in Abraham's shadow. Some commentators make matters worse for Sarah by following manuscripts that give the attribution of faith to Abraham instead of Sarah, and turn Sarah

---

1. Also, possibly, Ruth as she had moved from Moab and then later married an Israelite in Bethlehem and produced Obed.
2. Gal. 4.22-23.
3. Heb. 11.11.

into mere receptacle for, or incubator of, the promised son.[1]

In 1 Pet. 3.6, Sarah's obedience and verbal subservience to Abraham are held up as the model behaviour of a wife in the Christian community, and are also used to reinforce the claim that the Christians are the rightful children of Abraham. But Sarah's story in Genesis showed her to be a woman of initiative, for example in persuading Abraham to a course of action he had not thought of, namely, the impregnation of Hagar,[2] and in persuading him afterwards that it was fine for her to renege on her commitment to that pregnancy when it suited her upset feelings to do so—hardly the behaviour of a sweet-natured, docile, submissive wife. The New Testament author has abused Sarah by using her as a cipher of ideal, obedient wifehood.[3]

Rebekah

Rebekah in the Hebrew Bible is a partisan mother who supports, and even leads, her younger son Jacob in the usurpation of his brother's rights.[4] But in the New Testament she is no more than the dutiful wife and mother doing the most important thing she can do—in male perception—which is to conceive children and to do so by one man only, her husband Isaac. Paul, in Rom. 9.10, voices these particular details, highlighting not only what constitutes the key role of wives but also the exclusiveness of Isaac's sexual rights over Rebekah's body. The patriarchs produced sons with more than one woman, but Rebekah could be mated with only one male, her husband. And the credit for the success of Jacob over Esau is here not laid at the door of any actions or words of Rebekah but is attributed to God.

Tamar, Rahab, Ruth and Bathsheba (as Wife of Uriah)

Tamar, Rahab (as Boaz's mother), Ruth and the wife of Uriah, all women of 'suspect' character—by which connotation, as

---

1. A.T. Hanson, 'Hebrews', in D.A. Carson and H.G.M. Williamson (eds.), *It is Written: Scripture Citing Scripture: Essays in Honour of Barnabas Lindars, SSF* (Cambridge: Cambridge University Press, 1988), pp. 292-302 (pp. 298-99).

2. Gen. 16.

3. This Sarah is reminiscent of one of the 'Stepford wives'.

4. Gen. 27.

stated above, the reader understands sexual irregularity as defined by father or husband or brother—are brought into Matthew's genealogy of Jesus,[1] possibly as a means of lessening the farouche quality of Mary's marital credentials. It is unlikely that women who had been considered 'unsatisfactory' in the Hebrew Bible's telling of their tales would be ushered into pride of place at the beginning of two Gospels, had there not been some compelling reason to include them, such as a means of countering charges of Mary's unsuitability as the mother of the messiah. The women are made use of without the reader being alerted to their function. They are turned into props for the author's hidden agenda and are objectified by this transaction.

Women as General 'Types'

Stories told about individual women in the Hebrew Bible have sometimes been reduced in the New Testament to generalities. An example is the sequence of stories about independent women who, while making use of wells, encounter the hero of the narrative to whom they later become betrothed.[2] Rebekah, Rachel and Zipporah meet their future husbands at wells, and, in their narratives, Rachel and Zipporah are presented as independent women pursuing successful careers, and Rebekah as unusually communicative among the young women of her town. In the New Testament, however, these once fully fledged characters are represented by one person only—in the guise of an unnamed woman, a woman at a well, a woman whose 'career' is, if anything, suspect and who is, therefore, definitely not about to become betrothed to the symbolic bridegroom Jesus: (un)namely the woman of Samaria.[3]

1.   See also Bredin, in this volume.

2.   See the discussion of these 'type-scene' stories in R. Alter, *The Art of Biblical Narrative* (London: George Allen & Unwin, 1981), pp. 47-62.

3.   A clear pointer to the intertextuality of the stories is the fact that Jacob's connection with the well is verbalized by the woman in the story.

Women Relinquish 'their' Deceitfulness

In Hebrew Bible narratives deceit in the service of the male heroes is often accounted righteous,[1] and that same authorial strategy operates in the New Testament. So in Heb. 11.31, as in the Hebrew Bible,[2] Rahab's survival is laid at the door of her friendly welcome to Israelite spies because deceitful behaviour, if partisan towards the side favoured by the author, is regarded as praiseworthy. Similarly, in Jas 2.25, Rahab, in parallel with as highly lauded a character as Abraham, is considered to be justified by her good works. Treachery like this is not counted deceitful.

No such rehabilitation, however, is possible for Jezebel, who is portrayed as having practised her deceits on behalf of enemies. Thus in Rev. 2.20 we find Jezebel credited with more than the crimes listed against her in the Hebrew Bible, namely with having called herself a prophet and having taught and beguiled God's servants into practising immorality and eating food sacrificed to idols. Jezebel's partisan behaviour in favour of her former habits and religion, which could have been evaluated as loyalty to her roots, was denigrated in the Hebrew Bible and now in the New Testament has been elaborated into even more unrighteous actions, perhaps in terms more relevant for a Christian audience.

Another insidious method of reducing the status of women in texts is to show that the women described in the texts *deserve* to be outwitted or subjugated because they are liable to be underhand and programmatically use deceptiveness to achieve their purposes. This particular technique of innuendo occurs in the biblical texts and is frequently adopted unnoticed, or uncritically, in many commentaries on the texts; even writers who describe the technique do not take the trouble to condemn it. So, for example, Aycock claims that the male authors of Genesis depict in their story images where 'women threaten chaos and perfidy'...'mainly as a narrative device to lend emphasis to the character values it highlights' and cites the

---

1.   Fuchs, 'Who Is Hiding the Truth?', p. 142.
2.   Josh. 2 and 6.

descriptions of the 'equivocal moral qualities' of Eve, Sarah, Lot's daughters, Rachel and Leah, and Potiphar's wife.[1] But nowhere in his article does he criticize these character values, contenting himself with describing the narratives in language that mirrors the perspective of the original author/s. It is possible that he distances himself from the stance of the texts but this is not made clear throughout, and he makes such statements as, for example on p. 482, 'a patriarch visiting or residing under the dominion of another male unintentionally commits an offence that is attributed to the intrigues of a woman' without challenging the *imported* insinuation about the woman created by his secondary use of the word 'intrigues'. In this I take issue with him; it is not enough to report instances of narrative manipulation of the reader; some disagreement with the use of that technique should follow, not least as a preventative measure against the same, unnoticed, misprision happening again in the reading of his text.

Esther Fuchs dismantles male-centred evaluations of Hebrew Bible texts, particularly with respect to the portrayal of women as treacherous.[2] She sees any manipulation carried out by active, resourceful women as the best response of the powerless when trapped within a dominant and dominating system. She also calls attention to a hypocritical tendency in texts which imply that a woman's 'deception is acceptable and even recommended when her motives are selfless and when she attempts to promote the cause of man'.[3] As far as women characters are concerned it seems to her that the writers are presenting a totally one-sided view—especially as 'the deceptive acts of Abraham, Jacob, or David' are not fore-grounded or apostrophized to the same extent.[4]

Following the argument of Fuchs, and examining the use of the 'bride-in-the-dark' motif in the stories of Lot's daughters, Leah, Tamar and Ruth, James Black draws similar conclusions about the bias of the texts. He takes a stand against the casual use of language which is slighting to women, asking that

1. Aycock, 'Potiphar's Wife', pp. 481-82.
2. Fuchs, 'Who Is Hiding the Truth?', p. 137.
3. Fuchs, 'Who Is Hiding the Truth?', p. 142.
4. Fuchs, 'Who Is Hiding the Truth?', p. 143.

readers resist in particular the use of emotive phrases about women, such as 'clever wenches' or 'stratagem'. He concludes that women's manipulations give evidence of no more than 'women's means to act'.[1]

The Haemorrhaging Woman

Sadly, perhaps, in the New Testament texts even that power of deceptiveness is stripped from women characters; they are deprived of even that weapon or strategy of survival in a male-dominated culture—and text. For the woman who touches Jesus' garment confesses at once to him,[2] even though there is no chance she can be identified in the throng.[3] Apparently, she is so innocent and meek that she blurts out her guilt—if that be the right word. Certainly, in two Gospels she is described as if she were a suppliant begging for mercy on the ground before a mighty king—Jesus.[4]

An Adulteress

Another women exhibiting anything but the expected streetwise characteristics of a confirmed recidivist is the woman taken in adultery.[5] She is verbally innocent, even naïve, for she makes no excuse, denies nothing, covers nothing up, does not blame her partner and says only, 'No one, Lord', when asked who condemns her.[6] If we contrast her speech and behaviour with Potiphar's wife the conclusion is inescapable: the adulterous woman has nothing of the force and power of the Hebrew Bible character found in a comparable situation.[7]

---

1.   J. Black, 'Ruth in the Dark: Folktale, Law and Creative Ambiguity in the Old Testament', *Journal of Literature and Theology* 5 (1991), pp. 20-36 (pp. 35, 22, 23).

2.   Mk 5.24-34; parallels in Mt. 9.20-22 and Lk. 8.43-48.

3.   Mk 5.33; Lk. 8.47.

4.   Mt. 9 eliminates this self-abasement of the woman.

5.   Jn 8.4.

6.   Jn 8.3-11.

7.   Gen. 39; see also the interpretation of the motives for the actions of Potiphar's wife supplied by L.E. Donaldson, 'Cyborgs, Ciphers and Sexuality: Re-Theorizing Literary and Biblical Character', *Semeia* 63 (1993), pp. 81-96 (pp. 86-93). Note that in this account Donaldson does not revision the story as if Potiphar's wife presented a 'true' account of

The Woman at the Well in Samaria

Similarly, in John 4, the woman at the well in Samaria is actually put to the test by Jesus, in the style of an agent provocateur, to see if she will be deceptive about her marital status. She does not essay deception; she replies with a truthful evasion and receives a sharp reply which strips her of her cover. Seemingly, John's Jesus knew the truth about her all along, and has been practising deceit himself—in the form of entrapment. Whatever privileges this Jesus reserves to himself in the matter of truth telling, she can have no privacy with which to screen her life; the veil of the civil circumlocution is not to be available to her.

Sapphira

The ultimate punishment falls on Sapphira who is struck down dead by God for her deceptiveness, in apparently keeping back money from the Christian community.[1] On close scrutiny of the story, this punishment seems to have been rather unfair, for, at the very beginning of the account, we discover that the lie she tells is not a deceit of her own but the working out of a commitment to her husband's original lie. She is punished for that very loyalty and subservience to a husband's will that the New Testament elsewhere praises so highly in wives!

Who is Being Deceptive?

Suppose, however, that we accept Fuchs's understanding that the characterization of Hebrew Bible women as deceptive is a mis-description of women; then the lack of this quality in women in the New Testament could well be another and opposite mis-description. Both are male fantasies in which women are endowed with extremes of behaviour that invite and authorize either outwitting or domination.

---

events (as, for example, Bach would encourage)—rather she uncovers a more 'acceptable' set of motives, namely male bonding and power sharing, for the narrator-interpreted actions than his attributed motive of unbridled lust on the part of Potiphar's wife.

1. Acts 5.1-11.

Intertextual References between the Testaments

Intertextual reference from the Hebrew Bible to the New Testament, by means of verbal references to known characters or stories, damages named women; their range of abilities narrows (see discussion on Tamar, Ruth and Rahab above). But, even more, it damages unnamed women, for they do not have the 'protection' of an original characterization. Unnamed women, such as widows and maidens, become ciphers that may be manipulated to suit narrative needs.

Women as Decision Makers

Some young women of the Hebrew Bible have their own careers, such as shepherding, and they contribute to discussions and take a valuable role in problem solving; for example, the maidservant in the story of the healing of Naaman;[1] but in the New Testament, young women, such as the wise and foolish virgins,[2] are merely dependent and attendant on men. Hagar, as Sarah's maidservant, plays an extremely powerful role in the Hebrew Bible narrative,[3] but Caiaphas's maidservant's skills in observation are put to the purpose of discomfiting one of Jesus' key disciples—perhaps too sly an action for a male character.[4]

Women as Sisters

Among women described as relatives of other characters the only sisters of note in the New Testament are the symbolic sisters of Jesus who represent all women who carry out God's will,[5] and the exasperated Martha apostrophizing her absorbed sister Mary.[6]

David McCracken believes that the quality of 'character' in the biblical narration is especially vivid and instructive when two characters interact in a heated or crisis situation,[7] and

1.   2 Kgs 5.2-3.
2.   Mt. 25.1-13.
3.   Gen. 16.
4.   Mk 14.66-69; and parallels in Mt. 26.69-70, Lk. 22.56-57 and Jn 18.17.
5.   Mk 3.35; and parallels in Mt. 12.50 and Lk. 8.21.
6.   Lk. 10.38-42.

makes much of the characterization of Martha, claiming that she continues to *live* in her interaction with Jesus. In my view, this reading is controverted by the text, where Martha is given no space, time or even voice to make a reply to Jesus' approving comment about Mary. McCracken goes so far as to deny that the Martha of that pericope is reified in it. But to my mind that is exactly what happens to her. The character Martha does not have life in her own story, *pace* the reading of Alexander;[1] she is not able to learn anything from that interaction. The story is not really about her—she is merely a prop or prompt in Jesus' storyline.

But sisters as rivals, like Leah and Rachel,[2] or as co-workers, like Zipporah's sisters,[3] or as heiresses, like Job's daughters,[4] are unknown.

Conclusions

Patriarchy suppresses women in texts by means of various literary devices. Their activities are curtailed, their range of activities and skills is restricted. They lean more heavily on the male characters than women do in 'real life'. By means of the 'familiar double-think…a dominant social group simultaneously assigns certain necessary but unpopular tasks to a helot class and denigrates their importance'.[5] The New Testament displays these features to a marked extent, according to the methods and criteria outlined above. The women characters create no more than the frame in which to see the important (male) characters more clearly.[6]

In the New Testament the women of the Hebrew Bible are maltreated literarily. They lose status, force, role, interest and character. Their faded portrayal allows them to merge into the

7. D. McCracken, 'Character in the Boundary: Bakhtin's Interdividuality in Biblical Narratives', *Semeia* 63 (1993), pp. 29-42 (pp. 32-33).

1. Alexander, 'Sisters in Adversity'.
2. Gen. 29–30.
3. Exod. 2.16-19.
4. Job 42.15.
5. Alexander, 'Sisters in Adversity', p. 170.
6. Reinhartz, 'Anonymity', p. 132.

background—they do not appear to *deserve* any attention from the reader.

Bathsheba loses her name and becomes the second-hand wife of her ex-husband. .Lot's wife is reduced from an interesting character cameo to an Aunt Sally in a cautionary tale. Pharaoh's daughter is indeed mentioned in the praise of the heroes of the faith in Hebrews 11 but merely as someone to be spurned. The widow of Zarephath was unexpectedly chosen by God in her own story and is unexpectedly chosen by Luke in his. The Queen of Sheba is reduced from regal peer to female sycophant stunned by the magnificence of Solomon and, by implication, Jesus. A woman with persistent haemorrhaging is an unpleasant reminder of life gone wrong, and while the purpose of the discussion in Leviticus 15 is to show how she may take up the reins of her life again, the issue in the gospels is not about the woman's future at all. There she is dealt with almost literally in passing and Jesus' encounter with her functions as a prologue to the healing of the younger as yet unproductive woman, both of which healings serve to highlight the supreme healing, cleansing and life-bringing power of Jesus and, by corollary, the Christian church.

Sarah and Rebekah become successful and appropriate breeding stock; they have no other life in the New Testament texts. Rahab, as in the Hebrew Bible, has her deceits evaluated as virtues because she supported the Israelites against the inhabitants of the town in which she had lived and worked— what most would regard as treason. And Jezebel has her previously condemned faithfulness to her imported habits and religion exaggerated into anachronistically described crimes against religion in order to serve the rhetoric of Revelation.

The story of the Samaritan woman drawing water at Jacob's well carries many symbolic motifs in its own telling,[1] but it also carries echoes of messages from the stories of other women in the Hebrew Bible. This woman, however, can initiate nothing

---

1. See M.C. de Boer, 'John 4.27—Women (and Men) in the Gospel and Community of John', in Brooke (ed.), *Women in the Biblical Tradition*, pp. 208-30, for a differently focused study of the androcentrism in this story.

important—save perhaps the amazing of the disciples;[1] she may act only as a messenger between different groups of men.

The woman taken in adultery is practically invisible. She does nothing, resists nothing and speaks only the negative phrase, 'No one, Lord'. She serves much the same role as the woman with the issue of blood and, similarly, displays the protective non-aggression of Jesus towards 'faulty' human beings and, perhaps symbolically, Christian attitudes towards 'faulty' human institutions such as Judaism.

Readers of both genders should be able to see that texts, and especially these biblical texts, portray a mixture of reality and what the authors wish reality to be. Valid and successful readings of any texts depend on maintaining an awareness of the texts' tendencies to lead the reader by the nose. New Testament readers will benefit from constantly being alert to this continuous, though usually subliminal, aspect of authorial intent.

Male readers must take some share in neutralizing the androcentrism of texts, by deconstructing it as they read now; and female readers have to slough off complicity in the restriction of their freedom and powers. Female readers have to take seriously the warning that reading the New Testament will damage their self-esteem, 'immasculate' them,[2] and male readers have to realize that such texts contain dangerous elements of fantasy which can beguile and corrupt.[3]

Valid and successful readings of reality, such as happen when we reflect on our lives and work and plan ahead, similarly depend on all readers accepting just how much of their reality—and their texts—is time-conditioned.

---

1. De Boer, 'John 4.27', pp. 223-30.
2. Durber, 'The Female Reader', p. 187.
3. Clines, 'Why is there a Song of Songs?', p. 26.

'OLD WINE IN NEW WINESKINS': THE REFASHIONING OF MALE HEBREW BIBLE CHARACTERS IN NEW TESTAMENT TEXTS

Heather A. McKay

Introduction

While women in the Hebrew Bible are depicted mainly in the restricted modes allowed to them by patriarchy and frequently operate in the background of the stories,[1] many male characters radiate powerful qualities throughout the narrative. Among male Hebrew Bible characters only the young, such as Ishmael (Gen. 16, 17 and 21), or the disabled, such as Mephibosheth (2 Sam. 4.4, 9) 'deserve', or submit to, subjugation at the hands of powerful, dominant males.

These weaker male characters are patronized by their treatment at the hands of the biblical authors in much the same way as women characters: they do not act as subjects in their own right, but function as objects, submitting to, and having their future decided by, the powerful, successful males. Patronizing is the form that patriarchy takes when it is applied by powerful males to other, less dominant, males. Throughout the Hebrew Bible, the acquisition of power and of the right to self-determination characterizes successful males in the hypothetical 'real life' portrayed there, and in the narrative worlds of the various texts.

Being patronized is quite as demeaning to a male as being subjected to patriarchy is to a female, although the male victim understands an implicit promise from his societal group that in

---

1. See my article 'Only a Remnant of Them shall be Saved', above, for my feminist critique of the way female Hebrew Bible characters are reused by New Testament authors.

mature life he will assume a more powerful role over those younger, as well as those other-gendered, than he.[1] In biblical texts, narrative domination of 'inferior' fictive males is used, along with subjugation and silencing of women characters, as another means of reinforcing the norms of patriarchy, and, for that reason, this rhetorical manoeuvre can be uncovered, and recognized for what it truly is, by the application of the methods of feminist criticism.

However, the treatment of male Hebrew Bible characters re-appearing in the New Testament is not identical to the treatment of female characters making the same transition. For women characters, we found that the process of diminution or other misrepresentation was continued and intensified, whereas for male characters the tailoring process begins at this point.

So, while within the Hebrew Bible we find that intertextual references enhance the image of powerful biblical men, such as Abraham, who are praised in the Prophets and the Psalms, in the New Testament a different set of narrative rules applies. The powerful male Hebrew Bible characters are no longer afforded the protection 'due' under patriarchy to such venerable figures; in Gospels and letters alike they succumb to being patronized by the New Testament authors. Intertextual references, often on the surface laudatory, on close inspection can be seen to damage these men. By four principal means New Testament authors manhandle and recycle male characters from the Hebrew Bible.

1. Important Hebrew Bible figures, depicted as having close access to God's mind, such as Abraham and Moses, become reduced to donors who supply authority and divine authentication to the character Jesus.
2. Ambiguously evaluated Hebrew Bible characters, such as Aaron, are used as negative role models in the New Testament to encourage or castigate backsliders and other less than successful characters.
3. Hebrew Bible characters with particular and memorable attributes, such as Joseph with his foreknowledge of God's plans through dreams, lend their names to transpose ready-made character traits to New Testament characters who are being introduced to the reader.

1.   For females suffering under patriarchy there is no such guaranteed emancipation.

4. Negatively evaluated Hebrew Bible characters, such as Balaam and Cain, are used to facilitate the portrayal of certain New Testament persons or groups as butts of insult or mockery.

Hebrew Bible Characters as Accreditors of Jesus

To achieve the enhancement of the character Jesus necessary to the purpose of the Gospel narratives, male characters from the Hebrew Bible have their existence as powerful actants in their own right *progressively* removed; they function as psychological quarries from which the authors take qualities to aggrandize the persona of Jesus.[1]

On occasion the familiar characters do appear as recognizable summaries of their original Hebrew Bible portrayals but, more often, their names, and with them their personae, are used simply to supply positive labels for Jesus. The enhancement of the character Jesus in the New Testament narrative, from wayward, itinerant rabbi to supremely accredited agent of God, depends on the annexing of powerful attributes from those Hebrew Bible characters who are certain to be revered by the implied audience of the New Testament texts.

So, we find that characters such as Abraham, Moses, Elijah, David (as both king and as Psalmist) and Solomon all function in this affirming way in the New Testament.[2] The character Jesus, in some way, reveres each of them, yet always emerges from the relevant section of narration superior to them, and with their best traits incorporated into his character.

Other named male characters, including archangels, Gabriel and Michael,[3] and prophets, Isaiah, Jeremiah and Jonah,[4] are

---

1. This is in direct contrast to the treatment of women characters from the Hebrew Bible whose powerful characters traits are simply eliminated. See discussion in McKay, 'Only a Remnant'.

2. Some characters, such as Noah, and their stories are also used more neutrally in ways that emphasize continuity between these *new* Scriptures and the old.

3. Gabriel: Lk. 1.10-38; Michael: Jude 9; Rev. 12.7.

4. Isaiah: Mt. 3.3; 4.14; 8.17; 12.17; 13.14; 15.7; Mk 1.2; 7.6; Lk. 3.4; 4.17; Jn 1.23; 12.38-41; Acts 8.28-30; 28.25; Rom. 9.27-29; 10.16, 20; 15.12; Jeremiah: Mt. 2.17; 16.14; 27.9; Jonah: Mt. 12.39-41; 16.4; Lk. 11.29-32.

similarly put to the service of the character development of Jesus. In the Hebrew Bible these angels are powerful divine beings,[1] yet—to the New Testament writers—they are not as powerful as the human character Jesus nor do they hold as much authority in the cosmic domain as Jesus does in his role as the Christ. Prophets in the Hebrew Bible are portrayed as interpreters or commentators, giving reliable, because divinely generated, analyses of current situations and supplying accreditation to reliable speakers of God's words—whether political or cosmic. In the New Testament narratives these prophets, particularly Isaiah and Jeremiah, continue that role in the service of the character Jesus.

Abraham[2]

Abraham provides the paradigm for what happens to male characters from the Hebrew Bible at the hands of New Testament authors. In the New Testament he is reduced from the combined roles of rags-to-riches ancestor of the Hebrews and confidant of God to a symbol of divine authorization for Christian ethno-cultic development plans. When the New Testament authors have finished rewriting him he figures as no more than a genealogical mascot argued over by rival religio-political groups. The writers' repeated technique, of re-describing Abraham's deeds in laudatory language followed by stories and discussions that show how infinitely superior Jesus is,[3] is followed—with some variations—in both Gospels and letters.[4]

---

1.   Gabriel: Dan. 8.16; Michael: Dan. 10.13, 21.

2.   Much of my discussion on Abraham has been stimulated by, and set in contrast with, the work of Jeffrey Siker, both in papers given by him at meetings of the Society for Biblical Literature and in his book: J.S. Siker, *Disinheriting the Jews: Abraham in Early Christian Controversy* (Louisville, KY: Westminster/John Knox Press, 1991).

3.   Cf. Siker, *Disinheriting the Jews*, p. 140, who claims that the narrative pattern 'progressively subordinates Abraham to Jesus'.

4.   Cf. A.T. Lincoln, 'Abraham Goes to Rome: Paul's Treatment of Abraham in Romans 4', in M.J. Wilkins and T. Paige (eds.), *Worship, Theology and Ministry in the Early Church: Essays in Honor of Ralph P. Martin* (JSNTSup, 87; Sheffield: JSOT Press, 1992), pp. 163-79 (p. 164), who concludes that 'Paul appropriates Abraham for his gospel'.

In Romans.[1] The author of Romans 4 values descent from Abraham,[2] faith in God[3] and circumcision—in that order. He specifically demotes any righteousness gained by the actions of Abraham—and, implicitly, righteousness gained by any similar actions of Abraham's descendants. He locates the attribution of righteousness, given to Abraham in Genesis, exclusively within the context of his faith. Thus, those among the Jews or Gentiles who display faith like Abraham's can be construed as Abraham's descendants. Because the promise depended ultimately on faith—not birth or *bᵉrît*—these believers can also be inheritors of the promise.[4] By combining all these points, the writer is able to eliminate circumcision as a prerequisite for acceptability to God, on the grounds that Abraham was God's designated confidant long before he was circumcised (Rom. 4.12).

Returning to this point in Romans 9, the author makes use of the differences between Isaac and Ishmael, and between Jacob and Esau (Rom. 9.6-13), to prove that neither the name Israel, nor genetic descent from Abraham, automatically makes people 'children of Abraham'.[5] That relationship is forged through trust and through agreement to continue in the established promise relationship with God. Since they meet those criteria, the writer can envisage his followers as the new Israel.

In Galatians. In Galatians 3, the writer esteems his hearers' descent from Abraham, faith like Abraham's and the secondary receipt of blessing from Abraham—in that order (Gal. 3.6-9). He claims that through Christ the special divine blessing flows also to Gentiles—his implied audience. Then, developing the idea of

1.   I shall make no assumptions as to the authorship of any of the New Testament texts discussed here, other than of male gender, using such general terms as 'the writer' throughout.

2.   Also in 2 Cor. 11.2.

3.   Rom. 4.16 especially.

4.   Rom. 4.13-16; cf. R.B. Hays, '"Have We Found Abraham to Be Our Forefather according to the Flesh?": A Reconsideration of Rom. 4.1', *NovT* 27.1 (1985), pp. 76-98 (p. 97).

5.   Cf. C.K. Barrett, 'The Allegory of Abraham, Sarah, and Hagar in the Argument of Galatians', in J. Friedrich, W. Pöhlmann and P. Stuhlmacher (eds.), *Rechtfertigung: Festschrift für Ernst Käsemann zum 70. Geburtstag* (Tübingen: Mohr, 1976), pp. 1-16 (p. 14).

promise, used in Romans, as a way of including faithful Gentiles, he separates and distinguishes the receipt of blessing *by law* and the receipt of blessing *by promise*—implying also that the second is better because more original to God's purpose (Gal. 3.13-17).

In Galatians 4 Abraham is referred to, but only because he had two partners, Hagar and Sarah (Gal. 4.30–5.1). Abraham is not central to the argument here, the point made relating only to the different status of the descendants of the two women.[1] The author uses the stories from Genesis to call to mind the relation, yet distinction, of Isaac and Ishmael. By recalling the rivalries and hostility between the brothers,[2] he almost implies that the Christians should extrude Jews from any inheritance of Abraham, in the way Ishmael was excluded from Abraham's estate (Gal. 4.30).

In Hebrews. The writer of Hebrews uses the name of Abraham to identify Jews, or those faithful to the new covenant, as those people with whom God is particularly concerned (Heb. 2.16); for him, descent from Abraham exactly identifies God's chosen people.[3] Later in the letter the particular salvific role of God's promise to Abraham and its role in ensuring the future of those faithful in Abrahamic mode is stressed (Heb. 6.13-15).

In Hebrews 11, the writer praises Abraham for his faith and includes him in the list of heroes of the past. But it is Abraham's payment of tribute to Melchizedek that provides the main point he makes; by this action Abraham authorizes Jews, including Levites, to give tribute and honour to Jesus (Heb. 7.1-10), for the

1.   By somewhat tortuous logic he depicts the Jews as the issue of Hagar—a slave woman, though coming from Sinai and so linked with the giving of the law—and the Christians as descendants of the free woman, Sarah. By this means he can depict Christians as 'free' and Jews as 'enslaved'; cf. Barrett, 'The Allegory of Abraham, Sarah, and Hagar', pp. 11-13, 16.

2.   Barrett, 'The Allegory of Abraham, Sarah, and Hagar', pp. 11-13.

3.   C.P. Anderson, 'Who are the Heirs of the New Age in the Epistle to the Hebrews?', in J. Marcus and M.L. Soards (eds.), *Apocalyptic and the New Testament* (JSNTSup, 24; Sheffield: JSOT Press, 1987), pp. 255-78 (p. 274).

new priesthood of Jesus replaces the old priestly order, the Levitical priesthood.[1]

In James. The writer of James does not reapply any of Abraham's charisma to Jesus, but uses the example of Abraham to encourage his audience to show their faith by means of good works. He claims that faith does not help a needy person as effectively as good works do, citing Abraham's near-sacrifice of his son (Gen. 22) as the 'work' that proved his faith (Jas 2.18-24). Only, according to James, *after* a person's faith is proven can righteousness be 'reckoned' to him or her.

In Mark. The author of Mark's Gospel mentions Abraham only once, as one of the trio of named patriarchs to whom the god of the Hebrews had made himself known (Mk 12.26-27). He finds that an afterlife for Abraham was affirmed by God in the burning bush story (Exod. 3.6), for, since God does not concern himself with other than living beings, the divine reference to the patriarchs, Abraham, Isaac and Jacob, implies that they have a continuing live existence with God after their deaths. This, to the writer, provides evidence of resurrection.

In Matthew. Matthew's Gospel introduces Abraham as a revered ancestor of unquestioned fame and religious respectability who validates Jesus' credentials as potentially the one who will fulfil Jewish hopes and expectations.[2] Later the writer repeats the Markan use of the burning bush story as affirmation of the reality of resurrection (Mt. 22.32). In Chapter 3, somewhat in opposition to this picture of continuity with Jewish tradition, the voice of John the Baptist, by reminding the readers of the far greater power of God—when it comes to the matter of generation, from stones even, of Abrahamic offspring —implies that physical descent from Abraham is not *on its own* enough to ensure that any people will fulfil God's plans (Mt. 3.9). And in the Gospel's rhetoric it is possible that the Jews are

---

1.   Cf. Siker, *Disinheriting the Jews*, pp. 89-97; and Anderson, 'Heirs of the New Age', pp. 260, 267.

2.   Mt. 1.1, 2, 1.17; 3.9; 8.11; Siker, *Disinheriting the Jews*, p. 87.

here being ironically equated with stones, and are, therefore, implicitly, lacking in true life.[1]

In Luke–Acts. In Luke, similar lines of argument are followed,[2] with the addition of a couple of new threads. First, the appellations 'daughter of Abraham' (Lk. 13.16) and 'son of Abraham' (Lk. 19.19) are used to indicate a Jewish woman and, in the case of the reformed Zacchaeus, a faithfully observant Jewish man.

Secondly, Father Abraham—a title that highlights his role as ancestor—is described as having an afterlife both contented and sentient in a place indicated by the phrase 'Abraham's bosom' in which other fortunate deceased persons can also find themselves (Lk. 16.22-30), while less deserving persons endure eternal suffering in Hades. In his story of the rich man and Lazarus, the author elaborates the simple idea of afterlife found in Matthew and Mark to a place where continued human-like activity takes place.

The ways in which Abraham is appealed to in Luke valorize two groups of people: the pious poor and the outcasts, even the ultimate outcasts—the Gentiles.[3] Thus, while Jews are not *a priori* excluded from God's promises, they do have to be of a particularly pious and receptive cast of mind to be *certain* of inclusion.

The use of Abraham in Acts is closely similar. The author repeats the identification of God as the god of Abraham, Isaac and Jacob,[4] and as the maker of the covenant with the ancestor Abraham;[5] he refers to the special relationship of Abraham with God's puposes for his chosen people (Acts 7.2.), and uses the phrase 'sons of the family of Abraham' as an indicator of Jewish males (Acts 13.26). However, the ambiguity of his attitude towards Jewish inclusion in God's promises remains

---

1.   The Hebrew pun on *bānîm* 'sons' and *ᵃbānîm* 'stones' would, however, provide adequate motive for the use of the phrase.

2.   Lk. 1.55, 73; 3.8, 34; 13.28; 20.37.

3.   Siker, *Disinheriting the Jews*, pp. 103-27.

4.   Acts 3.13; 7.2, 32.

5.   Acts 3.25; 7.8-17.

unresolved,[1] while Gentile inclusion continues to be a mainstay of his writing.

In John. In chapter 8, the discussion involving Abraham indicates that, in the author's conception, Jewish self-understanding and self-confidence rest firmly on a belief in descent from, and religious continuity with, the patriarch. However, the writer then proceeds to divert the full weight of both Abraham's historical prestige and dignity, and also his perpetual closeness to God's heart and will, to the authentication of Jesus.[2] Jesus is thereby empowered to supersede even Abraham in terms of alignment with the being of God, and Abraham figures nowhere else, and in no other guise, in John.

So, while, as we saw above, the author of Luke distinguishes within the category of the 'sons of Abraham'—or descendants of Abraham—those who could more readily be included in God's promises because of piety and humility, the arguments in John frame that same distinction in terms of two groups of descendants of Abraham: genetic descendants (*sperma Abraam*) and spiritually faithful descendants (*tekna Abraam*).[3] The author of Luke does not go so far as to exclude Jews from becoming true children of Abraham, if they wish, but John's author begins to imply that Jewish descent could be something of a handicap to becoming true children of Abraham.

As he sees it, both Jesus and the Jews are to be identified by their paternity, and by their desire to adopt, and their success in following, their father's ways. Abraham is a candidate for genetic fatherhood of both Jesus and the Jews, but do Jesus and the Jews both follow in Abraham's footsteps? John 8 implies not. And though God is also a candidate for paternity of both Jesus and the Jews, the discussion makes clear that Jesus' claim to having God for his father takes precedence over the Jews' claim. It turns out that—for this evangelist—the Jews have completely misconceived their roots: God is the father of Jesus and the Jews are the offspring of the devil.

---

1. Siker, *Disinheriting the Jews*, pp. 126-27.
2. Jn 8.31-59; cf. E.D. Freed, 'Who or What was before Abraham in John 8.58?', *JSNT* 17 (1983), pp. 52-59.
3. Siker, *Disinheriting the Jews*, pp. 135-39.

In his rhetoric, Abraham acts as a lever to separate the Jews from God and align them with the devil. The Jews claim descent from Abraham, but by the Gospel writer's—and the character Jesus'—criteria they patently disavow that claim by their negative behaviour towards Jesus. They cut themselves off from being 'children of Abraham'. This rhetorical manoeuvre succeeds because of the two senses of 'children of Abraham':[1] genetic descendants, 'seed of Abraham', and faith-evincing followers, 'children after his own heart'.

Later in John 8 the argument shifts and the replacement of Abraham as close confidant of God with Jesus as son of God and, therefore, even closer confidant of God is set in motion. The Jesus of John's Gospel speaks of Abraham's having an existence outside of time after his own death and of Jesus' sharing that existence before his physical birth. The Jews in the text seem to ignore that interpretation and react as if Jesus claimed to have lived an earthly life alongside Abraham—patently nonsense to them—though they might perhaps have accepted that Abraham could have seen Jesus in a vision.[2] The writer's claim that Abraham accepts Jesus sets those Jews who do not accept him at odds with their lauded forebear—thus yielding a verbal victory for his point of view.

Isaac

In the New Testament, as in the Hebrew Bible, the amount of text devoted to Isaac is significantly less than that devoted to Abraham and to Jacob.

In the Letters. A reference indicating Jesus' similarity to Isaac—as far as being the beloved son of a father who was willing to sacrifice his son towards a greater good—has been noted in Rom. 8.32.[3] This text shows the writer's reasoning about Jesus'

---

1. See also Siker's analysis of the separation of the necessity of being of the 'seed of David' from messiahship (Siker, *Disinheriting the Jews*, pp. 138-39).

2. Siker, *Disinheriting the Jews*, p. 140.

3. T.F. Glasson (*Moses in the Fourth Gospel* [SBT, 40; London: SCM Press, 1963], p. 98), points out that the language regarding the 'sparing

death, in which he links the near-sacrifice of Isaac by Abraham at God's behest with the actual sacrificing of Jesus by God for the sake of the world.[1]

Later in Romans, Isaac is named as an important ancestor of the Jews, apparently as a means of rendering less central Abraham's role of key ancestor (Rom. 9.7, 10). By incorporating Isaac, as well as Abraham, as vital forebear, Abraham is made less crucial to the arguments—whether Jewish or Pauline— since Abraham's ancestry also of the non-favoured Arab races, through Ishmael, is hinted at. The Jews are indeed the descendants of Abraham, but through the line of Isaac. God's arbitrary —perhaps even capricious—and certainly unpredictable choice of certain people as favourites is made use of to show that Jesus was God's new, even if unexpected, choice of agent to redeem his people.

Similarly, the writer of Gal. 4.28 names Isaac, with his day-by-day subjection to life's indignities, implicitly at the hands of his older brother Ishmael, as a surety to his audience that one does not have to be a second Abraham to be included in God's promises; the ordinary—even the easily cowed—among them are also valued.

In Hebrews, Isaac represents both the vital link in the chain between Abraham and his descendants[2]—the inheritors of the promise—and the means,[3] cited also in James,[4] of the proof of Abraham's supreme faith. In his own right, as an active *subject*, Isaac stands for nothing in particular, although he seems to be portrayed as prefiguring the death and resurrection of Jesus in the discussion of his role, in Genesis 22, as *object* of near slaughter, and also, therefore, of quasi-resurrection.[5]

---

not of the son' used by Paul in Rom. 8.32 is similar to that used in the LXX of Gen. 22.12.

1.   See also A.C. Swindell, 'Abraham and Isaac: An Essay in Biblical Appropriation', *ExpTim* 87 (1975), pp. 50-53.

2.   Heb. 11.9-17.

3.   Heb. 11.18.

4.   Jas 2.21.

5.   Heb. 11.17-19; Glasson, *Moses in the Fourth Gospel*, p. 99.

In the Four Gospels and in Acts. The Gospels of Luke, Matthew and Mark all mention Isaac only in association with Abraham and Jacob. In Mark, this happens once, in the passage relating to the burning bush as evidence of resurrection, already explained for Abraham above, but in Matthew and Luke there are two other references to the three patriarchs: one in Jesus' genealogy and the other in a description of those seated at the top table in the kingdom of heaven.[1] In Acts, Isaac has again this same role of named patriarch—nothing more.[2]

Little is made of Isaac in the New Testament. He is present only as an accompanying person, along with Abraham and Jacob. He has no valuable qualities to be put to the service of the character Jesus, apart from the precedent of his role of non-resistant object of sacrifice. John's Gospel ignores Isaac completely.

Jacob

Jacob, in the Hebrew Bible, was noted for the interest—if not always admirability—of his character. In the New Testament he again commands attention on that basis.

In the Letters. In Rom. 9.13, the fact of Jacob's being beloved of God, while his twin brother Esau was hated, is restated as another means of justifying the acceptance of unlikely people into receipt of God's promises. This section of Romans recalls the original uncertainty of the success of the patriarchal family and credits its final success to God's commitment to it. God chose that family, so God made sure that family received his blessings—as promised. The writer implies that his followers will receive exactly similar special attention from God, and identical acceptance within God's plans. In the Hebrew Bible, the whole nation of Israel can be indicated by the one word, Jacob, and the writer repeats that usage when he refers to the final inclusion of Gentiles with Jews in God's chosen people at the end of time (Rom. 11.26).

In Hebrews, Jacob is mentioned only as a recipient or transmitter of blessings, as when Isaac blessed him, and also

1. Mt. 1.2; 8.11; 22.32; Lk. 3.34; 13.28; 20.27.
2. Acts 3.13; 7.8, 32.

when he blessed his children,[1] a useful illustration of a key image in the discussion on faith in Hebrews 11.

In the Four Gospels. Jacob receives similar treatment to Isaac, appearing in the reference to Moses at the burning bush (as cited above for Abraham) in all three Synoptics, and appearing in Matthew and Luke along with the other patriarchs in the genealogy and in the description of the heavenly banquet.[2]

But Jacob is also present by allusion, if not by name, in Jn 1.51, where the voice of Jesus promises Nathanael that he will 'see the heaven opened and angels ascending and descending upon the Son of Man'. This is an allusion to Jacob's vision at Bethel (Gen. 28.11-17), where Jacob dreams of himself and the Lord standing where they can see angels going up and down a ladder that reaches from earth to heaven. This reading points to Jesus' equation—by God, the source of the 'open heaven' phenomenon and line manager of the angels—with the ancestor Jacob. An alternative reading claims that Jesus is likened to God and Nathanael to Jacob, and infers that all future disciples of Jesus are being promised similar visions of the 'open heaven'.[3]

John 4, in the story of the woman at the well of Sychar in Samaria, goes further than equating Jesus with Jacob. There the author draws together themes from Israel's past, themes that are associated with the patriarch Jacob, and that are reapplied to Jesus. One idea is that of Jacob as provider of life-giving water by means of Jacob's well. Jesus outdoes that action by offering 'living water'.

Then the author sets up—only to subvert—a *faux* betrothal type-scene,[4] in which a woman meets an important stranger at a well. This woman, however, will not become the bride of Jesus, yet she points to his role as symbolic bridegroom. Jacob

---

1. Heb. 11.9, 20, 21.

2. Mt. 1.2; 8.11; 22.32; Lk. 3.34; 13.28; 20.37; Luke adds a reference to the house of Jacob in the Magnificat, Lk. 1.33, but none to Jacob himself.

3. J.H. Neyrey, 'The Jacob Allusions in John 1.51', *CBQ* 44 (1982), pp. 586-605; cf. M. Morgen, 'La promesse de Jésus à Nathanael (Jn 1.51) éclairée par la haggadah de Jacob-Israël', *Recherches des sciences religieuses* 67.3 (1993), pp. 3-21 (p. 20).

4. See discussion in McKay, 'Only a Remnant'.

became the bridegroom of two important ancestresses of Israel, but Jesus will be the bridegroom of Israel herself.

The theme of the ascendancy of Jesus over Jacob is suggested to the reader repeatedly throughout the whole scene, by means of the dialogue and interaction between Jesus and the woman of Samaria and by means of allusions and symbolism. Perhaps even the deceptive questioning of the woman by Jesus[1] is a way of showing his superiority over Jacob, famous for his divinely tolerated deceits.

Other Heroes of Israel's Past Who Authenticate Jesus

Moses, David, Elijah, Abel, Adam and Solomon are used in New Testament texts in such a way as to bring credibility to the prophetic and messianic roles ascribed to Jesus. Some of them— particularly Moses—also provide accreditation and enhancement of Jesus' persona. Abel provides a typical figure of innocent, undeserved death. Generally speaking, these characters fare no better than the patriarchs at the hands of the New Testament authors and are patronized by what is written about them.

Moses

Admittedly, reverence is shown to Moses by the writers—but to different degrees by the various characters in the narratives, and in ways that produce different effects in the reader.

Through each of the four Gospels Moses' force and power as a character or personality, validated by the Torah—the five Books of Moses—is diminished and faded as the power of Jesus is developed or, as the writers claim, 'revealed'. That is to say, Jesus becomes more important *at the expense of Moses*. So Moses appears in a range of roles, all of which are positively evaluated, but he progressively surrenders status. At the beginning of each Gospel he is introduced as ancestral leader, then as teacher and lawgiver, and as epiphane in the story of Jesus' transfiguration. But, by the end of each Gospel, he is depicted as a mere author or provider of a holy book. And in the letters similar narrative transferences of power take place.

---

1. See discussion in McKay, 'Only a Remnant'.

In the Letters. Although, in Romans and in 1 Corinthians, Moses is positively evaluated as revered leader and law-giver,[1] in 1 Cor. 10.1-4, the rock from which Moses produced water in the desert is revealed to be Christ.[2] Christ, as source, is more important, and closer to God, than the mere functionary and rock-tapper Moses.

In 2 Corinthians, the diminution of Moses' status continues: Moses' veil becomes a symbol of masking the truth, of hiding God's glory, and of the obfuscation of God's truth.[3] The law of Moses, originally God's law, and as such to be venerated and kept, has become no more than 'your law' or 'their law', perhaps at one time God's law, but now ill-interpreted and therefore not worthy of full obedience.[4]

In Hebrews 3 the writer reveres Moses as a member of God's household but, as soon as the reader has accepted the high tribute to Moses that that description represents, the picture changes and the role of Jesus—as builder of God's house— outranks the role of Moses as if he were no more than a part of the *fabric* of God's house.[5] Heb. 3.3 explicitly states that 'Jesus is worthy of more glory than Moses'.[6] The play on the meanings of 'house/household' allows this quick change from the elevation of Moses as a privileged member of God's household to the abasement of Moses as a servant in God's household. At the same time, there is concomitant elevation of Jesus—as son and joint designer/builder of God's house/household—to a status far above that of Moses.

Later in the letter Moses briefly reassumes the status he had in Exodus. He is again regarded as having been the mediator between God and people when the story of the giving of the law on Sinai is retold in Heb. 9.19 and where the continuing force of the laws of Moses is described (Heb. 10.28). But other references

1. Rom. 5.14; 9.15; 10.5, 19; 1 Cor. 9.9; 10.2.
2. Glasson, *Moses in the Fourth Gospel*, p. 48.
3. 2 Cor. 3.7, 13, 15; cf. U. Mauser, 'Paul the Theologian', *HBT* 11 (1989), pp. 80-106 (p. 88).
4. Glasson, *Moses in the Fourth Gospel*, p. 92.
5. Heb. 3.1-6; cf. T.G. Smothers, 'A Superior Model: Hebrews 1.1– 4.13', *RevExp* 82 (1985), pp. 333-43 (pp. 340-41).
6. Glasson, *Moses in the Fourth Gospel*, p. 69.

to Moses, somewhat unfairly, recount his 'sin of omission' in not attributing priestly status to the tribe of Judah from which Jesus would be descended (Heb. 7.14), and demote Moses from any special role in the writer's new configuration of the relationship among people, priest, God and Temple (Heb. 8.5-7). Even the encounter of Moses with God at the burning bush is retold only to point out that Moses' trembling shows how terrifying God actually is (Heb. 12.21).

In the list of heroes of the faith (Heb. 11.24-28), Moses is accounted faithful because he eschewed Egyptian power and luxury in order to live humbly with the Hebrew slaves, and, according to the author, preferred suffering for the Christ to the treasures of Egypt. This makes Moses out to be a willing servitor of Christ, and so aware of his future existence. Such a belief permits the author to count to Moses' detriment some other so-called 'failings' with respect to foreknowledge about Jesus.

In Mark. In Mark Moses appears first as one who commands, and whom Jesus follows without demur, in the story where Jesus tells the leper he has healed to give thanks *as Moses commanded* (Mk 1.44; 10.3). Later Moses is presented as one who speaks to Jews through the wise sayings of the command-ments (Mk 7.10). Later still he appears with Elijah as an equal supernatural authenticator of Jesus' religious significance and aid to the disciples' understanding of Jesus' role in Judaism (Mk 9.4-5). But, finally, he is much reduced in status, being presented merely as one who wrote down rules (Mk 12.19), or as one who, perhaps unwisely, permitted certain behaviours, such as divorce (which freedom Jesus 'rightly' rescinds—Mk 10.4), or as one who provided laws (Mk 12.19), or who long ago created a book (Mk 12.26).

This Gospel frequently contrasts Jesus with Moses and Elijah, and with 'the prophets of old', in order to begin to provide the reader with answers to the question as to what type of prophet Jesus actually was.[1] The answer given, generally, in the Gospels

1. R.A. Horsley ('"Like One of the Prophets of Old": Two Types of Popular Prophets at the Time of Jesus', *CBQ* 47 [1985], pp. 435-63 [p. 435]), frames the pertinent question as: 'Since this fellow is obviously a prophet, what sort of a prophet or which one is he?'

is that Jesus is portrayed with characteristics from all types of prophet: the action type, or charismatic leader and freedom fighter against tyrannical foreign oppression, the oracular type of prophet,[1] or as a (the) prophet who is to come, an eschatological prophet.

In Matthew. Matthew's Gospel presents a similar schema to Mark's,[2] but adds to the scriptural residue of Moses' authority the physical and symbolic idea of 'Moses' seat', a position of power and authority made use of by 'scribes and Pharisees' within the Jewish community (Mt. 23.2). The Matthaean texts criticize the Pharisees for the way they place Moses firmly in their nation's past as a long defunct law-giver whose name and authority are now being put to the service of another authority-seeking group, themselves. We can, however, wryly recognize the similarity of this procedure to the parallel annexing of Moses' authority by the pro-Jesus writers of the New Testament.

Matthew's infancy narrative includes obvious parallels with the story of Moses: the sojourn in Egypt, and, in particular, the hair's-breadth escape from the massacre of young male children by the wicked king.[3] If anything, the baby Jesus allegedly has had more care expended by God to ensure his survival than the baby Moses enjoyed.

The author of Matthew adds to Mark's account of the transfiguration the detail that Jesus' face shone like the sun (Mt. 17.1-8). So although Jesus has been in company with Moses on the mountain and has therefore been validated by him, Jesus also takes over a renowned characteristic of Moses, the glowing face, shining as Moses' face had after his close encounter with God.[4] The reader is left to assume that now it is only Jesus' face

---

1.   Horsley, 'Like One of the Prophets of Old', p. 460.

2.   Mt. 8.4; 17.3-4; 19.7-8; 22.24.

3.   Mt. 2.13-21; cf. Glasson, *Moses in the Fourth Gospel*, pp. 21-22; D.J. Harrington, 'Birth Narratives in Pseudo-Philo's Biblical Antiquities and the Gospels', in M.P. Horgan and P.J. Kobelski (eds.), *To Touch the Text: Biblical and Related Studies in Honor of Joseph A. Fitzmyer, S.J.* (New York: Crossroad, 1989), pp. 316-24 (pp. 321-22).

4.   Exod. 34.29; Glasson, *Moses in the Fourth Gospel*, p. 70.

that shines, while Moses' face is no longer radiant. Since this Gospel had earlier raised the question as to whether Jesus was the prophet who was to come, as promised by Moses,[1] the transference of the divinely generated luminescence to Jesus' face reads like confirmation of that suggestion.

In Luke–Acts. The author of Luke–Acts adopts the same pattern as that of the author of Matthew[2] in his use of Markan material,[3] though he adds different items to the picture.

Rather than replay the story of Moses' birth in his infancy narrative, the writer refers instead to Jesus' family's faithful observance of the law of Moses—particularly the laws of purification after childbirth—and thereby highlights Jesus' membership of an observant Jewish family (Lk. 2.22).

The Lukan account of the transfiguration makes Jesus and Moses out to be rivals,[4] even though the alteration in Jesus' face is made less of than in Matthew's account.[5] Other parallels between the two include the feeding of the five thousand (Lk. 9.10-17), including the question about Jesus' role as *a* prophet (Lk. 9.10-17), Jesus' journeys, the appointing of the 'seventy' (Lk. 10.1-17), and Jesus' exodus to Jerusalem (Lk. 9.31).

The Lukan account refers to Moses, as also to Abraham, in the story of Lazarus and the rich man (Lk. 16.29, 31). In this version of the story, neither Abraham nor Moses is reckoned to have the skill and power to convince reluctant Jews, though neither will Jesus have such power.

Because the figure of Moses as a shepherd of God's people is a well-known biblical theme, not only in the narrative of the burning bush but also in the Psalms and the Prophets,[6] the writer

1. Mt. 11.3; cf. Lk. 7.20.

2. Lk. 5.14; 9.30, 33; 20.28, 37.

3. Thus Luke, in 19.9, in a way similar to Matthew, uses the phrase 'son of Abraham' to indicate a Jewish male.

4. R.E. O'Toole, 'The Parallels between Jesus and Moses', *BTB* 20 (1990), pp. 22-29 (p. 22).

5. Lk. 9.28-36; see also the extended discussion of this topic in D.P. Moessner, '"The Christ Must Suffer": New Light on the Jesus–Peter, Stephen, Paul Parallels in Luke–Acts', *NovT* 28.3 (1986), pp. 220-56.

6. Exod. 2.2; Ps. 77.20; Isa. 63.11; Lk. 15.3-7; Glasson, *Moses in the Fourth Gospel*, pp. 95-96.

indirectly implies, in the parable of the lost sheep, that Jesus is better than, or at least as good as, Moses. Jesus is characterized as *the* good shepherd who searches indefatigably for those who stray.

In Luke, the actions of John the Baptist develop the comparison of Jesus with Moses by sending messengers to find out whether Jesus is the one who is to come (Lk. 7.18-23). But the author finally puts Moses completely into Jesus' hand when he describes Jesus as interpreting 'Moses and all of the prophets' clearly to the people, and implies that 'Moses and all of the prophets' foretell the life and works of Jesus (Lk. 24.27, 44). And he makes this same point again in Acts, twice, once in each of Paul's defences before Agrippa and Caesar.[1]

At points in the narrative of Acts a rivalry between Jesus and Moses surfaces: first, in Peter's claim that Jesus is the prophet greater than Moses whom Moses himself promised (Deut. 18.15); secondly, when there is a charge made against Stephen of blasphemy against Moses as well as against God;[2] and thirdly, during the discussion about circumcision and its relation to 'keeping the law of Moses'.[3] The debate highlights a rivalry between the teachings of Jesus and the teachings of Moses, and by casting the disagreement in terms of rival human interpretations of divine laws, the law of Moses is no longer seen to be co-terminous with the law of God. However, in Stephen's speech (Acts 7.2-53), Moses is given his full role in Israel's history, and no pejorative comparisons are made between him and Jesus. Rather Jesus is likened to Moses as a means of explaining *Jesus* to the hearers.[4]

Later, in Acts 13.38-39, the theme of competition between Moses and Jesus returns. A forgiveness beyond that offered by the law of Moses is offered to the audience through Jesus Christ. The juxtaposition of the two names suggests a replacement and superseding of Moses by Jesus, and, in this matter, Jesus is dominant.[5]

1.   Acts 26.22-23; 28.23.
2.   Acts 3.22; 6.11-14.
3.   Acts 15.1-21; 21.21.
4.   O'Toole, 'The Parallels between Jesus and Moses', pp. 25-26.
5.   Cf. O'Toole, 'The Parallels between Jesus and Moses', p. 28.

In John. In John, Moses is treated rather differently. There are three quite distinct and yet concurrent arguments. One is that Jesus *is very like* Moses, the second is that Jesus *is* the prophet like Moses whom Moses promised to the people in the future, and the third is that Jesus *is greater than* Moses. Moses is present on every page of this Gospel, either by direct reference or by allusion.

Throughout John there is a great deal of wilderness and exodus imagery, including echoes in the temptation narrative,[1] law-giving,[2] references to *the* prophet,[3] and to the bronze serpent.[4] Over and over again, there are allusions to actions carried out by Moses and to the discourses of Moses.[5] There is an expectation that there will be a second deliverer who will bring a second deliverance, like the exodus from Egypt. There will be 'bread of life' or 'living bread' just as there was manna. Jesus is the implied completion of all these hopes.

From the first chapter of John (Jn 1.17), Jesus and Moses are cast in the parallel roles of forerunner and fulfiller, for there Moses is described as a lawgiver, while Jesus is said to bring grace and truth. Later in the first chapter the author makes the point—which will become a running thread throughout this Gospel—that Jesus is *the prophet*, the one foretold by Moses and by other prophets.[6] At Sychar, the Samaritan woman gives voice to the expectation of the coming of the messiah who will be a great teacher, as Moses was also (Jn 4.25), and later decides that Jesus is he (Jn 4.25-39).

In John, the two rival groups, Jews and Pharisees and followers of Jesus, are cast in the roles of, respectively, disciples of Moses and disciples of Jesus, in the story of the healing of the man born blind (Jn 9.27-28). The groups are portrayed as in dispute, at loggerheads, as rivals for the stewardship of God's power on earth.

1.   Glasson, *Moses in the Fourth Gospel*, pp. 15-19.
2.   Glasson, *Moses in the Fourth Gospel*, pp. 20-26.
3.   Glasson, *Moses in the Fourth Gospel*, pp. 27-32.
4.   Num. 21; Glasson, *Moses in the Fourth Gospel*, p. 34.
5.   See the full discussion of all these allusions in Glasson, *Moses in the Fourth Gospel*.
6.   Jn 1.45; Deut. 18.15-22.

David

David is present, in both Gospels and letters, as tribal eponym and renowned regal ancestor, with a vital role as purveyor of useful prooftexts—by means of 'his' Psalms.

In the Gospels David also functions as an ancestral precedent and excuse for Jesus and his disciples when they are taken to task by Pharisees for breaking the Sabbath by rubbing ears of grain and eating them. The defence made was that David committed a similar profane act by taking, sharing and eating the shewbread in the Temple when he and his warriors were hungry.[1]

In addition to making use of narratives about David, David's own writings were useful to the Christian authors. The Psalms supply one of the most crucial prooftexts employed in Christian apologetics—the first verse of Psalm 110:[2]

> The Lord said to my Lord,
> Sit at my right hand,
> till I make your enemies your footstool.

In the Synoptic Gospels[3] this text is represented as words spoken by David and quoting a statement made by God to some other being whom David would also recognize as his (David's) lord. If that interpretation be granted by the reader, and if the lord in question be the Christ, then Jesus' sonship of David has to be seen, by the reader, in a light other than that of merely physical descent.[4] Jesus is a 'son of David' by birth, but is also far greater than David by God's appointment to the role of Christ.

The figure of David is used in four capacities at once in this cleverly constructed argument: as renowned tribal ancestor, as famous king from the past, as writer of sacred texts and as implied admirer of Jesus. How faithfully this deals with the

1.   Mt. 12.1-8; Mk 2.23-28; Lk 6.1-5.
2.   Mt. 22.41-46; Mk 12.35-37; Lk 20.41-44.
3.   Cf. Acts 2.23-36, where this, and a similar, point are made.
4.   R.H. Gundry, *Matthew: A Commentary on his Literary and Theological Art* (Grand Rapids, MI: Eerdmans, 1982), pp. 450-51; W.L. Lane, *The Gospel according to Mark: The English Text with Introduction, Exposition and Notes* (NICNT; Grand Rapids, MI: Eerdmans, 1974), pp. 435-36; J.A. Fitzmyer, *The Gospel according to Luke X–XXIV* (AB, 28a; Garden City, NY: Doubleday, 1985), pp. 1310-11.

character David of the Hebrew Bible is a moot point, but one of the strongest points made about Jesus in the New Testament is this argument, and it is made by means of the character David— as portrayed by the New Testament writers.

Elijah

Elijah's fame as a prophet, his personal charisma and his honest commitment to God's cause are used in the Gospels to authenticate Jesus as an important prophet.[1] Likewise, along with Elisha,[2] Elijah is used to excuse the locations of, and the social backgrounds of recipients of, Jesus' healing miracles.[3]

Elijah appears with Moses in the synoptic transfiguration narratives, and, although in Matthew and Luke he is secondary to Moses, he is the first of the two to be mentioned in Mark's account.[4] Elijah is present as both prophet and forerunner of Jesus, while Moses is present as 'the prophet *par excellence*',[5] and symbol of the written Scriptures.[6] However, in Mark, Jesus is not to be confused with either of these two famous prophets; he is greater than both Elijah and Moses, being the final consummation of God's sending of prophets and embodying the fulfilment of Scripture.

In the crucifixion narrative in Matthew and in Mark there is a suggestion, or a misprision, that Jesus calls to Elijah for some reason, but the possible role of Elijah at such a juncture is far

---

1. Mt. 16.14; Mk 6.15; Lk. 9.8. Elijah is also used to identify and characterize John the Baptist as a trustworthy herald of good news about the messiah in Mt. 11.14.

2. See Lk. 4.27, where the location of Jesus' miraculous cures in Galilee is excused by reference to Elisha's curing of Naaman alone of the lepers in Syria.

3. See Lk. 4.25-27, where God's particularity in sending Elijah to one widow in Zarephath is adduced as a parallel supporting the claim of God's sending Jesus to Galilee.

4. See discussion on Moses above.

5. M.D. Hooker, '"What Doest Thou Here, Elijah?" A Look at St Mark's Account of the Transfiguration', in L.D. Hurst and N.T. Wright (eds.), *The Glory of Christ in the New Testament: Studies in Christology in Memory of George Bradford Caird* (Oxford: Clarendon Press, 1987), pp. 59-70 (p. 63).

6. Hooker, 'What Doest Thou Here, Elijah?', p. 68.

from clear (Mt. 27.46-49; Mk 15.34-36). Other New Testament references to Elijah merely highlight his close, prayerful relationship with God, his humanness and the efficacy of his, and therefore of other human, prayers (Rom. 11.2; Jas 5.17).

Abel

In Matthew and Luke, Abel represents the first of a series of prophets—sent by God—whose blood was shed by hostile groups (Mt. 23.35; Lk. 11.51). To the writer of Hebrews he typifies the faithful giver of acceptable offerings to God, and the archetypal victim, the efficacy of whose innocent (righteous) blood is surpassed only by that of Jesus, acting as mediator of the new covenant (Heb. 11.4; 12.24).

Seeing Abel as the great innocent of the Hebrew Bible does no damage to the character as originally portrayed, but the casting of Abel as a prophet seems to be taking unfair advantage of a 'dead' character who cannot speak for himself. The Christian authors have changed a silent farmer (Abel says nothing in the Genesis narrative) into a professional wordsmith—a prophet.

Adam

Rom. 5.4 likens Adam to Jesus as being vitally important in human history but also contrasts them, seeing Adam as death-bringer and Christ as life-bringer. The same point is made twice more in 1 Corinthians, expanding the contrast between Adam and Christ to include the difference between Adam's receipt of God's life-giving spirit and Christ's giving it to others (1 Cor. 15.22, 45).

Adam's life and role in the creation narratives are completely ignored; only his unique status and his bringing of death are noteworthy to these writers. The former quality also belongs to Jesus as Christ, and the latter, disastrous, attribute is finally reversed by Jesus as Christ—the 'work' of the second Adam supersedes and redeems the 'work' of the first.

Solomon

Solomon appears in Matthew's, but not Luke's,[1] genealogy of

---

1. See Gundry, *Matthew*, pp. 14-17, for a discussion of the two genealogies.

Jesus (Mt. 1.6-7). The writer has used the list of David's descendants, supplied in 1 Chron. 3.5, 10-16, to create an ancestry for Jesus that shows strong precedents for his appropriateness as a messianic king. Solomon's greatness as a king is the attribute to be transferred to Jesus.

Later in Matthew, this time paralleled in Luke, Solomon's splendour is made little of by Jesus in a comparison with God's providential care of the 'lilies of the field'.[1] The third allusion to Solomon in Matthew, also paralleled in Luke, refers to his renowned wisdom and the fact that the Queen of Sheba made a long journey to discourse with him.[2] This theme is introduced solely for the purpose of pointing out that Solomon's wisdom is put in the shade by the more penetrating wisdom of Jesus.

Solomon is objectified by this use by the New Testament authors; only the very narrowest understanding of his attributes is expected of the reader in order to conclude that if Jesus outranks Solomon on these parameters, Jesus is indeed a wise and mighty king.

Jonah

The book of Matthew refers to Jonah twice, the second time quoting part of the first and longer section; Luke incorporates the longer section only.[3] The writer of Matthew imports Jonah's story for two features: one is the period—three days and nights—that Jonah spent inside the fish, which he uses as a foreshadowing[4] of Jesus' time in the tomb, and the other is Jonah's powerful preaching, which converted even such hardened sinners as the Ninevites of his day. Luke's account, however, takes up only the theme of Jonah as originator of the repentance of all Nineveh and implies that Jesus will cause repentance more widespread even than that.

The name of the character Jonah is used as a 'catchword',

1. Mt. 6.29; Lk. 12.27. There are no Hebrew Bible references to Solomon having resplendent clothes, but much other magnificence is attributed to him.

2. Mt. 12.42; Lk. 11.31; cf. my discussion of the character 'the Queen of Sheba' in 'Only a Remnant'.

3. Mt. 12.39-41; 16.4; Lk. 11.29-32.

4. Fitzmyer, *Luke X–XXIV*, p. 931.

almost as a metaphor to bring particular points into readers' minds. The full vigour and daring of the Hebrew Bible character is ignored by the New Testament writers. This is a patronizing use of the quirky Hebrew Bible character.

Hebrew Bible Characters as Types of Failures or Misunderstanding

Other Hebrew Bible characters are used to portray the natures of misguided religious predecessors or of partly committed waverers, for example, Aaron and Esau.[1]

Aaron

Aaron is used in Stephen's speech in Acts (7.39-41), as a reminder of how a person quite central to God's plans for Israel fell into apostasy and led others astray. This is faithful to the Hebrew Bible story of Aaron, but is only one part, and the most discreditable, part of his story.

The writer of Hebrews uses Aaron as the type of an important line of religious leaders, later displaced and replaced through God's initiative in providing a better leader—Jesus (Heb. 5.4). No one, he claims, would put themselves forward for that role, but would take it up only if God chose them for the role. Later, he uses the name of Aaron to indicate the former (inadequate) priesthood which has been replaced by the priesthood of Christ (Heb. 7.11).

Aaron as Moses' brother, colleague and companion does not feature in the New Testament; he is introduced only as a means of bringing his failings and inadequacies to notice, and to aggrandize the image of Christ as new High Priest.

Esau

The writer of Rom. 9.13 quotes the text of Mal. 1.2-3, where the voice of God states that he has loved Jacob and hated Esau, and then uses this text to distinguish those Israelites to whom God shows mercy from those whom God rejects. This is a rhetorical means of devaluing physical descent from Abraham as the

---

1.   Cf. also Korah, Lot and the pharaoh of the exodus story.

means of entry to the new Israel. Thus, an implied Ishmael[1] and a named Esau function as symbols of God's non-favouring of *certain* of Abraham's descendants.

Esau is used in two completely contradictory ways. First, in Heb. 11.20, Esau is the recipient of the faithful Isaac's blessing, and a parallel example to Jacob. Then, in Heb. 12.16-17, Esau's stupidity, thoughtlessness and carnality in selling his birthright of double portions for a single meal is, quite plainly, ridiculed. Esau's later frantic desire also to be blessed by his father is said to have been fruitless and his tears are used as a warning to the readers of Hebrews lest they behave in similar unwise ways.

Perhaps either of these rhetorical uses of Esau would be fair comment on its own, but the writer undoubtedly maltreats the Hebrew Bible character Esau when both these ploys are used within forty verses of each other.

Esau is of no interest to the Gospel writers; possibly there was no obvious role in their polemic for this type of ancestral 'Aunt Sally'.

Hebrew Bible Characters Providing Traits for New Characters

Some New Testament characters incorporate characteristics of familiar Hebrew Bible characters; for example, Joseph has dreams which are recognized as being sent from God, as did the patriarch Joseph. Judas sells a friend to foreigners for money, as Judah did his brother, Joseph. Ananias tells lies, like the Hebrew Bible prophet, Hananiah. Each New Testament character harnesses attributes from their Hebrew Bible predecessors and namesakes.[2]

Joseph/Joseph

Because of the story of Joseph's dreams in the Hebrew Bible,[3] readers' expectations of a series of dreams received by a person named Joseph (Mt. 1.20; 2.13, 19) are that they are truthful, reliable dreams. So, no argumentation to rule out non-divine

1. See discussion above on Abraham in Romans.
2. Cf. also Levi and Matthew, Joshua and Jesus, Jair and Jairus, Simeon and Simeon.
3. Gen. 37.5; 40.8-9, 16; 41.15, 17, 25; 42.9.

sources for the dreams, such as the influence of demons, is required from the Gospel writer. Joseph can accept, and act promptly in response to, these dreams. His behaviour is authenticated because it follows exactly the sequence of behaviour of his famous ancestor.[1]

Judah/Judas

Judah is the brother of Joseph who persuades the others not to kill him, but to sell him to foreign traders for twenty shekels of silver (Gen. 37.26-28). Judah is also the son of Jacob who persuades his father to send his remaining favourite, Benjamin, to Egypt to meet the disguised Joseph, and who guarantees the safety of Benjamin on his own recognizance (Gen. 43.3-15).

Some scholars have seen in this namesake of Judas (the two names are identical in Greek) some less wicked motivations for the behaviour of the Judas of the Gospels. There are the parallel ideas of handing over one of one's close companions to aliens for money, and there is the idea of standing guarantor for the life of another with one's own life.[2]

The name of Judah certainly carries those resonances and adds them to the picture the reader forms of Judas either as being similar to Judah or as an opposite.

Hananiah/Ananias

The prophet Hananiah, of Jeremiah 28, is notable for being a liar; that is how Jeremiah refers to him—and in less than a year Hananiah is dead.

Ananias (the same name in Greek) in Acts 5 is a very similar character, with a very similar fate.[3] Readers, on hearing his name, would instantly suspect the character of some blatant deceit.

---

1. Cf. R.E. Brown, 'The Annunciation to Joseph (Matthew 1.16-25)', *Worship* 61 (1987), pp. 482-92 (pp. 488-89).

2. See the fuller discussion of this point in H.A. McKay, *Good Friday and the Old Testament: A Study Guide for Lent*, forthcoming.

3. However, the Ananias in Acts 23 bears no resemblance to Hananiah.

Hebrew Bible Characters with an Unexpected Afterlife in the New Testament

Some Hebrew Bible characters are not channelled directly into Jesus' story and character portrayal, but have an afterlife in the New Testament that is at odds with their original character-ization in the Hebrew Bible. This is particularly the fate of Balaam.

Balaam

Balaam, in the New Testament, no longer faithfully delivers the unwelcome word of God, unwelcome because the person commanding his skills at the time desires to hear an opposite prediction. In the New Testament that faithfulness to his calling as a seer, and his true delivering of God's word—as portrayed in the Numbers text—have been ignored or subverted and Balaam is pilloried.

His maltreatment—if that be the appropriate name for what happens to Balaam elsewhere in the Hebrew Bible—begins in other, perhaps later, Hebrew Bible texts. They paint a less than favourable picture of Balaam. In Deut. 23.5, Josh. 24.9-10 and Neh. 13.2, the impression is given that Balaam did try to curse the Israelites—as he had been paid to do—but that God turned that cursing into a blessing. Set against that is the text in Mic. 6.5. where Balaam's resistance to Balak, and, therefore, faithfulness to his calling seem to be affirmed. But the New Testament texts present a development beyond even the derogatory texts of the Hebrew Bible.

In 2 Pet. 2.15, Balaam is apostrophized for having, apparently, loved the gain he got from wrongdoing, and the readers are expected to shun such a lifestyle. Similarly, Rev. 2.14 assumes that Balaam functioned as a teacher, and that he taught Barak to force the Israelites to sin by indulging in eating food sacrificed to idols and in immorality.

These two texts seem at first sight to refer to a totally different character from the Balaam of the Hebrew Bible, worse even than the less favourable depiction of him in some Hebrew Bible texts. Perhaps their purpose is polemic, attacking other powerful speakers within the local community, such as the 'false teachers' of 2 Pet. 2.1. The name 'Balaam' functions as no more than a tag to allow insults to be levelled at these (implied) others.

Cain

In Hebrews 11, Cain is mentioned in passing, and as a contrast to his more divinely favoured brother, Abel (Heb. 11.4), but elsewhere in the New Testament he is used as a pariah, a symbol of traits to be avoided at all costs, in particular feelings opposed to love, such as hate and, possibly, feelings with a satanic origin,[1] and an evil way of life (1 Jn 3.12; Jude 11).

Conclusions

Enhancement of the Character Jesus

Playing a small role in the creation of a completely holy, righteous and acceptable character for Jesus are Isaac, Jacob, Abel, Adam, Solomon and Jonah. Each of these Hebrew Bible characters contributes to the enhancement of the character Jesus.

Isaac and Abel call to mind the sacrifice of a beloved innocent. Jesus does not gain any qualities directly from Jacob, except, perhaps, a skill in casuistry, but is shown, in John, to outrank Jacob on most counts. Jacob provides continuity with the past, via Jacob's well, but is superseded by Christ, the giver of living water.

Adam has uniqueness which Jesus must also claim, but Jesus must also reverse Adam's death-bringing role. Jesus as the Christ *and* second Adam achieves these two aims and more than outdoes his famous forebear.

Solomon brings style, magnificence, aplomb and wisdom; the risen Christ will have more majesty than he. Jonah proves that preaching can prompt great repentance, and authorizes the claim that even the repentance of Nineveh can be improved upon by Jesus, whose preaching will bring the whole world to repentance.

1.   R. Schnackenburg, *The Johannine Epistles: Introduction and Commentary* (trans. R. Fuller and I. Fuller; Dublin: Burns & Oates, 1992), p. 179.

However, these minor characters add only one or two attributes each to the enhancing of the character Jesus. More central qualities and an inner stability and reliability are provided by the key figures Abraham, Moses, David and Elijah.

The favoured and powerful Abraham is used in the letters to provide invitations to hearers to regard themselves—whatever their character type—as suitable for inclusion in God's promises. He is also used in the Gospels to give qualities to Jesus, namely the appellations of agent and confidant of God.

In many ways, however, the Hebrew Bible character Moses has to be handled even more delicately than the character Abraham. He has many of the qualities, skills and attributes that the New Testament writers wish to accord to Jesus, and he had among the Jews of the time a large and faithful following, though some of those were also committed to accepting Jesus' teachings. Differentiating those two male characters in such a way that the qualities of Moses were seen to be duplicated and also surpassed in Jesus, and so that it became more attractive to the readers to commit their allegiance to Jesus, and less attractive to continue as disciples of Moses, presented a considerable challenge to the New Testament writers.

The writer of the Pauline letters and the writer of Hebrews use similar tactics. They distinguish between Moses and Jesus by ascribing a divine quality to Jesus as Christ and limiting Moses firmly to human status. Thus Moses becomes little more than an agent—as in the provision of water from the rock—and he is clearly less important then either the rock or the source of the water.

In Mark, there is a demotion of Moses and concomitant promotion of Jesus through the course of the Gospel. At the beginning Jesus himself reveres Moses as giver of divine laws, but by the end Jesus has reversed Moses' ruling on divorce. Matthew's Gospel takes a similar tack, though there are additional parallels between Moses and Jesus in the birth narrative and in the account of Jesus' shining face at the transfiguration. There is also, possibly envious, criticism of the scribes' and Pharisees' (ab)use of the power given to them by 'Moses' seat'.

In Luke, Jesus is portrayed in ways that compare and contrast him with Moses, but the implied readers are left in no doubt as to who is more important for their salvation. Admittedly, Moses was with God in the beginning; he began things well and executed important functions in the history of Israel, but Jesus is the leader for the present and future. Jesus can bring the new Israel into a close relationship with God, a new Israel that welcomes the pious and the penitent—from whatever community. The insidious voice of the narrator implies that Moses is *limited*, limited to the past, and limited in his dealings to the group of tribes of Israel wandering in the wilderness, but Jesus is without limits.

In John the fullest and most argumentative discussion of the points of similarity and contrast of Jesus and Moses, of ascendancy and demotion, of value for the past and value for the present and future, is made.[1] Just as, in John, we found the harshest reduction of the power and status of Abraham with respect to God and the Jews, so also we find the greatest transfer of the qualities of Moses to Jesus—as the bronze scorpion was held up at Moses' instigation to cure the fever-ridden Israelites in the desert (Num. 21.6-9), so Jesus would be lifted up on the cross to bring eternal life to his followers (Jn 3.14).

The character David, familiar from the Hebrew Bible, is no longer recognizable as the same 'person'; he has been re-created for their own purposes by the New Testament authors.[2] As a result of their skilful writing, King David inflates the importance of his peasant descendant.[3] As for Elijah, Jesus is all that Elijah was, and more.

To be convincing as the messiah, Jesus must outshine all these, and outdo them in all their qualities. He must be seen to be God's closest confidant through all time since before creation, the supremely perceptive prophet, teacher and law-giver, the

1. Jn 1.17, 45; 5.46; 7.23.
2. J.M. Bassler, 'A Man for All Seasons: David in Rabbinic and New Testament Literature', *Int* 40 (1986), pp. 156-69 (p. 156), who states that the New Testament authors 'were primarily interested in using David to promulgate their own views'.
3. Cf. Bassler, 'A Man for All Seasons', p. 163, who puts it as follows: 'the figure of David fades in the literary presence of his son'.

appropriate king for Israel, and a charismatic champion of the oppressed people of Israel. The New Testament authors' subtle and wide-ranging narrative use of Abraham, Moses, David and Elijah achieves that object.

Role Models for Struggling Christians

The ambiguity of the characters Aaron and Esau allows them to be used either in mitigation of backsliding or as role models for repentant sinners.[1] The new priesthood of Christ can be set above that of Aaron and the humble repentant believer can succeed at least as well—if not better than—Aaron or Esau.

They display negative qualities that Christians should eschew. Apostasy, weakness, greed, and short-sightedness are successfully presented as wrong by the writers' references to these characters and their stories, though redemption and assimilation remain possible for people like them.

Role Models for New Testament Characters

Importation of ready-made character traits into characters with supporting roles in the New Testament writings is accomplished by using the names of famous Hebrew Bible characters. The New Testament writers can say much more about a character by this means than by traditional descriptions. Thus Joseph has dreams on which it is quite proper to act immediately, Judas has the hint of a more innocent motivation for his actions in the passion narrative, and Ananias can be more quickly seen for the fraud that he turns out to be.

Rhetorical Means for Venting Spleen

Used as butts for insult and derision are Balaam and Cain. To some extent their Hebrew Bible stories authorize this treatment, but in the New Testament this verbal abuse is carried to excess. As a successful rhetorical manoeuvre, this ploy allow for the expression of venom at these named defaulters, and for the concomitant expression of opprobrium at the implied counterparts in the communities of the readers. In a religious movement

---

1.   As discussed above, Isaac is used to encourage the ordinary, and Jacob those with less than perfect characters, to believe that they also will be welcome in the 'new Israel'.

promoting love and forgiveness, these two characters are made use of to allow the expression of very vicious human sentiments indeed.

Summary Conclusion

Throughout the New Testament faithfulness to the original Hebrew Bible depiction of male characters has been sacrificed to the goals of persuasion and conversion. The Hebrew Bible characters have been patronized and objectified to provide a brilliant character for Jesus and to create comfortable role models for the new generation of Christians.

GENTILES AND THE DAVIDIC TRADITION IN MATTHEW

Mark R.J. Bredin

The aim of this essay will be to examine the presence of the four women in the Matthean genealogy, and to reach some conclusion as to why Matthew[1] included them. Special attention will focus on the social setting and changes which the Matthean community underwent. This will facilitate greater understanding of the motives which necessitated placing the women in the genealogy. It will be seen, also, that these motives were instrumental in Matthew's development of the traditions concerning the four women, and Jesus' encounter with a Canaanite woman (15.21-28), and may account for his interest in Abraham (see especially 1.1 and 8.11).

The opening chapter of Matthew's Gospel begins with a genealogy, a genre common to the Hebrew Bible. It begins: 'The book of the genealogy of Jesus Christ'. The attention of the reader is then drawn to two important figures from the Hebrew Bible: David and Abraham. It is said that Jesus was the heir to these two great figures—'the son of David, the son of Abraham'. The genealogy continues: 'Abraham was the father of (ἐγέννησεν, lit. 'he begat') Isaac'. This is typical of genealogies found in the Hebrew scriptures; compare Gen. 5.1: 'the book of the genealogy'; also: 'and x was the father of (ἐγέννησεν) y' (Gen. 5.6 and elsewhere). This follows a typical form until v. 3 where one finds: 'and Judah the father of (ἐγέννησεν) Perez and Zerah by Tamar'. In v. 5 one has: 'and Salmon the father of (ἐγέννησεν) Boaz by Rahab', and 'Boaz the father of (ἐγέννησεν) Obed by Ruth'. Then again in v. 6: 'and David was the father of

---

1. When referring to the author of Matthew's Gospel I shall write 'Matthew' without making any assumptions as to precisely who this figure is.

(ἐγέννησεν) Solomon by the wife of Uriah'. The author of
Matthew's Gospel is following a traditional genealogical structure until v. 3, when it is broken with the addition of Tamar,
then again with Rahab and Ruth.[1] The pattern is broken again in
v. 6, but in a different way. In v. 6, the woman's name is not
mentioned; she is described in reference to her husband Uriah,
as 'wife of Uriah'. There are then three breaks in the traditional
literary pattern.

Interest in the reason or reasons for Matthew's inclusion of
the four women is not new. This interest has resulted in many
theories. It is not my intention here to assess the merits or
demerits of each.[2] The arguments that Matthew included the
women because of their Gentile status seem compelling except
in the case of Bathsheba. Bathsheba, contrary to scholarly
opinion, is not a Gentile-Hittite.[3] The argument that Bathsheba
is a Gentile-Hittite because of the way she is designated must be
questioned, as one may note that Bathsheba is mentioned as
'daughter of Eliam'. There is an Eliam mentioned in 2 Sam.
23.34, who is included among a list of 37 great warriors, and is
probably the father of Bathsheba. Eliam is the son of Ahithophel
who is from Gilo, which is another name for Giloh, as
mentioned in Josh. 15.51. Giloh belonged to the inheritance of
Judah, and was a village somewhere in southern Judah (see

1.   There is some debate as to the exact identity of Rahab. The name
is undocumented in the Scriptures; Hebrew texts do record a women
named רָחָב, the harlot of Jericho (Josh. 2.1, 3). J. Quin writes: 'The Ραχαβ
of Mt. 1.5 ought not to be translated with Rahab, the name of the harlot
of Jericho': 'Is Rachab in Matthew 1.5 Rahab of Jericho?', Bib 62 (1982), pp.
225-28. See R.E. Brown for the opposite argument: 'Rachab in Matthew
1,5: probably is Rahab of Jericho', Bib 63 (1982), pp. 79-80. In spite of the
difference in Greek spelling and the dating difficulty (the biblical Rahab
lived at the time of the conquest, nearly two hundred years before Boaz),
most scholars conclude that it is virtually certain that Matthew means
the Rahab of the conquest. See A.T. Hanson's article also, 'Rahab the
Harlot in Early Christian Tradition', JSNT 1 (1978), p. 54.

2.   See W.D. Davies and D.C. Allison, A Critical and Exegetical
Commentary on the Gospel according to St. Matthew (Edinburgh: T. &
T. Clark, 1988), I, pp. 170-72.

3.   See C.L. Blomberg, 'The Liberation of Illegitimacy: Women and
Rulers in Matthew 1-2', BTB 22 (1992), p. 145.

Josh. 15.20). Can one not therefore surmise that Bathsheba's father was from Judah? The fact that Bathsheba married a non-Israelite does suggest the possibility that Eliam was not a Judahite. However, the evidence would seem to support the opposite conclusion. Eliam's father, Ahithophel, was councillor to David, and therefore again presumably a Judahite (2 Sam. 15.12). So it does seem that Bathsheba was a Judahite. This would militate against her inclusion because of her Gentile origins. However, in returning to the designation 'wife of Uriah', it is Uriah who is the salient figure here in the genealogy. Matthew's desire is to draw attention to the figure of Uriah. Uriah was certainly non-Israelite, and was considered a righteous man. He refused to sleep with his wife while his comrades were out fighting, and was named a man of valour (2 Sam. 23.39). It must remain a possibility, therefore, that the mention of Uriah is meant to recall him and not Bathsheba.[1] The motive for this would seem to be connected with Matthew's Gentile interest.

A further motive behind Matthew's inclusion of the Gentiles concerns their righteousness. Amy-Jill Levine expresses it well when she writes: 'Tamar acts when Judah unjustly refuses; Rahab recognizes the power of the Hebrew God and so protects the scouts; Uriah (who is named in the genealogy, whereas Bathsheba is not named)—unlike David—displays fidelity to his commission and his fellow soldiers; and Ruth, following Naomi's advice, moves Boaz to action'.[2]

It is usual in studies regarding the reasons for the inclusion of the four women to concentrate on the arguments concerning whether they were sinners, or righteous, or whether they showed initiative. On the whole, there are arguments for all the above solutions based upon the Hebrew biblical and later rabbinic traditions regarding the women. However, the inclusion of the first three women and Uriah as righteous Gentiles fits into the context of post-70 CE Judaism. The purpose here is to examine Matthew's inclusion of the women against the

1. A.-J. Levine, 'Matthew', in C.A. Newsom and S.H. Ringe (eds.), *The Women's Bible Commentary* (London: SPCK; Louisville, KY: Westminster/John Knox Press, 1992), pp. 252-63, esp. p. 252.
2. Levine, 'Matthew', p. 253.

wider background of his Gospel, aided by a study of the community in relation to its social context. Therefore, it is important to have some understanding both of the community which first received the Gospel, and of the issues which led the final writer/redactor to preserve and develop the traditions which he and the community received. This will demand answers to questions such as where the community was located, under what kind or kinds of political rule the community stood, and from which strata of society its members were drawn. A further point, some knowledge of the contentious issues which effected changes in the early church, is significant for Matthew's construction of reality, and the way traditions contained in the Gospel were developed. An assessment of the general Gospel context in the light of the problems of the early church, and the way Hebrew biblical traditions and traditions about Jesus have been developed and reinterpreted in reference to that context (especially the story of the Canaanite woman in 15.21-28), will facilitate a reconstruction of Matthew's reason for drawing attention to four righteous Gentiles in the first few verses in the opening chapter of his Gospel.

The date of writing of Matthew's Gospel is thought to be post-70 CE. It was certainly used in Syria around 115 CE by Bishop Ignatius, who quoted Mt. 3.15 in his letter to the Smyrneans. The Gospel is also used in the *Didache*, a writing which originated in Syria about 100 CE. As the Gospel shows an awareness of the Temple destruction which occurred around 70 CE (see 22.7; 24.9, 21), it would be fair to surmise a dating around 80–90 CE. This dating will be significant in understanding some of the problems that the community was facing, which will be looked at later.

The question of placing the Gospel is problematic. It seems to have its setting in Syria, probably Antioch; however, it has a distinct ring of 'Palestine' to it. Texts such as 10.5-6 point to the placing of the Gospel in 'Palestine'. Matthew uses texts from the Hebrew Bible and the Septuagint, and shows an awareness of scribal teaching. There is a Semitic touch to some of his Greek, such as a Jewish reader would appreciate. Aramaic terms are left untranslated, and Matthew leaves unexplained references to Jewish customs, such as hand-washing traditions, unlike

Mark who does explain for his Gentile readers (Mk. 7.3-4).[1] Further, it would appear from some texts that the Matthean community experienced the 66–70 CE war: 'It will be a time of great distress; there has never been such a time from the beginning of the world until now, and will never be again,' (24.21).[2] Also see Mt. 22.1-14 (the parable of the wedding feast) which reflects the destruction of Jerusalem; a similar parable is also found in Lk. 14.16-24. However, Matthew adds: 'The king was angry, and he sent his troops and destroyed those murderers and burned their city' (22.7). This verse intimates that the destruction was real and painful to some of the Matthean community living in Jerusalem. This would argue for a strong awareness of the volatile Palestinian setting on the part of the community.

Continuing with the Palestinian setting, it is interesting, but not altogether surprising in view of the escalating situation since 44 CE culminating in the Jewish war of 66–70 CE, to observe an anti-Gentile tendency in Matthew's Gospel. Anti-Gentile feeling was considerably kindled in the years following 44 CE when Claudius made Palestine into a Roman province, setting up a procuratorship, which Josephus portrays as showing little understanding or perception of its Jewish subjects (see especially *Ant.* 20.11.1; also Tacitus's *Historiae*, v. 9). The anti-Gentile tendency can be seen in 6.7, where the Gentiles are given as an example of how not to act: 'And in praying do not heap up empty phrases as the Gentiles do' (see also 6.32). In 5.47, Gentiles are belittled again, with the words: 'And if you salute only your brethren, what more are you doing than others? Do not even the Gentiles do the same?' In 18.17, the Gentile is compared to the tax-collector, the tax-collector being one of the most despised because he contracted with the Roman authorities

---

1. For example, the Aramaic word רקא is represented by ρακα (*raka*) in Mt. 5.22. In 27.6 the Hebrew קרבן is represented by κορβαναν (*qorbanan*); κορβαν (*qorban*) appears in Mk 7.11 but is translated for the audience. Note also 23.5 for the wearing of phylacteries, thus suggesting Matthew's audience were used to this sort of custom. See R.T. France, *Matthew* (Leicester: Inter-Varsity Press, 1985), pp. 17-18 for more detail.

2. Compare with Josephus's description of this period (*War* 5.12.3).

to gather taxes, at a profit to himself: 'If he refuses to listen to them, tell it to the church; and if he refuses to listen even to the church, let him be to you as a Gentile and a tax-collector'.

My proposal is that the Matthean community was set in Palestine and was able to practise its religion in relative peace until the war broke out, causing the community to flee to the regions of Syria. In Acts 8.1 we are told of a persecution and, consequently, a dispersion of Jerusalem Christians. Since later in Acts we read of Christians alive and well in Jerusalem (9.26, 9.31), but also again of those who were scattered (11.19-20), we may assume that there were two groups, one remaining, and one dispersed. These are generally held to be τοὺς Ἑβραίους (the Hebrews) of Acts 6.1 remaining, and the Hellenistic Christians being scattered, Matthew's community being the former. Josephus speaks of the outrage of Jews at the execution of James and Simon by Alexander (46–48 CE; *Ant.* 20.9.1). The situation in Palestine during this period was volatile. There was probably an increasing suspicion of the followers of Jesus, especially when it was reported that they were teaching against Moses and circumcision (Acts 21.21). However, they were secure enough to remain in Jerusalem until the period of the war. Many of these followers of Jesus would have defended their Jewish identity, and would have been accepted for their Jewishness by most. Acts 21.17-26 shows a strong desire to assuage fears and suspicions that the community was anti-Temple and anti-Torah. This affirmation of the Jewishness of the Matthean community accounts for its antipathy towards Gentiles. It may even account for vv. 10.5-6, which will be looked at later.[1] It may also be the cause of Jesus' harsh words to the Canaanite woman: 'οὐκ ἀπεστάλην εἰ μὴ εἰς (πρoς in 10.6) τὰ πρόβατα τὰ ἀπολωλότα οἴκου Ἰσραήλ' ('I was sent only to the lost sheep of the house of Israel', 15.24, see p. 108). It is plausible to see in these words a polemic against the Gentile mission in Antioch, which the twelve apostles were ambivalent about, as can be seen from Gal. 2.8-9.[2] However, the Syrian connection still

---

1. The commissioning of the Twelve appears elsewhere in Mk. 6.7-13 and Lk. 9.1-6. In neither Mark nor Luke are the restricting words regarding the disciples going only to the lost house of Israel to be found.

2. E.P. Sanders acknowledges this possibility, too, when he writes,

existed, and this will be shown to be significant later on.

From this it is possible to see a group of Christian Jews, living quite closely with their non-Christian Jewish contemporaries. H. Maccoby writes, 'first-century Pharisaism allowed for a variety of religious styles, in addition to the norm'.[1] Maccoby argues for this lenience which allowed for much diversity in its ranks by pointing to the disagreements and differences of attitude, for example, between the more lenient House of Hillel and the more severe House of Shammai. Acts' account of Gamaliel, the Pharisaic teacher, who counsels caution in persecuting the Christians (Acts 5.34-42) is an example of Jewish leniency before the war. So it is possible to see the followers of Jesus being able to live without too much trouble in Palestine, and probably in Jerusalem, and taking a fairly conservative view on breaks from Torah. The picture of first-century Palestine is one of many groups with various interpretations of Torah. The behaviour of the different groups varied, but on the whole toleration ruled the day.

It is fair to extrapolate, from the above data which point to the Jewishness of Matthew's community, that the community had probably not changed its structures of worship or organization much from its pre-Christian days. It seems quite plausible to see the community as having adopted the structures of its parent religion, and remaining a fairly cohesive group. R.T. France calls Matthew's Gospel 'A Gospel of the Church'.[2] This Gospel is the only one to include the term ἐκκλησία (church) (16.18; 18.17). Linking in with Acts, it does seem possible to argue that the Matthean community would fit the group which we read about in Acts 6.1, that is τοὺς 'Εβραίους (the Hebrews). They adopted and developed traditions which supported their setting in Jerusalem, and embraced traditions said to go back to Jesus which defended their anti-Gentile stance.

However, although this picture holds together some of the

'Matt 10.5f. could conceivably show that there was a hard-line group not mentioned in Galatians, one which positively opposed a Gentile mission'; *Jesus and Judaism* (London: SCM Press, 1985), p. 220.

1. H. Maccoby, *Judaism in the First Century* (London: Sheldon Press, 1989), p. 27.

2. France, *Matthew*, p. 20.

data, it exists in tension with other data within the same Gospel. It is important to observe the presence of this tension. In ch. 10 tension is found especially between vv. 5-6 which oppose the missionary activity of the Hellenists: 'Go nowhere among the Gentiles...', and vv. 17-18 which support it: 'Beware of these people; for they will deliver you up to councils, and flog you in their synagogues, and you will be dragged before governors and kings for my sake, to bear testimony before them and the Gentiles'. Mission to the Gentiles is here an assumed fact. The saying was put into the mouth of Jesus later to help support the community in its missionary activity to the Gentiles.[1] The story of the Canaanite woman would also appear to be in tension with 10.5-6.[2] In the story we read the words of Jesus about the mission being only to the House of Israel, which would support some Jewish readers who were not happy with mission to the Gentiles; thus far it coheres with 10.5-6.[3] Then suddenly the scene changes and Jesus affirms the woman, in complete contrast to his previous words to her. Tension and contradiction within one chapter and then within one story are surely significant. My proposal is that Matthew has intentionally placed differing and opposing traditions developed within his community in this way, and that his audience would understand the significance, just as they would understand the four women within the genealogy. The positioning points to the existence of a debate which is going on within the community, and this debate hypothesis is crucial to the placing of the four women within the genealogy.[4] This will be shown to be so later.

It could be argued that this debate hypothesis is based upon a contradiction and tension between particular sources which

1.   Sanders, *Jesus and Judaism*, p. 220.

2.   See also Mt. 21.43; note the emphasis upon God's rejection of Israel and his acceptance of Gentiles.

3.   It also coheres with what we know for certain about the historical Jesus, that is, that he restricted his ministry to Jews (see E.P. Sanders and M. Davies, *Studying the Synoptic Gospels* [London: SCM Press, 1989], pp. 305-309).

4.   My feeling is that Mt. 21.43 and 22.1-14 could also be traditions used within the debate to support the mission and the view that God accepts Gentiles, and that the mission is not simply to the house of Israel.

could better be accounted for by assuming various redactors, or alternatively that Matthew was not as concerned with contradictions as a PhD student might be. First, this might be the case if the contradictions and tensions were separated by a few thousand words, but not when separated by a few verses. Secondly, such a methodology in solving contradictions within texts is only legitimate if there is no other way of accounting for them.[1] My proposal offers another way.

The debate hypothesis can be further strengthened by the Syrian connection. Eusebius informs us that the Jerusalem community was able to escape the doomed city before the Roman siege of Palestine.[2] Also, Mt. 24.15-16 reads: 'So when you see the desolating sacrilege spoken of by the prophet Daniel, standing in the holy place...then let those who are in Judea flee...'. It is the contention here that a Jewish Christian community based in Jerusalem fled from the city. Caution must be used in accepting Eusebius's account.[3] However, it still seems possible that a Christian community did flee before Jerusalem was destroyed, as I am sure many non-Christian Jews did, and Mt. 24.15-16 appears significant in pointing to a fleeing community. Even if they did not escape, there is no reason to think that a Jewish Christian community did not survive. At the beginning of this article, the question of the Syrian/Palestinian origin to the Gospel was raised. The Syrian question has significance now. At some point within the lifetime of the Matthean community it moved away from Jerusalem. The siege of Jerusalem (66–70 CE) would be a possible time, which would fit in with the writing of the Gospel around 80–90 CE, and its later presence in Syria. A reconstruction of events would be that during the exodus from Jerusalem, the Matthean community fled to Syria (something akin to the great trekkers' move forward to the northern Transvaal in South Africa). Eusebius mentions a community which fled from Jerusalem to Pella; it seems likely that a community fled not only to Pella as according to Eusebius, but also to Antioch and the surrounding rural areas of Syria.

1.   Sanders and Davies, *Studying the Synoptic Gospels*, p. 202.
2.   Eusebius, *Eccl. Hist.* 3.5.3.
3.   Maccoby also adds his criticism here; see *Judaism in the First Century*, p. 130.

Antioch and the surrounding areas would seem an acceptable place to go for both non-Christian Jews and Jewish Christians fleeing Jerusalem. Even if they did not flee but stayed on in Jerusalem to fight the Gentiles, it is possible that they were dispersed by the victorious Gentiles to Antioch as well as many other places. The contention here is that in some way or other the Matthean community found its way to Syria, with many settling in Antioch. Antioch offers the place and setting which account for the way in which Matthew's Gospel developed into its final form, while the Palestinian background is significant for the way in which the community's traditions developed and for the issues that they faced in their altered sociological setting.

It is a great irony that the community found itself in Antioch, the place of so much conflict a little earlier between the dominant Jewish leadership of James and Peter representing the Hebrew group against the Hellenists. Fortunes had changed for the better for the Hellenistic Christians, and the Hebrew group was on new territory. There is no reason at all to expect that life would have been easy for the Hebrew Matthean community. Socio-economic and socio-cultural changes effect changes in terms of beliefs, and in terms of where one's commitments lie, either with the old or the new ways. It should be expected that within the community of displaced Hebrews, attitudes would have varied from one individual and family to another. This sociological phenomenon can be observed in ethnic minority groups settling into new areas, so also in Syria.[1] It seems fair to suppose that there were no few problems for the Matthean community. Riches writes: 'The social pressures on Jews in the first century were such as to make it increasingly difficult for them to sustain their own community norms and they therefore took certain paths of action to enable them to deal with these problems'.[2] In the Matthean setting, we are dealing with a

---

1. J. Riches, 'The Sociology of Matthew: Some Basic Questions Concerning its Relation to the Theology of the New Testament' (SBLSP; Atlanta, GA: Scholars Press, 1983), p. 267. Riches, a New Testament sociologist, acknowledges that looking for analogies in the history of other religious movements is a legitimate methodology when attempting to explain how ancient religious communities develop.
2. Riches, 'The Sociology of Matthew', p. 269.

community living in a situation different from that in Palestine. The sociologist's question, therefore, regarding the relationship of belief and altered setting is important. We may assume that beliefs would have been modified.[1] In this discussion, it is important to look at the situation that existed for Matthew's community in Syria in order to contrast it with what is known about its previous setting in Palestine.

To do this one must first ask how the non-Christian Jews were faring in post-70 CE society. Unfortunately, there are no detailed historical accounts regarding the years following 70 CE. One can at best surmise the situation. J. Neusner writes regarding the effects that the destruction of the Temple had on Jewry: 'first, a profound sense of disorientation because of the loss of the temple, second, confusion about how it was to be restored'.[2] The main leader group would now have been the Pharisees, who were led by Johanan ben Zakkai. The Temple destruction, for Judaism, marks the beginning of a tendency towards uniformity which demanded more observance of the practical obligations of the law, which can be seen later in the Mishnah and other Jewish writings. One should also see that such practices replaced the previous emphasis upon the Temple.[3] This would not have gone well for the Matthean community, who had up until then been able to exist as one of the many and diverse sects within Judaism.

It is not difficult to see that the altered social setting would

1. This is not to say that society is the all-dominant factor, for society is also modified.

2. J.H. Hayes and J.M. Miller, *Israelite and Judean History* (OTL; London: SCM Press, 1977), p. 665.

3. It could be argued that most Jews had not given up hope regarding the Temple until after the second revolt by Simon bar Kochba in 132 CE. However, *b. Soṭ.* 15.11-13 would seem to support the demise of hope in the Temple. This text speaks about the conditions in Jerusalem after the Temple was destroyed, which were not too hopeful. An exiled community would be likely to be even less hopeful, and would rather be more concerned with establishing new foundations for their community which would facilitate the survival of their identity. See also *ARN* ch. 4: Rabbi Joshua beholding the Temple in ruins cried out: 'Woe to us!…that this, the place where the iniquities of Israel were atoned for, is laid waste'.

demand a greater need for cohesion for the Jews in a now exiled situation, and the new emphasis upon the Torah would have drawn the disparate groups together. The relationship between the non-Christian Jews and the Christian Jews would be one of extreme tension. The anti-Jewish tendency in Matthew's Gospel can be accounted for by this. Texts in Matthew indicating that the community was now separated from the synagogue would be 4.23: ἐν ταῖς συναγωγαῖς αὐτῶν (in their synagogues); see also 9.35; 10.17; 12.9; 13.54. In 23.34 Jesus, referring to the scribes and Pharisees, says: 'some of whom you will kill and crucify, and some of whom you will scourge in your synagogues...'. Such words from Jesus would support the community when they were being oppressed in their own separate synagogues. The phrase συναγωγαῖς ὑμῶν (your synagogues) is significant in telling us about the developments. See also 5.11: 'Blessed are you when men revile you and persecute you...', and 10.23; 23.34. Stanton makes an acute observation when he writes:

> Like many a minority group which feels itself rightly or wrongly to be under threat from a dominant group from which it has parted company, Matthew's community uses polemical denunciations to justify its own position. This suggested setting for the evangelist's anti-Jewish polemic perhaps explains the harshness of the words....[1]

As was said earlier, Matthew's community was not fond of the Gentiles. Schuyler Brown observes: 'Matthew's gospel points to the tragic predicament of the community'.[2] The predicament is one of confusion which results from the antipathy of the community towards Gentiles, and its ostracism from its parent tradition. On the one hand, its members are being rejected by their own Jewish community, and on the other hand they are left with the Gentile Christians. The strong feelings against the Gentiles should not be played down. In the years leading up to the war beginning about 44 CE attitudes were hostile towards Gentiles (see Josephus, *Ant.* 20.11.1).

The movement towards a more exclusive Judaism would have

---

1. G. Stanton, *The Gospels and Jesus* (The Oxford Bible Series; Oxford: Oxford University Press, 1990), p. 78.

2. S. Brown, *The Origins of Christianity* (Oxford: Oxford University Press, 1988), p. 112.

left many in the Matthean community frustrated and, consequently, put the conversion of Israel beyond the realms of
possibility for some. It is at this point that the Matthean
community started to debate seriously the Gentile missionary
question, concerning the nature of its own attitude towards the
Gentiles and the Gentiles' place in salvation history, that is,
within the Davidic tradition. In the Gospel the debate is seen
from the perspective of Matthew and his supporters, who
would be in favour of the mission to the Gentiles; but an
appreciation of the argument of their opponents can be seen in
that Matthew frequently addresses the traditions which would
have been used against this position (as previously noted).[1] The
presence of the four women in the genealogy and the story of
the Canaanite woman would have been used at certain points in
the debate. The tradition of God's promise to Abraham that he
would be a blessing to all peoples (Gen. 12.1-3) also finds a place
in Matthew's Gospel, and may be a consequence of the debate
(see especially 1.1 and 8.11). In 8.11 many will come from east
and west to sit at table with Abraham in the kingdom of heaven.
Note that in the Lukan version (Lk. 13.29) Abraham is not
mentioned, which underlines the significance of this tradition
for the Matthean community. The link between the traditions,
especially the four Gentiles and the Canaanite woman, is that
they concern engagement in mission, association with Gentiles
and the question of the Gentiles' place in the scheme of salvation
history. Those within the community who were either ambivalent or simply opposed to any engagement with Gentiles would
have seen the community's move towards the Gentiles as hasty,
and to others it was quite simply an act tantamount to apostasy
borne of the desperation of the moment (that is the desperate
period of persecution of Christians by Jews). They would have
drawn upon a different tradition which can be seen in the setting
of the twelve disciples being sent out for missionary work (see
above). This group would have taken to heart the words: 'Go

1. I do not exclude Gentiles from the Matthean community at this
point. I expect that Matthew's supporters would have been Gentiles.
Stanton (*The Gospels and Jesus*, p. 79) acknowledges that Matthew's was
a mixed community. Mt. 21.43 would intimate the strong presence of
non-Jews.

rather to the lost sheep of the house of Israel' (10.6). Such words must have been popular for they appear again when Jesus speaks to the Canaanite woman (15.21-28). The group against mission to Gentiles had a good argument. Jesus did restrict his mission to 'Palestine';[1] he left no teachings to indicate that eventually a time would come when a mission to Gentiles should be undertaken.[2]

The other, more liberal, group had to respond to those taking a more literalistic position regarding Jesus. This group would have seen the task as being one of relating Jesus to the new situation. It was, therefore, left to them to develop the community's traditions in such a way as to support a new approach coming out of the altered socio-cultural setting. The story of the Canaanite woman is one such tradition along with the three women and Uriah in the genealogy. The question, as has already been noted, was how Jesus understood the place of Gentiles in the scheme of Israel's salvation history, that is the Davidic tradition. The Davidic tradition has its biblical origins in 2 Samuel 7, especially v. 16: 'And your house and your kingdom shall be made sure for ever and ever before me; your throne shall be established for ever.'

Herein lie the words of hope for all Jews. This tradition

---

1. See Sanders and Davies, *Studying the Synoptic Gospels*, pp. 305-309.

2. J. Jeremias's monograph, *Jesus' Promise to the Nations* (SBT, 24; London and Nashville: Abingdon Press, 1958), holds a contrary view; see esp. p. 62. Jeremias accepts that Jesus did limit his ministry to Israel, but that he predicted the proclamation to all the world by God's angel, and that Israel would be excluded from the kingdom. Jeremias's basis is that Jesus was in full agreement with the Old Testament on the ingathering of Gentiles, but that Jews were not. However, it seems extreme to say that there was a universal understanding of Gentiles being excluded from God's kingdom; there was great ambivalence, and this is reflected in the texts from around this time and later (see Sanders, *Jesus and Judaism*, p. 214). I do not believe that Jesus had any ideas of excluding Gentiles, but it does seem difficult to understand the later controversies in Acts if Jesus had explicitly taught about a later Gentile mission. The ambivalence we see in the texts regarding attitudes towards Gentiles supports my proposal of confusion within the Matthean community. There was uncertainty regarding attitudes towards the Gentiles and their place within the Davidic line.

needed to be developed and modified for the altered socio-cultural and socio-economic setting. The whole Matthean community was convinced that Jesus was the son of David, the royal messiah, heir to the the throne of David. It is my proposal that the genealogy would originally have been used by the anti-Gentile group to defend the exclusive Davidic tradition against the pro-Gentile supporters, but obviously without the presence of the four women, and the 'son of Abraham'. The anti-Gentile group would probably have drawn upon Isaiah 7, maintaining that they were the true remnant, שְׁאָר־יָשׁוּב ('a remnant will return', Isa. 7.3).[1] However, Matthew and his pro-Gentile supporters drew upon the traditions of the four women, supplemented by Yahweh's promise to Abraham (Gen. 12.1-3). Consequently, they pointed out that the Davidic line had Gentile blood; further, there was the promise that through the Davidic line all Gentiles would be blessed.

This is followed by another argument using the tradition of the Canaanite woman of 15.21-28, which probably began its tradition history in 1 Kgs 17.8-24, where Elijah heals a Gentile woman's son. Similarities are the setting, Sidon (see 1 Kgs 17.9, compare Mt. 15.21); in both stories a healing of the woman's offspring was involved, and in both stories there is on the part of the woman righteous anger at being treated badly by the prophet. Since Matthew and Mark (Mk. 7.24-30) have only 13 words in common out of 120, that Matthew depended upon Mark for his account must be questioned. More likely, the tradition had a long history, and developed in several ways to fit the particular *Sitz im Leben*. Matthew continues with the Davidic theme by placing the nationalistic title 'son of David' upon the lips of a Canaanite woman: 'Have mercy on me, O Lord, Son of David' (15.22). This would cause the opposition's ears to prick up, especially in the light of the genealogy. The

---

1. שְׁאָר יָשׁוּב ('a remnant will return') is the name given to Isaiah's son. The name is significant in relation to Isaiah's message to the Davidic family. The Matthean community would certainly be aware of this chapter, for Immanuel is drawn on later in Mt. 1.23. The text of Isaiah is dependent upon the Davidic/Zionist tradition, and the need to develop such a tradition. The Matthean community would also see themselves as the inheritors and mediators of this tradition.

designation Χαναναία (Canaanite) is a *hapax legomenon* in the New Testament and would connect with the women in the genealogy. If the four women's presence in the Davidic line was not enough of an argument against the anti-Gentile group, the identification of Jesus as the son of David by a Canaanite woman certainly would be. The designation Χαναναία may possibly have been a device to connect her with Rahab and Tamar who, though never designated Canaanites, would certainly have been identified within that national group. It is also quite possible to see Χαναναία as a designation for an outcast. Support for this lies in several texts from the Mishnah.[1] While this may be supporting a later understanding of the word, the argument still stands; the term is laden with meaning and allusions.

Still with the Canaanite woman, we read the words of the opposition spoken by Jesus against the woman which are seen also in 10.5-6. Is this Matthew responding again to the debate, perhaps with 10.5-6 in mind? The opposition readers would be patting each other on the back this far in the story, and seeing in themselves the reaction of the honoured twelve disciples. However, Matthew, the shrewd debater that he is, twists the whole debate around, and has the woman put right before Jesus, and leaves the disciples' noses out of joint, with Jesus saying to the woman: ὦ γύναι, μεγάλη σου ἡ πίστις ('O woman, great is your faith!'; 15.28, compare 8.10).

Conclusion

It is my proposal that the inclusion of the four women, the designation of Jesus as 'son of Abraham', and the story of the Canaanite woman can be accounted for by seeing traditions developing out of a debate (not necessarily unfriendly) within the community. The motion being addressed was that the Davidic tradition argued against mission to the Gentiles, and necessitated living apart from them. The pro-Gentiles creatively drew together traditions either directly from the Hebrew Bible or traditions having already developed out of the Hebrew Bible to mitigate this interpretation of the Davidic tradition, and to assuage the passions which this debate had engendered: Tamar,

1.   *Maʿas. Š.* 4.4; *ʿErub.* 7.6; *Qid.* 1.3.

Rahab, Ruth and Uriah were, consequently, interpolated as critiquing factors into the genealogy. The mention of the three women would recall righteous Gentiles, and more specifically the mention of Uriah would recall his righteousness against David's wickedness. Also, the tradition of God's promise to Abraham of a universal blessing to all nations, and the tradition of a Hebrew prophet visiting Sidon and healing the offspring of a righteous Gentile woman, showed that the Davidic tradition endorsed a movement towards the Gentiles.

SARAH'S SEMINAL EMISSION:
HEBREWS 11.11 IN THE LIGHT OF ANCIENT EMBRYOLOGY*

Pieter W. van der Horst

Many translators and commentators have racked their brains over Heb. 11.11:

πίστει καὶ αὐτὴ Σάρρα στεῖρα δύναμιν εἰς καταβολὴν σπέρματος ἔλαβεν καὶ παρὰ καιρὸν ἡλικίας.

The problem is obvious: καταβολὴ σπέρματος is the *terminus technicus* for a seminal emission by a male person or animal.[1] So it would seem impossible to say that Sarah received power to emit semen. Hence there are many evasive translations: 'Through faith even Sarah herself received strength to conceive seed' (KJV); 'By faith even Sarah herself received strength to conceive' (NEB); 'It was by faith that even Sarah got strength to conceive' (Moffatt); 'It was equally by faith that Sarah was made able to conceive' (JB); 'Also by faith Sarah personally received potency for conception' (Berkeley Version); 'By faith Sarah herself received power to conceive' (RSV). A different solution is found in the following translations: 'It was faith that made Abraham able to become a father, even though...Sarah herself could not have children' (GNB); 'By faith he received power of procreation, even though he was too old—and Sarah herself was barren' (NRSV). This translation reflects a cutting of

*   Originally published in D.L. Balch, E. Ferguson and W.A. Meeks (eds.), *Greeks, Romans and Christians* (Festschrift A.J. Malherbe; Minneapolis: Fortress Press, 1990); repr. in P.W. van der Horst, *Hellenism–Judaism–Christianity: Essays on their Interaction* (Kampen: Kok–Pharos, 1994), pp. 203-23. Reprinted by permission.
    1.   See the instances collected in Bauer–Aland's *Wörterbuch* s.v. καταβολή 2, and especially the many passages in J.J. Wettstein, *Novum Testamentum Graecum* (Amsterdam: Dommerian, 1752, II), pp. 425-26.

the Gordian knot based upon the way our text is printed in the UBS *Greek New Testament* (3rd edn): πίστει—καὶ αὐτὴ Σάρρα στεῖρα—δύναμιν εἰς καταβολὴν σπέρματος ἔλαβεν καὶ παρὰ καιρὸν ἡλικίας. As Bruce Metzger explains in a note in the *Textual Commentary to the Greek New Testament*, this way of printing the text is based upon the assumption that Abraham, who is the grammatical subject in vv. 8-10 and in v. 12, most probably is also the subject in v. 11, and the words καὶ αὐτὴ Σάρρα στεῖρα are a parenthetical and Semiticizing circumstantial clause ('even though Sarah was barren'), as Matthew Black had already proposed.[1] The authors of the *Translator's Handbook on the Letter to the Hebrews* also opt for this solution, albeit not without hesitation.[2]

In commentaries on Hebrews, one finds a variety of other solutions to the problem. H. Windisch assumes that the text is corrupt; if it were about Sarah, one would expect εἰς ὑποδοχὴν σπέρματος, but since the author uses καταβολὴ σπέρματος, which can only be said of Abraham, there must be a textual corruption.[3] O. Michel, H. Braun, H.-F. Weiss, and H.W. Attridge assume that an original dative αὐτῇ Σάρρᾳ has been misread as a nominative αὐτὴ Σάρρα, and thus one should translate, 'By faith he [Abraham] received power, together with Sarah, to deposit seed'. They find less likely the solution to regard the words καὶ αὐτὴ Σάρρα στεῖρα as a later gloss or to take them as a circumstantial clause (although Weiss finds the latter more probable).[4] A.F.J. Klijn assumes that the author has

1. B.M. Metzger, *Textual Commentary to the Greek New Testament* (London: United Bible Societies, 1975), pp. 672-73. M. Black, *An Aramaic Approach to the Gospels and Acts* (Oxford: Brill, 3rd edn, 1967, pp. 87-88). Black here refers to K. Beyer's discussion of the 'Zustandssätze' in his *Semitische Syntax im Neuen Testament* (Göttingen: Vandenhoeck & Ruprecht, 1961), pp. 117-119.

2. E.P. Ellingworth and E.A. Nida, *Translator's Handbook on the Letter to the Hebrews* (London: United Bible Societies, 1983), p. 261. Cf. also the remark in the *Translator's New Testament* (London: British and Foreign Bible Society, 1973), p. 528.

3. H. Windisch, *Der Hebräerbrief* (Tübingen: Mohr, 1913), pp. 92-93.

4. O. Michel, *Der Brief an die Hebräer* (Göttingen: Vandenhoeck & Ruprecht, 6th edn, 1966), pp. 395-96; H. Braun, *An die Hebräer* (Tübingen: Mohr, 1984), pp. 358-59. H.-F. Weiss, *Der Brief an die Hebräer* (Göttingen:

mixed two different thoughts, one about the faith of Abraham and one about Sarah's becoming pregnant.[1] H.W. Montefiore says that one should not press the expression δύναμιν εἰς καταβολὴν σπέρματος to have a literal meaning; the translation 'power to conceive' can stand.[2] H.A. Kent proposes as the least forced solution the following translation: 'By faith Sarah received power with regard to [Abraham's] depositing of the seed'.[3] And so one could go on listing solutions by commentators.[4]

As far as I have been able to see, it is only C. Spicq who assumes that the author may have literally meant what he seems to write. In his earlier commentary, Spicq only remarks that the ancients believed that a woman, as well as a man, could emit semen; for evidence he refers to an article by H.J. Cadbury.[5] In his later commentary, Spicq says that some pre-Socratics (Empedocles, Parmenides and Democritus) believed that women emit their own semen, and that the physician Galen had the same opinion, and he quotes Lactantius as stating that Varro and Aristotle shared this view.[6] Cadbury and Spicq seem to me to be on the right track. In this contribution it will be demonstrated that the view that women had their own seminal emissions was not an eccentric, but a quite current opinion in antiquity and that this idea did not remain limited to Greek scholarly circles, but penetrated into other strata of society as

Vandenhoeck & Ruprecht, 1991), pp. 587-88; H.W. Attridge, *The Epistle to the Hebrews* (Philadelphia: Fortress Press, 1989), p. 325.

1.   A.F.J. Klijn, *De brief aan de Hebreeën* (Nijkerk: Callenbach, 1975), p. 123.

2.   H.W. Montefiore, *The Epistle to the Hebrews* (London: A. & C. Black, 1964), p. 194.

3.   H.A. Kent, *The Epistle to the Hebrews* (Grand Rapids: Baker, 1972), p. 226.

4.   A good and recent survey is to be found in P. Ellingworth, *The Epistle to the Hebrews* (Grand Rapids: Eerdmans, 1993), pp. 586-89.

5.   C. Spicq, *L'épître aux Hébreux* (Paris: Gabalda, 1953), II, pp. 348-49; H.J. Cadbury, 'The Ancient Physiological Notions Underlying John I 13 and Hebrews XI 11', *The Expositor* (ser. 9) 2 (1924), pp. 430-39.

6.   C. Spicq, *L'épître aux Hébreux* (Paris: Gabalda, 1977), p. 188.

well. It will also be demonstrated that this theory was well known in early Judaism.[1]

Preliminary Remarks

Three preliminary remarks are in order here. First, it should be borne in mind that, although it was known since Herophilus[2] that women had ovaries, the ovum itself was unknown throughout antiquity (and remained so until it was discovered with a microscope by C.A. von Baer in 1827).[3] Secondly, when the ancients discussed female seminal emission, this probably had little or nothing to do with observation of the so-called G-spot (documented by W. Grafenberg in 1950[4]), but it did have to do with a theoretical problem in their doctrines of heredity. Thirdly, this theoretical problem was created by the observation that the widespread and traditional notion that the father alone makes the child and provides the substance for its coming into being and development could not explain why children often resemble their mothers. This traditional theory already occurs in 'a context innocent of pretensions to biological investigation',[5] namely, in Aeschylus's *Eumenides* (ll. 657-61.), where the god Apollo says:

> This too I will tell you and mark the truth of what I say. She who is called the child's mother is not its begetter, but only the nurse of the newly sown embryo. The begetter is the male, and

1.   Cadbury was the first to study Heb. 11.11 in the light of 'ancient physiological notions' (see p. 114 n. 5), but his evidence is extremely limited and he does not discuss at all the relevant rabbinic material.

2.   On Herophilus, the famous third-century BCE Alexandrian anatomist, and his role in ancient medical science, see H. von Staden, *Herophilus: The Art of Medicine in Early Alexandria* (Cambridge: Cambridge University Press, 1989).

3.   See for the details J. Needham and A. Hughes, *A History of Embryology* (Cambridge: Cambridge University Press, 2nd edn, 1959). When ovaries were discovered in the Hellenistic period, they were regarded as the depositories of female sperm and called testes!

4.   See A.K. Ladas, B. Whipple and J.D. Perry, *The G-Spot and Other Recent Discoveries about Human Sexuality* (London: Corgi Books, 1983).

5.   Thus G.E.R. Lloyd, *Science, Folklore and Ideology: Studies in the Life Sciences in Ancient Greece* (Cambridge: Cambridge University Press, 1983), p. 86.

she as a stranger preserves for a stranger the offspring, if no god blights its birth.[1]

Aeschylus here clearly reflects the common assumption of the superiority of the male role, a theory that had obvious implications for the evaluation of the position of women. As G.E.R. Lloyd states, 'The question must still be pressed, on what grounds alternative views—dissenting from the assumption of the determining role of the male and allotting equal importance to the female—were put forward'.[2]

Alternative views were developed by some of the pre-Socratic philosophers.[3] The doxographical excerpt in Censorinus, *De die natali* 5.4, clearly states:

> On another point as well these authors [namely, the philosophers] have divergent opinions, namely whether an embryo originates solely from the seed of the father, as

1. Translation (slightly adapted) by H. Lloyd-Jones, *The Eumenides by Aeschylus. A Translation and Commentary* (Englewood Cliffs, NJ: Prentice–Hall, 1970), pp. 51-52. Cf. also Euripides, *Orestes*, ll. 552-53.

2. Lloyd, *Science, Folklore and Ideology*, p. 87.

3. What follows is based largely upon E. Lesky, *Die Zeugungs- und Vererbungslehren der Antike und ihr Nachwirken* (Mainz: Akademie für Wissenschaft und Literatur, 1951). Other and shorter presentations can be found in W. Gerlach, 'Das Problem des "weiblichen Samens" in der antiken und mittelalterlichen Medizin', *(Sudhoffs) Archiv für Geschichte der Medizin* 30 (1937–38), pp. 177-93; T. Hopfner, *Das Sexualleben der Griechen und Römer von den Anfängen bis ins 6. Jahrhundert nach Christus* (Prague: Calve, 1938), I.1, pp. 132-36; P.M.M. Geurts, *De erfelijkheid in de oudere Griekse wetenschap* (Nijmegen: Dekker en van de Vecht, 1941); E. Lesky and J.H. Waszink, 'Embryologie', *Reallexikon für Antike und Christentum* 4 (1959), pp. 1228-42; H.-J. von Schumann, *Sexualkunde und Sexualmedizin in der klassischen Antike* (Munich, 1975), pp. 102-104; Lloyd, *Science, Folklore and Ideology*, pp. 86-94. A. Rousselle, *Porneia: On Desire and the Body in Antiquity* (Oxford: Blackwell, 1988), pp. 27-32, is idiosyncratic. A short survey of other (more primitive, often magical) theories of conception in the ancient world is F. Kudlien, 'Zur Erforschung archaisch-griechischer Zeugungslehren', *Medizinhistorisches Journal* 16 (1981), pp. 323-39. A survey of the study of ancient gynaecology in general can be found in D. Gourevitch, 'Les études de gynécologie antique de 1975 à aujourd'hui', *Centre Jean Palerne, Université de Saint-Etienne, Informations* 12 (March 1988), pp. 2-12 (I owe this reference to the kindness of Dr M. Stol).

> Diogenes and Hippo and the Stoics have written, or also from
> the seed of the mother, which is the view of Anaxagoras,
> Alcmaeon, Parmenides, Empedocles, and Epicurus.[1]

The five authors mentioned as defenders of the view that female semen is also needed to form an embryo were not the only ones—we will meet others later—nor were their theories uniform. There existed at least three different theories on the coming into being of human sperm: (1) the encephalo-myelogenic doctrine; (2) the pangenesis doctrine; and (3) the hematogenic doctrine.

Three Greek Theories

The encephalo-myelogenic doctrine[2] holds that there is a continuum of 'brains–spinal marrow–sperm'; hence 'sperm is a drop of brain', as Diogenes Laertius (8.28) presents Pythagoras's view. And the Pythagorean (?) Alcmaeon of Croton is reported to have said that sperm is ἐγκεφάλου μέρος (Aetius 5.3.3). Although this theory was rather quickly superseded by the pangenesis doctrine, its influence is still noticeable in Plato's *Timaeus*. In *Tim.* 77D Plato speaks of the 'generative marrow', and in 91A he says that 'marrow runs from the head down the neck and along the spine and has, indeed, in our earlier discourse been called seed' (referring back to 73C, 74B, 86C).[3] And although Aristotle speaks out strongly against this theory,

---

1. N. Sallmann, *Censorini de die natali liber* (Leipzig: Teubner, 1983), p. 8 *ad locum*, gives the pertinent references to the fragments of the authors mentioned, as does R. Rocca-Serra, *Censorinus: Le jour natal* (Paris: Vrin, 1980), p. 45 (his French translation is at p. 8). In 6.5 and 6.8 Censorinus discusses Parmenides' and Anaxagoras's ideas on the role of female semen.

2. Discussed by Lesky, *Zeugungs- und Vererbungslehren*, pp. 9-30; but see especially the extensive discussion in R.B. Onians, *The Origins of European Thought about the Body, the Mind, the Soul, World, Time, and Fate* (Cambridge: Cambridge University Press, 1988 [1951]), *passim*. A concise doxographical account of several theories on this matter is to be found in Aetius, *Placita* 5.3-11 (in H. Diels, *Doxographi Graeci* [Berlin: de Gruyter, 4th edn, 1965], pp. 417-22).

3. Translation by F.M. Cornford, *Plato's Cosmology* (London: Routledge & Kegan Paul, 1937), p. 356.

which gave an extra impetus to its decline, even in the imperial period it still had some adherents, albeit by then in various amalgamated forms.[1]

It is clear that this doctrine in principle leaves room for a female contribution in the process of conception, the brains–marrow–semen continuum not being restricted to males. And, indeed, we find that several of its adherents adopt the *epikrateia* principle as far as heredity is concerned. This principle of ἐπικράτεια (predominance) is best illustrated by the short statement in Censorinus, *De die natali* 6.4: 'Alcmaeon said that the sex of that parent would be realized [namely, in the embryo] whose semen was most abundant [namely, in coition]' (frag. 24A14 Diels–Kranz). That is to say, if the woman's sperm prevails in quantity, a girl will be born, and if the man's, a boy. This principle, that the seed of either parent can be 'over-powered' by the other's seed, is not limited to Pythagorean circles, but occurs with various modifications in several ancient theories of sex differentation (again, in spite of Aristotle's oppo-sition to every double seed-theory; see especially *De generatione animalium* 1.20).[2] The existence of female semen and the occurrence of female ejaculation is the necessary basis of the *epikrateia* principle and is affirmed by authors such as Parmenides (frag. 28B18 D–K),[3] Empedocles (frag. 31B63 D–K), Democritus (frag. 68A142 D–K), and several Hippocratic writers (see below). Let us look briefly at two theories concerning sex differentation that imply a double-seed doctrine.

Empedocles thought that some parts of the embryo had their origin in the man's seed and others in the woman's seed. However, he seems to have combined this with a theory about the determining influence of the temparature of the seed (or the

---

1. On which see Lesky, *Zeugungs- und Vererbungslehren*, pp. 20-22.

2. For example *De gen.* 1.20, 727b33-36: 'Some think that the female contributes semen in coition because the pleasure she experiences is sometimes similar to that of the male, and also is attended by a liquid discharge; but this discharge is not seminal'.

3. On this difficult fragment, preserved only in a late and free Latin rendering (and beginning with *femina virque simul Veneris cum germina miscent* ['When a woman and a man together mix the germs of love']), see the discussion by J. Mansfeld, *Parmenides en Zeno: Het leerdicht en de paradoxen* (Kampen: Kok-Agora, 1988), pp. 76-77.

uterus).[1] A late traditon (in Censorinus, *De die natali* 6.6-7) schematizes this theory as follows:

Mw + Fw > Mm   Mc + Fc > Ff   Mw + Fc > Mf   Mc + Fw > Fm
(M = male; m = resembling the male parent; F = female; f = resembling the female parent; w = warm seed; c = cold seed; > indicates result.)

Even though this tradition may perhaps not fully go back to Empedocles himself, it gives a fairly good idea of one of the ancient theories of sex differentiation and heredity. Parmenides' view on this matter is different, because he has a combination of a double-seed doctrine with a left-right theory.[2] This is the theory that the sex of the child is determined by its position in the left or right part of the uterus (right for males and left for females). A later modification of this theory by Anaxagoras (frag. 59A107 D–K) seems to have introduced the idea that the sex of the embryo was determined by the part (left or right) of the body from which the seed had been formed.[3] This results in the following schema:

Mr + Fr > Mm   Ml + Fl > Ff   Mr + Fl > Mf   Ml + Fr > Fm
(M = male; m = resembling the male parent; F = female; f = resembling the female parent; r = seed formed in the right part of the body; l = seed formed in the left part of the body.)

Later, other amalgamated forms of the left-right theory and of other pieces of embryological speculation developed, and it is probable that these theories had become widely accepted even outside scientific circles.[4]

Anaxagoras brings us to the second theory concerning the

1. On the problems caused by the lack of clarity in the doxographic tradition on this point see Lesky, *Zeugungs- und Vererbungslehren*, pp. 31-38. The relevant fragments are 31A81, 31B63, 31B65 D–K.

2. See esp. Lesky, *Zeugungs- und Vererbungslehren*, pp. 39-69; O. Kember, 'Right and Left in the Sexual Theories of Parmenides', *Journal of Hellenic Studies* 91 (1971), pp. 70-79; G.E.R. Lloyd, 'Parmenides' Sexual Theories', *Journal of Hellenic Studies* 92 (1972), pp. 178-79.

3. On the ambiguities in the doxographic tradition about Anaxagoras's embryology see Lesky, *Zeugungs- und Vererbungslehren*, pp. 51-61.

4. Lesky (*Zeugungs- und Vererbungslehren*, p. 62), points to passages in Varro, Pliny the Elder, and Horapollo that seem to indicate that these theories had become popular lore.

origin of semen, the so-called pangenesis doctrine, of which he is the *auctor intellectualis* (see frag. 59B10 D–K).[1] This theory was refined in the school of the atomistic philosophers. According to Aetius (*Plac.* 5.3, 6), Democritus said that sperm is formed from all parts of the body, like bones and flesh and sinews (frag. 68A141 D–K). Democritus is also quoted as saying: 'Coition is a slight attack of epilepsy, for man gushes forth from man and is separated by being torn apart with a kind of shock' (frag. 68B32 D–K). He believed that in women, too, sperm was formed from all parts of the body. Aristotle tells us that the *epikrateia* principle was an important factor in Democritus's embryological system:

> Democritus of Abdera also says that the differentiation of sex takes place within the mother; however, he says, it is not because of heat and cold that one embryo becomes female and another male, but that it depends on the question which parent it is whose semen prevails–not the whole of the semen, but that which has come forth from the part by which male and female differ from one another (*De gen.* 4.1, 764a6-11 = frag. 68A143 D–K).

The pangenesis doctrine was the dominant theory in several Hippocratic writings, especially in *On Airs, Waters, Places; The Sacred Disease; On Generation; On the Nature of the Child;* and *On Diseases* IV.[2] A few quotations will suffice. *On Generation* 8.1-2 says: 'Sperm is a product which comes from the whole body of each parent...[The child] must inevitably resemble each parent in some respect, since it is from both parents that the sperm comes to form the child'. *On Generation* 4.1 says: 'A woman also emits something from her body, sometimes into the womb, which then becomes moist, sometimes externally as well, if the womb is open wider than normal... If

---

1.   On the question of who is to be credited with the invention of this theory Lesky (*Zeugungs- und Vererbungslehren*, pp. 70-72.), is to be corrected; see A. Preuss, 'Galen's Criticism of Aristotle's Conception Theory', *Journal of the History of Biology* 10 (1977), pp. 68-85, esp. p. 72.

2.   See the references in Lesky, *Zeugungs- und Vererbungslehren*, p. 77, and in I.M. Loney, *The Hippocratic Treatises 'On Generation', 'On the Nature of the Child', 'Diseases IV'* (Berlin and New York: de Gruyter, 1981), esp. pp. 19-21.

her desire for intercourse is excited, she emits semen before the man'.[1] *On Diseases* IV 32.1 says: 'The sperm, coming from all parts of the body both of the man and the woman to produce a human being and falling into the uterus of the woman, coagulates'.[2] An interesting new feature is that the author of *On Generation* stresses that 'both male and female sperm exists in both partners' (7.1). This thesis, in fact a principle of complete parity, results in the following schema:[3]

M+/F+ > M   M-/F- > F   M-+/F+- > M or F   M+/F- > M or F   M-/F+ > F or M

(M = male; + = male determining sperm; F = female; – = female determining sperm; M or F / F or M = depending upon the *epikrateia*)

We see here a far-reaching theory with immensely important implications for an anthropology in which equality of the sexes is sought.

The third theory, the hematogenic doctrine, holds that semen originates from the blood—in fact, is nothing but blood in a certain state of coagulation. It is not certain who the author of this theory was,[4] but it was already held by Diogenes of Apollonia (frag. 64B6 D–K), as is clearly stated in a long quotation from his work by Aristotle (*Historia animalium* 3.2, 511b31-512b10). Aristotle himself is the one who promoted this theory to its influential position,[5] which it held until far into the Middle

1. Translation by Loney (see previous note). At p. 119, Loney makes the pertinent comment: 'The question of what the mother contributes to the formation of her child has an obvious importance socially, legally, and economically, as well as on a more personal level. The kind of relevance this question had is illustrated by the passage in the *Eumenides* of Aeschylus (ll. 657-666) in which Apollo supports the case of Orestes by the argument that it is the father who forms the embryo, while the mother nourishes it and preserves it.'

2. The three Hippocratic treatises *On Generation, On the Nature of the Child* and *On Diseases* IV originally formed one whole; see, besides the work of Loney, also R. Joly, *Le niveau de la science hippocratique* (Paris: Les Belles Lettres, 1966), pp. 70-119, esp. pp. 111-16 ('L'infériorité de la femme').

3. Lesky, *Zeugungs- und Vererbungslehren*, p. 84.

4. For discussion see Lesky, *Zeugungs- und Vererbungslehren*, pp. 120-25.

5. On Aristotle see Lesky, *Zeugungs- und Vererbungslehren*,

Ages. Aristotle's *De generatione animalium*, book I, is our main source for his ideas on spermatogenesis. Of course, the basic principle is teleology. Aristotle holds that the woman contributes to the embryo nothing but ὕλη (matter)—that is, she is the *causa materialis*—whereas the man contributes τέλος (end), εἶδος (form), ἀρχὴ τῆς κινήσεως (source of movement)—that is, the *causa finalis*, the *causa formalis*, and the *causa efficiens*. This male contribution is semen, but the female contribution is not semen but menstrual blood (τὰ καταμήνια). Semen is a residue of food. The body converts food into blood by means of a process of 'concoction' (πέψις). Blood is the substance from which flesh, bones, and so on come into being. Because in childhood all (food >) blood is needed for the growth of the body and its parts, no semen or menstrual blood is produced. Once the body has become fully grown, it produces a residue (περίττωμα) of blood (< food), and in a process of further concoction, this residue is transformed into semen or menstrual blood. The essential element in this process of concoction (food > blood > semen) is bodily heat. Because males have greater bodily heat than females, males' blood can be 'cooked' enough to reach the stage of semen; females can never reach this stage and hence can produce no semen, only (menstrual) blood.[1] In the process of fertilization the semen brings form and movement into the matter (ὕλη) of the menstrual blood. The state of aggregation of this blood changes only by the impact of the greater heat of the semen, 'for the menstrual blood is semen not in a pure state, but in need of working up' (*De gen. anim.* 1.20, 728a26). Only semen in a pure state can 'inform' the powerless female matter so as to make it develop into an embryo. It is clear that in Aristotle's version of the hematogenic doctrine, the female contribution to embryogenesis is very much reduced as compared with the pangenesis and the encephalo-myelogenic doctrines.[2]

pp. 125-59, and V. Happ, *Hyle: Studien zum aristotelischen Materie-Begriff* (Berlin and New York: de Gruyter, 1971), pp. 746-50.

1. Happ, *Hyle*, p. 747, puts it concisely: 'Die Katamenien sind also sozusagen "halbgares" Sperma, das Sperma ist "gares" Menstruationsblut'.

2. See J. Morsink, 'Was Aristotle's Biology Sexist?', *Journal of the History of Biology* 12 (1979), pp. 83-112.

Aristotle heavily influenced not only Stoic doctrines of spermatogenesis,[1] but also the doctrines of the medical school of the so-called Pneumatics, founded in the first century CE by Athenaeus of Attaleia.[2] More important in this respect, however, is the influential Galen, since this great physician tried to combine Aristotelian elements with insights of pre-Socratic and Hippocratic writers as regards embryology.[3] Galen did assume on the one hand that women contribute their own sperm, but on the other hand he followed Aristotle in attributing a much lower value to this contribution: female sperm is by far less perfect, thinner, and colder than male sperm. During coition, female sperm is expelled from the 'ovaries' in such a way that both kinds of semen meet in the womb, mix, and form a membrane; thereafter, the female sperm serves only as food for the male semen in its development into an embryo (see for all this especially Galen's extensive treatise *De semine*).[4] As a real

1. It should be noted, however, that whereas Aetius in *Plac.* 5.5, 2 states that Zeno, like Aristotle, did not believe that women produce sperm, the same doxographer says about the Stoics in general (*Plac.* 5.11, 4) that they believe προΐεσθαι καὶ τὴν γυναῖκα (that the woman also produces [sperm]). On the Stoics see also Censorinus, *De die natali* 5.4, quoted above.

2. Lesky, *Zeugungs- und Vererbungslehren*, pp. 163-77. F. Kudlien demonstrates also the Stoic influence on the Pneumatics in his article 'Pneumatische Ärzte', PWSup 11 (1968), pp. 1097-108.

3. See R.E. Siegel, *Galen's System of Physiology and Medicine* (Basel and New York: Karger, 1968), I, pp. 224-30; Preuss, 'Galen's Criticism of Aristotle's Conception Theory'; M. Boylan, 'Galen's Conception Theory', *Journal of the History of Biology* 19 (1986), pp. 47-77; J. Kollesch, 'Galens Auseinandersetzung mit der aristotelische Samenlehre', in J. Wiesner (ed.), *Aristoteles: Werk und Wirkung* (Festschrift P. Moraux; Berlin: de Gruyter, 1987), pp. 17-26.

4. See also the notice on Galen by Nemesius, *De natura hominis* 25, 247 (ed. M. Morani [Leipzig, 1987], pp. 86-87): Γαλήνος δὲ καταγινώσκων Ἀριστοτέλους λέγει σπερμαίνειν μὲν τὰς γυναῖκας καὶ τὴν μῖξιν ἀμφοτέρων τῶν σπερμάτων ποιεῖν τὸ κύημα ('But Galen scorns the view of Aristotle, and says that women do produce semen, and that it is the mingling of the two kinds of semen that produces the embryo'). Galen's theory of the reproductive system as presented in his *De usu partium* books 14 and 15 is excellently summarized by M. Tallmadge May, *Galen on the Usefulness of the Parts of the Body* (Ithaca, NY: Cornell University Press, 1968), I, pp. 56-58, cf. also II, pp. 631-32 n. 24.

eclectic, Galen tries to run with the hare and hunt with the hounds. Nonetheless, despite Aristotle's influence, Galen maintains the concept of female sperm: ψευδῶς λέγεται τὸ μόνου τοῦ πατρὸς εἶναι τὸ σπέρμα ('it is falsely said that sperm is only from the father') (*De sem.* 2.1), and he transmits his theory to many a writer in the Middle Ages.[1]

We could go on discussing ancient Greek testimonies concerning female seed,[2] but I will turn now to a few references to Latin authors who discuss the Greek theories. In Lucretius's *De rerum natura* 4.1208-87, we find an interesting passage on matters of procreation. I quote ll. 1208-17 in the prose translation of R.E. Latham:[3]

> In the intermingling of seed it may happen that the woman by a sudden effort overmasters the power of the man and takes control over it. Then children are conceived of the maternal seed and take after their mother. Correspondingly, children may be conceived of the paternal seed and take after their father. The children in whom you see a two-sided likeness, combining features of both parents, are products alike of their father's body and their mother's blood. At their making, the seeds that course through the limbs under the impulse of Venus were dashed together by the collusion of mutual passion in which neither party was master or mastered.[4]

This is a very clear instance of a double-seed theory based upon the pangenesis doctrine combined with the *epikrateia* principle. The influence of earlier philosophers is obvious. Less influenced

---

1.   Gerlach, 'Das Problem des weiblichen Samens', pp. 190-93. The physician Soranus, too, takes an eclectic position: females as well as males emit sperm (*Gyn.* 1.30-31), but female sperm does not contribute to the formation of the embryo (*Gyn.* 1.12). See O. Temkin, *Soranus' Gynecology* (repr. Baltimore: Johns Hopkins University Press, 1991 [1956]).

2.   Short but interesting doxographic accounts on this matter can be found in Aetius, *Plac.* 5.3-9, esp. 5.5 (on the question εἰ καὶ θήλεα προίενται σπέρμα); cf. H. Daiber, *Aetius Arabus: Die Vorsokratiker in arabischer Überlieferung* (Wiesbaden: Otto Harassowitz, 1980), p. 487 (on *Plac.* 5.3).

3.   *Lucretius: The Nature of the Universe* (Harmondsworth: Penguin, 1951), p. 168.

4.   Cf. also Lucretius, *De rerum natura* 4.1227-32.

by philosophers is Ovid, who warns women in his *Ars amatoria* 3.767-68: 'It is not safe to fall asleep during a meal, for much can happen during sleep that one may feel ashamed of.' It is probable that the poet is making an allusion here to the phenomenon of female wet dreams. The pseudo-Aristotelian author of the tenth book of *De generatione animalium* states that when women have erotic dreams, they too emit semen into the region in front of the womb (10.2, 634b30-31).[1] And other authors discuss the same phenomenon.[2]

The material surveyed so far covers the period of roughly 500 BCE to 200 CE. It has shown us that throughout this period a theory about female semen had its place side by side with a theory that denied females a contribution to embryogenesis. Widely differing ideas circulated concerning the origin of human semen. I have briefly discussed three of them, and we have seen that all three left room for one or other form of a double-seed theory. Even Aristotle, the most staunch opponent of the idea of female semen, did not deny that a woman contributed her *katamenia* to the embryogenesis and that this menstrual blood was in fact from the same origin as male semen, albeit that it had stopped halfway in its development into semen *pur sang*. We have seen that many philosophers, physicians, poets, and others held that the contributions of men and women to the formation of a fetus were strictly equal.

Jewish Theories

If, however, we want to make it a probable thesis that the author of Hebrews could have known such a theory, it does not

---

1. Aristotle himself denies that the occurrence of wet dreams in women has anything to do with the emission of sperm (*De gen. anim.* 2.4, 739a20-26), but it is apparent from this passage that the occurrence of nocturnal emissions in women had been used as one of the arguments that females, as well as males, emit sperm. Cf. also *Hist. anim.* 10.6, 637b28.

2. See Hopfner, *Sexualleben*, p. 134, and especially A. Rousselle, 'Observation féminine et idéologie masculine: Le corps de la femme d'après les médecins grecs', *Annales (économies, sociétés, civilisations)* 35 (1980), pp. 1100-1101.

suffice to point out its existence in the Greco-Roman world. We will have to demonstrate that a Jewish author—and this the author of Hebrews certainly was—could have known such a theory, either because it had penetrated into early Jewish circles or because similar ideas were already current in Jewish tradition itself.

Let us first go back in history and look at whether ancient Israel could possibly have met such a theory in one of its surrounding cultures. When we turn to Egypt, we do not find any evidence. This matter has been studied extensively by the Dutch Egyptologist B.H. Stricker in his impressive multi-volume enterprise *De geboorte van Horus*, but in this elaborate commentary on an ancient Egyptian embryological treatise, he has not been able to point to any unambiguous passage from Egyptian literature that supports a double-seed theory.[1] If we continue our search in Mesopotamia, the harvest is far from rich, but perhaps there is something to be found. There is an ancient Mesopotamian potency incantation in which the following line occurs: 'If either a man or a woman is [...?] and their semen flows copiously...'[2] The most recent editor of this text remarks that the Babylonian word *rihutu* (sperm) is 'here used exceptionally of a woman's secretions'.[3] However, it should be conceded that this cuneiform tablet is partly restored here and that, even if the restoration would seem acceptable, this single instance would stand too isolated to enable us to speak of a double-seed theory in Mesopotamia.[4]

When we turn to the Old Testament, again we find only one single text that could perhaps be interpreted as implying a theory of female seed. The text is Lev. 12.2: 'Say to the people of

1. B.H. Stricker, *De geboorte van Horus* (5 vols.; Leiden: Ex Oriente Lux, 1963–1989); see esp. vol. II (1968), p. 131.

2. See R.D. Biggs, *SA.ZI.GA: Ancient Mesopotamian Potency Incantations* (Locust Valley: Augustin, 1967), p. 66. The text is usually referred to as BAM 205.40.

3. Biggs, *SA.ZI.GA*, p. 68. See also the comments in the review by R. Labat in *Bibliotheca Orientalis* 25 (1968), p. 357a, and M. Stol, *Zwangerschap en geboorte bij de Babyloniërs en in de Bijbel* (Leiden: Ex Oriente Lux, 1983), p. 5.

4. In *CAD*, V (1984), p. 349b, our passage (BAM 205.40) is quoted but not translated, being too uncertain.

Israel: If a woman *tazri'a* and bears a male child, then she shall
be unclean seven days; at the time of her menstruation she shall
be unclean'. The word *tazri'a* is the *hiphil* of *zr'* (to sow), a
causative form which is used in the Old Testament only here and
in Gen. 1.11-12, where it is said of plants in the sense of 'produce
seed, yield seed, form seed'. When a form of *zr'* means 'to
become pregnant, to be impregnated', the *niphal* form is always
used (see, for example, Num. 5.28; Nah. 1.14). Because the *hiphil*
form can hardly mean anything else than 'to make seed',
commentators have got into trouble over this verse and proposed emendations of the text, because they found the thought
expressed impossible.[1] But one should beware of over-hasty
conclusions and leave open the possibility that the author of
Leviticus 12 may have meant what he seems to write, that is,
that a woman can produce semen. This remains uncertain. We
shall see later, in fact, that this is exactly what the rabbis
understood this biblical verse to mean. However, before looking
at the rabbinic evidence, let us cast a quick glance at earlier
postbiblical Jewish material.[2]

The earliest postbiblical passage to be quoted is *1 En.* 15.4,
where the Ethiopic text runs as follows:

> Surely, you [namely, the Watchers], you (used to be) holy,
> spiritual, the living ones, (possessing) eternal life; but (now)
> you have defiled yourselves with women and with the blood
> of flesh you have begotten children; you have lusted with the
> blood of the people [or: after the daughters of men],[3] like them
> producing blood and flesh, (which) die and perish.[4]

1.   See, for example, A.B. Ehrlich, *Randglossen zur hebräischen Bibel*
(repr.; Hildesheim: Olms, 1968 [1909]), p. 40: 'Bei der durch *zr'*
ausgedrückten Handlung kann das Weib nur als der passive Teil
gedacht werden; vgl. Num. 5:28. Aus diesem Grunde ist für das hier
unmögliche *tazri'a* entschieden *tizra'* zu lesen' (!).
2.   A very short and incomplete survey of this material can be found
in Cadbury, 'Ancient Physiological Notions', pp. 433-34, and in Lesky and
Waszink, 'Embryologie', p. 1241.
3.   On the text-critical problem here see M. Black, *The Book of Enoch
or 1 Enoch* (Leiden: Brill, 1985), p. 152.
4.   Translation (slightly adapted) by E. Isaac in J. H. Charlesworth
(ed.), *The Old Testament Pseudepigrapha* (Garden City, NY: Doubleday,
1983), I, p. 21. The square brackets are mine, the round brackets are

The expression 'with the blood of flesh you have begotten children' would seem to be a reference to an Aristotelian theory of the καταμήνια (menstrual blood) as one of the two components in the generative process. That this theory was known in Jewish circles seems certain in view of *Wis.* 7.1-2: 'In my mother's womb I was sculpted into flesh during a ten months' space, curdled in blood by virile seed and the pleasure that is joined with sleep' (καὶ ἐν κοιλίᾳ μητρὸς ἐγλύφην σάρξ δεκαμηνιαίῳ χρόνῳ, παγεὶς ἐν αἵματι ἐκ σπέρματος ἀνδρὸς καὶ ἡδονῆς ὕπνῳ συνελθούσης).[1] David Winston rightly points out in his commentary that the author here reflects passages like Aristotle's *De gen. anim.* 1.19-20. The same probably holds true for *4 Macc.* 13:20: 'There [in their mother's womb] do brothers abide for a similar period and are moulded through the same span and nurtured by the same blood and brought to maturity through the same vitality'[2] ([τῆς μητρῴας γαστρὸς] ἐν ᾗ τὸν ἴσον ἀδελφοὶ κατοικήσαντες χρόνον καὶ ἐν τῷ αὐτῷ χρόνῳ πλασθέντες καὶ ἀπὸ τοῦ αὐτοῦ αἵματος αὐξηθέντες καὶ διὰ τῆς αὐτῆς ψυχῆς τελεσφορηθέντες). And we can add Philo, *Quaest. in Gen.* 3.47:

> The matter of the female in the remains of the menstrual fluids produces the fetus. But the male (provides) the skill and the cause. And so, since the male provides the greater and the more necessary (part) in the process of generation, it was proper that his pride should be checked by the sign of the circumcision.[3]

And compare his *Op. mundi* 132: '[The menstrual blood] too is said by physical scientists to be the bodily substance of embryos' ([τὰ καταμήνια] λέγεται γὰρ οὖν καὶ ταῦτα πρὸς ἀνδρῶν φυσικῶν οὐσία σωματικὴ βρεφῶν εἶναι).[4]

Isaac's. The passage refers, of course, to Gen. 6.1-4.

1. The translation is by D. Winston, *The Wisdom of Solomon* (Garden City, NY: Doubleday, 1979), p. 162. See also his commentary on pp. 163-64.

2. Translation by M. Hadas, *The Third and Fourth Books of the Maccabees* (New York: Ktav, 1953), p. 213.

3. The translation of the Armenian version is by R. Marcus in the LCL edition.

4. Translation by F.H. Colson and G.H. Whitaker in the LCL edition.

These five passages all clearly use Aristotelian terminology or show reminiscences of it, so one cannot but conclude that at least this form of the hematogenic doctrine of seed was known in educated Jewish circles. And it has been suggested that it is against this background that one should consider a passage in the New Testament, Jn 1.13: οἳ οὐκ ἐξ αἱμάτων οὐδὲ ἐκ θελήματος σαρκὸς οὐδὲ ἐκ θελήματος ἀνδρὸς ἀλλ' ἐκ θεοῦ ἐγεννήθησαν. The expression ἐξ αἱμάτων ἐγεννήθησαν ('were born of blood')[1] is best explained against the background of an Aristotelian *katamenia* theory. Be that as it may, the evidence for knowledge of (originally) Aristotelian theories in Judaism does not prove the existence of a theory of female semen. As far as I know, there is no direct evidence for that outside rabbinic literature. However, it should be borne in mind that knowledge of Aristotle's ideas very probably implied knowledge of the ideas he combatted so firmly, that is, knowledge of double-seed theories. It may be pure coincidence that these theories are nowhere mentioned (besides being a testimony to Aristotle's influence and prestige), for we meet them often in early rabbinic literature.

In the Talmud and the Midrashim, we find the same variety of opinions as in Greek (or Latin) literature. Of course, there is the traditional theory that the woman does not contribute anything to the formation of the embryo, for example in *Lev. R.* 14.6.[2] This need not detain us here, although it is interesting to see that in one of the passages that reflect this view, we find a marked concurrence with, if not influence of, Greek terminology: in *Gen.*

1.   For the plural αἵματα cf. Euripides, *Ion* 693, ἀλλῶν τραφεὶς ἐξ αἱμάτων, and see, besides the commentaries on Jn 1.13, especially Cadbury, 'Ancient Physiological Notions'.

2.   See e.g. J. Feliks, 'Biology', *EncJud* IV (1972), pp. 1019-22; I. Simon, 'La gynécologie, l'obstétrie, l'embryologie et la puériculture dans la Bible et le Talmud', *Revue d'histoire de la médecine hébraïque* 4 (1949), pp. 35-64; J. Preuss, *Biblisch-talmudische Medizin* (repr.; Wiesbaden: Otto Harassowitz, 1992 [1911]), pp. 434-504; ET *Biblical and Talmudic Medicine* (trans. F. Rosner; New York: Sanhedrin, 1978), pp. 375-431 (Gynecology and Obstetrics). Unfortunately I have not been able to consult the dissertation by E. Szarvas, *Les connaissances embryologiques et obstétricales des Hébreux jusqu'à l'époque de clôture du Talmud* (Paris, 1936).

R. 17.8 we read: 'Why does a man deposit sperm within a woman while a woman does not deposit sperm within a man? It is like a man who has an article in his hand and seeks a trustworthy person with whom he may deposit it'. The word used here for the verb 'deposit' is a *hiphil* form of *pqd*, which, according to the dictionaries, means 'to give in charge, to deposit'. When one looks up καταβάλλω and καταβολή in Liddell–Scott–Jones, one finds there exactly the same meaning, '(to) deposit'. This can hardly be coincidence, and I am inclined to detect here the influence of Greek terminology for seminal emission.

That there was indeed Greek influence on rabbinic embryology[1] is proved beyond any doubt by several passages, of which I will quote only the most illuminating.[2] The Aristotelian position seems to be reflected in the short remark in *b. Ket.* 10b: 'It has been taught in the name of Rabbi Meir: Every woman who has abundant (menstrual) blood has many children'.[3] A combination of an Aristotelian and a double-seed theory (as in Galen) is found several times—for example, in a baraita in *b. Nid.* 31a:

> Our rabbis taught: There are three partners in (the conception of) man, the Holy One, blessed be He, his father, and his mother. His father supplies the semen of the white substance out of which are formed the child's bones, sinews, nails, the brains in his head and the white in his eye. His mother supplies the semen of the red substance out of which is formed his skin, flesh, hair, blood, and the black of his eye. The Holy One, blessed be He, gives him the spirit and the breath, beauty

1. Greek influence on rabbinic anthropology in general was proved long ago by R. Meyer, *Hellenistisches in der rabbinischen Anthropologie* (Stuttgart: Kohlhammer, 1937).

2. Some passages are discussed by F. Rosner, *Medicine in the Bible and the Talmud* (New York: Ktav, 1977), pp. 173-78. Cf. also D.M. Feldman, *Birth Control in Jewish Law: Marital Relations, Contraception and Abortion as Set Forth in the Classic Texts of Jewish Law* (Westport: Greenwood Press, 1980), pp. 132-40. Several passages are also mentioned by Stricker, *De geboorte van Horus*, II, pp. 121-25 with notes.

3. I use throughout the Soncino translation of the Talmud and the Midrash Rabbah.

of features, eyesight, the power of hearing, the ability to speak
and to walk, understanding and discernment.

Almost identical passages can be found in *b. Qid.* 30b, *Qoh. R.*
5:10, 2, *Midrash Yetsirat ha-Walad*,[1] and others. The Aristotelian element is, of course, that the menstrual blood is
regarded as the female contribution to the embryogenesis
(although, in a sense, quite different from the Stagirite), whereas
the fact that the *katamenia* are explicitly called 'semen' here
classes this statement with the double-seed theory.

The double-seed theory is also explicitly referred to in *b. B.
Qam.* 92a, where the rabbis discuss the fact that in Gen. 20.18
('For the Lord had closed up all the wombs in the house of
Abimelech'), the Hebrew text has two forms of the verb 'close',
the infinitive and the finite verb (MT has *ʿaṣor ʿaṣar*):

> Rabbi Eleazar said: Why is 'closing up' mentioned twice? There
> was one closing up in the case of males, semen, and two in the
> case of females, semen and the giving of birth. In a baraitha it
> was taught that there were two in the case of males, semen and
> urinating, and three in the case of females, semen, urinating
> and the giving of birth. Rabina said: Three in the case of males,
> semen, urinating and anus, and four in the case of females,
> semen and the giving of birth, urinating and anus.

Interestingly enough, within the framework of a double-seed
theory, the rabbis developed their own version of the *epikrateia*
principle. This version simply held that if a man emits his semen
first, the child will be a girl, but if the woman emits her semen
first, the child will be a boy (see, for instance, *b. Ber.* 54a, *Nid.*
70b-71a).[2] This theory—strange at first sight—of crosswise sex
determination was supported by an exegesis of Lev. 12.2 and
Gen. 46.15 (Lev. 12.2 being the only Old Testament text
discussed above). In *b. Nid.* 31a we read the following discussion:

> Rabbi Isaac citing Rabbi Ammi [or: Assi] stated: If the woman
> emits her semen [*hiphil* of *zrʿ*, as in Lev. 12.2!] first, she bears a
> male child, if the man emits his semen first, she bears a female
> child; for it is said: 'If a woman emits semen and bears a male

1. German translation of this midrash in A. Wünsche, *Aus Israels
Lehrhallen* (repr.; Hildesheim: Olms, 1967 [1909]), III, p. 221.
2. These and other passages are discussed by Rosner, *Medicine in the
Bible and the Talmud*, pp. 173-78.

child' [Lev. 12.2]. Our Rabbis taught: At first it used to be said that if the woman emits her semen first, she bears a male child, and if the man emits his semen first, she bears a female child, but the Sages did not explain the reason, until Rabbi Zadok came and explained it: 'These are the sons of Leah whom she bore unto Jacob in Paddan-Aram, with his daughter Dinah' [Gen. 46.15]. Scripture thus ascribes the males to the females and the females to the males.

This last sentence makes clear how Gen. 46.15 was understood: because this biblical text speaks of 'sons of Leah' and of 'his daughter Dinah', Scripture evidently implies that the fact that sons were born was due to Leah and that a daughter was born was due to Jacob. This fact, combined with the datum that the unique *hiphil* form of *zr‹* in Lev. 12.2 implies female seminal emission, seems to lead inevitably to this specifically rabbinic doctrine of sex differentiation.[1] The obvious problem of a double pregnancy with both a male and a female embryo was solved as follows: 'It may equally be assumed that both [man and woman] emitted their semen simultaneously, the one resulting in a male and the other in a female' (*b. Nid.* 25b and 28b).

In this context it should be added that, although the Targumim on Leviticus all have a verb meaning 'to become pregnant' for the *hiphil* of *zr‹* in Lev. 12.2, and the halakhic midrash *Sifra* has no remarks *ad locum*, the haggadic midrash *Lev. Rabba* 14.9 remarks on our verse:

> It [namely, the determination of the embryo's sex] may be likened to two artists, each of whom executes the likeness of the other; thus it is always that the female is formed from [the seed of the] man and the male from [the seed of the] woman. This is indicated by what is written...[Lev. 12.2 and Gen. 46.15]. The process may be likened to two entering a bath house: whichever perspires first is the first to come out.

Several other aspects of rabbinic embryology betray the influence of Greek medical and philosophical ideas, but I have limited myself to the concept of female seed. It may be clear that

1. The sequel of this passage in *Nid.* 31a goes on to discuss this theme but need not be reproduced here. All embryological, sexological, and gynecological lore in the tractate *Niddah* betrays a great deal of knowledge of Greek medical theories.

this concept was not the fruit of an indigenous development of Jewish ideas about semen, nor was it the result of exegesis of Lev. 12.2 and Gen. 46.15. The fact that these biblical texts are only adduced in a context of discussion of *epikrateia* as the dominant principle of sex determination makes it highly probable that these biblical passages were only taken into service *a posteriori* as a scriptural prop to this theory. The Greek theory had probably already been adopted by the rabbis before the exegetical justification was there. It seems to me that in this respect, too, the rabbis were indebted to Hellenistic culture.[1]

Conclusion

I have surveyed evidence for a theory of female semen from approximately 500 BCE to approximately 500 CE. I have demonstrated that there was continuous support for this theory during this millennium (and the demonstration could have covered the next millennium as well).[2] What has become overwhelmingly evident is that nothing prevents us from assuming that the author of Hebrews could easily have had knowledge of this widely current idea (much more current than Cadbury and Spicq had surmised). The fact that this author uses the term καταβολὴ σπέρματος, whereas in most other texts about female seminal emissions this term is not used—the most current terms are προΐεσθαι, ἀποκρίνειν, ἐκκρίνειν σπέρμα, σπερμαίνειν—is not a valid objection, since these other terms were used indiscriminately for male and female emissions as well. Hence we cannot but concur with Cadbury, who said 70 years ago: 'The author of Hebrews meant what he seems to say'.[3]

1. For another example in the field of embryology see P.W. van der Horst, 'Seven Months' Children in Jewish and Christian Literature from Antiquity', in *Essays on the Jewish World of Early Christianity* (Freiburg/Göttingen: Universitätsverlag/Vandenhoeck & Ruprecht, 1990), pp. 233-47.

2. For the persistence of this doctrine in the Middle Ages in Greek, Latin and Hebrew literatures, see Needham and Hughes, *Embriology*; Gerlach, 'Problem'; Lesky, *Die Zeugungs- und Vererbungslehren*; and Rosner, *Medicine*.

3. Cadbury, 'Ancient Physiological Notions', p. 439. On p. 430

It should be added in fairness, however, that nine centuries before Cadbury, an early commentator on our epistle, the Byzantine exegete Theophylactus, wrote in his *Exposition in Epistulam ad Hebraeos* 11.11:

> 'She received strength for a seminal emission': That is, she obtained strength to receive and retain Abraham's seed that was emitted into her. Or, because those who have studied these matters in detail say that a woman, too, in a sense, produces seed of her own, perhaps the words 'for a seminal emission' should be taken to mean this: 'so that she herself too could emit semen' ("δύναμιν εἰς καταβολὴν σπέρματος ἔλαβεν"· τουτέστι, ἐνεδυναμώθη εἰς τὸ ὑποδέξασθαι καὶ κρατῆσαι τὸ καταβληθὲν εἰς αὐτὴν σπέρμα τοῦ Ἀβραάμ. "Ἡ ἐπειδή φασιν οἱ ταῦτα ἀκριβωσάμενοι, καὶ τὴν γυναῖκα οἷόν τι σπέρμα ἀφ' ἑαυτῆς συνεισάγειν, μήποτε οὕτως ἐκληπτέον τὸ "εἰς καταβολὴν σπέρματος" ἀντὶ τοῦ "εἰς τὸ καταβαλεῖν καὶ αὐτὴν σπέρμα").[1]

Cadbury rightly remarks on sexological notions of the ancients: 'Such notions as they had, they were wont to express with directness without euphemism and false delicacy even in untechnical writing, as in poetry and religious literature'.

1. *PG* 125, p. 348. On the knowledge of double-seed theories among patristic authors of the earlier period (second to fourth centuries CE) see esp. Waszink, 'Embryologie', pp. 1242-44, and also his monumental *Tertulliani De anima* (Amsterdam: Meulenhoff, 1947), pp. 342-48.

Part II

WOMEN AND THE FEMININE:
NEW TESTAMENT WOMEN CHARACTERS

MARY'S CALL

Bea Wyler

Call Narratives in the Hebrew Bible

In a course on Isaiah, I came across N. Habel's article 'The Form and Significance of the Call Narratives'.[1] Habel's point in this paper is that 'call accounts of the Old Testament are based upon a literary structure which requires further clarification and research'.[2] He then elaborates the literary structure of call narratives in detail. In order to illustrate his thesis, he applies the pattern to a number of biblical figures, beginning with Gideon and Moses, then focusing on the classical prophets. I presented Habel's findings in a seminary session of the Rabbinical School at the Jewish Theological Seminary of America, where we were to discuss personal histories that lead us into the Rabbinate. Before I summarize Habel's paper I need to add that, curious as I am, I tried to apply the pattern to additional biblical figures who were not on Habel's list, in particular to a number of women, especially Old Testament women. However, studying the Hebrew Bible together with Christian students had also sensitized me to New Testament questions. But since at that time I was not at all familiar with the text of the New Testament, I asked for help from someone for whom the New Testament has the power of Holy Scripture: Was there a New Testament text with the pattern of call narratives that referred in some way to Jesus of Nazareth? My Catholic colleague taught me that a *special* call to enter divine service was naturally superfluous for Jesus, but I should check in

---

1. N. Habel, 'The Form and Significance of the Call Narratives', *ZAW* 77 (1965), pp. 297-323.
2. Habel, 'Call Narratives', p. 297.

the Gospel of Luke for Mary, Jesus' mother.

The literary structure of call narratives has six components. These can vary widely in form, length and wording. The six features of the pattern are best recognized in the call to Gideon, in Judg. 6.11-17. This is the pattern:

1. The Divine Confrontation (vv. 11b-12a): 'Gideon was beating out wheat in the wine press...and the angel of Adonai appeared to him...' The call happens 'out of the blue', while Gideon is busy with his daily routine as a farmer. However, it is a time of historical crisis in Israel (Midian is attacking). Although the call marks the initial divine interruption in the life of the called, the caller is not God but rather a heavenly messenger.[1]

2. The Introductory Word (vv. 12b-13): '...and said to him, "Adonai is with you, mighty man of valor!" And Gideon said to him, "Pray, sir, if Adonai is with us, why then has all this befallen us?...but now Adonai has cast us off..." '. An introductory word precedes the direct commission. It is a personal communication, usually introduced by אמר. Its function is to spell out the specific basis for the commission: it is both explanatory and preparatory. The greeting ה' עמך, 'God is with you!', at the very beginning of the encounter establishes the peculiar personal relationship between God and the individual who is being called. But Gideon's response is quite sharp and has an undertone of despair. He links the present situation of hopeless crisis with the past relationship between the saviour God and Israel, and remains in a state of rational consciousness during the whole conversation.

3. The Commission (v. 14): 'And Adonai turned to him and said, "Go in this might of yours and deliver Israel from the hand of Midian; do not I send you?"' The direct command is formulated in the imperative and, to underline its strength, a rhetorical question concludes the commission act. Gideon's function is that of deliverer, and it is through him that divine deliverance will be revealed. Thus Gideon is not only a deliverer, but also a messenger: he mediates God's historical intervention in Israel. It is worth noting that now it is God who speaks to

1.   Hebrew מלאך; compare Gen. 22.11, 15; 48.16; Exod. 3.2.

Gideon, thus emphasizing the ultimate source of the divine command.

4. The Objection (v. 15): 'And he [Gideon] said to him, "Pray, my Lord, how can I deliver Israel? Behold, my clan is the weakest in Menasseh, and I am the least in my family"'. From Gideon's human perspective he is totally inadequate to meet the task. Gideon is the youngest representative in the weakest of the clans of Menasseh—how could he possibly be capable of saving Israel?! This contrasts directly with God's perception of this same individual. Like Israel, whom Gideon represents, Gideon is chosen by God's grace from insignificant past to prominent and preferred status.[1]

5. The Reassurance (v. 16): 'And Adonai said to him, "I am indeed with you! And you shall smite the Midianites as one man"'. Gideon's initial question whether God was with the Israelites in any recognizable way, and his subsequent objection that he was completely inadequate for the task, are answered by divine reassurance. *Indeed* God is with him and, therefore, Gideon will smite the enemy. Characteristically, the reassurance repeats the essence of the commission's content. God's demand is thus made inescapable.

6. The Sign (v. 17): 'And he said to him, "If I have found favor with You, then show me a sign that it is You who speaks with me"'. Gideon asks for supporting assurance that God had spoken, not for proof that Adonai will conquer Midian: if God has *really* spoken, it will undoubtedly happen. The quest for the sign means additional confirmation that he *indeed* was the mediator of God's word.

Gideon's call is the most suitable for establishing the literary pattern of call narratives, since it is complete with all six components being clearly discernible. As mentioned before, this pattern is applicable in varying forms to a wide range of biblical characters. Habel continues with the call of Moses before he applies it to the classical prophets. In the case of Moses the text of the call becomes much longer (Exod. 3.1-12), but this is not the main difference. God offers the sign before Moses asks for it.

1.   Habel, 'Call Narratives', p. 300.

However, it is unusual that the sign's fulfillment is delayed to a much later time, namely *after* Moses has followed the divine call. Habel observes that,

> whereas the sign of Gideon is requested as confirmation prior to the execution of his commission, that of Moses (in Exod. 3) is unsolicited and takes place after the performance of his command.[1]

While Isaiah's call is quite an extensive text and is surprisingly placed as late as the sixth chapter (Isa. 6.1-13), Jeremiah's call is brief, terse and placed at the very beginning of the book (Jer. 1.4-10). The most elaborate call narrative is found in Ezekiel. The divine confrontation includes nothing less than 28 verses, namely the whole of the first chapter, Ezekiel's famous vision of the chariot; the completion of the call pattern continues far into the third chapter (Ezek. 3.11). Another unusual case is Abraham's: the pattern is not applicable on his first call to enter divine service (Gen. 12.1-3). However, Abraham is called several more times, and these texts follow the pattern beautifully (for instance, Gen. 15.1-5; 17.1-5).

Women's Calls: Sarah and Mrs Manoah

Sarah's call (Gen. 18.9-14) is indirect: the messengers talk to her husband Abraham, and he answers on her behalf. However, Sarah is the first to be mentioned to have heard the message (v. 10). Her objection, too, is unusual on two counts. While the narrator mentions that the two of them might be too old for having children, Sarah bursts out laughing (actually she bursts 'in' laughing, she laughs inside herself: בקרבה). God's reaction, expressed again towards Abraham, is more rebuke than reassurance and, consequently, Sarah does not ask for a sign but rather tries to defend her reaction.

An incredibly funny call narrative tells the story of Samson's parents, Manoah and his nameless wife, who have a most physical encounter with a divine messenger (Judg. 13.2-20). In fact there are *two* call narratives, both announcing the conception of the same child, namely one for the mother (Judg. 13.2-11)

---

1. Habel, 'Call Narratives', p. 305.

and one for the father (Judg. 13.11-20).[1] Even though each call is complete in itself, they are intertwined, since each of them plays a crucial role in the other one. For the purpose of this paper, the emphasis is on the call to Samson's mother (Judg. 13. 2-11). After her first experience with the stranger (vv. 3-5),[2] she gives her husband a detailed report (vv. 6-7), and mentions that she did not ask the awesome-looking man with the strange message for his name, even though she recognizes him at this point in the narrative as a 'man of God'. Forgetting to ask for the name functions as the objection,[3] which is supported by Manoah who does not know how to care for the baby yet unconceived and therefore requests the repetition of the instructions (!). Another issue is unusual in the call of Samson's mother: God appears only through the messenger, who furthermore *is* the actual sign.[4] On the other hand, Manoah's request for God's help is heard by *God*, even though a messenger comes to fulfill it.

It is quite obvious from the cases of Sarah and Mrs Manoah that calls for women are of a unique character—if one wants to name them 'calls'. The two cases discussed are annunciation stories. However, since all the elements of the call pattern are included, the annunciation of a birth—expressed to barren women at that!—has to be understood as a variation of the classical call, particularly since God has some important plans for the child to be born. In both cases the conception of a long-awaited child underlines the commission, which makes the husbands' presence in the stories understandable, although their

---

1. Since the conception of Samson is announced to both his parents, the two separate accounts can be read as one *single* call addressed to the couple. However, recognizing the six-step pattern in this case is admittedly a bit tricky. The entire encounter with Mrs Manoah, vv. 3-11a, has to be understood as an elaborate form of steps 2 and 3, the introductory word and the commission. The questions, including 'are you the man?' (vv. 11b-12) signify Manoah's mild objection (step 4), both expressing disbelief and hope. The reassurance (step 5) is short and to the point (vv. 13-14), while the sign (step 6) takes a whole discussion between the angel and Manoah (vv. 15-20).

2. 1, confrontation: vv. 2-3a; 2, introductory word: v. 3b; 3, commission: vv. 4-5.

3. 4, objection: vv. 6-8.

4. 6, sign: v. 11b.

participation in begetting the child is enigmatic[1] to say the least. It is thus significant that the women do not act on their own but in company (Mrs Manoah) or in the shadow (Sarah) of their husbands. Consequently, they share the fulfillment of their task with their husbands. The achievement is not theirs alone, as it is in the case of Gideon, Moses or the prophets. It is necessary to add that the commission in women's calls is not always in the realm of childbearing.[2] However, for the purpose of this paper, Sarah's and Mrs Manoah's encounters with the divine in the context of their childlessness are suitable texts for comparison.

Mary is Called

In the New Testament the literary pattern of call narratives is used in a most impressive way in Lk. 1.26-38, in the annunciation to Mary. The person called is not the main protagonist, but his future mother. Thus, in common with Sarah's and Mrs Manoah's cases, in Mary's case the conception of a child is the issue of the commission, although hers is not a child long awaited. Mary is not known to be a barren woman. Pregnancy has not been an issue in her life yet, since she is unmarried. She will not therefore have to share the fulfillment of the call with her husband as a partner; rather, the virgin birth must have been a tremendous challenge for Joseph of Nazareth. Nevertheless, this does not mean that Mary fulfills the call for herself alone—it is rather her son who 'participates' in her following the call. In the words of the authors of *Mary in the New Testament* the sharing of the call becomes even more unequal, Mary being the loser: 'Discussing Mary in the Gospels we must

1. Note that in Judg. 13.9, Manoah's wife's second encounter with the divine messenger happens with her husband *explicitly* absent, even though it is he who asks for the instructions to be repeated.

2. See Deborah (Judg. 4) and Esther (Est. 4). Interestingly enough in both of these cases the messengers to call them into service are not heavenly at all, but rather very human: Barak and Mordechai. The issue of childbearing is modified in the story of the midwives Shiphra and Puah (Exod. 1.15-21), and it is their *fear of God* alone which serves as 'messenger' .

not let our inquiry obscure the fact that the evangelist's primary interest is in Jesus, not in Mary'.[1]

The text of Mary's call follows the pattern established in the Hebrew Bible (the 'Old' Testament) in such pure and clear ways that an audience familiar with the text of the Hebrew Bible must have noticed the similarity at once. It is necessary to take a close look at this text, which contains all six components of the call pattern.

1.   The Divine Confrontation (vv. 26-27[2]): 'In the sixth month the angel Gabriel was sent from God to a city of Galilee named Nazareth, to a virgin betrothed to a man whose name was Joseph, of the house of David; and the virgin's name was Mary'. Habel notes in his study on Hebrew Bible characters in call narratives:

> The initial divine confrontation is portrayed in a manner which tends to emphasize the disruptive and overwhelming character of the call encounter which could not be readily described in terms of a normal everyday occurrence.[3]

This observation certainly seems to apply to Mary, too, although if one assumes that the messenger was not recognized by her as being Gabriel, one might claim that a stranger visiting a young woman was perhaps not so disruptive and over-whelming an experience, certainly not at this stage of the plot, even though she was betrothed. The most surprising aspect of this first step of the call, however, is that both protagonists, in fact all three, are introduced by name. By comparison, neither the man of God nor Manoah's wife has a name; and Moses is born of two nameless parents (Exod. 2.1), of whom only their tribal kinship is known.

2.   The Introductory Word (vv. 28-30): 'And he came to her and said, "Hail, O favored one, the Lord is with you!" But she was greatly troubled at the saying, and considered in her mind what sort of greeting this might be. And the angel said to her,

1.   E.R. Brown, K.P. Donfried, J.A. Fitzmyer and J. Reumann (eds.), *Mary in the New Testament* (New York: Paulist Press, 1978), p. 20.

2.   All New Testament translations are from The New Oxford Annotated Bible, 1977.

3.   Habel, 'Call Narratives', p. 317.

"do not be afraid, Mary, for you have found favor with God"'. Since Sarah is not addressed directly, the two women are not comparable at this stage. Mary is also unlike Mrs Manoah, who is greeted by the divine messenger with the direct exclamation 'You are barren, you have no children!' (Judg. 13.3). Mrs Manoah is introduced with a severe flaw for a woman of her time. By contrast, Mary is greeted like Gideon with a most positive attribute: 'O favored one!' is just as beautiful as 'You mighty man of valor!'—if one disregards the fact that neither of them is addressed by name. Furthermore Mary is assured, like Gideon and Moses, that God is 'with her'. Habel understands this segment to be of 'semi-confessional' nature:

> The call of the prophet or mediator establishes a historical connection between Yahweh's past and present involvement in Israel's history.[1]

This may well have been the intention of Luke's author, when he chose the rather 'masculine' formula of 'God is with you' in Mary's personal call narrative. Her first reaction is one of 'great trouble', and when she 'considers in her mind what sort of greeting this might be', the overwhelming rupture with her everyday life becomes evident. In this Mary resembles Sarah, who has an 'inner' reaction, too; but Sarah's disbelief is replaced by Mary's curiosity and wonder. Mary is quite different from Mrs Manoah, who seems to have entered the first confrontation with no hesitation whatsoever but rather full of curiosity. Mary's reaction of doubt also echoes Gideon's, who asks questions how it is possible that God is with him/them whereas Israel's situation is so bad.

3. The Commission (vv. 32-33): 'And behold, you will conceive in your womb and bear a son, and you shall call his name Jesus. He will be great, and will be called the Son of the Most High; and the Lord God will give to him the throne of his father David, and he will reign over the house of Jacob for ever; and of his kingdom there will be no end'. Habel observes that

> The actual commissioning of the person involved is regularly couched in the terms of a direct personal imperative which

---

1. Habel, 'Call Narratives', p. 318.

embraces the essential goal of the task assigned...The command, however, is more than 'Go and say!' For Moses and Gideon it is basically, 'Go and save'. For Isaiah it is tantamount to 'Go and damn!' The role is the same but the goal is reversed. In each case it becomes apparent that the commission involves a range of activities which is beyond the range of the individual's natural ability.[1]

Mary's commission is parallel to that of other women: 'Go and have a child!' is a commission which is perfectly within the range of normal women's lives. However, for all three women—Sarah, Mrs Manoah and Mary—having a child is not within their natural ability, for two are barren and one is not yet married. The commission 'Go and have a child!' can be understood as an invitation to become normal women (in biblical terms). Their calls thus mean that they should engage in the normal, not in the exceptional—which is quite different from farmer Gideon's or shepherd Moses' call. For Sarah and Mrs Manoah this is a joyful perspective; for Mary it is a source of 'great trouble'. There is yet another, the crucial, difference in Mary's commission to have a child. In Sarah's and Mrs Manoah's case the emphasis is on the women, not on the child, while in Mary's case it is clear from the beginning onwards that the focus is on the son. This aspect is enhanced by the fact that Jesus is named by the divine messenger, while Isaac is named by his father (Gen. 21.3) and Samson by his mother (Judg. 13.24). The way in which the greatness of Mary's son is announced makes it clear that Mary is just the 'instrument' to bring forth this son. In other words, the call is *not really* meant for her, even if she is the addressee as well as the one to execute the commission.

4.   The Objection (v. 34): 'And Mary said to the angel, "How shall this be, since I have no husband?"'. This echoes a number of objections. Sarah basically says 'How can this be? I (with my husband) am too old' (Gen. 18.11-12). Moses responds with 'who am I?' (Exod. 3.11), while Jeremiah exclaims, 'I cannot even speak, I am too young' (Jer. 1.6). Gideon's reaction points to the impossibility of the circumstances. Only Mrs Manoah is

---

1.   Habel, 'Call Narratives', p. 318.

immediately and completely willing to fulfill the exceptional task; she has, in her excitement, just forgotten a few details. Mary is a combination of those variants. She points to her state of being unmarried, hence her inability to meet the task; but, since she is betrothed, conceiving will soon be in the realm of her possibilities. Her objection, in other words, is not very convincing. Habel points to an important aspect in the objecting person which, based on the factors mentioned, does not fully apply to Mary.

> To object to a divine commission or decision may not be merely a sign of the prophet's innate humility or sense of inadequacy, but rather a part of his office as servant, mediator and agent of Yahweh. For the prophetic 'I' must be viewed both as the prophet's ego in dialogue with Yahweh as well as in action for Yahweh.[1]

5.   The Reassurance (v. 35): 'And the angel said to her, "The Holy Spirit will come upon you, and the power of the Most High will overshadow you; therefore the child to be born will be called holy, the Son of God"'. According to Habel,

> The reassurance incorporates a direct divine response which forcefully answers the specific objection of the person commissioned by reaffirming the previous command.[2]

Mary's specific objection is not responded to; rather the commission is powerfully repeated. In none of the calls mentioned in Habel's paper does the person called appear so totally without a choice than here. In the divine formula 'I am indeed with you', which is in Mary's call implied but not explicitly expressed, the finality of the divine commission and the inevitability of the divine mission are bound together. Habel again:

> Once the word has been spoken and the decree made public the divine plan must go in effect. This feature gives us a further insight into the concept of prophetic compulsion...The spoken word from heaven is inescapable. It must take its destined

---

1.   Habel, 'Call Narratives', p. 319.
2.   Habel, 'Call Narratives', p. 319.

course and the person to whom it is directed must become its vehicle.[1]

6. The Sign (vv. 36-37): 'And behold, your kinswoman Elizabeth in her old age has also conceived a son; and this is the sixth month with her who was called barren. For with God nothing will be impossible'. (And v. 38: 'And Mary said, "Behold, I am the handmaid of the Lord; let it be to me according to your word." And the angel departed from her'.) This is the one exception in all the call narratives where the fact that the same has happened to other people functions as a sign: it must be true, because 'with God nothing is impossible'. The annunciation of John the Baptist's birth thus functions as an example for the forthcoming birth of Jesus. In Sarah's call also God insists that nothing is impossible, but there is no other pregnant old woman around to support the divine promise; indeed, Sarah has to wait another three chapters until God remembers her and she conceives a child (Gen. 21.1). However, Elizabeth's pregnancy is sufficient proof for Mary: under these conditions she easily accepts the announced events and enters into the divine service.

Concluding Remarks

The similarities between the call narratives of Gideon, Moses and the prophets on the one hand and the annunciation narratives of Sarah, Mrs Manoah and Mary on the other hand are striking. Luke is the only text outside the canon of the Hebrew Bible which facilitates some questions concerning this usage of a literary pattern. Is the way in which Luke reports the stories around Jesus' birth historically authentic? Or is 'his' formulation, based on a well-known pattern, an attempt to root the events around Jesus' life in the Hebrew Bible, thus writing an 'extension' of the latter? By using biblical features and language forms, is his intention to write Holy Scripture, or are his writings closer to the early midrashic tradition? Is the account as we have it today original as from Jesus' lifetime, or does it include

---

1. Habel, 'Call Narratives', p. 319.

the contribution of the evangelists, or gospel writers, [who] themselves select, shape, modify and embellish the material they inherited?...Is any...access to stage one blocked forever by the work of the evangelists (stage three) and the needs of the Christian communities, who freely created pronouncement stories..., miracle stories, and other units developed in a stylized form to answer questions or support practices of the early church (stage two)?[1]

Since so much has already been written on these questions, and, in addition, I lack the necessary depth in New Testament scholarship, I do not intend to attempt answers. However, as a rabbinic Jew, I am interested to know what is going on here in terms of the role of (Jewish) women in first century CE Palestine, particularly since Mary is not the only eminent New Testament woman. Can we learn anything about it from this New Testament text? Is Mary given this prominent role by the author of Luke because everybody needs a mother? But then, Moses' mother too should be a well-known figure! And what about King David, whose mother is totally unknown (1 Sam. 16)? Why does Jesus need parents at all? There are so many Hebrew Bible heroes who simply exist and have no particular family background worthy of mention. And furthermore, as for Jesus' lineage, which is as a matter of course concerning his role as messiah, the *father* is crucial, but not the mother. Does the outstanding place of Mary (and Elizabeth in Lk. 1.5-25) at the beginning of one of the Gospels hint at a more valuable place for women *in general* in the early Christian communities as compared with the early rabbinic communities of the time Luke was written? Is it a homage, with an intended side-effect of appeal to all women whose participation in the new communities will become eminently important? Conclusive answers based on this one text are not possible. However, it is awesome to recognize how well the author knew his Bible (the Hebrew

1. See G. O'Collins: 'Jesus', in M. Eliade (ed.), *Encyclopedia of Religion* (New York: MacMillan, 1987), VIII, p. 16. The four Gospels include material that has gone through three stages of development. Stage one covers the period of Jesus' ministry—'reports'; stage two covers the time of preaching about him—'traditions'; stage three covers the contribution of the Evangelists— 'midrash'.

Bible, the only canon then existing) and how he used his knowledge and skill to provide his audience with an important female hero, a young woman at that, who has been functioning as a role model for generations. The author of Luke obviously knew exactly what he was doing. Even if one is not interested in learning about his religious intentions or in doing a contextual reading, even if one does not read Luke as Scripture, the author left us an excellent piece of literature.

THE FOREMOTHERS AND THE MOTHER OF JESUS[*]

Jane Schaberg

The New Testament infancy narratives are of tremendous significance for any understanding of the image and reality of woman in the West, because they are the source of the Christian virgin-mother ideal. These texts have been read traditionally as making a unique claim: that Jesus the messiah was virginally conceived—that is, that his mother became pregnant solely by the power of divine creativity, and not as a result of sexual intercourse.[1] But have the New Testament texts been properly understood? I think that they have not; in fact they *could* not have been within the confining structures of patriarchal religion.

Reading as a woman reads,[2] and as a reader resisting some aspects of the authors' thought,[3] I propose that Mt. 1.1-15 and Lk. 1.20-56; 3.23-38 were originally about an illegitimate conception, not a virginal conception. It was the intention—or better, an intention—of Matthew and of Luke to hand down the tradition they inherited: that Jesus the messiah had been illegitimately conceived during the period when his mother Mary was betrothed to Joseph. At the pre-Gospel stage, this illegitimate conception tradition (probably originating in the circle of

---

*   First published in *Concilium* 26 (1989), pp. 112-19; reprinted by permission.

1.   See R.E. Brown, *The Birth of the Messiah* (Garden City, NY: Doubleday, 1977); J.A. Fitzmyer, *The Gospel according to Luke I-IX* (AB; Garden City, NY: Doubleday, 1981).

2.   The hope is that this reading will bring us closer to a more inclusive human reading.

3.   See J. Fetterly, *The Resisting Reader* (Bloomington: Indiana University Press, 1978); E. Showalter (ed.), *The New Feminist Criticism* (New York: Pantheon, 1985).

the family of Jesus) had already been understood theologically as due in some unexplained way to the power of the Holy Spirit.

Both evangelists worked further with this potentially damaging and potentially liberating material, each developing his own brilliant and cautious presentation. Their caution and their androcentric perspectives, as well as the history of interpretation of the narratives, make this aspect of their meaning difficult to perceive. They took for granted the illegitimacy tradition, of which Christians soon became unaware. In both accounts, Jesus' biological father is absent and unnamed, but adoption by Joseph incorporates the child into the Davidic line. Both evangelists express the faith conviction that in spite of his human origins, the child will be God's, since the Holy Spirit is ultimately responsible for this conception. In both Gospels this conviction is presented by depicting an angelic announcement that the pregnancy is divinely ordained. The story of Jesus' illegitimate conception and of his full acceptance as God's child and of Israel is the story that anticipates and prepares the reader for the final message of resurrection. The infancy narratives attempt as well to initiate the reader into a new framework of social values and realities in the community of the resurrected one, where the last are to be first and the claims of patriarchal power and dominion abolished.

Reading the New Testament narratives in terms of an illegitimate conception, rather than a virginal conception, offers a consistent explanation of many small details. None of the explanations offered here, taken alone, is convincing enough to challenge the traditional interpretation of the Infancy Narratives. But the cumulative effect of these explanations does pose that challenge. There is space here only to examine four elements of the Matthean narrative.[1]

---

1. My book, *The Illegitimacy of Jesus* (San Francisco: Harper & Row, 1987), includes further discussion of Mt. 1, treatment of the Lukan Infancy Narrative, of the pre- and post-Gospel illegitimacy tradition, and discussion of the feminist implications of my reading.

1. *The Genealogy*

Matthew begins his Gospel with the genealogy of Jesus Christ (1.1-17). An unusual feature of this genealogy is the mention of four women: Tamar, Rahab, Ruth, and the wife of Uriah. Why did Matthew choose these particular women as the 'fore-mothers'? What do they have in common, which may prepare the reader for the story of Mary that follows? A careful look at the stories of the four in the Hebrew Bible shows that their sociological situations are comparable.[1] 1. All four find themselves outside patriarchal family structures: Tamar and Ruth are childless young widows (then Tamar is later pregnant by her father-in-law); Rahab is a prostitute (if the Rahab in Joshua is the one Matthew is thinking of); Bathsheba is an adulteress and then a widow pregnant with her lover's child. 2. All four are 'wronged' or thwarted by the male world. Without claiming a full feminist consciousness for the authors of these narratives, we can claim an awareness, however dim, that society was patriarchal, and that this caused suffering for women in certain circumstances. 3. In their sexual activity[2] all four risk damage to the social order and their own condemnations. Accusation of improper sexual conduct is actually made in the case of Tamar, implicit in the case of Rahab, avoided in Ruth's case by the secrecy of Boaz, and levelled in Bathsheba's case against her partner. 4. The situations of all four are righted by the actions of men who acknowledge guilt and/or accept responsibility for them, drawing them under patriarchal protection, giving them identity and a future, legitimating them and their children-to-be. The mention of the four women is intended to lead Matthew's reader to expect another story of a woman who becomes a social misfit in some way; is wronged or thwarted; is party to a sexual act which places her in great danger; and whose story has an outcome which repairs the social fabric and ensures the birth of a child who is legitimate or legitimated.

1. See S. Niditch, 'The Wronged Woman Righted', *HTR* 72 (1979), pp. 143-49.
2. Or in Ruth's case, perhaps only suspicion of sexual activity (see the commentaries on Ruth 3.4, 7-9, 12-13).

Further, what do these stories of the foremothers have in common theologically, and what is the reader led to expect theologically? The stories show a significant *lack* of miraculous, direct intervention on the part of God, to right the wrongs, or remove the shame, or illuminate the consciousness, or shatter the structures. The stories are instead examples of the divine concealed in and nearly obliterated by human actions, and they share an outlook which stresses God as creator of the context of human freedom. Matthew leads his reader to expect a story which will continue this subtle theologizing. It will be a story marked by lack of miraculous, divine intervention, a story rather of divine accommodation to human freedom in the complexity of near-tragedy.

2. *The Marital and Legal Situation*

In the Palestine of the first century CE the marriage of a young girl took place in two stages. First came the betrothal, which was a formal exchange in the presence of witnesses of the agreement to marry, and the paying of the bride price. The betrothal constituted a legally ratified marriage, since it began the girl's transfer from her father's power to her husband's, giving the latter legal rights over her, and giving her, for many purposes, the status of a married woman. The betrothal could be broken only by his divorce of her, and any violation by her of his marital 'rights' during this period (when she continued to live in her father's house for about a year) was considered adultery. The second stage was the marriage proper, the transfer of the girl to her husband's home where he assumed her support. Only at this point did she definitely pass into her husband's power. It was normally assumed that the girl was a virgin at the time of her betrothal, and, at least in Galilee, also at the time of her completed marriage.

In Mt. 1.18-25, Mary is described as having been found pregnant in the period between the betrothal and the completed marriage, before she and Joseph 'came together', probably meaning before Mary was brought to Joseph's home. Joseph's reaction in v. 19 makes it plain that he is not responsible for the pregnancy (and v. 25 will underline this). Adultery or rape are two normal ways Joseph has of explaining the pregnancy with which he is confronted. The case of a betrothed virgin's sexual intercourse with someone other than her husband during the period of betrothal is handled in the Hebrew Bible only in Deut. 22.23-27, the text many scholars think is alluded to by both evangelists.

> If there is a betrothed virgin (MT *nš^arâ b^etûlâ*; LXX *pais parthenos*) and a man meets her in the city, and lies with her, then you shall bring them both out to the gate of the city, and you shall stone them to death with stones, the young woman because she did not cry for help, though she was in the city, and the man because he violated his neighbor's wife; so you shall purge the evil from the midst of you.[1] But if in the open country a man meets a young woman who is betrothed, and the man seizes her and lies with her, then only the man who lay with her shall die. But to the young woman you shall do nothing; in the young woman there is no offence punishable by death, for this case is like that of a man attacking and murdering his neighbour; because he came upon her in the open country and though the betrothed young woman cried for help there was no one to rescue her.

It is important that we try to determine as far as possible how this law was applied in Matthew's time, and the range of options that would be presented in such a case as he describes, involving pregnancy. 1. There is evidence that in a hearing before a judge or judges there would be an effort to go beyond Deuteronomy and not make everything turn on the scene of the act. For example, according to Philo, it had to be questioned whether she cried out and resisted, or co-operated willingly, or even whether she *could* cry out and resist, or was gagged and bound, overcome by superior strength, and whether the man had accomplices.[2] 2. There is evidence also of a less severe legal system in the first century, according to which the death penalty would not be enforced for an adulteress, but divorce was probably obligatory. 3. There may have existed in some circles as

---

1. The commentaries refer to this case as 'seduction'; the man 'seizes' the virgin who does not resist; this is considered adultery on the part of both.

2. Philo, *Spec. Leg.* 3.77-78.

well a rigorous *halakah* which required the layman (as well as the priest) to divorce even a raped woman; under a less severe *halakah*, divorce of the raped woman by the layman was not obligatory but probably allowed. 4. If no hearing was held, the woman may have been presumed guilty, and divorce would be the outcome, possibly on trivial grounds. 5. Concerning the fate of children of an adulteress, Sir. 23.22-26 contains harsh words: her cursed memory and disgrace live on in them (cf. Wis. 3.16-19), and punishment falls on them (perhaps the assembly's decision that they are illegitimate, and the husband's rejection of them as his heirs). They are piously wished premature deaths and sterile unions. We can suspect that the children of raped women or women only suspected of adultery were also such social misfits. 6. Finally, let me mention what has been called 'the humane provision of Israel's regulations concerning adoption': the ruling principle was that any male child accepted under the rule of the head of a family was considered his son in all respects.[1]

In Matthew's opening lesson on righteousness and Torah, Joseph, 'a just man' (that is, Torah-observant), and unwilling to expose his wife to public disgrace, 'resolved to divorce her quietly' (1.19). The logic of the story[2] indicates that Joseph felt himself obligated, or allowed, to divorce rather than complete the marriage. I take this to mean that he ruled out the hearing to determine whether Mary had been seduced or raped, thus shielding her (and himself) from public shame and questioning, from the possibility of conviction on the charge of adultery, with its most likely punishment of a degrading divorce, attendant indignities and bleak future, and perhaps from the reasonable likelihood that rape could not be proven.

The angelic message in vv. 20-21, however, urges the home-taking, the completion of the marriage. 'Joseph, son of David, do not be afraid to take Mary your wife into your home, for the

---

1. C. Tchernowitz, 'The Inheritance of Illegitimate Children according to Jewish Law', in G.A. Kohut (ed.), *Jewish Studies in Memory of Israel Abrahams* (New York, 1927), pp. 402-403.

2. The phrase about the Holy Spirit in v. 18 is read by most critics as an aside to the reader.

child begotten in her is through the Holy Spirit'. One critic comments, 'The angel, by removing the suspicion of adultery and of violence, makes Mary acceptable to her husband'.[1] In my judgment, hometaking would remove the suspicion of adultery; a Torah-observant man would probably not complete the marriage with an adulteress. But the hometaking would *not* remove the suspicion of rape: a Torah-observant layman, following the *halakah* that allowed him to marry a raped woman, could proceed with the marriage. Since in his Gospel Matthew insists that the Torah is valid and must be interpreted without relaxation (5.18-19), on the hermeneutical principle of the priority of the love command, we can say he intends the angelic solution to the dilemma to be a righteous and legal one. It is also the most merciful alternative offered by the Law. Joseph, accepting the pregnant Mary into his home, accepts responsibility for the child she is carrying. The words to Joseph in 1.21, 'You will call his name Jesus', are equivalent to a formula of adoption. Joseph, by exercising the father's right to name the child, acknowledges Jesus and thus becomes his adoptive and legal father.

3. *The Role of the Holy Spirit*

What does Matthew mean when he says in v. 18 that Mary was found pregnant 'through the Holy Spirit', and in v. 20 that 'the child begotten in her is through the Holy Spirit'? Few modern critics think that these verses refer to anything but a virginal conception, a counter-explanation to human paternity. It is rapidly becoming a scholarly consensus, however, that the idea of a virginal conception is found nowhere but in the two New Testament infancy narratives, and that there are no real parallels in the Hebrew or Greek Bible, in intertestamental literature, or in the Pauline or Johannine writings; nor is the idea alluded to anywhere else in the New Testament. Critics generally agree that there are no real pagan parallels either, since pagan myths consistently involve a type of *hieros gamos*

---

1.   A. Tosato, 'Joseph, Being a Just Man', *CBQ* 41 (1979), p. 551.

or divine marriage, with pregnancy resulting from sexual penetration of some sort.[1] My suggestion for reading Matthew is a simple one: since nothing in the context of Matthew 1 requires us to read the phrases in terms of a virginal conception, they should be read against the wider Jewish and Christian background. This means they should be read in a figurative or symbolic sense.

In all the relevant Jewish and New Testament literature, divine begetting presupposes and does not replace human parenting. There are texts that speak of divine begetting to stress that God's power is the ultimate source of human life and generation, or to stress that God sometimes communicates a special spiritual dimension of life to humans, over and above or within human existence. In this latter sense Paul and John speak of the Christian begotten by the Spirit or by God.

In the light of these texts, Mt. 1.18, 20 can be read to mean that the Holy Spirit empowers this birth as all births are divinely empowered, that this child's existence is willed by God, that God is the ultimate power of life behind and in this as in all conceptions. My sense is that Matthew means more than—but not less than—this. In the situation he has described, this dimension of meaning is extremely significant: this child's existence is not an accident or mistake, and is not cursed. But Matthew is also clearly speaking about the election of this child from the womb for a role in Israel's history: Jesus will save his people from their sins (1.21), and will be called Emmanuel (1.23). Further, this begetting constitutes him Son of God in a special sense, as the one who sums up in his existence the whole history of Israel. Jesus is begotten through the Holy Spirit in his human paternity; he is one with God from his conception.

4. *Isaiah 7.14*

Between the angel's words to Joseph and Joseph's obedience to those words, Matthew inserts his first fulfillment citation: 'All this took place to fulfill what the Lord had spoken by the

---

1. See R.E. Brown, *The Virginal Conception and Bodily Resurrection of Jesus* (New York, 1973).

prophet: "Behold, the virgin (*parthenos*) will conceive and will give birth to a son and they will call his name Emmanuel"'. The sign offered by Isaiah to King Ahaz during the Syro-Ephraimite war in the eighth century BCE was the imminent birth of a child naturally conceived, who would signal God's presence and care for Judah. The Greek translation of Isaiah's Hebrew ʿalmâ (young woman) by *parthenos* (virgin) does not indicate a miraculous conception. Rather, the Greek translator simply meant that one who is *now* a virgin will conceive by natural means. Matthew himself added the citation to a pre-existing narrative or body of infancy tradition.

But why, of all the texts available to him, did Matthew choose this one to elucidate and support his story of the origins of Jesus? I think it is likely that the word *parthenos* played a role in his choice. But Matthew was not thinking of a virgin conceiving miraculously, but of the law in Deut. 22.23-27 concerning the seduction or rape of a betrothed virgin, the law he presupposes in his presentation of the dilemma of Joseph. Although he does not quote the law, this is the catchword association that triggered his use of Isa. 7.14. This would mean that he understood the text as the Greek translator did, referring to one who *was* a virgin and who conceived naturally. The placement of the citation underscores the way the divine assurance overturns Joseph's decision to divorce Mary.

The problem before Matthew was to make theological sense of a tradition concerning the illegitimate pregnancy. If we pause for a minute and ask what texts and traditions were available to him to be used for such a purpose we find that none would be clear and unambiguous choices. No text in the Hebrew Bible I can think of fully vindicates a wronged woman who has been seduced or raped, or legitimates the child born of such a union— much less prepares for the startling thought that this might be the origin of the expected messiah. There were, in fact, no texts and traditions ready at hand for such a theological task. Matthew had to create out of fragments easily misunderstood, and one of these is Isa. 7.14.

The virgin betrothed and seduced or raped is, then, in the great Matthean paradox, the virgin who conceives and bears the child they will call Emmanuel. His origin is ignominious and tragic, but Matthew's point is that his existence is divinely willed; his messiahship was not negated by the way he was conceived. The wording in which the New Testament conception story survives is 'when scrutinized closely, curious and equivocal'.[1] This is due not to the desire to be enigmatic, nor to the stress and strain of presenting a novel notion of divine begetting without human paternity (a virginal conception). It is due rather to something more difficult: the effort to be honest, discreet and profound, dealing with material that resisted—and still resists—the theologian's art: the siding of God with the outcast, endangered woman and child.

5. *Conclusions and Response*

In this interpretation of Matthew 1, God 'acts' in a radically new way, outside the patriarchal norm but within the natural event of human conception. The story of the illegitimacy of Jesus supports the claim Luke makes, that Mary represents the oppressed who have been liberated. But Matthew's version, with its focus on Joseph, is androcentric, primarily about and for males; it does not confront the causes or structures of oppression. It is not the story of the mother of Jesus. By linking her story, however, with those of the four women listed in the genealogy, Matthew implies that salvation history is not essentially a male enterprise. We can carry the implication further to challenge our deepest prejudices and presuppositions, by breaking the silence of the silent night.

1. G. Vermes, *Jesus the Jew: A Historian's Reading of the Gospels* (London: Collins, 1973), p. 221.

ELISABETH AND MARY—NAOMI AND RUTH: GENDER-RESPONSE CRITICISM IN LUKE 1-2*

Arie Troost

Speaking about the use of the Hebrew Bible or the LXX in the New Testament implies, among other things, notions of authorship. The possibility that certain intertexts are present 'in' the text depends to a high degree on a reader's preconceived ideas about who the anonymous or pseudonymous author could have been, what this author would have wanted to say, and the literary traditions and social locations by which this author might have been framed. Conversely, it is equally possible that a reader's selection and evaluation of intertexts contributes to readerly knowledge concerning the author of the text.[1] In this article I intend to demonstrate how gender, both the reader's and the author's, can play a decisive role in this two-way process.

On the one hand, we have to allow that the reader's gender influences the way the anonymous or pseudonymous author is viewed and gendered.[2] On the other hand, the (conventional)

* Parts of this article were previously read to the Colloquium Biblicum Lovaniense 1992 and to the SBL 1993 International Meeting in Münster, Germany. I would like to thank Athalya Brenner, Jan Willem van Henten and Anja Kosterman for their many helpful suggestions.

1. On what is *in* the text see J. Culler, *On Deconstruction: Theory and Criticism after Structuralism* (London/Henley: Routledge & Kegan Paul, 1983), pp. 73-78. On the use of the notion of 'framing' instead of 'context' see J. Culler, *Framing the Sign: Criticism and its Institutions* (Oklahoma Project for Discourse and Theory; Norma, OK. and London: University of Oklahoma Press, 1988), p. xiv.

2. See A. Brenner and F. van Dijk-Hemmes, *On Gendering Texts: Female and Male Voices in the Hebrew Bible* (Biblical Interpretation, 1; Leiden: Brill, 1993).

presupposition of a gendered author influences the way a gendered identity of the reader is constructed and reinforced.[1] In both cases the choice and evaluation of intertexts is one of the focal points of gender construction.[2] I will propose a 'gender-response criticism' in order to give an account of this two-way traffic of the interpretation process—whereby a reader is both gendered and gendering, both responding to gender and attributing gender.

The present study of Lk. 1.5–2.52 (hereafter referred to as Lk. 1–2) focuses on certain items in conventional interpretations of this narrative. These items include a vision of Elisabeth and Mary as two unequal mothers, both of whom play instrumental roles in the fulfilment of divine promises of progeny.[3] It will be argued that these items are not necessarily 'in' the text. This will provide the material for an inquiry—in Part II—into the relationship between readerly gender positions, and assumptions about the gendered author of the text. I will conclude with a

---

1. See J. Bekkenkamp, *Canon en Keuze: Het bijbelse Hooglied en de Twenty-One Love Poems van Adrienne Rich als bronnen van theologie* (Kampen: Kok Agora, 1993), pp. 11-44.

2. The use of the terms 'author', 'gender' and 'reader' might leave a more confident impression then intended. For a theoretical discussion of these concepts, see R. Barthes, 'La mort de l'auteur', *Mantéia* (1968), repr. in *Le bruissement de la langue: Essais critiques IV* (Paris: Seuil, 1984), pp. 61-67; ET 'The Death of the Author', in *Image, Music, Text* (New York: Hill & Wang, 1977), pp. 142-48; M. Foucault, 'Qu'est-ce qu'un auteur?', *Bulletin de la Société française de Philosophie*, Séance du 22 Février 1969, 64 (1969), pp. 73-104; ET 'What is an Author?', in *Language, Counter-Memory, Practice: Selected Essays and Interviews* (ed. D.F. Bouchard and S. Simon; Ithaca, NY: Cornell University Press, 1977), pp. 113-38; N.K. Miller, *Subject to Change: Reading Feminist Writing* (Gender and Culture; New York: Columbia University Press, 1988); Brenner and van Dijk-Hemmes, *On Gendering Texts*; A. Troost, 'Reading for the Author's Signature: Genesis 21.1-21 and Luke 15.11-32 as Intertexts', in A. Brenner (ed.), *A Feminist Companion to Genesis* (The Feminist Companion to the Bible, 2; Sheffield, Sheffield Academic Press, 1993), pp. 251-72; R. Braidotti, 'What's Wrong with Gender?', in F. van Dijk-Hemmes and A. Brenner (eds.), *Reflections on Theology and Gender* (Kampen: Kok Pharos, 1994), pp. 49-70.

3. See A. Troost, 'Als Elisabet en Maria elkaar spreken: over het nemen van het woord', *Schrift* 140 (1992), pp. 60-64.

comparison of Elisabeth and Mary with Naomi and Ruth, as an example of gender-response criticism (Part III). The comparison helps to highlight Elisabeth and Mary as women who, like Naomi and Ruth, cooperate in facing their social and religious locations. There is evidence that, in this respect, Elisabeth and Mary do not represent a rare phenomenon in the Graeco-Roman world of early Christianity.

Part I: Where Elisabeth and Mary Speak to Each Other

It is generally acknowledged that, in Luke 1–2, there is a parallelism between John and Jesus. First their respective births are announced (1.5-25; 1.26-38). Then, after a central section concerning Elisabeth and Mary (1.39-56), the birth stories proper are related (1.57-80; 2.1-40).[1] Though more sophisticated divisions have been proposed, this simple parallelism between two annunciations and two nativities grouped around the meeting between the two mothers remains at the very core of the interpretations for these two chapters.[2] The analogy between

1. For this simple division, see for example, A. Plummer, *A Critical and Exegetical Commentary on the Gospel according to S. Luke* (ICC; Edinburgh: T. & T. Clark, 4th edn, 1901), p. 6; E. Klostermann, *Das Lukasevangelium* (HNT, 5; Tübingen: Mohr, 3rd edn, 1975), p. 363; A. Loisy, *L'évangile selon Luc* (repr.; Frankfurt: Minerva, 1971 [1924]), p. 77; J.M. Creed, *The Gospel according to St. Luke* (London: Macmillan, 1975 [1930]), p. 6; K.H. Rengstorf, *Das Evangelium nach Lukas* (NTD, 3; Göttingen: Vandenhoeck & Ruprecht, 14th edn, 1969), pp. 51-52; W. Grundmann, *Das Evangelium nach Lukas* (THKNT, 3; Berlin: Evangelische Verlagsanstalt, 4th edn, 1966), p. 46.

2. More sophisticated divisions have been proposed by, for example, M. Dibelius, *Die urchristliche Überlieferung von Johannes dem Täufer* (FRLANT, 15; Göttingen: Vandenhoeck, 1911), p. 67; K.L. Schmidt, *Der Rahmen der Geschichte Jesu: Literarkritische Untersuchungen zur ältesten Jesusüberlieferung* (repr.; Darmstadt: Wissenschaftliche Buchgesellschaft, 2nd edn, 1969), p. 315; E. Burrows, *The Gospel of the Infancy and Other Biblical Essays* (London: Burns & Oates, 1940), pp. 4-6; R. Laurentin, *Structure et théologie de Luc I-II* (EBib; Paris: Gabalda, 1957), pp. 26-33 (much like Dibelius); G. Voss, 'Die Christusverkündigung der Kindheitsgeschichte im Rahmen des Lukasevangeliums', *BK* 21 (1966), p. 112 (goes back to Laurentin); W. Wink, *John the Baptist in the Gospel Tradition* (SNTSMS, 7; Cambridge: Cambridge University Press,

John and Jesus does not mean that the two children are equal in status. On the contrary, as the narrative proceeds, Jesus' importance appears to grow at the expense of John's, until—in Lk. 3.16—John is not even worthy of unfastening the straps of Jesus' sandals. We see a growing opposition between John and Jesus in Luke 1–2: the chronological order is inverted in favour of a qualitative order, hence Jesus takes precedence.

It therefore seems productive to read Luke 1–2 in the tradition of the Genesis narratives of conflict between brothers, in which the latter-born takes over the first-born's position.[1] Such stories are narrated of Cain and Abel (Gen. 4.3-16), Noah's sons (Gen. 9.20-27), Ishmael and Isaac (Gen. 16; 21.1-21), Esau and Jacob (Gen. 25.21-34; 26.34-8.9; 32.2-33.10), Er and Onan (Gen. 38.2-10), Zerah and Perez (Gen. 38.11-30), and Ephraim and Manasseh (Gen. 48). Of a slightly different character is the rivalry between Joseph and his older brothers (Gen. 37, particularly between Reuben and Judah, embodying a rivalry within

---

1968), p. 59 (repeats Dibelius); A. George, 'Le Parallèle entre Jean-Baptiste et Jésus en Lc 1-2', in A. Descamps and A. De Halleux (eds.), *Mélanges Bibliques* (Festschrift B. Rigaux; Gembloux: Duculot, 1970), pp. 147-71, repr. in A. George, *Etudes sur l'œuvre de Luc* (SB; Paris: Gabalda, 1978), pp. 43-65 (goes back to Dibelius); J.A. Fitzmyer, *The Gospel according to Luke I-IX* (AB, 28; Garden City: Doubleday, 1981), pp. 313-14 (obviously mainly informed by Laurentin, although confessing major indebtment to Dibelius). The introduction of semiotic analyses served to reinforce this parallelism: R. Laurentin, *Les évangiles de l'enfance du Christ. Vérité de Noël au-delà des mythes. Exégèse et sémiotique—historicité et théologie* (Paris: Desclée, 1982); A. Gueuret, *L'Engendrement d'un récit: L'évangile de l'enfance selon saint Luc* (LD, 113; Paris: Cerf, 1983). See the discussion by R.E. Brown, *The Birth of the Messiah: A Commentary on the Infancy Narratives in Matthew and Luke* (Garden City, NY: Doubleday, 1977), pp. 248-53.

1.   See J.P. Fokkelman, *Narrative Art in Genesis: Specimens of Stylistic Analysis* (repr.; Biblical Seminar, 12; Sheffield: JSOT Press, 2nd edn, 1991); S. Niditch, *Chaos to Cosmos: Studies in Patterns of Creation* (Scholars Press Studies in the Humanities, 6; Chico, CA: Scholars Press, 1985); D.W. Forsyth, 'Sibling Rivalry, Aesthetic Sensibility, and Social Structure in Genesis', *Ethos: Journal of the Society for Psychological Anthropology* 19 (1991), pp. 453-510.

rivalry;[1] 42–45; 50.15-21).[2] To these well-known Genesis stories
we can add the reversal between Samuel and the other,
nameless children of Elkanah (1 Sam. 1–2), later transposed to a
reversal between Samuel and Hophni/Pinehas in relation to the
priest/father Eli (1 Sam. 2.12–4.1a). This reversal is ultimately
concluded by the birth of Ichabod and the death of his mother,
Pinehas's wife (1 Sam. 4.19-22), which serves as a narrative
counterpart to the birth of Samuel and his naming by his mother
Hannah (1 Sam. 1–2.11).[3]

As I have argued elsewhere, in these stories two (groups of)
children are substituted for each other by means of a reversal.[4] I
called it the substitution-by-reversal paradigm. In this paradigm
the children change places in relation to their father but their
substitution is, in a number of instances, legitimated by a kind of
inequality, even rivalry, between their mothers: Hagar and
Sarah (Gen. 16.4-6),[5] Leah and Rachel (Genesis 30), Hannah
and Penninah (1 Sam. 1.6-7). The inequality of the mothers is
traced back to the circumstances of conception, responsibility for

---

1.   In determining Joseph's fate, Judah is the first to object to murder
(Gen. 37.21) but Reuben, the eldest, is the first to suggest a line of action
aimed at returning Joseph to his father (v. 22). Then Judah proposes to
sell Joseph off (vv. 26-27). As Judah's plan eventually wins out (v. 28)
and Reuben's plan fails (v. 29), the younger brother triumphs. The
Reuben–Judah opposition is echoed in the second Joseph narrative,
Gen. 42.37 and 43.9 (see Forsyth, 'Sibling Rivalry', pp. 490, 498).

2.   A rivalry between Adam and Jesus should not be included in this
list (as Forsyth ['Sibling Rivalry], p. 461, does, calling it an 'implicit
rivalry'), because this is a Christian narrativized theological construct
(see 1 Cor. 15.45) of a different order than the stories mentioned here (see
Niditch, *Chaos to Cosmos*, pp. 85-105). As for the narrative of Noah's
sons (Gen. 9.20-27), I do not see why Forsyth includes this one in his
inventory without returning to it in his discussion of the separate
stories (but see Niditch, *Chaos to Cosmos*, pp. 50-55).

3.   For the parallel between the birth of Ichabod/the wife of Pinehas
and the birth of Samuel/Hannah, see J.P. Fokkelman, *Narrative Art and
Poetry in the Books of Samuel. IV. Vow and Desire (1 Sam. 1-12)* (Assen:
Van Gorcum, 1993), who regards 1 Sam. 1–4 as one narrative act, denying
the existence of an independent Ark narrative.

4.   Troost, 'Reading', pp. 264-65.

5.   But not in Gen. 21.8-13! See Troost, 'Reading', pp. 259-64.

which is at times attributed to God, whose plans have to materialize.

This same mechanism seems to be at work in Luke 1–2, albeit in a less outspoken way. The responsibility for both births is attributed to God, while earthly fatherhood is almost excluded (1.18, 34). The preeminence of Jesus over John is related to their mothers in the visitation scene (1.39-56). In comments on this scene, John's jumping up in Elisabeth's womb and Elisabeth's subsequent words to Mary (1.41-45) are often considered not only an expression of John's recognition of Jesus' superiority, but also of Elisabeth's unworthiness vis-à-vis Mary. Such a thought is voiced as early as Origen who, in his *Homilies on Luke*, commenting on Lk. 1.43, says, 'The words of Elisabeth are in perfect accord with those of her son. This one [John] actually called himself unworthy to be at the side of Christ, just as Elisabeth called herself unworthy of the coming of the Virgin'.[1] This line of thought has been followed since Origen by many scholars.[2]

As feminist biblical critics have demonstrated, rivalry between women as mothers occurs in societies where women's identity is linked to the bearing of (legitimate) children.[3] Rachel's words to Jacob, 'Give me sons/children, or I shall die' (Gen. 30.1) are symptomatic in this respect. In these and other stories, women are viewed as instruments in obtaining divinely promised progeny. The same seems to obtain for Elisabeth and Mary. There is Elisabeth's 'shame among the people' (*oneidos*), taken away by God through a pregnancy that is 'done to her' (1.25). Mary's consent leaves the road open for the angel, God and/or

1. Origen, *Homiliae in Lucam* 7.5, Frag. gr. 22 (H. Crouzel, F. Fournier and P. Périchon [eds.], *Origène: Homélies sur S. Luc. Texte latin et fragments grecs* [SC, 87; Paris: Cerf, 1962], pp. 480-81). My translation.

2. See Laurentin, *Structure*, pp. 23-42, 148-63, and the literature cited there.

3. See for example, E. Fuchs, 'The Literary Characterization of Mothers and Sexual Politics in the Hebrew Bible', in A.Y. Collins (ed.), *Feminist Perspectives on Biblical Scholarship* (Society of Biblical Literature: Biblical Scholarship in North America, 10; Chico, CA: Scholars Press, 1985), pp. 117-36; A. Brenner, 'Female Social Behaviour: Two Descriptive Patterns within the "Birth of the Hero" Paradigm', *VT* 36.3 (1986), pp. 257-73; repr. in Brenner (ed.), *Genesis*, pp. 204-21.

Spirit (1.38), after which Mary states that her 'humiliation' (*tapeinōsis*) is noticed (1.48), counting herself among the humiliated (1.52). Moreover, both women are subservient to the birth of two very special children, a prophet—more than a prophet (7.26)—and a saviour.

The comparison of Luke 1–2 with this biblical substitution-by-reversal paradigm serves to highlight the application of two conventional interpretations. The one concerns the inequality between Elisabeth and Mary, which corresponds to the inequality between John and Jesus. The other concerns their motherhood as fulfilment of divinely announced births. Both interpretations should be treated with suspicion. I would venture in advance that these conventional interpretations are primarily motivated by androcentric and religious concerns.[1] It remains to be seen whether there really is—in Luke 1–2—an opposition between Elisabeth and Mary that is appropriately described in terms of the 'unworthiness' of the former by comparison to the latter. Besides, whether the narrative roles of Elisabeth and Mary are limited to instrumental motherhood, serving the fulfilment of divine plans, remains questionable. With these questions in mind, it is time to turn to the narrative.

First Observation: Who Acts?
When we direct our attention to the narrative, three narratological observations can be made regarding Elisabeth and Mary.[2] A first observation relates to how the fabula-layer actors

1. According to U. Busse the existence, in Luke's Gospel, of an opposition between John and Jesus is questionable. Still, he retains the instrumental function of these women as mothers of two divinely announced children precisely because of explicit religious concerns ('Das "Evangelium" des Lukas: Die Funktion der Vorgeschichte im lukanischen Doppelwerk', in C. Bussmann and W. Radl [eds.], *Der Treue Gottes trauen: Beiträge zum Werk des Lukas* [Festschrift G. Schneider; Freiburg: Herder, 1991], pp. 161-77).

2. The narratological model is described systematically and comprehensively in M. Bal's Dutch book, *De theorie van vertellen en verhalen: Inleiding in de narratologie* (Muiderberg: Coutinho, 5th rev. edn, 1990). The English version of this introduction (*Narratology: Introduction to the Theory of Narrative* [Toronto: University of Toronto Press, 1985]) is equally comprehensive but reflects earlier thoughts on

are invested as characters in the story layer.[1] Both Elisabeth and Mary are strongly marked as independently acting subjects, especially when compared to Zachariah and Joseph.[2]

Zachariah does not act independently. His function as a priest is derived from birth (1.5), he officiates according to the service roster (1.8), and it is his turn by lot to enter the temple (1.9). His words in 1.18 confirm his own inability to act, and express his doubts that the angel's words will prove true, precisely when his prayer (see 1.13) is about to be fulfilled! Afterwards his words confirm what is already a fact, that is, the name-giving by Elisabeth (1.63). Only after this does Zachariah burst out into a lengthy prophecy (1.68-79). In that, however, he has already been preceded by Elisabeth and Mary (1.42-55). Joseph does not act autonomously either. He sets off, forced by Caesar's decree, for his family's native city (2.1-4). Joseph does not play a narra-

narratology, in the sense that it shows more confidence in the possibility to describe what is 'in' the text. More detailed theoretical description of the model is provided in M. Bal, *Femmes imaginaires: l'ancien testament au risque d'une narratologie critique* (Utrecht/Paris: HES/Nizet, 1986), pp. 58-131. A very useful scheme of the narratological model in which the various subject positions are differentiated is given in M. Bal, *Death and Dissymmetry: The Politics of Coherence in the Book of Judges* (Chicago: University of Chicago Press, 1988), pp. 248-49.

1. A three-layer distinction between fabula (events and actors structured along logical, spatio-temporal principles), story (the material of the fabula ordered and presented from a certain vision, for instance characterization), and text (discursive structures) is at the basis of the narratological model used here (see Bal, *Narratology*, pp. 3-10).

2. The term 'independent' is used here in a strict narratological sense, meaning that there is no actor, however remote, acting as a 'sender' (*destinateur*; see A.J. Greimas and J. Courtés, *Sémiotique: Dictionnaire raisonné de la théorie du langage*, II [Paris: Hachette, 1979], pp. 94-95). One should not assume *a priori* that God is a 'sender' (as in the semiotic analyses by Laurentin, *Les Evangiles*, and A. Gueuret, 'Sur Luc. 1, 46-55: Comment peut-on être amené à penser qu'Elisabeth est "sémiotiquement" celle qui a prononcé le Cantique en Lc 1,46?', *Bulletin du Centre protestant d'études et de documentation. Supplément* [Paris, April 1977], pp. 3-11; *idem, L'Engendrement*), which would be a conflation of narratological and theological devices. It is possible to recognize the commitment of Mary to the humiliated, or to the cause of God or Israel's hopes as a 'sender' (A.J. Greimas and J. Courtés, *Sémiotique*, II [Paris: Hachette, 1986], pp. 66-67).

tive role of any consequence.

Elisabeth and Mary, on the other hand, do act independently. On the fabula layer there is no actor, such as a function or decree or even God or an angel, impelling them to act as they do. On the story layer they are invested with many qualities, leaving an impression of independence. Mary stands up of her own accord and sets off (1.39). Both Elisabeth and Mary show insight into the actions of God (1.42-55). Elisabeth names John (1.60) although the angel had foretold that Zachariah would do this (1.13), revealing the name 'John' only to him. Elisabeth and Mary keep the series of events concerning the births of John and Jesus going. They play a central role, expressed by the central place occupied by their meeting in Luke 1–2.

Second Observation: The Distribution of Speech
A second narratological observation concerns the variety of terms denoting speech (or non-speech) in Luke 1–2. The variety is extraordinary, as the following inventory shows. Terms for denoting or representing speech (or non-speech) include: speaking, talking, calling, starting or continuing to speak, proclaiming, keeping silence, beckoning, being mute, considering, exclaiming, nodding, praising, asking, prophesying, shouting loudly, pronouncing as happy, communicating by divine inspiration, asking questions, contradicting.[1] There are

---

1.   Speaking (*eipon*, 17 times—18 times including variant 2.15; *legō*, 5 times; *to eirēmenon*, once, 2.24), talking (*laleō*, 14 times including 2.15, of which twice 'not being able to speak', 1.20, 22), calling (*kaleō*, 14 times! See K.L. Schmidt, 'καλέω', *TWNT* III [1938], pp. 488-92), starting or continuing to speak (literally 'responding', *apokrinomai*, 3 times, 1.19, 35, 60), proclaiming (*euaggelizomai*, only twice, 1.19; 2.10), keeping silence (*siōpaō*, once, 1.20), beckoning (*dianeuō*, once, 1.22), being mute (*kōphos*, once, 1.22), considering (*dialogizomai*, once, 1.29), exclaiming (*anaphōneō*, once, 1.42, *hapax* in New Testament; variant *anaboaō*, New Testament further only in Mt. 27.46), nodding (*enneuō*, once, 1.62, *hapax* in New Testament), praising (four synonyms: *eulogeō*, 6 times - 7 times with variant 1.28; *aineō*, twice, 2.13, 20; *doxazō*, once, 2.20; *anthomologeomai*, once, 2.38, *hapax* in New Testament), asking (*aiteomai*, once, 1.63), prophesying (*prophēteuō*, once, 1.67), shouting loudly (*kraugē megalē*, once, 1.42; varia lectio *phōnē megalē* also in 1.44), pronouncing as happy (*makarizō*, once, 1.48, in New Testament further only in Jas 5.11), communicating by

also a few terms representing writing: writing, issuing a decree, registering.[1] Next to this diversity of phrases denoting speaking and writing, there is also variation in phrases for responding to speech and writing. Thus, speech is said to be possible; it takes place; is talked about; is made known, kept, considered and understood.[2] What is said elicits belief, disbelief and confusion.[3] Speeches and wonderful things are heard; what is heard is taken to heart, and Zachariah's prayer is heard.[4] What is written elicits surprise; it takes place either as word of Scripture or as decree of Caesar.[5]

It would therefore not be too much to view this text as an illustration of different ways to introduce, communicate and respond to speech.[6] From this variety, at least two conclusions could be drawn bearing on the question of gender. First, the

---

divine inspiration (*chrēmatizō*, once, 2.26), asking questions (*eperōtaō*, once, 2.46), contradicting (*antilegomenon*, 2.34, see J.D.M. Derrett, ''Ἀντιλεγόμενον, φομφαία, διαλογισμοί [Lk 2:34-35]: The Hidden Context', *Filología Neotestamentaria* 6. 12 [1993], pp. 207-18).

1. Writing (*graphō*, 3 times, 1.3, 63; 2.23), issuing a decree (*exēlthen dogma*, once, 2.1), registering (*apographomai*, 3 times, 2.1, 3, 5; in New Testament further only in Heb. 12.23).

2. *rēma*, 9 times: *ouk adynatei*, 1.37; *gignomai*, 1.38; 2.15; *kata to*, 1.38; 2.29; *dialaleō*, 1.65, in New Testament further only in Lk. 6.11; *gnōrizō*, twice, 2.15, 17; *syntēreō*, 2.19 and *diatēreō*, 2.51, in New Testament further only in Acts 15.29; *symballō*, once, 2.19, in New Testament only in Luke–Acts; *syniēmi*, 2.50.

3. *logos*, 4 times, 1.2, 4, 20, 29: *pisteuō*, 1.20, 45; *ouk episteuō*, 1.20; *diatarattō*, 1.29, *hapax* in New Testament.

4. What is heard (*akouō*, 7 times) is taken to heart (*ethento en tei kardiai*, once, 1.66); the prayer is heard (*eisakouō*, once, 1,13).

5. All are surprised (*thaumazō*, 1.63); it happens as written/said in the Law (2.23-24) and according to Caesar's decree (*egeneto*, 2.1-5).

6. A point of reflection has to be the degree of significance that could be attributed to the use of many synonyms or near synonyms, such as terms of praise and terms of 'making known'. Are they to be understood as just an expression of the wish for stylistic variation? Or do they reflect semantic differences as well? See H.J. Cadbury, 'Four Features of Lukan Style', in L.E. Keck and J.L. Martyn (eds.), *Studies in Luke–Acts* (London: SPCK, 2nd edn, 1976), pp. 87-102; G. Mussies, 'Variation in the Book of Acts', *Filología Neotestamentaria*, 4.8 (1991), pp. 165-82, and the literature cited there (pp. 171-74), and *idem*, 'Variation in the Book of Acts (Part II)', *Filología Neotestamentaria* (forthcoming).

variation in terms for denoting speech coincides with the distribution of narrative roles among women and men (discussed in the previous section). And secondly, there is interaction between the text layer (on which speech is situated) and the fabula layer. In this interaction, Mary's vision plays a decisive role. I will now explain these two conclusions.

The variation in terms denoting speech coincides with the narrative roles of women and men. Sometimes the coincidence is rather traditional, at least in our eyes, while at other times traditional role patterns are broken. One instance of traditional attribution of speech-acts is the naming of John (1.59-66). When Elisabeth gives John his name, the bystanders are not willing to accept this name. Although Elisabeth is the only parent able to speak, the (non)listeners turn to the father, Zachariah, who has previously lost his power to speak and now has to communicate by means of a writing tablet. This attitude of the bystanders is surprising. Because of their unwillingness to accept the name given by the mother, they deprive themselves of their ability to speak and turn to nodding instead.[1]

Another instance of traditional attribution of speech is found in the presentation at the temple (2.22-38). In this scene we hear the words of Simeon (2.25-35), while the words of Hannah the prophetess are not cited (2.36-38). This is surprising, as a prophetess is someone whose vocation requires speech.

Although the instances cited above would nowadays be consid-

---

1.   The unwillingness of the listeners to accept the name proposed by Elisabeth seems to arise from her deviation from the custom that an (eldest) son has to be named after relatives (G. Mussies, 'Name Giving after Relatives in the Ancient World: The Historical Background of Luke I, 59-63 in Connection with Matt. I, 16 and XIII, 55', in P.W. van der Horst and G. Mussies [eds.], *Studies on the Hellenistic Background of the New Testament* [Utrechtse Theologische Reeks, 10; Utrecht: Theological Faculty Utrecht University, 1990], pp. 65-85). The question is whether name-giving in the ancient world is something that had to be done by the father. Unfortunately Mussies does not address this question. Apparently, the instances in the Hebrew Bible where the mother names her child outnumber by far the cases in which the father gives the name (F. van Dijk-Hemmes, *Sporen van vrouwenteksten in de Hebreeuwse bijbel* [Utrechtse Theologische Reeks, 16; Utrecht: Theological Faculty, Utrecht University, 1992], pp. 159-66).

ered rather traditional distributions of speech, the question is whether the same applies to Luke 1–2. I think that it does, because the instances cited disturb the narrative movement. Why is Hannah called a prophetess, when she is not allowed to speak? The existence of listeners whose commitment to Zachariah is such that they refrain from their own ability to speak, although Zachariah has only forfeited his power to speak and not his ability to hear (1.20a), converges oddly with the fact that the one who actually speaks, Elisabeth, is not taken at her word.[1] This disturbs the narrative movement to the extent that the angel's words are partly falsified: the name-giving is performed by Elisabeth, not by Zachariah (cf. 1.13). It seems reasonable to recognize here gender-role patterns that are traditional, in so far as the characters are socially framed by the narrative.[2]

Other instances, however, show an attribution of speech-acts that breaks through traditional role patterns. The priest Zachariah loses his power to speak because he questions the fulfilment of the angel's words. From a priest in the temple one might expect more confidence where an angel's speech is concerned, especially since Zachariah is called, like Elisabeth, 'irreproachable' (1.6). Zachariah is not able to speak before the people gathered in the temple (1.22), whereas one would expect him to bestow the priestly blessing on the people.[3] In contrast to

1.   One might object that *kōphos* (1.22) means *mute* as well as *deaf*. The text makes clear that Zachariah is mute (1.20, 22, 64). There is no indication of Zachariah's being deaf.

2.   The question to what extent these traditional gender role patterns could be framed in broader historical (social, economical) structures of the Graeco-Roman world exceeds the aim of this article. I intend to return to this question elsewhere.

3.   Num. 6.24-26. See Sir. 50, 11-21 and *m. Tam*. 6.3-7.3 (par. *m. Soṭ* 7,6), discussed by Str–B, II, pp. 75-76; F. O'Fearghail, 'Sir 50,5-21: Yom Kippur or the Daily Whole-Offering?', *Bib* 59 (1978), pp. 301-16, esp. 305-306 n. 7; E. Schürer, *The History of the Jewish People in the Age of Jesus Christ (175 B.C.-A.D. 135)* (ed. G. Vermes, F. Miller and M. Black; Edinburgh: T. & T. Clark, 1979), II, pp. 292-308, esp. 306, 453 n. 137. But the link between the priestly benediction and the temple is not mentioned in the Torah: S. Safrai in *idem* and M. Stern (eds.), *The Jewish People in the First Century: Historical Geography, Political History, Social, Cultural and*

this, Elisabeth cries out her blessings of Mary with a loud cry (1.42), which is even more striking since no one else is present.

In the meantime Joseph, descending from David's house and ancestry line (1.27; 2.4; cf. 3.23-31), does not speak at all. This is surprising, as one might expect for someone of Davidic descent some characterization proving this descent. In contrast to this, Mary sings a true psalm of praise expressing her faith in the Servant of the Davidic house.

Hence, in the cases of Elisabeth/Zachariah and Mary/Joseph, the traditional attribution of speech-acts is broken. In the other instances, however, the traditional attribution of speech-acts is confirmed. This confirms the general impression that 'Luke's' treatment of women and men is not unambiguous.[1] This conclusion should be broadened by paying attention to the ambiguous words of the angel(s).

As we have seen, many actors in Luke 1–2 are paired off: Elisabeth/Zachariah and Mary/Joseph, John and Jesus, Simeon and Hannah. The shepherds in the field and the teachers in the temple could be added to these pairs. God and the angel, however, do not seem to have a narrative counterpart. This exception is obvious, one might say, for it is part of the religious ideology of this narrative that God and the angel as mouthpiece have no counterpart.[2] But a closer look at the story shows that this conclusion is premature. God and angel actually do find their counterparts in Caesar Augustus and Caesar's decree (2.1).

Both God and Caesar remain in the background. On the fabula layer they only appear in so far as they are represented verbally through other actors. In this way, angel and decree

Religious Life and Institutions, II (CRINT, I; Assen/Amsterdam: Van Gorcum, 1976), pp. 865-907, esp. 885-90.

1.   Recently argued by M.R. D'Angelo, 'Women in Luke–Acts: A Redactional View', *JBL* 109. 3 (1990), pp. 441-61.

2.   Brenner points to an example of this narrative phenomenon from the book of Esther. She argues that King Ahasuerus has no narrative counterpart, as this would run counter to kingship ideology ('Literary Strategies in the Book of Esther' [Lecture in the University of Leiden: Department of Biblical Studies, September 15, 1989]; 'Looking at Esther through the Looking Glass', in *idem* [ed.], *A Feminist Companion to Esther, Judith and Susanna* [The Feminist Companion to the Bible, 7; Sheffield: Sheffield Academic Press, 1995], pp. 71-80).

represent God and Caesar. There is a tension between God/
angel on the one hand and Caesar/decree on the other. This
tension is acted out between angel and decree, while on the
actions of God and Caesar we are only informed through the
embedded speeches. God/Caesar and angel/decree should
therefore be regarded as a double pair, like Elisabeth/Zachariah
and Mary/Joseph.[1] What is, exactly, the character of Caesar's
decree and of the angel's speech?

Caesar's decree is extremely powerful.[2] It is a written speech-
act, invested with the authority of foreign occupation. It says
that 'the whole *oikumene*', that is the whole cultivated world,
should be 'registered' (2.1). Indeed, this 'registering' happens
(2.2), as everyone is 'going to be registered' (2.3), including
Joseph who is 'to be registered' with Mary (2.5). The repetition
of 'registering' indicates the effectiveness of the decree Joseph is
subjected to.[3]

The angel does not operate by writing but through speech,
which is equally powerful. The angel's words, to which
Zachariah and Mary are apparently subjected, do materialize
because 'with God no word is impossible' (1.37). Awareness of
this act-like character of the angel's speech is voiced by the
shepherds who set out to 'see this word/thing [spoken by the

1.   According to V.K. Robbins, there is also a tension between, on the
one hand, God/angel in Lk. 1.26-56 and, on the other hand, the
emperor/King Agrippa in Acts 25.13–26.32, representing 'an inner
tension in the discourse of Luke-Acts' ('Socio-Rhetorical Criticism: Mary,
Elizabeth and the Magnificat as a Test Case', in E.S. Malbon and E.V.
McKnight [eds.], *The New Literary Criticism and the New Testament*
[JSNTSup, 109; Sheffield: Sheffield Academic Press, 1994]).

2.   In the following interpretation of the decree and the angel's words
as powerful speech-acts, and of the various ways to respond to these
speech-acts, I am indebted to a lecture by M. Bal, 'Zelf-reflekties: Het
bijbelboek Esther en de (on)macht van het geschreven woord' (Lecture at
Utrecht University: Women's Studies in Theology, March 15, 1990).

3.   See P.W. Barnett, 'ἀπογραφή and ἀπογράφεσθαι in Luke 21-5',
ExpTim 85 (1973–74), pp. 377-80. This repetition is the more remarkable
in the light of the use of lexical variation in Luke–Acts. *apographe* is, in
the Hellenistic period, the common technical term for an official
statement on behalf of the census held every 14 years; *apographesthai* is
'to deliver in an official statement (on behalf of the census)' and hence
the census itself.

angels] that has happened' (2.15).[1] But there is a difference
between angel and decree and, consequently, between Joseph,
Zachariah and Mary in their respective narrative roles. Let us
take a closer look at what actually happens.

The words of the decree directly turn into action. An unambiguous exercise of power occurs as the decree manipulates
society. The same seems to be the case with the angel's speech to
Zachariah, whose objections are immediately punished, while
Elisabeth seems only to observe what has happened to her. But
in Mary's case there is discussion. Why is Mary not punished,
like Zachariah, with cessation of speech? The objections of both
are almost identical! My answer would be that it is their
different status in society, of which gender is a constituent, that
makes the difference.

The text gives but scant information concerning Mary. The
narrator says that Mary is 'troubled' (1.29). It is the angel's
response that informs us of Mary's position. Her question is
responded to with the allocation of divine protection and
acceptance for the child that will be born. These words are in
accordance with Mary's position, as she expresses it herself in
the Magnificat. There Mary expresses in retrospect her state of
tapeinsis (humiliation), of which God/angel has promised to
make sense.[2]

By consenting to the angel's words (1.38) Mary undoubtedly
helps the movement of the narrative as programmed by God/
angel. In this sense she certainly fulfils the actantial role of
helper.[3] As a consequence, one could ascribe to her an instrumental function. But this is only valid in a narrative programme
directed at the birth of Jesus. It now appears that Mary also
manages to safeguard 'her' own narrative programme, which is
to obtain divine protection in humiliation and acceptance of a
child born outside marriage as a child of God. Here lies the
difference between the 'irreproachable', male temple priest and

1.   S.D. Moore, *Mark and Luke in Poststructuralist Perspectives: Jesus
Begins to Write* (New Haven and London: Yale University Press, 1992),
pp. 116-20.

2.   For an interpretation along partly similar lines, see Robbins,
'Socio-Rhetorical Criticism'.

3.   Greimas and Courtés, *Sémiotique I*, p. 10, s.v. 'Adjuvant'.

the unmarried, pregnant young woman.

Zachariah is an outsider whose position is not jeopardized. After all, he is not going to be pregnant: Elisabeth is. He only gets what he has asked for, as his prayer is heard (1.13). But he doubts whether the angel's words can materialize. He fails to recognize that God is about to perform a miracle birth in the best Israelite tradition. As his question is not informed by reflection on his position, he is not competent in interpreting the angel's prophetic words concerning the future. He simply has nothing to add. This is semiotically expressed by his muteness.

Unlike Zachariah, Mary shows herself competent in dealing with the angel's speech. Her speech voices a different and gendered vision of a different status; her concern is for facing the social awkwardness of her position, and for the child to be born. While claiming her own subjectivity, she recognizes the power of the angel's words to materialize. She uses her insight to make herself part of this materialization. She asks protection for herself and assistance in bearing the consequences of the announced pregnancy. This is readily granted by the angel, and the dialogue is concluded by Mary's consent. An agreement is reached. From now on, Mary is able to represent God's narrative presence through speech and action while, at the same time, she remains herself, someone able to stand up and go to Elisabeth.

It is important to notice that, from this moment on, the narrative programmes of Mary and God/angel match each other. This explains the double character of the visitation scene, the intertextuality of which is sometimes brought to bear on Mary's maternal aspect and at others linked to a combative tradition leading from Deborah and Judith to Mary. Thus, Elisabeth's expression, 'blessed are you among women' (1.42b), places Mary in the tradition of Jael and Judith (Judg. 5.24; Jdt. 13.18). In those texts Jael and Judith are blessed in the same words because they saved their people by killing the enemy.[1]

1.   F. van Dijk-Hemmes, 'Gezegende onder de vrouwen: een moeder in Israël en een maagd in de kerk', in *idem* (ed.), *'t Is kwaad gerucht, als zij niet binnen blijft: Vrouwen in oude culturen* (Utrecht: HES, 1986), pp. 123-47; J.W. van Henten, 'Judith as a Female Moses: Judith 7-13 in the light of Exodus 17; Numbers 20 and Deuteronomy 33:8-11', in van

Similar ambiguity could be attributed to the Magnificat: it is sometimes characterized as a birth song, intrinsically connected to the narrative; and at others as a warrior's victory song, like those of Miriam (Exod. 15.21), Deborah (Judg. 5.2-32) and Judith (Jdt. 16.1-17)—seemingly out of place in Luke 1 and probably inserted here from another literary tradition.[1] Interestingly Hannah's song (1 Sam. 2.1-10), like the Magnificat, also has the same ambiguous characterization.

Third Observation: Elisabeth and Mary Confirm Each Other
A third observation has to do with the speeches of Elisabeth and Mary in the visitation scene (1.39-56). On closer inspection of this scene, we find a kind of merging of both characters. Elisabeth and Mary address each other in terms reflective of their own situations.[2] Mary's greeting of Elisabeth reminds us of the salutation of Mary by the angel. Elisabeth confirms the annunciation to Mary, addressing her with a blessing. But what Elisabeth conveys to Mary concerns herself as well. Elisabeth, too, is pregnant with a divinely promised child. The expression 'blessed are you among women, and blessed the fruit of your womb' (1.42c), refers back to herself too.[3] Afterwards Elisabeth pronounces a beatitude (1.45) which is repeated by Mary (1.48b).

Elisabeth's beatitude is remarkable. She praises Mary because

Dijk-Hemmes and Brenner (eds.), *Reflections*, pp. 33-48; J.W. van Henten, 'Judith as Alternative Leader: A Rereading of Judith 7-13', in Brenner (ed.), *Esther, Judith and Susanna*, pp. 224-52.

1. P. Winter, 'Magnificat and Benedictus—Maccabean Psalms?', *BJRL* 37 (1954), pp. 328-47. Winter suggests that the author of the Magnificat might have been a woman. However, by specifying her as 'a mother of warriors', he neglects the Jael and Judith allusions, putting her rather in the male-identified position of the mother of Sisera! (p. 345). M. de Groot seems to regard the Magnificat as a woman's text ('Maria en Elisabeth', in C.J.M. Halkes and D. Buddingh [eds.], *Als vrouwen aan het Woord komen: Aspecten van de feministische theologie* [Kampen: Kok, 2nd edn, 1978], pp. 35-41; repr. in *De Vrouw bij de Bron: Fragmenten intuïtieve theologie* [Haarlem: Holland, 1980], pp. 32-40). Van Dijk-Hemmes ('Gezegende'), does not speak out on this matter.

2. De Groot, 'Maria en Elisabeth', in *De Vrouw bij de Bron*, p. 33.

3. *eulogōmenos o karpos tēs koilias sou.*

of her faith that the word spoken to her would come to fulfilment (1.45). But it should be noted that Elisabeth has already been introduced as one who keeps the commandments and is righteous before God (1.6). For this reason, one would expect the word of Deut. 28.1, 4 to be applied to Elisabeth herself: 'If you listen carefully to the voice of YHWH your God and keep all his commandments with care...blessed will be the fruit of your womb...'.[1] Nevertheless, it is Elisabeth who speaks these words to Mary (1.42c). Therefore one could say that, in the visitation scene, there occurs a merging of the narrative roles and characterization of Elisabeth and Mary. It would be possible to substitute one for the other without making much difference with regard to the narrative sequence.

This narratological 'merging' is textually ambiguous; hence it facilitates several variant readings. One example is that the words of Elisabeth to Mary (1.42b) are, according to many text witnesses, anticipated in the annunciation to Mary (1.28). Far more intriguing is the fact that some early versions of the New Testament attribute the Magnificat to Elisabeth. Thus, three Old Latin manuscripts read in 1.46a, 'and Elisabeth said'.[2] The Latin version of Origen's *Homilies on Luke* (7.3) mentions the existence of codices attributing the Magnificat to Elisabeth,[3] although the other references in both the Latin versions and Greek fragments of these *Homilies* read 'Maria' as its author.[4] For this reason, many scholars qualify the passage on Elisabeth (*Luc. Hom.* 7.3) as an interpolation by Origen's Latin translator, Jerome.[5] There are also indications of an attribution of the

1. *eulogēmena ta ekgova tēs koilias sou*, LXX Deut. 28.4.
2. *et ait Elisabeth*. The MSS concerned are Vercellensis (a) and Veronensis (b), from the fourth–fifth centuries, and Rehdigeranus (l, first hand) from the seventh–eighth centuries.
3. *Invenitur beata Maria, sicut in aliquantis exemplaribus repperimus, prophetare. Non enim ignoramus, quod secundum alios codices et haec verba Elizabeth vaticinetur.* (Origen, *Luc.Hom.* 7.3, in M. Rauer [ed.], *Origenes Werke IX: Die Homilien zu Lukas* [GCS 49.2; Berlin: Akademie Verlag, 2nd edn, 1959], p. 43.10).
4. Origen, *Luc.Hom.* 7.8 and 8 (Rauer, *Homilien*, pp. 46.22; 47.6; 47.17-18; 48.7; 49.7; 50.1-2); Origen, *Fragmenta e catenis in Lucam* 37, 39 and 40 (Rauer, *Homilien*, pp. 242.3-4; 243.3; 243.1).
5. Already Tischendorf, but notably O. Bardenhewer, 'Ist Elisabeth

Magnificat to Elisabeth in some Latin and Armenian versions of Irenaeus's *Against the Heretics*,[1] and in a Latin sermon by Nicetas of Remesiana (fifth century CE).[2]

This issue has caused much debate.[3] Some scholars defend the text-immanent view that the reading 'Elisabeth' should be preferred. On the other hand, the evidence from biblical and patristic literature for the reading 'Mary' is overwhelming. Different solutions have been proposed. One solution is the

die Sängerin des Magnificat?', *BibS(F)* 6 (1901), pp. 187-200.192; and T. Zahn, *Das Evangelium des Lukas ausgelegt* (KNT, 3; Leipzig/Erlangen, 4th edn, 1930), pp. 748-49.

1.   Irenaeus's testimony is divided. *Adv. Haer.* 3.10.2 reads in the Latin MSS *Maria clamabat...Magnificat anima mea Dominum*, whereas *Adv. Haer.* 4.7.1 reads in the major Latin MSS Claromontanus and Vossianus *Sed et Elizabeth ait: Magnificat anima mea Dominum*, the other Latin MSS reading *Maria* (A. Rousseau and L. Doutreleau [eds.], *Irénée de Lyon, Contre les Hérésies, Livre III* [SC, 210-11; Paris: Cerf, 1974], pp. 118-19; *idem, Irénée de Lyon, Contre les Hérésies, Livre IV* [SC, 100.1-2; Paris: Cerf, 1965], pp. 456-57; and the early discussion on the Armenian versions by E. Ter-Minassiantz, 'Hat Irenäus Lc. 1,46 Μαριάμ oder Ελεισάβετ gelesen?', *ZNW* 7 [1906], pp. 191-92).

2.   *De utilitate hymnorum* (previously referred to as *De psalmodiae bono*) 9, 13-16: *Ergo in euangelio inuenies primum Zacchariam, patrem magni Iohannis, post longum illud silentium in hymnis uoce prophetasse, nec Helisabeth, diu sterelis, edito de repromissione filio Deum de ipsa anima magnificare cessauit.* And *UtHym* 11, 11:...*cum Helisabeth Dominum anima nostra magnificat* (C.H. Turner, 'Niceta of Remesiana II. Introduction and Text of *De Psalmodiae Bono*', *JTS* 24 [1923], pp. 225-52).

3.   The discussion was initiated by Fr. Jacobé (pseudonym for A. Loisy), 'L'origine du Magnificat', *Revue d'histoire et de littérature religieuses* 2 (1897), pp. 424-32, and by A. von Harnack, 'Das Magnificat der Elisabet (Luk. 1, 46-55) nebst einigen Bemerkungen zu Luk. 1 und 2.', SPAW 27 (1900), pp. 538-58; repr. in A. von Harnack, *Studien zur Geschichte des Neuen Testaments und der Alten Kirche. I. Zur neutestamentlichen Textkritik* (AKG, 19: Berlin/Leipzig, 1931), pp. 62-85. Surprisingly, Harnack does not even mention Jacobé's article. Harnack continued his argument in 'Zu Lc I,34.35.', *ZNW* 2 (1901), pp. 53-57, to which A. Hilgenfeld ('Die Geburt Jesu aus der Jungfrau in dem Lucas-Evangelium', *ZWT* 44 [1901], pp. 313-17) quickly responded in highly negative terms. A review of the subsequent discussion is presented by S. Benko, 'The Magnificat: A History of the Controversy', *JBL* 86 (1967), pp. 263-75. A recent semiotic contribution is Gueuret, 'Sur Luc. 1, 46-55'.

conjecture that the Magnificat was originally only introduced by
'and [she] said', parallel to the introductory formula to the song
of Hannah (1 Sam. 2.1).[1] This conjecture cannot be defended, as
no textual witness exists without a proper name in the introductory formula of Lk. 1.46. Another solution has been sought in the
utilization of different sources, such as for example a 'Baptist
Document'.[2]

This discussion clearly would not make much sense without
the possibility of substituting 'Elisabeth' for 'Mary' or vice
versa. Could it not be that the textual variants are just an
indication or expression of the same narrative reciprocity
between the two women already encountered during the
narratological analysis? As we have seen, this narrative
reciprocity is such that both women could easily be substituted
for each other. The discussion of the supposedly original reading
reflects, I suspect, the readerly convention according to which
Mary takes precedence over Elisabeth.[3]

As the annunciation scenes have demonstrated, the
subjectivity of Zachariah and Mary is connected to their
competence in reflecting on their location within society, of
which gender is a constituent. Mary's self-reflective competence
has led her not to become a mere object of ongoing events.
Instead, she has managed to obtain divine protection and
assistance as a response to her 'humiliation'. Thus, she is able to
develop a line of action in which her own subjectivity coincides
with the representation of God's plan. In the visitation scene we

1.   But the occurrence of the name of Anna in 1 Sam. 2.1 in the
Alexandrinus and the Lucianic texts might be due to Christian interests
because of the parallel between the song of Hannah and the song of
Mary.

2.   P. Vielhauer, 'Das Benedictus des Zacharias (Luk. 1,68-79)', *ZTK* 49
(1952), pp. 255-72; Winter, 'Magnificat'; F. Neirynck, 'Visitatio B.M.V.
Bijdrage tot de Quellenkritik van Lc. 1-2', *Collationes Brugenses et
Gandavenses* 6 (1960), pp. 387-404.

3.   As is clearly demonstrated by Benko, when he says that Luke—by
prefixing chs. 1 and 2 to his Gospel—'satisfied a popular desire which
sought to give Jesus higher honours than John, and Mary than
Elizabeth...And thus it came to pass that a Jewish hymn of praise, first
adopted as a song of Elizabeth, the mother of John, was quickly
attributed to Mary, the mother of the Christ' ('Magnificat', p. 275 n. 15).

encountered a mutual confirmation of the subject positions of Mary and Elisabeth. Elisabeth's subjectivity becomes clear through her competence in addressing Mary as the recipient of divine promises made in the Law, of which Elisabeth herself partakes. Mary's subjectivity becomes clear through her act of extending the angelic promise of protection and assistance to Elisabeth and all the 'humiliated' people, of which Mary is herself a part.

I have now made three narratological observations, pleading against reading an opposition between Elisabeth and Mary and, instead, suggesting reciprocity between the two. The observations concern (1) the central role of Elisabeth and Mary as autonomous actors in the fabula and as characters in the story; (2) their competence in handling speech effectively; and (3) the resemblance between their narrative positions and, subsequently, a narrative fusion. What are the consequences of these conclusions for gendering the author, reader and text of Luke 1–2?

Part II: Toward a Gender-Response Criticism

What does 'to gender a text' mean? Athalya Brenner and Fokkelien van Dijk-Hemmes have outlined some principles pertaining to this problem.[1] They focus their analysis on how female and male gender positions are constructed *within* the text. The concept of 'voice' is important. When the overall vision presented by the text converges with a female or male character in the text, Brenner and van Dijk-Hemmes are prepared to recognize a female or a male voice within the text. These female and male voices are called F and M voices respectively.

There is an epistemological problem involved. How does one arrive at the knowledge of what is 'in' the text?[2] Brenner addresses this problem when she explains that recognition of gender positions in the text could be ascribed to the interests of a gendered reader. As she says, 'Gendering texts depends to a large extent on the reader's membership of a gender'.[3]

1. Brenner and van Dijk-Hemmes, *On Gendering Texts*.
2. Troost, 'Reading', p. 252.
3. Brenner and van Dijk-Hemmes, *On Gendering Texts*, p. 8.

Consequently, Brenner allows for the possibility of a dual-gendering of biblical texts, in the sense that 'F readers will listen to F voices emanating from those texts', while 'M readers will hear themselves echoed in them. This is to say that, in many cases, two parallel readings are possible.'[1]

Brenner's thesis that 'the reader's membership of a gender' is a constituent of the gendering of a text should be specified. In the first place, there is the reader's specific location in time and space (to borrow a central notion in the work of Adrienne Rich which has been used in the more recent work of Nancy K. Miller).[2] Female or male readers are socially and ideologically framed in various locations. These framings are constituents of the way a reader is gendered, but also of the way a reader genders. By 'location' a specific point on the time–space axis is meant on which a certain reader operates, a point where gender emerges and is responded to. In the second place, the reader's more or less conscious beliefs concerning authorship are inherent to a gendered reader's specific location. Of special significance are preconceived ideas about how a female or male author might write.

Although Brenner rightly emphasizes the difference that women and men as gendered readers embody in their relation to the text, the differences that separate women among themselves and men among themselves as interpreters of biblical texts should be stressed. The significance of a dual-gendering of biblical texts related to a dual-gendered readership should by no means be underestimated, as it is part of the history of the biblical texts as well as of their interpretation. But the existence of variables in various socio-cultural framings should also be

1.   Brenner and van Dijk-Hemmes, *On Gendering Texts*, p. 9.

2.   A. Rich, 'Notes toward a Politics of Location (1984)', in *Blood, Bread, and Poetry: Selected Prose 1979-1985* (New York: Norton, 1986; London: Virago, 1987), pp. 210-31. Part II of my essay was inspired by N.K. Miller, *Getting Personal: Feminist Occasions and Other Autobiographical Acts* (New York and London: Routledge, 1991), especially the chapters on 'Dreaming, Dancing, and the Changing Locations of Feminist Criticism, 1988' (pp. 72-100) and 'Philoctetes' Sister: Feminist Criticism and the New Misogyny' (pp. 101-20), both originally read as papers to the Women's Studies Department of Utrecht University, in 1988 and 1990.

recognized. In the following this insight will be examined in relation to some multiple-gendered readings of Elisabeth and Mary in Luke 1–2. For the sake of clarity these readings are arranged in two series, one reader-oriented (to examine the role of location), and one author-oriented (to examine the role of assumptions concerning authorship). Of course, it will appear that these two, location and assumptions, cannot be kept separate.

Reader-Oriented Interpretations

The reader's location accounts for the specific interpretive traditions she or he brings to bear on a text, as well as for the readerly commitments with which the text is approached. But social factors and ideological position can cause substantial differences *between* members of the same gender. In my opinion, this explains why F readers do not always read F texts, nor do M readers inevitably read M texts. Let me explain this point by comparing three divergent interpretations of the Lukan birth narratives.

The first interpretation is the result of reading the scene of the annunciation to Mary as a suspicious, resisting reader. I propose to do so by framing the passage in Luke by the broader literary type-scene of the biblical annunciations, as described by Esther Fuchs.[1] Fuchs, who is a highly resistant reader of Hebrew biblical narrative, argues that the annunciation stories continue to present, in an ever-increasing degree, the mother as the true heroine of the narrative whereas the father's narrative role decreases in importance until his near-absence in 1 Samuel 1 and 2 Kings 4. Fuchs warns us that this growing importance of motherhood is ideologically suspect, for the father's role is taken over by the male-constructed God. Fuchs concludes that the mother's growing narrative importance represents gender

---

1. Fuchs, 'Literary Characterization', who elaborates on R. Alter, 'How Convention Helps us Read: The Case of the Bible's Annunciation-Type Scene', *Prooftexts* 3 (1983), pp. 115-30. See also Brown, *Birth*, p. 156; J. Schaberg, *The Illegitimacy of Jesus: A Feminist Theological Interpretation of the Infancy Narratives* (San Francisco: Harper & Row, 1987), pp. 104-10, and her article in this volume.

politics and serves patriarchal interests by focusing on the control of human reproduction.

Fuchs confines her study to the annunciation stories of the Hebrew Bible. Lk. 1.26-56 is therefore not included in her typology, although the narrative seems to fit the picture described by her perfectly well. Interpreting the Lukan narrative as another instance of the annunciation type-scene, the following aspects come to the fore. From a narrative point of view, the mother Mary is the main acting subject, while the man is of no consequence as an actor. The dispatching subject is God who speaks/acts through the intermediary angel. God is also the beneficiary, at least on the primary (narrator's) level of narration.[1] The basic question is whether this God is gendered as a male or, at least, could be said to take side with fatherhood. A crucial passage in this respect is the angel's speech to Mary in Lk. 1.35b, '[the] holy ghost will come over you and [the] power of the most high will overshadow you'. These words are usually regarded as a declaration of 'divine infusion' and, as a consequence, are gendered as male. Mary's response to the angel (1.38a) is accordingly appreciated as an act of submission to this divine presence. Whether this is an appropriate judgment will be discussed in the next section. At the present stage of the discussion my conclusion is that, reading as a suspicious and resisting reader together with Fuchs, androcentric elements are brought to the fore which could be said to be 'in' the text. The question is whether such an interpretation is, in this case, compelling and necessary.

How do you know that you are reading an androcentric or gynocentric text? Do you not rather read conventional interpretation that constructs the text as such? One should, for instance, wonder whether the verbs 'overcome' and 'overshadow' (*eperchomai* and *episkiazō*, 1.35) should be invested with such strong sexual connotations, and whether Mary's response should not be assigned a different narrative role. In order to find an answer to these and other questions, let me discuss a second interpretation.

The second interpretation is gleaned from a feminist utopian

---

1. On levels of narration, see Bal, *Narratology*, pp. 134-49.

novel by Charlotte Perkins Gilman titled *Herland*.[1] In this novel, three North American men explorers by chance arrive at an unknown hidden country. This country appears to be Herland, inhabited by a society consisting entirely of women. One of the most remarkable phenomena, at least in the men's eyes, is that these women give birth solely to girls, and they do so without the interference of men. This is a fact the male visitors find extremely hard to accept. Somewhere in this country, they insist, there must be men. When the women ask the men to tell them about the country they come from, the men set off to tell some of the master narratives of their own culture. When mentioning the virgin birth, the three men have to admit that such a thing does not exactly mean a miracle to these women. In fact, as they perceive, 'the story of the Virgin birth *naturally* did not astonish her...'[2]

Herland is quite a humorous story. Gilman mocks conventional ideas of what is feminine and what is masculine, what is manly and what is womanly, what is culturally learned and what is biologically determined male or female behaviour.[3] As the *Herland* women demonstrate, women do have the power to alter society and to control nature in their own interest. By relating the virgin birth to Herland, Gilman seems to invite the reader to ponder the possibility that no male is involved in the biblical birth narratives, be it a human or divine character. The objections raised by the three male explorers resemble traditional objections against the virgin birth. They all hold the 'somewhere-there-must-be-a-man' position. Returning to the Lukan narrative, we find—on the basis of our narratological analysis—that a divine conception is not completely necessary. Besides, as we have seen, the women in Luke 1–2 are in control of the narrative programme, while male actors and God—on an embedded level—play a minor role.

1. Written in 1915 and serialized in Gilman's monthly magazine, *The Forerunner*, volume 6 (1915). First published separately as *Herland* (introduction by A.J. Lane; New York: Pantheon, 1979). See also *The Yellow Wallpaper and Other Writings* (ed. and introduction by L.S. Schwartz; New York: Bantam, 1989).
2. Gilman, *Herland* (1979 edn), p. 110; emphasis added.
3. Gilman, *Herland* (1979 edn), p. xiii.

Gilman's concern is the critique of society within the first feminist wave, a critique of the way society deals with women and children. Gilman's utopia is not merely a piece of literary art, but also and primarily a political document. Its aim is to introduce profound changes into society precisely through its literary merits and references to one of the basic books that same society accepts as canonical. Ruth Levitas, who studied the use of the 'utopia' concept in feminist works, called Gilman's novel 'an exploration of the kind of society that might emerge if the needs of children (and their mothers) were genuinely prioritised'.[1] Gilman's theological visions bear on the way she chooses to symbolize this utopian reality.[2] In doing so, she demonstrates how difficult it is for men to give up thoughts of dominance. The 'somewhere-there-must-be-a-man' position is emblematic of this difficulty.

This position is clearly present in the interpretation of the verbs *eperchomai* and *episkiazō* (1.35). Moving from narratological to lexical analysis, we find that these verbs evoke Septuagintal language and that, in the LXX, they are nowhere used as euphemisms for sexual intercourse.[3] Rather, as Jane Schaberg and others have not failed to notice, they indicate empowerment and protection.[4] This reminds us that the Herland women do not understand why God is personalized at all—rather they believe

1. R. Levitas, *The Concept of Utopia* (New York: Philip Allan, 1990), p. 109.

2. Compare C.P. Gilman, *His Religion and Hers* (New York: Century, 1923) who pleads for a 'birth-based religion' concerned with collectively preserving future human life.

3. *Contra* P.W. van der Horst, whose argument that *episkiazō* in Lk. 1.35 includes sexual activity is not convincing, as (1) it is based on only one very remote parallel, (2) it works by mere suggestion, (3) it ignores the LXX references in Lk. 1.35 ('Peter's Shadow: The Religio-Historical Background of Acts V.15', *NTS* 23 [1976–77], pp. 204-12, esp. pp. 211-12; repr. in van der Horst and Mussies [eds.], *Studies*, pp. 153-63; repeated in 'Der Schatten im hellenistischen Volksglauben', in M.J. Vermaseren [ed.], *Studies in Hellenistic Religions* [EPRO, 78; Leiden: Brill, 1979], pp. 27-36, esp. p. 30 n. 10).

4. Schaberg, *Illegitimacy*, pp. 112-17 and the literature cited there.

in a Pervading Power, an Indwelling Spirit, a Maternal Pantheism.[1]

The studies on Luke by Schaberg provide the third interpretation I would like to discuss with regard to the reader's location. In her studies on the New Testament infancy narratives she addresses the question whether there is a divinely inspired 'virgin birth' in Luke 1.[2] Like Joseph Fitzmyer[3] she does not think so, although Fitzmyer afterwards changed his mind on this point.[4] Schaberg gives a multilayered interpretation of the infancy narratives. A summary might do injustice to the care and critical sense with which she presents her arguments. I will confine myself to some of them.

Schaberg regards Lk. 1.20-56 as representing an old tradition bearing on an illegitimate conception of Jesus during the period of Mary's betrothal to Joseph.[5] One of the elements indicating this tradition is the word *tapeinōsis* in the Magnificat (1.48a). Usually, this term is taken to mean 'humiliation'. In this sense the word is found in the LXX in birth narratives, such as the angel's speech to Hagar in the desert (Gen. 16.11), Leah naming her son Reuben (Gen. 29.32) and Hannah's vow (1 Sam. 1.11). Hannah's words are almost literally parallel to Mary's words. Together with the Leah passage, they seem to refer to humiliation arising from barrenness (the Hagar passage being a bad parallel because, as Schaberg says, this is 'a case not of barrenness but of oppression'[6]). The word occurs in many other instances with no birth connection, where it describes difficult

---

1.   Gilman, *Herland* (1979 edn), p. xv.

2.   Schaberg, *Illegitimacy*, pp. 80-84; *idem*, 'Luke', in C.A. Newsom and S.H. Ringe (eds.), *The Women's Bible Commentary* (London: SPCK; Louisville, KY: Westminster/John Knox, 1992), pp. 275-92.

3.   J.A. Fitzmyer, 'The Virginal Conception of Jesus in the New Testament', *TS* 34 (1973), pp. 541-75; repr. in *To Advance the Gospel: New Testament Studies* (New York: Crossroad, 1981), pp. 41-78.

4.   J.A. Fitzmyer, 'Postscript (1980)', in *To Advance the Gospel*, pp. 61-62; *idem, Luke*, p. 338; see Brown, *Birth*, pp. 299-301.

5.   Schaberg, *Illegitimacy*, pp. 78-144; 'Luke', pp. 282-85.

6.   Schaberg, *Illegitimacy*, p. 99.

circumstances or a state of misery.[1] This would concur with the use of *tapeinos* in Lk. 1.52b.[2]

The question raised by Schaberg is 'in what way the reader of Luke's narrative could think of Mary as experiencing humiliation'.[3] The references to the birth narratives do not apply, because in Mary's case being barren is not the issue. Rather, it is uncontrolled loss of virginity that constitutes the problem here (uncontrolled, that is, by patriarchal structures). For this reason, Schaberg investigates the meanings of the verb *tapeinoō* in the LXX. There the word is often used for the sexual humiliation of a woman through seduction or rape: the rape of Dinah (Gen. 34.2), of the so-called concubine of the Levite (Judg. 19.24; 20.5), of David's daughter Tamar (2 Sam. 13.12, 14, 22, 32), the women of Zion (Lam. 5.11), the legislation in Deut. 21.14, and the prophecy in Ezek. 22.10-11.[4]

The reference to sexual humiliation would especially make sense, according to Schaberg, in the light of the law in Deut. 22.23-27, which speaks of the seducer as having violated or humiliated (*ʿinnâ*; LXX *etapeinōsen*) the betrothed virgin. This law is closely reflected in Luke 1 (Lk. 1.27, 34, 48a). Schaberg believes Lk. 1.48a to contain a double allusion, to Hannah and to the law of Deuteronomy. 'The virgin betrothed to a man (1.27) was sexually humiliated. But her humiliation, like the barrenness of Hannah (and Elizabeth) was "looked upon" and reversed by God (1.52b)'.[5]

The Magnificat not only refers simply to the humble position of the *ʿănāwîm*, but also to the state of humiliation arising from being a single female parent in Graeco-Roman Judaea. These experiences are framed by the hopes of the *ʿănāwîm*, together with the promise of divine protection and empowerment. This is the new location of the betrothed virgin's experiences. Once again, Mary emerges as competent in wording. As Schaberg

---

1.   For example Gen. 31.42; Deut. 26.7; LXX 1 Sam. 9.16; 2 Sam. 16.12; 2 Kgs 14.26; 2 Esd. 19.9.

2.   The combination with *hupsoun* (Lk. 1.52) also in LXX Ezek. 21.31; Est. 1.1 (ed. Rahlfs) and Job 5.11.

3.   Schaberg, *Illegitimacy*, p. 99.

4.   See Schaberg, *Illegitimacy*, p. 101. Less obvious is Isa. 51.21, 23.

5.   Schaberg, *Illegitimacy*, p. 100.

makes clear, we thus find in a generally androcentric text some specific life experience of women, an experience that is unfortunately still recognizable today. The way the text calls the child 'a child of God' has, according to Schaberg, nothing to do with a divine conception taken literally, but indicates acceptance as 'a child of God' for those who endure much hardship in society, notably women and children.

As Schaberg herself lives in one of the larger cities of the USA, a city with enormous social problems, her concern is with the many, often very young, women in the larger cities of the world who have so-called illegitimate children, and with the struggle for life these women and their children have to face. Schaberg shows who should bear responsibility for so-called illegitimacy, a responsibility that cannot be passed onto God or Spirit, male or female. The question is not about the genealogy of the child, but how Mary could live with it. One should give credit to Schaberg for making visible again probable experiences of women framed by androcentric society of Graeco-Roman Judaea, and for making sense of them from a contemporary perspective.

I have now compared three different interpretations in order to clarify the role of the reader's location in gendering a text. This comparison illustrates that each reader is framed by certain locations, partly related to her or his gender, which determines his or her commitments and provides her or him with an interpretive tradition bearing on a certain text. Fuchs, a resisting reader, highlights the male interests in the literary tradition of the barren women. Gilman's utopia creates a women's society in which children are engendered without male interference at all. Schaberg reads a 'double tradition' in which male responsibility for a woman's humiliation is brought to light, together with a divinely empowered woman's utopian vision in which she gives voice to those without power. Differences in time and space, social factors and ideological stances generate different ways of gendering a text, allowing for a greater diversity than merely a 'dual-gendering of biblical texts' in 'two parallel readings'.

Author-Oriented Interpretations
The second constituent in gendering a text I would like to discuss is a reader's assumed 'knowledge' of the gender of a text's author. We have ample evidence that such knowledge matters. This knowledge is, of course, related to the reader's location. Particularly important are the reader's preconceived ideas of how a female or male author would write. In parallel with the term 'reader-response criticism',[1] I propose to use the term 'gender-response criticism'. By 'gender-response criticism' I mean an approach that acknowledges that a reader's assumed knowledge of the author's gender influences the analysis and interpretation of gender positions 'in' the text, while the reader's gender is of decisive influence to the way these gender assumptions are valued.

Let me explain this point by giving two examples, derived from the discussion at the turn of the century about the sources and original language of Luke 1–2. The first example is a theory put forward by Alfred Resch.[2] The second is provided by the Lukan studies of Adolf Harnack.[3]

Resch argued that the source for Matthew 1–2 and Luke 1–2 was a written Hebrew infancy gospel of Jesus, the *tôlᵉdôt yēšûʿa*.[4] In order to defend his case, Resch analyzed the Hebrew and LXX biblical references in Luke 1–2.[5] The most prominent intertext, according to him, is the book of Ruth. Resch was convinced that the conjectured infancy gospel must have been of approximately

---

1.   See for example J.P. Tompkins (ed.), *Reader-Response Criticism: From Formalism to Post-Structuralism* (Baltimore and London: The Johns Hopkins University Press, 1984).

2.   A. Resch, *Aussercanonische Paralleltexte zu den Evangelien. II.3. Paralleltexte zu Lucas* (TU, 10.3; Leipzig: Hinrichs, 1895); *idem*, *Ausserkanonische Paralleltexte zu den Evangelien. III.5. Das Kindheitsevangelium nach Lucas und Matthaeus unter Herbeibeziehung der aussercanonischen Paralleltexte quellenkritisch untersucht* (TU, 10.5; Leipzig: Hinrichs, 1897).

3.   Harnack, 'Magnificat'; *idem*, *Lukas der Arzt: Der Verfasser des dritten Evangeliums und der Apostelgeschichte* (Beiträge zur Einleitung in das Neue Testament, I; Leipzig: Hinrichs, 1906).

4.   Resch, *Paralleltexte zu Lucas*, pp. 812-23, 834; *Das Kindheitsevangelium*, pp. 10-29, 238-41, 319-34.

5.   Resch, *Paralleltexte zu Lucas*, p. 836.

the size of Ruth, and he recognized many parallels between the two texts. In both texts, he says, we read a family history, concerning the house of David, from which the messiah went forth. In both cases we read prophetic speeches pertaining to the Gentiles. And in both cases a genealogy is presented.[1] Finally, Resch sees lexical congeniality with the book of Ruth through numerous parallels, especially in the annunciation and visitation scenes.[2] On the basis of these references, Resch concluded that the Hebrew infancy gospel, and Lk. 1.5–2.52 with it, was arranged after the book of Ruth.[3]

Resch is very careful in conjecturing an author for this infancy gospel but, towards the end of his book, he points to Mary as the one whose notes or communications form a basis for this work. His main argument lies in the convergence of a moderate narrative characterization of Mary within the text, and the sober narrative style of Luke 1–2 as a whole.[4] Resch's argument is clearly based on his idea of how a woman like Mary might narrate. For why does he insist on the moderate aspects of Mary? And why does he play down Mary's active narrative participation? Furthermore, Resch's notions of authorship seem to influence his treatment of the Ruth parallel. For why does he relegate Ruth to the domain of family narratives?

The second example is derived from the Lukan studies by Harnack. Like William Hobart before him, Harnack was convinced that Luke was a well-educated Greek physician, the author of the third Gospel, including the first two chapters thereof, and Acts.[5] In fact, Harnack repeated many of Hobart's arguments in his study on Luke the physician.[6] Harnack tried to prove this thesis by analyzing the biblical references in some of the poetic sections in Luke 1–2: the Magnificat (1.39-56), Mary's dialogue with the angel (1.34-35), the Benedictus (1.68-79) and

1. Resch, *Das Kindheitsevangelium*, pp. 192-93.
2. Resch, *Das Kindheitsevangelium*, pp. 29-69.
3. Resch, *Das Kindheitsevangelium*, pp. 28-29, 319-20.
4. Resch, *Das Kindheitsevangelium*, pp. 323-24.
5. W.K. Hobart, *The Medical Language of St. Luke* (repr.; Michigan: Baker, 1954 [1882]).
6. Harnack, *Lukas der Arzt*.

the Gloria (2.14).[1] I will focus on Harnack's discussion of the Magnificat and the Benedictus, as his treatment of the other two sections is of a more technical character.

On a closer look, it appears that Harnack recognizes in these two texts mainly LXX references to the psalms and the prophets. Nevertheless, he regards the passages concerning Hannah in 1 Samuel, especially 1.11 and 2.1, 7, 10 as the most important references in the Magnificat. Harnack concludes that the Benedictus shows a priestly character, in accordance with the way Zachariah is characterized, while the Magnificat is dependant on Hannah's song, in accordance with the way Elisabeth is characterized.[2] For, it should be remembered, Harnack sided with those who thought that the Magnificat was originally ascribed to Elisabeth.

It would seem that Harnack, in his treatment of the Magnificat and the Benedictus, found himself in trouble somehow. On the one hand, he was convinced that the Magnificat and the Benedictus were both originally written in Greek by Luke. On the other hand, he wanted to account for the special character of Luke's *Sondergut*, in which Harnack included the gender-specific character of the Magnificat. He tried to solve this problem by assuming an oral source which he located in the four prophesying daughters of the evangelist Philip, mentioned in Acts 21.9. He based his claim on Papias's report that these women narrated miraculous stories.[3]

In Harnack's studies we again have an example of how preconceived ideas on how a woman or man might write influence the way in which the text is gendered. Harnack defends an active, prophetically styled, male-authored Greek original. The attention to women characters he attributed to women's sources, thus allowing for women's voices within the text. But why does Harnack not say that the Magnificat is a

1. Harnack, 'Magnificat'; 'Zu Lc I,34.35'; *Lukas der Arzt*, 'Über den Spruch "Ehre sei Gott in der Höhe", und das Wort "Eudokia"', *SPA* (1915), pp. 854-75, repr. in *idem, Studien*, pp. 153-79.
2. Harnack, 'Magnificat', in *Studien*, p. 84.
3. Harnack, *Lukas der Arzt*, pp. 69, 72; Papias *apud* Eusebius, *Eccl. Hist.* 3.39.9 (G. Bardy [ed.], *Eusèbe de Césarée: Histoire Ecclésiastique, I-IV* [SC, 31; Paris: Cerf, 1952]).

priestly and prophetic text? After all, the intertexts in the Magnificat and Benedictus are taken from the same sources. And why does he not say that the Benedictus reflects *fatherly* concerns? After all, Zachariah is the only one who addresses his child, 'And you, then, little child...' (1.76)!

It is obvious that the way Resch and Harnack conceived of the possible author's gender was conditioned by their own *location* as male liberal Protestant scholars in the history of religions school, in turn-of-the-century Germany. Although they showed interest in the question of gender, like many others in this school, their research was not motivated by feminist concerns. Their own agenda enabled them to explain the existence 'in' the text of rather 'unusual' elements, namely the Ruth parallel and the ascription of the Magnificat to Elisabeth. At the same time, however, the convictions they held about how a woman or man might write led them to interpret their findings in a rather androcentric fashion, and to gender the text accordingly. Would it be possible to interpret their findings in a less androcentric way? This question will be dealt with in the third and final part of this article.

Part III: The Ruth Parallel and Locating Luke's Text

The Ruth parallel and the attribution of the Magnificat to Elisabeth might be of help to trace evidence in Luke 1–2 of women's or men's responses to social, economical and cultural framings of the Graeco-Roman world toward the end of the first century CE. For, recently, good arguments have been put forward by feminist scholars to recognize in the book of Ruth voices from women's cultural traditions, especially through the cooperation of Naomi and Ruth expressed therein.[1]

1.   S.D. Goitein, 'Women as Creators of Biblical Genres', *Prooftexts* 8 (1988), pp. 1-33 (trans. from: 'nāšim kᵉyōṣᵉrōt sûgēy sifrût bammiqrāʾ', in *Iyyunim Bammiqra* [Tel Aviv: Yavne, 1957], pp. 248-317); Brenner, 'Female Social Behaviour', p. 273, repr. in Brenner (ed.), *Genesis*, p. 221; van Dijk-Hemmes, *Sporen*, pp. 169-71; C. Meyers, 'Returning Home: Ruth 1.8 and the Gendering of the Book of Ruth', in A. Brenner (ed.), *A Feminist Companion to Ruth* (The Feminist Companion to the Bible, 3; Sheffield: Sheffield Academic Press, 1993), pp. 85-114, and many other contributions in Brenner (ed.), *Ruth*.

Cooperation between women has also been identified by feminist scholars as a means to face male-oriented social structures in the period covered by Luke–Acts.[1] As the book of Ruth is the only larger narrative in the Hebrew canon in which a merging between the two female protagonists is also the centre around and through which the narrative evolves,[2] it might be fruitful to work out the comparison between Ruth and Luke 1–2.

The basic assumption is that Luke's text, like the book of Ruth, represents some elements of women's responses to social locations, and that these responses are voiced by 'a third text', namely feminist criticism.[3] It is to be assumed that voices of survival and utopian vision are intertwined in Luke 1–2. For that reason, the following investigation will be guided by perspectives expressing both Gilman's *Herland* and Schaberg's interpretation.

Harnack's substitution of Elisabeth for Mary reminds us that it is easy to do this, without turning Luke 1–2 upside down. From this point of view, the attention Resch gives to the book of Ruth gains a new light. On closer examination there are—apart from numerous minor lexical parallels with the book of Ruth, listed by Resch—quite a few possible narrative parallels between the two pairs of women in Ruth and Luke 1.[4]

1.   See especially M.R. D'Angelo, 'Women Partners in the New Testament', *JFSR* 6.1 (1990), pp. 65-86; and *idem*, 'Women in Luke-Acts'.

2.   See E. van Wolde, *Aan de hand van Ruth* (Inaugural Lecture, Tilburg; Kampen: Kok, 1993); *idem*, *Ruth en Noömi, twee vreemdgangers* (Baarn: Ten Have, 1993).

3.   The methodology applied here, I have described as a 'reading as if', based on a concept of 'diffuse intertextuality' (Troost, 'Reading', pp. 257-58).

4.   The following reading of the book of Ruth has benefited mainly from A. Brenner, 'Naomi and Ruth', *VT* 33.4 (1983), pp. 385-97, repr. in Brenner (ed.), *Ruth*, pp. 70-84; *idem*, 'Naomi and Ruth: Further Reflections', in Brenner (ed.), *Ruth*, pp. 140-44; P. Trible, *God and the Rhetoric of Sexuality* (Philadelphia: Fortress Press, 5th edn, 1987), pp. 166-99; J.M. Sasson, *Ruth: A New Translation with a Philological Commentary and a Formalist-Folklorist Interpretation* (Baltimore: The Johns Hopkins University Press, 1979; The Biblical Seminar, 8; Sheffield: JSOT Press, 2nd edn, 1989). Preliminary remarks on this narrative parallel in Brenner, 'Female Social Behaviour', pp. 269-71; repr. in Brenner (ed.), *Genesis*, pp. 217-19.

Naomi and Elisabeth are aged (Ruth 1.12a; Lk. 1.7, 18), Ruth and Mary are youthful. Like Naomi and Ruth, Elisabeth and Mary are kinswomen (Lk. 1.36), although the nature of this kinship is not clear. Naomi and Elisabeth have no children (left), nor prospects of children, which is referred to as 'bitterness' (Ruth 1.20-21) and 'shame' (Lk. 1.25). This situation entails social isolation: Naomi is not answered by the women of the town (Ruth 1.20-21); Elisabeth hides herself for five months (Lk. 1.24). Naomi's isolation is emphasized and then ameliorated by Ruth, who stays with her (Ruth 2.23) and mediates between Naomi and the outside world. Ruth's faithfulness to her mother-in-law (praised by Boaz in Ruth 2.11-12), is called by Boaz her first *ḥesed* (mutual solidarity, loyalty; LXX: *eleos*), over against her second *ḥesed*, which she bestowed on Boaz (Ruth 3.10).[1] Elisabeth's isolation is emphasized then ameliorated by Mary, who visits her in the mountainside and stays with her for three months (Lk. 1.39-40). During this visit, Mary voices, toward Elisabeth, God's *eleos* ('mercy', 'compassion') concerning those 'who fear him' (Lk. 1.50, 54). Obviously, this *eleos* concerns Mary but also includes Elisabeth (because of Lk. 1.6).

Ruth has to face the humiliation of being a widow and a stranger. Mary has to face the *tapeinōsis* of bearing a child while she knows no man (Lk. 1.34). Ruth and Mary share the benefit of being protected. Ruth seeks protection from the God of Naomi (Ruth 2.12) and from Boaz (Ruth 3.9). Mary receives protection and empowerment from God (Lk. 1.35).[2] In return, both Ruth and Mary consent to do what they are requested to do (Ruth 3.5; Lk. 1.38). Ruth calls herself Boaz's servant (Ruth 2.13; 3.9), Mary calls herself God's servant (Lk. 1.38). Ruth's attitude and action

1. The first *ḥesed* is determined in Ruth 1.14 as 'adherence' (*dbq*), the same word which is used in Gen. 2.24 for a heterosexual relation of a man to his wife; see Ruth 1.16-17. See M. Bal, 'Heroism and Proper Names, Or the Fruits of Analogy', in *Lethal Love: Feminist Literary Readings of Biblical Love Stories* (Bloomington: Indiana University Press, 1987), ch. 3, pp. 68-88, repr. with an afterword in Brenner (ed.), *Ruth*, pp. 42-69.

2. Argued by D. Daube, *The New Testament and Rabbinic Judaism* (School of Oriental and African Studies, University of London, Jordan Lectures in Comparative Religion, 2; London: Athlone, 1956), pp. 27-63. See Schaberg, *Illegitimacy*, pp. 117, 128.

toward Boaz is called a *ḥesed*, because through her deeds Boaz, apparently an elderly man with no children, regains a significant position within society.[1] Mary's attitude toward God/ angel enables her to embody God's *eleos* and to include Elisabeth and the humiliated people in it. Both Ruth and Mary are called 'blessed' for what they have done (Ruth 3.10; Lk. 1.42).

After the birth of Obed, the women of the town speak to Naomi and name Obed (Ruth 4.14-15); after the birth of John the neighbours speak to Elisabeth, establishing John's name (Lk. 1.58-66). Social isolation has come to an end. Naomi and Ruth are described as one widow during the session at the gates (Ruth 4.1-12). Finally, Naomi and Ruth emerge as a single mother (Ruth 4.17), unlike Elisabeth and Mary. Regarding Jesus, the narrative follows a distinctive track.

Naomi and Ruth, Elisabeth and Mary work together in facing their awkward position in society. Both in the book of Ruth and in Luke we find cooperation between the two women, to the extent that their narrative roles merge. Of course, there are also differences. The main difference is that the cooperation between Naomi and Ruth results in the end in a child that belongs to both of them, whereas in Luke we find a differentiation between the two children which, in traditional interpretations, has led to differentiating between the two women as well. Nevertheless, it does not seem unreasonable to say that 'Luke', at least in so far as the visitation scene is concerned, refers to the book of Ruth, particularly to the merging and cooperation of the two women therein.

This theme of cooperation seems to be connected with the use of the concept of *ḥesed/eleos*. The *ḥesed*, a term usually denoting the mutual relationship between God and people, is the expression of the nature of the mutual relationship between Ruth and Naomi, and between Ruth and Boaz. Its function in the Ruth scroll is the 'building up of the house of Israel' (Ruth 4.11) through Ruth's representation of God's *ḥesed*. The same could be said with regard to the *eleos* between God and Mary/ Elisabeth, and between Mary/Elisabeth and the humiliated. Elisabeth and Mary do not as much as allow God to work in them, but rather do they envision the fulfilment of the

---

1. Bal, 'Heroism', pp. 68-88.

humiliated people's expectations through their representation of God's *eleos* to each other. They are able to do so because their own position is involved.

Could this be regarded as evidence for the presence of women's responses to the complex social, economical and cultural locations represented by Luke 1–2?[1] As I have argued, the answer to this question depends on readerly ideas regarding women's or men's responses to various locations, and the locations deemed significant by the reader to frame their responses. If cooperation between women is supposed to be part of women's cultural traditions, as they are envisioned in *Herland*, the answer will undoubtedly be positive. I am inclined to defend this notion. Cooperation between women most probably reflects bare necessity in the Graeco-Roman world (as well as it did in the time and place of Ruth and Naomi).

In the Graeco-Roman world, as well as in the period of the second temple in Judaea, conservative tendencies alternated with tendencies aimed at social change, especially where women's roles were concerned.[2] There is ample evidence from New Testament times that women cooperated in facing the pressures of social and cultural locations, and managed to spread social and religious visions as well.[3] The same would apply to Luke 1–2. Here we find a fluctuation between traditional gender role patterns and surprising breakthroughs connected to women's recognition of God's presence in their

1. R.S. Kraemer, 'Women's Authorship of Jewish and Christian Literature in the Greco-Roman Period', in A.-J. Levine (ed.), *'Women Like This': New Perspectives on Jewish Women in the Greco-Roman World* (SBL Early Judaism and its Literature, 1; Atlanta, GA: Scholars Press, 1991), pp. 221-242. Brenner suggests that women's voices can be heard in Lk. 1 ('Female Social Behaviour', p. 273; repr. in Brenner [ed.], *Genesis*, p. 221). The following paragraphs present only a very brief outline of an answer to this question. I intend to discuss the matter more fully in my dissertation.

2. K.E. Corley, *Private Women, Public Meals: Social Conflict in the Synoptic Tradition* (Peabody, MA: Hendrickson, 1993); C. Safrai, 'Women in the Temple: The Status and Role of Women in the Second Temple of Jerusalem' (PhD dissertation, Catholic Theological University of Amsterdam, 1991).

3. D'Angelo, 'Women Partners', pp. 65-86.

locations. This recognition apparently carries the promise of social change. Thus, following Schaberg's perspective, something of the historical locations would become visible precisely by reading parts of Luke 1–2 as elements of a *Herland* utopia.

FROM NARRATIVE TO HISTORY:
THE RESURRECTION OF MARY AND MARTHA*

Adele Reinhartz

The women disciples of Jesus make only rare and brief appearances in the canonical Gospels. Of these shadowy figures, only two—the sisters Mary and Martha—emerge with any clarity. The three passages in which they appear (Lk. 10.38-42; Jn 11.1-44; 12.1-7) depict Martha in the acts of serving (Lk. 10.40; Jn 11.1-44), complaining (Lk. 10.41) and confessing (Jn 11.27), and Mary as engaged in studying (Lk. 10.39), mourning (Jn 11.20, 31), and anointing (Jn 12.3). We surmise that they, along with their brother Lazarus, constituted an independent Jewish household from which parents and spouses were absent. But the most important detail about them, from the evangelists' perspective, was their contact with Jesus, whom they apparently believed to be the messiah (Jn 11.27). This composite picture leaves many questions unanswered: What was the nature of their relationship to each other and to the man who was the focus of their activities? What were their places in, and feelings about, the various social and religious groups and institutions of their community? Were they historical figures, or role models for the early Christian churches? To answer these questions requires nothing less than an act of resurrection which would release Mary and Martha from the narratives and commentaries in which they are entombed, and make them breathe, act, and most important, speak to us.[1]

* Originally published in A.-J. Levine (ed.), 'Women Like This': New Perspectives on Jewish Women in the Greco-Roman World (SBL Early Judaism and its Literature, 1; Atlanta: Scholars Press, 1991). Reprinted by permission.
    1. For a detailed discussion of the methodology in this task, see

Such resurrections, far from being restricted to the prophets of old, are attempted regularly by scholars who draw on the narrative materials in the New Testament in order to compose the history of the early church. While we usually assume that the people named in the Pauline epistles were historical figures,[1] the same cannot be said for many of the others mentioned in early Christian literature. It is possible that all or some of the latter correspond to the 'real' women and men of the early movement, but the fact remains that they are known to us only through texts which, while claiming to tell a 'true' story, nevertheless exhibit many of the characteristics of fictional narrative.[2] The anonymous writers of these texts,[3] although often basing their accounts on early tradition, exercised great liberty in their choice of stories and had no misgivings about writing their own interests—as well as those of their communities—into their narratives. As a result, the Gospels actually present two simultaneous stories. The accounts of Jesus and his followers, situated in the early decades of the first century CE, at the same time reflect the experiences, concerns and theologies of the evangelists' implied audiences at the end of that century.[4] In so

B. Brooten, 'Early Christian Women and their Cultural Context: Issues of Method in Historical Reconstruction,' in A.Y. Collins (ed.), *Feminist Perspectives on Biblical Scholarship* (Atlanta, GA: Scholars Press, 1985), pp. 65-91.

1.   The historicity of Phoebe (Rom. 16.1), Prisca (16.3) and Junia (16.7), for example, is assumed by E. Schüssler Fiorenza, *In Memory of Her* (New York: Crossroad, 1986), pp. 171-72.

2.   The Gospels contain elements such as plot, characters, narrators, and implicit commentary, which are also characteristic of fictional narrative. R.A. Culpepper, *Anatomy of the Fourth Gospel* (Philadelphia: Fortress Press, 1983), is only one of many examples of attempts to analyze the Gospels by using the methodologies of literary criticism.

3.   Although it is customary, and convenient, to refer to the Gospels by the names of the individuals to whom they were traditionally attributed, it is the most recent scholarly consensus that the evangelists cannot be identified in any absolute way. It is likely, however, that the evangelists were male; hence my use of the masculine pronoun.

4.   This point is made by J.L. Martyn, *History and Theology in the Fourth Gospel* (Nashville: Abingdon Press, 2nd edn, 1979), p. 37 and *passim*; the same approach can be used with the other Gospels. For a discussion of implied audience and related terms (narrator, author,

doing, the narratives express not only the creativity but also the biases of their authors.[1]

What then do we make of Mary and Martha? The paucity of detail in the Gospels clearly indicates that the evangelists were not interested in describing the sisters for their own sakes. Rather, their inclusion serves other purposes, such as the presentation of a particular view of the life of Jesus and his significance for the implied audience. Nevertheless, the fact that they are mentioned by both Luke and John, and in different contexts, suggests that they were not evangelistic recreations but were already present in, or known to, a pre-redactional, shared stratum of tradition.[2] While this observation in itself does not demonstrate their historicity, it supports the assumption that Mary and Martha, or figures like them, did exist at the time of Jesus or in the early years of the Christian movement.

In our efforts to give these women life, we cannot simply exhume them intact from their narrative contexts and dust them off. If the evangelists, or the tradition from which they drew, turned real people into literary characters in the service of the narrative, so do we need to reverse that process. As we consider how others have mapped the path from narrative to history and then take some tentative steps along the trail ourselves, it will soon become apparent that the path is not clearly marked. Indeed, it seems to lead in several different directions. Nevertheless, by placing Mary and Martha at the centre of our

implied reader), see Culpepper, *Anatomy*, pp. 15-17, 205-27.

1.   With the advent of redaction criticism in the post-World War II period, this observation has become a cornerstone of Gospel criticism. See N. Perrin, *What is Redaction Criticism?* (Philadelphia: Fortress Press, 1969).

2.   Some scholars have argued for a direct literary knowledge of Luke on the part of John, especially in the anointing scenes (Jn 12.3-7; Lk. 7.36ff). See, for example, W.G. Kümmel, *Introduction to the New Testament* (trans. H.C. Kee; Nashville: Abingdon Press, rev. edn, 1975), p. 203. R.E. Brown, however, represents the majority view in stating that there is no direct literary contact between the Third and Fourth Gospels, but that there is the possibility of access to similar traditions as well as of cross-influences at an oral stage in the history of gospel composition. See Brown, *The Gospel according to John* (AB, 29; Garden City, NY: Doubleday, 1966), pp. xlv, xlvii.

investigation, and by paying attention to their roles as literary figures, we might glimpse something of their identities as Jewish Christian women. In the process, we may also catch sight of other women, those unnamed, silent and faceless individuals in the early church who knew and responded to these narratives.

Luke 10.38-42

The references to Mary and Martha in Luke come at the end of ch. 10. This chapter records the mission of the seventy (or seventy-two) disciples (10.1-24) and Jesus' subsequent conversation with a lawyer (10.25-37), which concludes with the parable of the good Samaritan (10.30-37).[1] Immediately after the parable, Luke notes that Jesus, presumably accompanied by his disciples (10.38), entered a village where he was received by Martha. While her sister Mary sat at Jesus' feet and listened to his teaching (10.39), Martha 'was distracted with much serving' (10.40). Annoyed with Mary's behaviour as well as with the apparent indifference of her guest, Martha asked Jesus, 'Lord, do you not care that my sister has left me to serve alone? Tell her then to help me' (10.40). Instead of the sympathy she expected, however, Martha received a gently worded rebuke: 'Martha, Martha, you are anxious and troubled about many things; one thing is needful. Mary has chosen the good portion, which shall not be taken away from her' (10.41-42).[2]

Attempts to recover the historical sisters from Luke's account require a judgment as to the meaning of Jesus' response in 10.41-42. Were these words spoken by Jesus himself, or were they placed in his mouth by the evangelist? Do they simply express approval of female discipleship ('sitting at his feet'), or are they a critique of an activity traditionally seen as female (serving at table)? These questions in turn require further investigation into the *Sitz im Leben* of the passage as well as the social mores of the Greco-Roman world. Does the pericope pertain to life in the

---

1.   All biblical citations are from the RSV, 1952.

2.   For a discussion of the textual problems in these verses, see J.A. Fitzmyer, *The Gospel according to Luke (X-XXIV)* (AB, 28a; Garden City, NY: Doubleday, 1985), p. 894, and B.M. Metzger, *A Textual Commentary on the Greek New Testament* (London: UBS, corr. edn, 1975), pp. 153-54.

time of Jesus in early first-century Palestine, or to the later situation of Luke's Diaspora community? Would the original readers have perceived serving at table to be women's work? Both the foreground and the background of the scholarly discussions of the historical sisters depend in large part on answers to these questions.

Ben Witherington III examines Lk. 10.38-42 in his *Women in the Ministry of Jesus: A Study of Jesus' Attitudes to Women and their Roles as Reflected in his Earthly Life*.[1] The main purpose of his book is to show that 'Jesus...not only countered the negative evaluations of women [that were prevalent in the Jewish environment], but also endorsed and extended women's rights beyond the positive evaluation' which Witherington admits also existed within first-century Judaism.[2] This aim sets the agenda for his book and also determines the contours of his exegesis. According to Witherington, the pericope is an accurate account of an event in the life of the historical Jesus, although written by Luke in his own language and style.[3] Jesus' words

> are neither an attempt to devalue Martha's efforts at hospitality, nor an attempt to attack a woman's traditional role; rather, Jesus defends Mary's right to learn from Him and says this is the crucial thing for those who wish to serve Him.[4]

Witherington does not dwell on the connotations of his statement, however. Instead, his principal interest is in contrasting the roles of Martha and Mary as portrayed in this passage with those of their non-Christian, Jewish contemporaries. First, he claims that it would have been questionable for a Jewish male to be alone with two women who were not related to him.[5] Secondly, he argues that Jesus, in condoning Mary's role as disciple, was breaking new ground. Although Jewish women could study, Witherington asserts that it was highly unusual for a rabbi to come into a woman's house and teach her.[6] Finally, he suggests that Martha's act of serving,

---

1. Cambridge: Cambridge University Press, 1984.
2. *Women*, p. 10.
3. *Women*, p. 101.
4. *Women*, p. 101.
5. *Women*, p. 101.
6. *Women*, p. 101.

though apparently seen by some to have been a traditionally female role, may have been atypical: 'In a Jewish context... women were not allowed to serve at meals if men were in attendance, unless there were no servants to perform the task'.[1] On these grounds, Witherington asserts the superiority of the early Christian movement to its Jewish matrix: Jesus frees humankind from the restraints imposed by Jewish law and custom. Though he does not explicitly say so, Witherington thus implies that Mary and Martha, in their allegiance to Jesus, have moved outside the Jewish community, and that their experience of liberation was typical of, or paradigmatic for, women in the early church.

While this analysis has its merits,[2] it is marred by a disturbing bias. It is also open to criticism on exegetical grounds. For example, it is not clear from the Lukan context that Jesus was alone with the two women.[3] Lk. 10.38 refers to a group of people travelling together; while only Jesus is specifically mentioned as having entered the house, is the reader to understand that the rest stayed outside? If Jesus were her only guest, why was Martha so preoccupied? Her words convey a feeling of harassment with which those who have provided hospitality for an unexpected, large crowd can identify. Furthermore, the text

1. *Women*, p. 101. Witherington contradicts himself here. On the one hand, he assumes that serving at table was a traditional female role (pp. 100, 103, 118), but on the other hand part of his argument is built on the notion that serving in mixed company was a radical act (pp. 101, 112).

2. For example, Witherington (*Women*, p. 100) is probably correct in saying that Luke was not interested in the story for the sake of the sisters but only insofar as it provided a vehicle for Jesus' words in 10.41-42.

3. For Witherington's argument, such as it is, see *Women*, pp. 101 and 190 n. 135. Withering cites Metzger, *Textual Commentary*, p. 153, in support of his claim, though in fact Metzger's comment refers only to the phrase 'in her house'. That the disciples are not specifically mentioned as having entered the house with him does not mean that we are necessarily to understand Jesus as having entered the house alone. Rather, it could simply mean that Jesus, as the central character, is the only one who needs to be mentioned. For parallels, see Gen. 12.14, in which only Abram is mentioned, though both he and Sarai have entered Egypt; Gen. 22.19, in which only Abraham is mentioned as having returned to his men, though Isaac apparently did too; for Lukan examples, see 2.4 and 7.6.

offers no indication that the contact between Jesus and the sisters was perceived to be unusual by Jesus, the women, any onlookers, or the narrator. John 4 offers a useful contrast: the Samaritan woman (4.9), the narrator (4.9) and the disciples (4.27) note the irregularity of Jesus' behaviour in stopping to converse with and request hospitality from a woman, and a Samaritan at that.

Next, Witherington's assertions concerning the place of women in Judaism are inadequately, if at all, documented. He cites no primary evidence, rabbinic or otherwise, for his claims that two women and an unrelated man could not be alone together, that women did not serve in mixed gatherings, or that women did not study. Although the role of women in first-century Judaism is a complex issue, Witherington's categorical statements appear to be the product of his apologetic interests rather than of an independent, critical examination of the relevant sources. In other words, his claim that 'a low view of women [in Judaism] was common, perhaps even predominant before, during and after Jesus' era'[1] is necessitated by his view that Jesus ushered in a new era of liberation from Judaism.[2]

A very different picture of Martha and Mary emerges in Elisabeth Schüssler Fiorenza's article entitled 'A Feminist Interpretation for Liberation: Mary and Mary: Lk. 10.38-42'.[3] As

1. Witherington, *Women*, p. 10. As sources for this assertion he cites several passages from the English translation of *Genesis Rabbah*, the Babylonian Talmud, Philo and Josephus, as well as some secondary sources. He does qualify his statement somewhat by saying that the views of Jeremias and Bonsirven are overly negative, and by citing J. Hauptman, 'Images of Women in the Talmud', in R.R. Ruether (ed.), *Religion and Sexism: Images of Women in Jewish and Christian Traditions* (New York: Simon & Schuster, 1974), pp. 184-212 as presenting a more balanced view.

2. The tendency to cast Christianity and its portrayal of women over against Judaism is not unique to Witherington. As Brooten ('Women', p. 72) comments, 'on the question of women, Judaism is regularly used as a negative backdrop against which to view early Christianity'. Brooten supports her observation by citing some of the most influential studies of women in the early church, including those of Joachim Jeremias, George Tavard, G.W. Trompf, Evelyn and Frank Stagg, Leonard Swidler, and Johannes Leipoldt.

3. *Religion and Intellectual Life* 3 (1986), pp. 21-36. See the similar

a Christian feminist historian and theologian, her perspective differs greatly from that of Witherington. Schüssler Fiorenza's goal is to take the '*ekklesia* of women...as the hermeneutical center and canon of a critical feminist interpretation and re-reading of the Bible'.[1] In doing so, she seeks to 'develop a new model of biblical interpretation that can explore and assess the oppressive or liberating dynamics of biblical texts and their function in the contemporary struggle of women for liberation'.[2] Her attempt at a critical re-reading and reappropriation of the text for contemporary women shapes her reconstruction of the figures of Mary and Martha, just as Witherington's agenda has shaped his.[3]

Yet although she operates explicitly from a feminist perspective, she avoids any comparison of Mary and Martha with Jewish or indeed other women outside the Christian movement, and hence she also avoids the anti-Judaism that characterizes so many other studies of Christian women.[4] Schüssler Fiorenza rejects both the theory that Luke's pericope is an accurate portrayal of an event in the life of Jesus and the claim that the words placed on Jesus' lips were spoken by him. Instead, she situates Luke's story in the context of the community to which he writes,[5] and sets Martha and Mary

treatment in her *Theological Criteria and Historical Reconstruction* (Protocol of the 53rd Colloquy: April 10, 1986; Berkeley: Center for Hermeneutical Studies in Hellenistic and Modern Culture, 1986), and, most recently, in *But She Said: Feminist Practices of Biblical Interpretation* (Boston: Beacon Press, 1992), pp. 51-76.

1. 'Lk. 10.38-42', p. 23; cf. *Criteria*, pp. 1-2.

2. 'Lk. 10.38-42', p. 23.

3. This is discussed in William Anderson's response to Schüssler Fiorenza's analysis in *Criteria*, pp. 17, 19, in which he bluntly comments that she 'has shaped the material to fit her prejudices'. For her own discussion of value-laden and value-free scholarship, cf. *Memory*, pp. xviff.

4. Cf. *Memory*, p. 105, in which she comments that 'historical recon-structions of Christianity over and against Judaism can be continuing resources for Christian anti-Judaism because they perceive Christian origins in light of the historical fact of Christianity's separation from and partial rejection of its Jewish roots and heritage'. See also *Criteria*, p. 6.

5. *Criteria*, pp. 29-30. According to Schüssler Fiorenza, this is linguistically signalled by the title *kyrios*, which appeals to the authority

squarely within the early Christian housechurch.[1]

In order to determine the import of the passage, Schüssler Fiorenza first engages in a limited literary-critical analysis. Her discussion, which underlines the androcentric dynamic of the text,[2] focuses on the nature of the contacts between Jesus and each of the sisters. She considers the relationship between Martha as host and Jesus as guest to be one of independent equals. This egalitarian relationship is rejected, however, by the Lukan Jesus in favour of one of dependency such as he has with Mary 'who chooses the position of a subordinate student' dependent on her master.[3] This, she argues, is not descriptive of the actual place of women in the time of Jesus. Rather, it represents the evangelist's own (androcentric) notions of what the role of women should be.[4] For Luke, Schüssler Fiorenza suggests, Martha and Mary represent women engaged in two different activities: Martha is actively engaged in preaching the word in the housechurch; Mary listens passively to the teaching of Jesus.[5] Luke criticizes the former model while urging the latter upon his readers, some of whom were likely women engaged like Martha in preaching activity. In Schüssler Fiorenza's words,

of the resurrected Lord. H. Waetjen (in *Criteria*, p. 36) suggests that on text-critical grounds the readings should be 'Jesus' and not *kyrios*. See Fitzmyer, *Gospel*, p. 893, who also seems to favour this reading. Such a shift in terminology does not, however, invalidate Schüssler Fiorenza's position, which can be supported with reference to other evidence of the evangelist's redactional activity (for example, the Lukan Sermon on the Plain, which betrays the author's specific interests). See H. Conzelmann, *The Theology of St. Luke* (trans. G. Buswell; Philadelphia: Fortress Press, 1961), pp. 45-46.

1. *Criteria*, p. 30.
2. *Criteria*, p. 29.
3. *Criteria*, p. 29.
4. *Criteria*, p. 29.
5. *Criteria*, p. 29. According to the Mishnah and Gemara, rabbinic disciples did not simply listen to their teachers, but they engaged in discussion with them. See also the dialogues between the Lukan Jesus and his disciples and would-be disciples (for example, 11.1-4; 8.39-50), and the comments by Waetjen in *Criteria*, p. 36.

> Lk. 10.38-42 pits the apostolic women of the Jesus movement
> against each other and appeals to a revelatory word of the
> resurrected Lord in order to restrict women's ministry and
> authority. Its rhetorical interests are to silence women leaders
> of housechurches who like Martha might have protested, and
> at the same time to extol the silent and subordinate behaviour
> of Mary.[1]

This reconstruction therefore presents the sisters as examples of
women who were not only members of the church, but also
leaders and preachers in their own right. As such, they were
thorns in the sides of some of the male members of the church
hierarchy. Luke, a member of this hierarchy, sought to alter the
situation by presenting the silent, sitting Mary as a behavioral
model preferable to that of the active and assertive Martha.

As our discussion has demonstrated, Ben Witherington and
Elisabeth Schüssler Fiorenza take different routes on their way
from the Gospel narrative to early Christian history, and they
arrive at different destinations. The fact that their pictures of
Martha and Mary bear the stamp of their respective agendas
leads one to suspect that this will be true of all such journeys;
there may in fact be no 'objective' destination at all. We will not
allow this suspicion to scuttle our own travel plans, but we
should plan our own itinerary carefully and, perhaps, buy some
cancellation insurance as well. In contrast to the primarily
historical approaches of Witherington and Schüssler Fiorenza,
our own journey will linger much longer at its point of
departure, that is, on a literary analysis of the Lukan narrative.
Only after so doing will we decide how far down the road to
history and in which direction our vehicle will carry us. The
following literary analysis of the pericope will focus on two
main points: its larger context in ch. 10 and in the Lukan Gospel
as a whole; and its characterization of Mary and Martha.

Although many scholars see little or no connection between
Lk. 10.38-42 and its immediate narrative context,[2] it is possible
to demonstrate otherwise. Chapter 10 begins with the sending

---

1.   'Lk. 10.38-42', p. 32.
2.   For a brief discussion, see Fitzmyer, *Gospel*, p. 892. Waetjen in
Criteria, p. 35, referring to the parable of the good Samaritan, also argues
that the larger context needs to be considered.

out of a large number of disciples who are given specific missionary instructions (10.4-11). Among these is the directive: 'Whenever you enter a town and they receive you, eat what is set before you' (10.8). This suggests that those who receive the disciples will also serve them by taking care of their physical well-being. For their part, the disciples heal the sick and preach the word (10.9). Receiving the disciples by serving them and hearing their word is tantamount to receiving and hearing Jesus and indeed God as well (10.16). If this is the case, then the women in 10.38-42, who serve Jesus and sit at his feet, epitomize true belief. This reading suggests that we have come upon Martha and Mary in the very act of conversion, of turning to Jesus as saviour.

What then is the significance of Jesus' rebuke? It may indicate that while serving, that is, taking care of physical needs,[1] and hearing the words are both elements of discipleship, concern for the former should not overshadow the importance of the latter. True service consists not only of attention to physical needs (and its accompanying distraction) but also, and primarily, of listening to the gospel. While serving others food and drink is an altruistic act, it should be placed in the same category as anxiety about one's physical needs, against which the Lukan Jesus cautions:

> Do not be anxious about your life, what you shall eat, nor about your body, what you shall put on. For life is more than food, and the body more than clothing...For all the nations of the world seek these things; and your Father knows that you need them. Instead, seek his kingdom, and these things shall be yours as well (12.22-23, 30-31).[2]

---

1.   Schüssler Fiorenza's decision to limit the meaning of *diakoneo* in this pericope to 'preaching' may be challenged. While preaching is clearly one meaning of the verb, other Lukan passages imply the broader translation of 'to serve'. Such service is ascribed not only to women (4.39; 8.3; 10.40) but also to male servants (17.8) and to Jesus himself (12.37; 22.26-27). Furthermore, Acts 6.2 uses the verb specifically to mean service at table, in contrast to preaching the word. For more detailed discussion, see Schüssler Fiorenza, 'Lk. 10.38-42', and H.W. Beyer, '*Diakoneuo, diakonia, diakonos*', *TDNT*, II, pp. 81-93.

2.   In his response to Schüssler Fiorenza, W. Anderson in *Criteria*, p. 19, also draws a connection between the two pericopes.

Even more significant for our analysis are passages such as 22.26-27 in which the Lukan Jesus inverts the conventional relationship between master and servant: 'Let the greatest among you become as the youngest, and the leader as one who serves. For which is the greater, one who sits at table, or one who serves? Is it not the one who sits at table? But I am among you as one who serves'. But what kind of meal is it that Jesus serves? The answer is: a spiritual one. Whereas Jesus' disciples serve him in various ways, he serves them by offering the word and eternal life. Lk. 10.38-42 may thus provide a graphic illustration of the inverted master–servant dichotomy. Though Martha is called upon to serve the Lord, it is Mary who provides him with an opportunity to serve her.

These parallels suggest that Jesus' remarks were not intended to limit women's activity to passive listening to the word preached by men, as Schüssler Fiorenza suggests. Nor do they depict women's new freedom to be disciples of a great teacher, as Witherington argues. Rather, they emphasize that while service to others is important, hearing the word for oneself is the essential ingredient of discipleship. Because Luke provides male and female examples of both serving and hearing the word, it would seem that a differentiation of gender roles is not his primary message. The place of Lk. 10.38-42 in the larger narrative and theological context of the third Gospel suggests that Jesus' words to Martha convey the evangelist's attitude toward discipleship in general, not his views on women disciples specifically.

A similar conclusion emerges from an analysis of the Lukan characterization of the sisters. As Schüssler Fiorenza notes, Martha and Mary are portrayed only in their relationship to Jesus.[1] While she interprets this as evincing Luke's androcentrism, the pericope is not manifestly concerned with issues of equality between men and women, or the subordination of women to men, or even the right of women to assume functions that an androcentric church would prefer to limit to men. A glance beyond the passages reveals that in the third Gospel all activities and relationships—whether associated with male or with female characters—are christocentric. This literary feature

1. 'Lk. 10.38-42', p. 29.

of the Gospel is inherent in the narrative itself, as the implied author points out in his address to Theophilus (Acts 1.1). Therefore the characterization of Mary and Martha should be understood less as androcentric than as christocentric. That the sisters are depicted only in their relationship to Jesus reflects not a male bias but the inevitable focus of the Gospel narrative.[1] In other words, had the same story been told about male siblings such as the brothers Zebedee (Lk. 5.10), the christocentric focus of their characterization would have been the same (cf. 5.1-11).

A second element of the characterization of Mary and Martha concerns its effect on the Gospel's implied audience. Clearly the evangelist, as implied author, would like his audience to understand and accept the point conveyed in the passage, whatever we understand that point to be. But I suggest that he does so by using the specific literary technique of frustrating and thereby modifying the expectations he imputes to his readership.[2] Such expectations are articulated by Martha in 10.38-42. The passage derives its impact from the fact that Martha initially appears to have justice on her side. It seems unfair that she should do all the work while her sister sits. The expectation that Mary should help serve is also implicit in and therefore reinforced by 10.8, in which service is a sign that one has received the disciples and accepted their message.

Jesus' unexpected reply therefore functions in the first instance to frustrate Martha's expectations as well as those of the implied readers: if Martha's complaint is justified and if Jesus is on the side of justice (cf. Lk. 6.32-49), why does he rebuke her? In the second instance, however, Jesus' words serve to modify and deepen the implied reader's understanding. Mary's act, while seemingly inconsiderate, is in fact the preferable one since it demonstrates the element of discipleship that Luke considers

1. This is not to deny Luke's overall androcentrism, which is evident in other passages (for example Acts 18.26-27.). But Waetjen in *Criteria*, p. 18, argues that most of Schüssler Fiorenza's arguments regarding Luke's androcentric bias are from silence and so are not particularly strong.

2. On this literary device as it pertains to the fourth Gospel, cf. my 'Great Expectations: A Reader-Oriented Approach to Johannine Christology and Eschatology', *Journal of Literature and Theology* 3 (1989), pp. 61-76.

central. In this way, the characterization of Martha and Mary becomes a vehicle for the Lukan theme that true disciples, like the sisters, will centre their actions on the Christ. True service consists not of caring for physical needs but of ingesting, and digesting, the message of the Gospel.[1]

In summary, our discussion of Luke's narrative has pointed us in a different direction than those taken by Witherington and Schüssler Fiorenza. It has suggested that the evangelist's narrative purpose is not to describe the ideal female disciple in particular, but to illustrate his views on discipleship in general. This observation does not acquit Luke of androcentrism or ignore the use that later ecclesiastics have made of this and other Lukan passages to bar women from positions of leadership.[2] Nevertheless, Luke's use of female figures to express his views on discipleship, while probably grounded in pre-Lukan tradition, at least implicitly attests to a role for women in his view of the church. Further, it suggests the willingness of the male members of his implied audience to derive a lesson from a story in which women are important characters.

These observations lead our attempts at historical reconstruction in two directions. If we assume that the evangelist is drawing upon a tradition ultimately rooted in historical fact, the story provides a glimpse of two sisters in the process of becoming believers in the Christ, through the missionary activity of the disciples or perhaps even Jesus himself.[3] If we see the

1.   The technique of frustrating and then modifying readers' expectations also appears in Lk. 8.19-21 (Jesus seems to reject the idea that honor is due to one's parents) and 9.60 (he appears to question the honor due to the dead). In both cases, Jesus shocks his narrative audience, and Luke shocks his readers, by subordinating well-established moral values to the radical message of salvation through the Christ.

2.   Indeed, this seems to be a part of Witherington's agenda: he exalts the traditional roles that women found meaningful in the early church and, by implication, should continue to find satisfactory today. See Witherington, *Women*, pp. 117-18, and Schüssler Fiorenza, *Criteria*, p. 5.

3.   In 10.2, Jesus seems to be implying that the seventy are sent out ahead of him; they therefore prepare the way for his own travels to specific communities. But 10.16 suggests that the entire chapter is intended also to support the idea that the apostles and later missionaries can be effective in bringing the word of God to the people, and that

passage as addressed to a particular community, we may catch sight, however briefly, of the women members of that community who would have seen the sisters as role models affirming the legitimacy of their discipleship.[1]

John 11.1-44

Mary and Martha appear as two of the central characters in the Johannine story of the raising of Lazarus. This final and most detailed sign[2] of Jesus' ministry serves as a catalyst for the sequence of events which culminate in Jesus' betrayal, trial and execution (cf. 11.47 onwards).[3] In comparison with Luke's passage, the portrait of the two sisters here is lavishly detailed. We are told they live in a village named Bethany (11.1), and have a brother named Lazarus (11.2). We also learn that Jesus loved all three siblings (11.3, 5).

Mary and Martha initiate the action by sending word to Jesus that their brother is ill (11.3). Behind this act lie the expectations that Jesus cares about Lazarus and, more important, that he has the ability to heal him. This latter expectation is implied by the narrator, who reports Jesus' puzzling response to the message: instead of rushing to Lazarus's bedside, Jesus stays two days longer where he is.[4] It is also expressed explicitly by Martha (11.21) and Mary (11.32) as well as by the Jewish crowd in Bethany (11.37). When Jesus does finally arrive, Lazarus is already dead and buried. Martha greets Jesus, and the two engage in a theologically charged discussion. First, she expresses her views that had Jesus been in Bethany, Lazarus would not have died, and that even now God would give Jesus what he

believing through the word of such a missionary is tantamount to receiving, and being accepted by, Jesus and God. Consequently it is difficult to say whether we are to see Mary and Martha as hearing the word initially from the disciples or from Jesus himself.

1. This point is also made by Schüssler Fiorenza, 'Lk. 10.38-42', p. 32.

2. Other signs are recounted in chs. 2, 4, 5, 6 and 9.

3. Brown (*Gospel*, pp. 118, 427) sees chs. 11 and 12 as added later to the plan of the Gospel, at which time the cleansing of the temple was moved from its place at the end of the ministry to the first Passover.

4. This pattern is similar to that in 2.1-11 and 4.48-54. See my 'Great Expectations' for discussion and bibliography.

asks (11.21-22). Jesus does promise that her brother will rise again (11.23), but Martha understands his comment to be a reference to the 'resurrection at the last day' (11.24). As a correction, Jesus makes a self-revelatory statement: 'I am the resurrection and the life; he who believes in me, though he die, yet shall he live, and whoever lives and believes in me shall never die. Do you believe this?' (11.25-26). The climax occurs with Martha's ensuing confession: 'Yes, Lord; I believe that you are the Christ, the son of God, he who is coming into the world' (11.27).

The narrative now turns to the meeting between Jesus and Mary. Upon hearing from Martha that Jesus had called for her (11.28), Mary rose, presumably from her mourning, and went to meet him outside the village; she was followed by the Jewish friends who had been consoling her (11.29-31). The Gospel recounts her mournful reproach: 'Lord, if you had been here, my brother would not have died' (11.32). Unlike Martha, Mary makes no further statement regarding Jesus or his power. Neither does Jesus respond to her directly; rather, followed by Mary (11.45), Martha (11.39) and the crowd (11.45) he immediately heads toward the tomb. Over Martha's practical objection (11.39), he has the stone removed from the entrance to the tomb (11.41) and, after a brief, audible prayer (11.42), he calls Lazarus forth (11.43-44). The remainder of the chapter recounts the responses of the Jewish witnesses to the sign (11.45) as well as that of the Jewish authorities (11.47-53) in a manner which emphasizes the impending passion.

Before offering our own literary analysis and historical reconstruction of the Johannine Martha and Mary, it will be instructive to look briefly at three other studies. Each finds particular details to be of interpretive significance, and each provides a different perspective on both the *Sitz im Leben* of the passage and the nature of Martha's confession.

The first study is that of Raymond E. Brown, who appended an article entitled 'Roles of Women in the Fourth Gospel' to his book *The Community of the Beloved Disciple*.[1] Brown's purpose was to examine the Johannine evidence pertinent to the

1. New York: Paulist Press, 1979, pp. 183-98; the essay was first published in *TS* 36 (1975), pp. 688-99.

contemporary debate about the role of women in the church.[1] Although he does not exclude the strong possibility that the fourth Gospel represents an early, possibly historical tradition,[2] he regards the Johannine women characters primarily as representative of the situation in the evangelist's community.

Brown focuses on two narrative details: the note in 11.3 that Jesus loved Mary and Martha; and the conversation between Martha and Jesus in 11.25-27. He claims that the description of the sisters as beloved of Jesus associates them with the Johannine disciple par excellence, the Beloved Disciple.[3] Though they are not equal to this male figure, the women are nevertheless considered to be true disciples.[4] This point is reinforced by Jesus' revelation of his mystery to Martha (11.25-26).[5] Her confessional response indicates that she has both understood his words properly and reached a level of true faith.[6] The parallel between Martha's confession here and that of Peter in Mt. 16.16, in Brown's view, exemplifies the fourth evangelist's deliberate tendency to give women a role traditionally associated with Peter.[7] This portrayal of Martha as a near equal to the Beloved Disciple and the synoptic Peter is for Brown a clue to the status of women in the Johannine community. He suggests that women were seen as recipients of revelation and therefore were esteemed members of the church. He does not, however, draw any conclusions with respect to women's position in the community's authority structure.

Brown's perspective is shared in some respects by Schüssler Fiorenza, who discusses the Johannine account in her article on

1. 'Roles of Women', pp. 183, 185.
2. 'Roles of Women', p. 185 n. 328.
3. 'Roles of Women', p. 191.
4. 'Roles of Women', p. 191.
5. 'Roles of Women', p. 191.
6. 'Roles of Women', p. 190. Here he has apparently revised the opinion expressed in *Gospel*, p. 434, that Martha's confession expresses a similar outlook to that of the Samaritan woman, namely, a developing but still partial faith.
7. 'Roles of Women', p. 190. Brown notes that the evangelist takes special care to do so. We may ask, however, how we can tell this to be the case. Do we see John's construction as deliberate because we expect he would most naturally give these roles to men?

Luke 10.[1] Like Brown, she uses the reference to Jesus' love for
the sisters in 11.3 to suggest that they should be grouped along
with the Beloved Disciple as disciples of Jesus.[2] She too
considers Martha's words in 11.27 to be a full christological
confession comparable to that of Peter in Mt. 16.16.[3] But
Schüssler Fiorenza goes beyond Brown in considering many
more details of the pericope and in suggesting that the narrative
reflects the role of women as leaders in the Johannine
community. In her description of the sisters as full disciples, for
example, Schüssler Fiorenza compares Martha's call of Mary
(11.28) with Andrew and Philip's call of Peter and Nathanael
(1.35-51). In my view, however, this comparison is inappropriate, since the two situations differ in one important manner.
Whereas Peter and Nathanael made their first contacts with
Jesus through Andrew and Philip and then became disciples as a
consequence of that contact, Mary is clearly already a disciple
prior to being called by Martha (cf. 11.3). Hence Martha's words
to her sister are not a call to discipleship but a literary device
designed to introduce the next narrative segment.[4]

In similar fashion, Schüssler Fiorenza takes the narrator's
comment in 11.31, 45, that the Jews who had been consoling
Mary followed her out of the house, as indicating that she had
followers among her people who then came to believe in Jesus.[5]
This reading implies that their following had something to do
with Mary's leadership. But this theory is not borne out by the
text, which states that those who believed did so because they
witnessed the raising of Lazarus (11.45).

Finally, for Schüssler Fiorenza, Martha's confession is evidence that she had become the spokesperson for John's
christological emphases: 'Martha represents the full apostolic
faith of the Johannine community just as Peter does for the
Matthean community'.[6] The implication is that Martha would

1. 'Lk. 10.38-42'.
2. 'Lk. 10.38-42', p. 32.
3. 'Lk. 10.38-42', p. 31.
4. Brown (*Gospel*, p. 435) comments that the entire scene in 11.28-33
does not really advance the story and, indeed, seems rather artificial.
5. 'Lk. 10.38-42', p. 32.
6. 'Lk. 10.38-42', p. 31.

have been seen by the community as a leader among the disciples, although Schüssler Fiorenza does not state whether this is in rivalry or in partnership with the Beloved Disciple.[1] In conclusion, Schüssler Fiorenza contrasts the Johannine passage favourably with Luke's account. She argues that John's portrait of Mary and Martha as disciples and community leaders 'indicates how women might have appealed to the leadership of women in order to legitimate their own ministry and authority'.[2]

Unlike Schüssler Fiorenza and Brown, Witherington situates some elements of the story (for example, Martha's rudimentary confession, Jesus' self-proclamation, the general outline of the sisters' encounter with Jesus) in the *Sitz im Leben* of Jesus, although he acknowledges that other details, including the resurrection of Lazarus, may be redactional.[3] Witherington too sees 11.3 as evidence that Mary and Martha were disciples of Jesus,[4] but his analysis differs from that of Brown and Schüssler Fiorenza in its evaluation of Martha's confession. According to Witherington, the Johannine Martha sincerely believes in Jesus and has faith in his power, but she does not come to a full confession of faith. Although 11.27 is the most complete confession encountered thus far in the narrative,[5] it falls short in that it does not go beyond the 'orthodox Pharisaic view of resurrection on the last day'.[6] For Witherington, the portrayal of Martha

1. Despite the high regard shown here for Martha, the fourth evangelist still sees the Beloved Disciple as primary. Though the disciple makes no full confession—indeed, he says little in the narrative—he is closely aligned with Jesus throughout the second half of the Gospel whereas Mary and Martha appear in only two chapters.

2. 'Lk. 10.38-42', p. 32.

3. Witherington, *Women*, p. 106.

4. *Women*, p. 106.

5. *Women*, pp. 108-109.

6. Witherington (*Women*, pp. 108-109) makes this judgment on literary-critical grounds: 'It is possible that the Evangelist has constructed his Gospel so that alongside the crescendo of the miraculous, we have a crescendo of confessions. This would mean that Martha's confession takes on new importance because of its place in the climactic episode of the series of signs'. Hence Thomas's confession would be the best of all, though it is accompanied by a critique voiced by the Johannine Jesus himself.

therefore conveys the message that women have a right to be taught even the mysteries of the faith and that they are capable of responding in faith with an accurate, if incomplete, confession. Hence they are also capable of being disciples of Jesus.[1] In contrast to Martha, he argues, Mary is not portrayed here in a sympathetic or favourable manner. She is simply presented as a grieving woman who points an accusatory finger at Jesus and thereby betrays an attitude of hopelessness and lack of trust.[2]

Behind the varied claims of these three studies lies a common picture of Mary and Martha as disciples, a picture which implies that women were fully accepted as members—and, if Schüssler Fiorenza is correct, even as leaders—in the Johannine community. There are two elements of the passage, however, which this picture omits: the literary technique used by the evangelist to create an impact on the reader and to deepen christological understanding; and the narrative clues which pertain to the place of these women within the Jewish community of Bethany. To these points we now turn.

My discussion of Lk. 10.38-42 noted that the exchange between Martha and Jesus serves to frustrate and then modify certain expectations of the evangelist's implied readers with regard to their understanding of discipleship. The same technique is at work in the conversation between Jesus and Martha conveyed in Jn 11.25-27. Here Martha's first words articulate her expectations concerning Jesus' love for Lazarus and his ability to heal him. That these expressions are echoed by Mary and by the Jewish crowds suggests that they were seen by the evangelist as characteristic also of his implied audience. Jewish in origin, these views were apparently held by those who were already Christians, since Mary and Martha were themselves followers of Jesus when they articulated them.

1. *Women*, p. 109. But Witherington is silent as to whether they might also have held positions of leadership. Perhaps his apologetic concerns simply prevent him from considering this as a possibility. Cf. *Women*, pp. 117-18.

2. *Women*, p. 109. While it is true that Mary is not as important in this story as Martha is, Witherington's comment goes beyond what is warranted by the text. In fact the seemingly unbalanced treatment of the sisters is corrected in the first pericope of the next chapter: there Mary, not Martha, is central to the narrative interests (12.1-7).

These expectations, however, are frustrated not only by Jesus' words concerning resurrection but also by his tarrying instead of responding immediately to the sisters' invocation. The inappropriateness of his response in itself challenges the expectations of the reader, and Jesus' comment to Martha in 11.25-26 serves to modify and correct them. Martha, and the implied audience, impute to Jesus the power to raise the dead at the last day and so imply a straightforward future eschatology. But Jesus' response asserts that she has misunderstood: resurrection is not future but present. This assertion is then demonstrated dramatically and forcefully by the resurrection of Lazarus. Martha's desire to see her brother alive has been realized magnificently, although not in the way she had imagined. Where she asked for healing, Jesus provided resurrection.

There is yet another important element to their conversation. Jesus' correction of Martha's christological understanding is immediately followed by her confession. She believes what Jesus has just told her, though she as yet lacks empirical evidence that his assertions are true. Like the nobleman whose son is healed (cf. 4.44-54), her belief is prior to the accomplishment of the sign. The sequence gains significance in light of Jesus' later remark to Thomas: 'Have you believed because you have seen me? Blessed are those who have not seen and yet believe' (20.29). This analogy settles the question of whether Martha's confession is rudimentary or profound. While her balking at the tomb might suggest otherwise,[1] her willingness to base her faith on Jesus' words implies that she is indeed one of the blessed. As in the Lukan passage, so here the attribution of a high confession to Martha would have served both to modify the expectations of the readers—women and men—and to legitimate the right of women to be active in the church.

To this point in our historical-critical study we have studied Martha and Mary primarily as representative of women in the early Christian community; very little has been said about them

---

1. Witherington (*Women*, p. 108) takes 11.35 to be a sign that her faith is not complete. Nevertheless, the narrative sequence in Jn 11 follows closely that of Mt. 16, in which Peter also follows his confession with a comment (16.22) which casts doubt on the fullness of his understanding. He is then clearly rebuked by the Matthean Jesus (16.23).

as Jewish women. This silence is appropriate with respect to the
Lukan passage which, *pace* Witherington, says nothing about
them as Jewish women.[1] The situation is different, however, for
Jn 11.1-44. In this passage the sisters are apparently engaged in
the traditional mourning rites of first-century Palestine.[2]
Further, they are consoled by the members of their community,
and these fellow Jews show no inclination to distance themselves from the mourners when Jesus arrives. The observation
that Jewish believers in the Christ were part of the general
Jewish community counters the impression created by 9.22,
which has tended to overshadow the discussion of the relationship between the church and the synagogue in the evangelist's
own *Sitz im Leben*.[3] In 9.22 the narrator states that 'the Jews
had already agreed that if anyone should confess [Jesus] to be
the Christ, he was to be put out of the synagogue'. Although it is
possible that Jews may have come simply out of kindness to
console even those mourners who had been excluded from the
synagogue, this seems a far-fetched way of avoiding the contradiction. Whether we seek an explanation for the contradiction or
add it to the list of Johannine narrative difficulties, we may at
least conclude that in the time of Jesus, if not of the evangelist,
there were women disciples who were integrated into their
Jewish communities.

As in my analysis of Lk. 10.38-42, the picture which emerges
from the portrayal of Mary and Martha in Jn 11.1-44 corresponds to the two levels on which the narrative may be read.
The passage depicts Mary and Martha as Jewish women who
live independently with their brother in Bethany. Fully integrated into the Jewish community, they nevertheless have a
close enough relationship with Jesus to call on him in time of
trouble. Furthermore, at least one of them, Martha, has a

1. The very placement of this story within the ministry of Jesus
would seem to imply that there was a Jewish context.

2. For discussion of Jewish mourning practices in the second temple
period, see E. Feldman, *Biblical and Post-Biblical Defilement and
Mourning: Law as Theology* (New York: Ktav, 1977), and S. Safrai and S.
Stern (eds.), *The Jewish People in the First Century* (CRINT, 2;
Philadelphia: Fortress Press, 1976), pp. 774-75, 781-85.

3. See Martyn, *History and Theology*, pp. 37-62; Brown, *Gospel*,
p. 380.

sophisticated understanding of his identity and his significance for those who believe in him. But the evangelist apparently writes not only to record an important event in the life of Jesus but also to speak directly to his audience. In using Martha to represent a true disciple who attains the profound understanding of resurrection that he wishes his community to share, the evangelist is also creating a strong role model for the women members of the church. Such a model authenticates both their membership as women and their right—like Martha's—to 'ask whatever you will, and it shall be done for you' (Jn 15.7).

John 12.1-7

I shall conclude my study with a brief look at Jn 12.1-7, which immediately follows the raising of Lazarus. In this scene Mary anoints Jesus at her home in Bethany, six days before his final Passover (12.1).[1] The occasion is a dinner in Jesus' honour at which Martha served (12.2). Mary silently 'took a pint of costly ointment of pure nard and anointed the feet of Jesus and wiped his feet with her hair' (12.3). For this act she is criticized by Judas, who complains sanctimoniously, 'Why was this ointment not sold for three hundred denarii and given to the poor?' (12.5). But Jesus, defending Mary, responds, 'Let her alone, let her keep it for the day of my burial. The poor you always have with you, but you do not always have me' (12.6-7).

Elisabeth Schüssler Fiorenza discusses this passage briefly because it provides a counterpoint to her study of Lk. 10.38-42. She notes that for John, in contrast to Luke, Mary is not the opposite of Martha but the counterpart to Judas; the true female disciple is an alternative to the unfaithful male disciple.[2] Her act both prepares Jesus for his burial and anticipates his command that the disciples wash each other's feet as a sign of the 'agape praxis of true discipleship'.[3] Hence Mary, like her sister in the

---

1. For a comparison of the various anointing scenes, see Witherington, *Women*, p. 110; Schüssler Fiorenza, *Criteria*, p. 3; and especially Brown, *Gospel*, pp. 449-54.

2. 'Lk. 10.38-42', p. 32.

3. 'Lk. 10.38-42', p. 32.

preceding pericope, is a model for female leadership in the Johannine community.[1]

Ben Witherington III, like Schüssler Fiorenza, sees Mary's anointing of Jesus as a prophetic act. From this evidence, he concludes that the Gospel writers may be implying that early Christian women legitimately assumed the role or tasks of the prophet.[2] His analysis differs from that of Schüssler Fiorenza in that he sees continuity, not contrast, between the Lukan and Johannine accounts: the Johannine sisters too are seen as having been liberated from the shackles of their Jewish past. Mary demonstrates this liberation by letting down her hair in the presence of men to whom she was not related, an act that, according to Witherington, was considered scandalous.[3] Martha's serving at table in mixed company, an act that violates the rules of Jewish practice, constitutes evidence of her liberation. She performs the function of a free servant to honour the one in whom she believes; 'liberty in Christ is not only freedom from customs which restrict love, but also freedom to take a lower place, to humble oneself to serve'.[4]

Witherington has read into his treatment of the Johannine pericope the theme of liberation from Jewish mores as he did in his discussing of Lk. 10.38-42. But neither the content nor the context of Jn 12.1-17 provides any hint of this theme. Witherington's comparison of this passage with the Lukan story is on firmer ground. In both cases, Martha—functioning as the head of the household—serves at table while Mary engages in acts of devotion and discipleship. In Jn 12.1-7, however, there is no rivalry between the two sisters; furthermore, Mary's acts in the Johannine passage go beyond the listening and learning of

---

1.   'Lk. 10.38-42', p. 32.

2.   Witherington, *Women*, p. 115. Witherington agrees with Brown that this possibly gave precedent for women to become deaconesses.

3.   Witherington's main source for this appears to be Jeremias, although he cites two rabbinic sources in English translation; *Women*, pp. 113, 194 n. 209.

4.   *Women*, p. 112. This exaltation of traditional female roles comports well with Witherington's apologetic motives. See *Women*, pp. 117-18.

Lk. 10.38-42 both to encompass prophetic elements and to provide a foil for Judas.[1]

Finally, with respect to context, the juxtaposed Johannine passages are among the last, climactic scenes of Jesus' ministry as well as key elements that advance the plot toward the all-important passion narrative. It is consequently not only the particular roles ascribed to Martha and Mary in the fourth Gospel but also the crucial juncture at which they appear that compel us to take them seriously both as characters and as vehicles for Johannine theology. In portraying Mary and Martha in acts of serving and anointing, Jn 12.1-7, like the other pericopes we have explored, presents the sisters as disciples. That they hosted a dinner for Jesus, at which others of his inner circle were present, implies that the sisters or women like them were also part of, or close to, this inner circle. Regardless of its historicity, the account would have served to affirm the full membership of women in all aspects of the Johannine community.

Conclusions

Our attempts to resurrect Martha and Mary from their narrative resting places have resulted not in a single picture of each sister, but in a multiplicity of images. The differences among these images are due primarily to the varying perspectives of the scholars who recreated them. Witherington, despite his concession that the Johannine anointing story may impute leadership positions to women, concludes that the account upholds the status quo. In his view, the unique feature of Jesus' women followers is that[2]

> the traditional roles of hospitality and service are seen by them as a way to serve not only the physical family but the family of faith. Being Jesus' disciples did not lead these women to abandon their traditional roles in regard to preparing food, serving, etc. Rather, it gave these roles new significance and importance, for now they could be used to serve the Master and the family of faith. The transformation of these women

1. Brown (*Gospel*, p. 435) points out that Mary is always at Jesus' feet.
2. Witherington, *Women*, p. 118.

involved not only assuming new discipleship roles, but also
resuming their traditional roles for a new purpose.

The tone of this and many other sections of his book implies that
modern Christian women should be satisfied with these roles as
well.

This is a view which Schüssler Fiorenza emphatically rejects.[1]
Instead, she declares:[2]

> A hermeneutics of remembrance can show that both Luke and
> the Fourth Gospel reflect the struggle of early Christian women
> against patriarchal restrictions of women's leadership and
> ministry at the turn of the first century...The critical explo-
> ration of the literary dynamics of Lk. 10.38-42 has shown that
> the androcentric tendencies of traditional and contemporary
> interpretations are not completely read into the text, but that
> they are generated by the text. Even a feminist interpretation
> that is interested in defending the story as positive for women
> perpetuates the androcentric dualism and patriarchal prejudice
> inherent in the original story. This text is patriarchal because it
> reinforces the societal and ecclesiastical polarization of women.
> Its proclamation denigrates women's work while at the same
> time insisting that housework and hospitality are women's
> proper roles...We ought to be not only good disciples but also
> good hostesses, not only good ministers but also good house-
> wives, not only well-paid professionals but also glamorous
> lovers.

This does not mean that patriarchal texts cannot be used in
preaching and teaching. Rather, since 'women and men have
internalized the androcentric and patriarchal tendencies of this
text as the word of God, Bible studies and sermons must
critically explore its oppressive functions and implications'.[3]

More difficult than identifying the views, assumptions and
contemporary concerns which shape such reconstructions of
Mary and Martha is labelling one's own. No doubt mine have
already been discerned by many readers. First, as a woman
scholar, I am fascinated by the opportunity to imagine women

1.   In *Criteria*, p. 5, she expresses this directly by questioning the
'scholarly' nature of Witherington's book and deploring its publication
in a distinguished New Testament series.
2.   'Lk. 10.38-42', pp. 32-33.
3.   'Lk. 10.38-42', p. 33.

back into a period of history in which their presence has often been ignored, forgotten or overshadowed. I stress here the element of imagination, not only because of the paucity of the evidence, but also because of the difficulties which are inherent in any attempt to do historical reconstruction on the basis of narrative alone.[1] I am more confident in our ability to say something about Martha and Mary as literary representations than as historical figures.

Secondly, unlike Witherington, Brown and Schüssler Fiorenza, I am not Christian but Jewish. Gospel texts do not undergird the theology or social structure of my religious community, nor can they be used for feminist critique and empowerment of women within that community. What does concern me is the manner in which the New Testament, the Mary and Martha stories included, has been used to legitimate anti-Jewish attitudes and a supercessionist theology. While I am concerned about the roles of women within the Jewish community and can offer a critique of their ambiguous portrayal in Judaism's foundational documents, I deplore superficial and apologetically motivated attempts to demonstrate the superiority of Christianity to Judaism on the basis of the respective roles they accord women.

In evaluating the process of historical reconstruction attempted above, we must consider whether we have in fact resurrected Martha and Mary from their fixed places in the Gospel texts. Have we been able to move from literary analysis to historical reconstruction of the sisters on the one hand, and of the first-century women who read and heard about them on the other? The answer, despite the hesitations expressed in this essay, seems to be a qualified yes, that is, as long as certain assumptions are maintained.

To reconstruct the sisters as historical figures, we must assume that the third and fourth Gospels bear witness to an early and authentic tradition. Since the portraits are for the most part complementary, we can with some imagination create a composite picture of two sisters living with their brother Lazarus near Bethany. Martha, the head of the household, and

1. For a discussion of the 'historical imagination' and its central role in the process of historical reconstruction, see Brooten, 'Women', pp. 67-69.

possibly the elder sister, has charge of such duties as greeting visitors and preparing and serving meals; however, she expects her younger sister to help. The three siblings have come to believe that Jesus is the messiah, although they continue to progress in their understanding of his message. As disciples, they are confident of his affection for them, and consequently they do not hesitate to ask him for help or to organize social functions in his honour. This latter function may indicate their presence in his inner circle as well as their leadership and influence over others outside the circle. Moreover, although their allegiance to Jesus is no secret, they are fully integrated into the Jewish community of Bethany, and they rely on and benefit from that community's emotional support in times of need. It is not therefore inconceivable that their examples may have influenced other Jews in Bethany to follow Jesus as well.

The evangelists told their tales not to address women only but to deepen the theological understanding of all readers. Nevertheless, women readers in the early church especially would likely have identified with Martha and Mary. For these readers, the sisters may have demonstrated the possibility that women independent of male supporters such as fathers and husbands could be active in the world. In addition, they may have affirmed the activity of women not only in the rank and file of the church but also in its inner circle of authority. Finally, Martha and Mary may have been seen as models of integration, according to which it was possible for women to view their belief in the Christ and active participation in the church as compatible with, and complementary to, other important elements of their lives.

This highly tentative reconstruction requires, in addition to many assumptions, an active historical imagination. Nevertheless, it seems that the process of which this double-focused and rather blurry picture is the result may indeed lead to new insights, not only about the history of the early church but also about the narratives—their implied authors, their theological and social agendas, and their literary ploys—from which we try to recreate that history.

SCRIPTURE AND THE FEMININE IN JOHN

Judith Lieu

No apology is needed for an essay on the fourth Gospel in a volume exploring interpretations and re-readings of the Hebrew Scriptures within the New Testament, for 'Scripture... is part of its very woof and warp'.[1] Equally, the fourth Gospel demands a place in any 'Feminist Companion', for the distinctive role women play within the narrative has made it a favourite resource for feminist readings. The faith displayed at key points in the narrative and in different ways by the Samaritan woman (4.4-42), by Mary Magdalene (20.1-2, 11-18), by the mother of Jesus (2.1-5; 19.25-27), and by Mary and Martha (11.1-44; 12.1-8) demand attention; more particularly, the primacy of the confession put in the mouth of the last-named (11.27), the missionary activity of the first (4.39), and Mary Magdalene's mission as 'apostle to the apostles' (20.17-18), have prompted reconstructions of the prominent role arguably played by women in the Johannine community, a prominence which may have been suppressed or lost in other Christian communities but which can become a model for the present.[2] At the same time the characteristic Johannine skill in narrative art, which is particularly displayed in the stories of the Samaritan woman or of Mary and Martha, has invited feminist literary readings.[3] To explore the

1. A.T. Hanson, *The Prophetic Gospel: A Study of John and the Old Testament* (Edinburgh: T. & T. Clark, 1991), p. 245.

2. See among others R.E. Brown, 'Roles of Women in the Fourth Gospel', in *The Community of the Beloved Disciple* (London: Chapman, 1979), pp. 183-98; E. Schüssler Fiorenza, *In Memory of Her: A Feminist Theological Reconstruction of Christian Origins* (London: SCM Press, 1983), pp. 323-34; S.M. Schneiders, 'Women in the Fourth Gospel', *BTB* 12 (1982), pp. 35-45.

3. M. de Boer, 'John 4.27—Women (and Men) in the Gospel and Community of John', in G. Brooke (ed.), *Women in the Biblical Tradition* (Lewiston, NY: Edwin Mellen, 1992), pp. 208-30; E. Eslinger, 'The Wooing of the Woman at the Well', *Literature and Theology* 1 (1987), pp. 167-83,

relationship between these two focal concerns is the obvious next step;[1] yet this cannot simply mean asking what part the Hebrew Scriptures have played in the presentation of the women in the Gospel, for the latter issue itself also empowers us to look for the wider potential, both positive and negative, of John's relation with Scripture.

Wisdom in the Prologue

The most obvious place to start is the Prologue of the Gospel (1.1-18), which, whether it was written first or last, now sets the agenda for the reader and informs her understanding of the drama which follows. Although John[2] explores the heavenly backcloth in terms of the Logos or 'Word', he is in fact drawing on Jewish traditions about Sophia or Wisdom.[3] Wisdom in these traditions is the expression of God's activity in creation, revelation, redemption, and this expression is echoed at each point by the Johannine 'Word'. It was Wisdom who was there at the beginning of God's creative activity (Prov. 8.22-23; cf. Jn 1.1), who was with God (Wis. 9.9; Sir. 1.1; cf. Jn 1.1-2), who can be associated with light and life (Wis. 7.6; 8.13; cf. Jn 1.4-5), who came to the world but experienced only rejection, except perhaps in Israel (Sir. 24.8; cf. Jn 1.10-11). The parallels can be, and have been, multiplied, perhaps to the point where one begins to wonder whether it is only the modern scholar, moving at ease in a printed text from one to another book of the 'wisdom

repr. in M. Stibbe (ed.), *The Gospel of John as Literature: An Anthology of Twentieth Century Perspectives* (NTTS, 17; Leiden: Brill, 1993), pp. 165-82; S.M. Schneiders, 'A Case Study: A Feminist Interpretation of John 4.1-42', in *The Revelatory Text: Interpreting the New Testament as Sacred Scripture* (San Francisco: Harper, 1991), pp. 180-99.

1.   Similarly M. Scott (*Sophia and the Johannine Jesus* [JSNTSup, 71; Sheffield: JSOT Press, 1992]) seeks to integrate the pivotal role of 'Wisdom' in John's Prologue and Christology with the significance of women in the Gospel; see further below.

2.   I follow normal conventions in so referring to the author of the Gospel and assuming his gender.

3.   This has become a truism in modern scholarship; see Scott, *Sophia*; J. Ashton, 'The Transformation of Wisdom: A Study in the Prologue of John's Gospel', *NTS* 32 (1986), pp. 161-86, and most modern commentaries.

literature', who can perceive the coherent profile which matches at each point the Johannine *Logos*. However, suspending such scepticism, our question must be, 'What does Sophia do for Jesus?'; or, perhaps, 'What does Jesus do for Sophia?'.

'Wisdom' is in both Hebrew and Greek (the form in which John may have known the Scriptures) lexically female, and from Proverbs onwards this gender becomes an essential part of the literary and religious symbolism represented by Wisdom;[1] Wisdom/Sophia[2] is personified, and is personified as a female figure. Thus, once the presence of 'Wisdom' behind 'the Word [who] became flesh' in the Johannine Prologue is recognized, it seems only a small step to say, with Martin Scott, that for John 'Jesus Christ is none other than Jesus Sophia incarnate' and 'the Prologue is at the same time an introduction to Jesus as Sophia, the feminine face of God'.[3] Scott goes on to argue that it is not just in the Prologue that Wisdom provides a framework for the Johannine picture of Jesus, but that throughout the Gospel she continues to do so; the main features of Jesus' experience can be paralleled by Wisdom thought and specifically by the figure of Sophia: his intimacy with God (Prov. 8.30), the 'I am' sayings and the identification with truth, life and light (Prov. 8.12-14, 35-36; Sir. 24), his role as teacher (Sir. 4.11-12), his relationship with the Law and with the Spirit (Sir. 19.20; Wis. 7.22), and even the 'signs' (Wis. 11).[4] This means, for Scott, that 'the point of John's Wisdom Christology is precisely that Jesus Sophia is not mere man, but rather the incarnation of both the male and the female expressions of the divine, albeit within the limitations of human flesh', and that John presents 'a Jesus Sophia who is a unique blend of the male and female (Jesus is a *man* who exhibits all the characteristic traits of the *woman* Sophia)'.[5]

This may well seem to meet the finest aspirations of a feminist exegesis, to offer a solution to the old dilemma, 'How can a

1. For example Prov. 8.1-21; 9.1-6; Wis. 6.12-16; Sir. 16.18-31; see among others C. Camp, *Wisdom and the Feminine in the Book of Proverbs* (Sheffield: Almond Press, 1985).

2. The use of the Greek term *sophia* acts as a reminder of her feminine gender.

3. Scott, *Sophia*, p. 170.

4. See Scott, *Sophia*, pp. 115-68.

5. Scott, *Sophia*, pp. 172, 174.

male saviour redeem women?', and to suggest a model for future theological and christological exploration. Unfortunately (!), it is self-evidently simply not true. John has no interest in 'wisdom'; the term itself is as ominously absent from this Gospel, replete with the religious symbolic language of its day, as is 'knowledge' (*gnosis*)—whose absence is often intepreted as deliberate and as a polemic against those (gnostic) systems which claimed individual enlightenment through 'knowledge'.[1] It is not merely a male patriarchal exegesis which has failed to observe the significance of the wisdom motifs behind John's Word/Logos (masc.!)—although such an exegesis is easy enough to demonstrate;[2] the Gospel itself betrays no interest in them. It is not, as suggested by G. Tavard, that 'the nuptial elements of the image of Sophia should be transferred to the image of the Logos, who then becomes the feminine companion of God, pregnant with creation',[3] but that in that transference all femininity has been lost.[4] So too, if there are parallels in the continuing ministry of Jesus, and several are extremely strained, they are neither unique to wisdom, nor 'characteristic of the *woman* Sophia'; they are in no sense part of her gendered character and cannot be said to be an expression of the feminine (aspect of the divine or whatever). Because wisdom is sometimes described with feminine imagery, and because that image sometimes appears to be used deliberately for its gendered qualities, this

1.   Scott acknowledges this, attributes it to the problems posed by the feminine gender of 'Sophia' and the historical masculine gender of Jesus, and sees it as compensated in part by the prominent role accorded women in the Gospel. Yet this does not explain why John can ascribe other lexically feminine epithets to Jesus: life, resurrection, truth.

2.   Thus C.H. Dodd (*The Interpretation of the Fourth Gospel* [Cambridge: Cambridge University Press, 1953], pp. 273-76) recognizes the role of Wisdom speculation but never refers to the gender of 'Sophia'.

3.   G. Tavard, *Women in Christian Tradition* (Notre Dame: University of Notre Dame Press, 1973), p. 41.

4.   Compare A.-J. Levine, 'Who's Catering the Q Affair? Feminist Observations on Q Paraenesis', in L. Perdue and J. Gammie (eds.), *Paraenesis: Act and Form* (*Semeia* 50; Atlanta: Scholars Press, 1990), pp. 145-62, p. 155 on Q: 'since Sophia is a conventional motif in Wisdom literature, her direct association with Jesus may be less a "feminizing" of the teacher than a "masculinizing" of the mythical source of that teaching'.

does not mean that wherever wisdom imagery is to be found, it is consciously gendered and always consciously so used.[1] Nowhere is this more true than in the fourth Gospel, which uses imagery and symbols from a wide range of religious traditions and redefines them all through the person of Jesus. Yet because this refocusing through Jesus is, as we shall see, characteristic of all aspects of Johannine thought, John cannot be blamed for deliberately and specifically suppressing the wisdom Christology or 'Sophialogy' of an earlier tradition.[2]

This is not to deny the theological potential of the scriptural exploration of 'wisdom' or the apparent loss of such exploration in the early church. In its use of imagery drawn from the wisdom traditions the fourth Gospel does draw us to richer resources of scriptural language than Christian theology has always made use of. But the fourth Gospel can neither decide nor guarantee the usefulness of 'wisdom' for christological (or trinitarian) reflection; for those for whom all such reflection must have New Testament authorization, such may be found in Paul (1 Cor. 1.18-30) and in the Q traditions within the synoptic Gospels (Lk. 7.35; 11.49-51; 13.34-35).[3] John, however, would eschew any reliance on scriptural authority which claims independence from a response to the encounter with Jesus.

Narrative Images

1. *The Meeting at the Well*
Leaving aside, for the moment, the mother of Jesus (2.1-10), Jesus' first encounter with a woman is with the Samaritan woman at the well at Sychar (4.4-42). It is a narrative whose rich detail naturally asks to be read as more than an example of

1. See on this the useful analysis by M. Williams, 'Variety in Gnostic Perspectives on Gender', in K.L. King (ed.), *Images of the Feminine in Gnosticism* (Philadelphia: Fortress Press, 1988), pp. 2-22. See also the discussion by C.M. Tuckett, 'Feminine Wisdom in Q?', in Brooke (ed.), *Women in the Biblical Tradition*, pp. 112-28.

2. On 'Sophialogy' see Schüssler Fiorenza, *In Memory*, pp. 130-40.

3. See the optimistic J.M. Robinson, 'Very Goddess and Very Man: Jesus' Better Self', in King (ed.), *Images of the Feminine in Gnosticism*, pp. 113-27, and the caution by Tuckett, 'Feminine Wisdom?'; also Levine, 'Who's Catering?'.

Jesus' pastoral skill in dealing with individuals; for this reason traditional scholarship has tended to see the woman, if not from the start then increasingly, as a cipher, serving to underline both the falsity of Samaritan religion and the sole locus of all true worship in Jesus, the theme of 4.20-24.[1] At first glance this reading may seem to ignore the repeated stress that she is not just a Samaritan but a woman (so 4.7, 9, [11], 15, 17, 19, 25, 27; Samaritan only in 4.7, 9, 39-40), but as a woman she can also be set within the well-known scriptural tradition which represents Israel as faithless wife, deserting her true husband in pursuit of others (Hos. 1–3; Jer. 2.20, 32-33). Generally, modern scholarship has tended to reject seeing in the woman's previous five husbands (4.18) an allegorical allusion to the seven (!) deities worshipped by the Samaritans according to 2 Kgs 17.29-32; a 'scriptural' affinity between women, sexual promiscuity and religious infidelity, however, has proved less controversial and has ensured the retention of her moral unreliability as a symbol of Samaritan religion.[2]

However, to put the focus on the status of the Samaritans in this way is to devalue both the richness of the narrative and its allusions, and the assertive role—unusual in John where most (male) characters have a puppet-like quality—which is played by the woman as Jesus' dialogue partner. To dwell on the woman's moral status, which is nowhere judged by the text, is to collude with an assumption that the woman must carry the blame— even in a society where she would not normally initiate divorce.[3] A reading of the narrative shows rather that it is her gender and not her ethnic origin nor her (obvious?) moral stature which shocks Jesus' disciples when they find him talking with her (4.27).

Moreover, for the reader familiar with the stories of Israel's past, an encounter between 'the hero' and a strange woman at a well must needs be laden with potential meaning. It was there

---

1. Note the first and second person plurals in these verses; most commentaries discuss this.

2. B.F. Westcott (*The Gospel according to John* [London: John Murray, 1889], p. 67) is typical when he sees a contrast between 'The woman, the Samaritan, the sinner' and 'the Rabbi, the ruler of the Jews, the Pharisee' (i.e. Nicodemus in ch. 3).

3. Assuming that it is divorce and not Levirite law which explains her marital history.

that Abraham's servant met and identified the future bride of Isaac, Rebekah (Gen. 24.11-27). More directly, Jacob himself waited by the well and not only met there his bride-to-be, Rachel, but also drew the water for the sheep she guarded (Gen. 29.1-14). Later, sitting by a well, Moses was to water the sheep of the seven daughters of a priest of Midian and receive one of them in marriage (Exod. 2.15-22). So when Jesus, who has already turned water into wine at a wedding (Jn 2.1-10), and who has been identified as the bridegroom who possesses the bride (3.29), now comes and sits by the 'well of Jacob' where he is encountered by a woman coming to draw water (4.6-7), our expectations are inevitably raised. But what are we to expect? The offer of water, which dominates the early part of the dialogue (4.7-15), also evokes a range of scriptural passages, some of which carry sexual undertones (Prov. 5.15-18; Song 4.12, 15).[1] Yet, instead of the desideratum of kinship which marks both Rebekah and Rachel, she is a Samaritan, *verboten*.[2] By the end of the story the woman will appear not as potential bride but as having had five husbands and now with one who is no husband (4.18); the conversation will have swerved from the 'living water' which, although he has no bucket, Jesus will offer to her, to the conditions of true worship (4.10, 20-23). Jesus will remain by the well requiring no sustenance but to do the will of him who sent him (4.34). There is no wedding feast, only the flocking to Jesus of the crowds who no longer need the witness of the woman (4.39-42). While we may be tempted to let the Pentateuchal models provide an alternative ending with 'the Samaritan woman [being] led in the direction of being both re-created and remarried through a union with Jesus',[3] this is precisely what does not happen.

On one proposed reading, these scriptural allusions provoke in the reader, and much more in the woman, false expectations. For a moment we, as readers, wonder whether Jesus will after

---

1. Both C. Carmichael ('Marriage and the Samaritan Woman', *NTS* 26 [1980], pp. 332-46), and Eslinger ('The Wooing'), draw attention to this.

2. J. Neyrey ('Jacob Traditions and the Interpretation of John 4:10-26', *CBQ* 41 [1979], pp. 419-37) recognizes the Jacob allusions but integrates this with an interpretation which stresses the replacement of previous husbands with a true one.

3. Carmichael, 'Marriage and the Samaritan Woman', p. 341.

all follow the pattern of the patriarchs before him; but quickly we assume the insider's superiority from our prior experience of the deeper significance of water (3.5) and of the inappropriateness of all mundane (mis)understandings of Jesus (3.4). The woman, however, is trapped in the misconceptions bred by the echoes of the past; Scripture is a snare to her, forcing her to extricate herself from her embarassment and carnal expectations—reflected in her innuendoes about 'water' and the progeny of Jacob (4.12)—by a sudden grasp at respectability and theological discourse in the volte-face of 4.20.[1] This reading is a sobering one: while traditionally the perspicacity and persistence of the 'outcast' woman of Samaria have been contrasted with the obtuseness of the male 'insider' of the previous chapter, Nicodemus, here she loses even those virtues; once again, Scripture is being used to devalue (the) woman and her feminine potential.

Yet, although John does indeed know that Scripture may mislead those who rely on it without true understanding (5.39-40), it is patently the imagination of the commentators and not the text which has supplied the woman's embarassment at the 'exposure' of her marital past and has read into Jesus' words, 'You have said well' (4.17), a rebuke and a rejection of the sexual or marital innuendoes of the scene. Instead it is the woman who takes the initiative and turns the conversation in a new direction, and the woman who, unlike the brides of Genesis and Exodus, has a voice. Unlike them, it is not her family nor her male relatives who determine her significance but her own discovered identity. Although the narrative is ultimately about Jesus, who is 'greater than our father Jacob' (4.12), the woman too shapes the action and mediates the confession 'Truly this is the saviour of the world' (4.42): endogamy is replaced by universal hegemony.

2. The Mother of all Living
A persistent tradition of interpretation has seen in the mother of Jesus a reflection on the figure of Eve.[2] Never spoken of by

---

1.   So Eslinger, 'The Wooing'.
2.   There is a large bibliography; see the brief discussion in T.K. Seim, 'Roles of Women in the Gospel of John', in L. Hartman and B. Olsson (eds.), *Aspects of the Johannine Literature* (CB.NTS, 18; Uppsala: Almqvist & Wiksell, 1987), pp. 56-73, pp. 61-62.

name, she is in this Gospel either 'his mother' or 'the mother [of Jesus]', or, when addressed by Jesus, simply 'woman' (Jn 2.4; 19.26)—an unusual maternal address often discussed in the commentaries.[1] So spoken of, she recalls to the predisposed reader the 'woman' who is also without name (Gen. 2.23: 'she shall be called "woman"'), and whose name, Eve, when acquired, means 'the mother of all life': indeed, for the Greek translation of the Scriptures her name is 'Life' (Gen. 3.20).

Despite John's predilection for the opening chapters of Genesis, this interpretation would carry little weight for the reader without any prior disposition, were it not for the little parable in Jn 16.21.[2] Here, Jesus, anticipating his coming departure, speaks of the joy it will bring to the world, the grief to the disciples. Yet their grief will be transformed to joy. There follows a mini-parable, a rarity in this Gospel: 'The woman when she is in labour has grief, because her hour has come. When she gives birth to the child, she no longer remembers her tribulation because of the joy that a human [man] has been born into the world'.[3] This woman, also identified only as a, or the, woman,[4] acts as a bridge to the mother of Jesus by the cross (19.26, 'woman'!): for John the cross marks the coming of the hour (12.23; 13.1; 17.1; cf. 19.27); equally she is a bridge to the mother of Jesus at Cana who was told that Jesus' hour had not yet come (2.4, 'woman'!). At the same time she recalls Eve; in Gen. 3.16 Eve was promised 'grief' in childbearing—a word which is not otherwise used of physical pain; it is this—the same word in the Greek ($\lambda\upsilon\pi\acute{\eta}$)— which the woman of Jn 16.21 experiences. In Gen. 4.1 Eve rejoices, or so we must assume, because she has acquired not a child but, unexpectedly, a man: 'With the help of the Lord I have

1. As is often pointed out this is not a rude address in Greek as it appears to be in English translation, but it remains unexpected and perhaps distant when used of one's mother.

2. On what follows see A. Feuillet, 'L'heure de la femme (Jn 17,21) et l'heure de la mère de Jésus (Jn 19,25-27)', *Bib* 47 (1966), pp. 169-84, 361-80, 557-73. J. Michl ('Der Weibessame [Gen 3,15] in spätjüdischer und frühchristlicher Auffassung', *Bib* 33 [1952], pp. 371-401, 476-505) notes that the identification of 'woman' in Jn 2.4 and 19.26 with Eve is not found until the sixteenth century. The links are clearer in Rev. 12.

3. Translations are my own unless otherwise indicated.

4. The article is used, but this could be generic.

acquired a man'; so too this woman experiences the joy that a man is born into the world. Elsewhere in the Gospel the one who has come into the world is Jesus (3.16; 6.14; 9.39 etc.).

A second, not incompatible, line of interpretation notes that this woman recalls Jerusalem as a woman in Isa. 66.7: 'Before she was in labour she gave birth; before her pain came upon her she was delivered of a son' (NRSV). From the Qumran hymns (1QH. 3.7-12) it appears that this verse was already being interpreted messianically.[1] A further source for the image might be Isa. 26.17-19, 'Like a woman with child who writhes and cries out in her pangs, when she is near her time, so were we because of you, O Lord; we were with child, we writhed...Your dead shall live, their corpses shall rise'. (NRSV). The woman whose grief will turn to joy points forward to the resurrection hope.

But what meaning can this have? Of Jn 16.21 Raymond Brown says,

> In harmony with the symbolism wherein the combined death and resurrection of Jesus is represented by the messianic birth of a child, John sees the disciples' suffering at the death of Jesus as *thlipsis* [tribulation] which precedes the emergence of the definitive divine dispensation.[2]

He goes on to interpret the scene before the cross in the light of 16.21 as the birthpangs: 'In this climactic hour men are recreated as God's children'; Mary (*sic*), evoking Zion, is the mother of all Christians/the Beloved Disciple; she is, at the same time, the New Eve.[3] The slipperiness of the symbolism is acknowledged here, but this interpretation similarly obscures the woman: both in experience and in Scripture, the birthpangs are suffered by the woman, not the child who is born; to transfer them implicitly to the messiah/Jesus or even to the disciples/the new community is to destroy the potency of the image and the intertextuality. But unlike Luke, who anticipates Mary's anguish (Lk. 2.35), John assigns to Jesus' mother no emotion at the cross, or before—she suffers no grief. Yet, in contrast to the other Gospels, it is only John who mentions her presence at the cross, and, doing so, puts

---

1.   See Hanson, *Prophetic Gospel*, pp. 185-86.

2.   R.E. Brown, *The Gospel According to John*, II (AB, 29a; Garden City, NY: Doubleday, 1970), p. 733.

3.   Brown, *John*, pp. 925-27.

her in first place and centres the scene on her. So, we must ask, is her presence necessary as a birthing?[1]

3. *The Woman in the Garden*

Before we follow this path further we should become aware of the other echoes of the primeval story in John's passion narrative. Alone of all the Gospels, John has Jesus' crucifixion and his burial—and so also the resurrection experiences—happen in the same place, and he alone identifies the location as 'a garden': 'There was in the place where he was crucified a garden, and in the garden a new tomb in which no-one had yet been laid' (Jn 19.41). Since it was also in a garden that Jesus was betrayed (18.2), the whole passion narrative becomes identified as belonging to a 'garden'.[2] The garden recalls the garden of Genesis 2–3, the scene of creation from the dust, of the tree of life, and of Adam and 'the woman'.[3] In the garden of the burial and resurrection too a woman is present and is, initially, addressed just as that: 'woman' (Jn 20.13, 15). This is Mary Magdalene who was also at the cross (Jn 19.25) but who has had no active role until now. It would be wrong to read into this Mary's presence elements from her depiction in the other Gospels where she seems to take a leading role which stretches back into Jesus' ministry (Lk. 8.2-3; Mk 15.40, 47; 16.1); for John she is as yet a character without a profile.[4]

1.   F.M. Braun (*La Mère des fidèles* [Paris: Casterman, 1953]) sees her presence as necessary as the enemy of the serpent (Gen. 3.15) at the moment of its defeat.

2.   The popular idea of 'the garden of Gethsemane' is a conflation of the Johannine garden and the synoptic 'place called Gethsemane' (Mk 14.32). On what follows see E. Hoskyns, 'Genesis I-III and St John's Gospel', *JTS* 21 (1920), pp. 210-18, and N. Wyatt, '"Supposing him to be the Gardener" (John 20,15): A Study of the Paradise Motif in John', *ZNW* 81 (1990), pp. 21-38.

3.   Wyatt ('"Supposing him to be the Gardener"') over-develops the associations by adding the 'king as gardener' motif from other ancient Near Eastern traditions (cf. Jn 20.15). See also M. Alexandre, *Le Commencement du Livre Genèse I-V: La version grecque de la Septante et sa réception* (Christianisme Antique, 3; Paris: Beauchesne, 1988), pp. 244-45 on Greek translations of 'garden'; Aquila uses John's Greek term while the Septuagint uses *paradeisos*.

4.   See on this and what follows J.M. Lieu, 'The Women's

The significance of the ensuing scene within a Johannine context has often been noted: she, fulfilling Jesus' own words imaging the good shepherd and his sheep (10.3), is called by name and recognizes his voice (20.16). Because she is commissioned with the message of Jesus' resurrection-ascension her role as 'apostle to the apostles' (20.17) has been celebrated in feminist reconstructions,[1] although perhaps with over-optimistic inattention to the ambiguity of that task: the message she bears is directed to Jesus' new brothers. If there is a new creation in this chapter it comes instead in Jesus' breathing into the disciples (20.21), as God breathed into Adam (Gen. 2.7): although John's use of 'disciples' is significantly neutral and rarely tied to a specific number of identified (male) followers, the description of the absent Thomas as 'one of the twelve [who] was not with them' (20.24) creates the supposition that this too was a male experience.[2]

There is in Scripture another woman in a garden, the woman of the Song of Songs (Song 5.1; 6.2). This woman can say, 'I sought him and did not find him, I called him and he did not answer me' (Song 5.6); in John, Mary Magdalene also seeks him (Jn 20.14) but it is he who calls her and demands her answer. The story teases us with its language of myrrh (see Song 5.5), which this Mary did not bring to the garden, but which another Mary had poured over Jesus' head (Jn 12.1-10), with the woman telling of how she had put off her garment and washed her feet (Song 5.3; cf. Jn 13.4-5). The second letter of John is addressed to a nameless 'elect lady' (2 Jn 1); most commentators would agree that she is not an individual but a personification of the church. It is a personification which may draw its imagery from the Song; for this woman too is 'elect' (Song 6.9)—and her love song was (to become) the song of Israel with her God.[3]

Resurrection Testimony', in S. Barton and G.N. Stanton (eds.), *Resurrection: Essays in Honour of J.L. Houlden* (London: SPCK, 1994).

1.   Schüssler Fiorenza, *In Memory*, p. 332; Brown ('Roles of Women', p. 190) notes the long history of this epithet.

2.   John rarely speaks of 'the twelve' (6.67-71), but an experienced reader would have known that this was an exclusively male group; in turn, this suggests that 'brothers' (20.17) is exclusive.

3.   That there is an echo of the Song in 2 John is suggested by M. Hengel, *The Johannine Question* (trans. J. Bowden; London: SCM

Once again, discernment of apparent echoes of the Hebrew Scriptures is easier than their interpretation. As we shall see, for John the primeval history is far more formative than Israel's 'salvation history', and this has its own importance for a feminist reading. But at the narrative level the presence of the woman in that evocation of 'the beginning' and in the fulfilment of 'the hour' seems both an essential element and resistant to any precise interpretation. Neither the mother of Jesus nor the 'new' woman in the garden is Eve; attempts to see a new Adam (Jesus) and new Eve (Jesus' mother) in the scene by the cross, or a new humanity or family, can only be made to fit the Johannine text by ignoring again the actual dynamics of the narrative. Yet these women are not accidental figures on the stage; in each case a woman is the essential and 'scriptural' mediator of narrative action.

4. *Birth and Rebirth*
One of the most distinctive models of the fourth Gospel is that of birth. '"In very truth I tell you, unless someone is born from above, they cannot see the Kingdom of God". Nicodemus says to him, "How can a man when he is old be born? Can he enter his mother's womb a second time and be born?"' (Jn 3.3-4). In the Prologue those who receive the word-in-the-world are given power 'to become children of God...born not of blood, nor of fleshly desire, nor of male desire but of God' (1.12-14). The images, 'born anew/from above', 'born of God', are not identical and should not be harmonized, even when the first letter John independently gives free rein to the assurance given true believers that they are born of God (1 Jn 3.9; 4.7; 5.1, 4, 18).[1] The background of this imagery of birth or birth anew remains elusive. Pagan parallels are inexact and of uncertain date, and do little to guide us. The description of Israel or of individuals as child(ren) or son(s) of God (Exod. 4.22; Deut. 32.5-6; Wis. 12.19-20) does not take us far enough. The passage which brings us closest is Deut. 32.18, 'You were unmindful of the rock that bore

---

Press, 1989), p. 170 n. 61, and was independently pointed out to me by my research student Ms Julie Harris.

1. See J.M. Lieu, *The Theology of the Johannine Epistles* (NT Theology; Cambridge: Cambridge University Press, 1991), pp. 33-39.

you, you forgot the God who gave you birth', which in turn reminds us of the maternal God of prophecy and psalmody (Hos. 11.1-4; Isa. 42.14; Ps. 139.13). Perhaps, then, Nicodemus is not totally deluded when he asks whether one can or must again enter the mother's womb: Johannine irony usually works not through total misunderstanding but through partial misunderstanding or through a level of truth which the speaker does not intend (as in Jn 11.49-52; 7.41-42). So here we should not think of a dualism in which that birth again/from above is alien to and contrasted with the birth from a mother: for John earthly experience is a 'sign' which points to and enfleshes divine truth. God is already the one who has carried you 'from the womb' (Isa. 46.3), and is already the one who has given birth to those who are called to recognize it.

5. *Women as Mediators of Scriptural Images of Salvation*
The mother of Jesus present at a marriage, the woman who comes to draw water, Mary and Martha mourning the loss of a brother and receiving the assurance of life, Mary anointing Jesus, the nameless woman giving birth, experiencing pain and joy— the women of the fourth Gospel mediate images of salvation which are drawn from the Scriptures. They are images which belong with the promise of nourishment, even nourishment by self-giving (6.51), of the gift of water to drink out of the belly/womb (7.37-39),[1] which Jesus himself both mediates and incarnates. There is more here than the fact that the other men of the Gospel are not mediators of scriptural hope, or that these images are drawn from the Wisdom traditions with their 'feminine' ethos. Through these images of nurture, with their mediators, the fourth Gospel returns us to a search through Scripture for alternatives to the traditional but largely un-Johannine language of king and kingdom, dominion and final judgment.

The Significance for a Feminist Reading of Attitudes to the Hebrew Scriptures and to Judaism

There is nothing transparent about John's Gospel. It invites the reader into an encounter with the text, with the Word who

---

1.   The same word in Greek; grammar and phrasing in 7.37-39 make it debatable whether 'his belly' refers to the believer or Jesus.

became flesh, an encounter in which there can be no neutrality. Yet in this encounter new possibilities are hinted at, old securities challenged. It is in these possibilities more than in any new certainties that the Gospel has most to offer.

As we have seen more than once, the opening chapters of Genesis are particularly important for John—far more so than the story of God's dealings with Israel, than exodus, covenant or prophetic promise. Jesus can only be understood by reaching back before Abraham (cf. Mt. 1.1) to the very beginning of creation (Jn 1.1; Gen 1.1). At the end Jesus breathes spirit into his disciples (Jn 20.22; Gen 2.7). In between, the murderous intents of Cain/Jews (8.44) are transcended when Jesus lays down his own life, while Eve's pain in childbirth issues in the birthing of the one 'who comes' (16.21: see above). The beginning is no longer a template for the cycle of domination and mortality but reveals its potential as life-giving power.

For John Scripture finds its goal and its meaning in Jesus. Because Jesus as goal defines the past there is no prior 'salvation history' or preparation for him: 'Before Abraham was I am' (Jn 8.58). Although it is this Gospel which speaks of Abraham's rejoicing (8.56), of Jacob's well and progeny (4.12) and of the manna given by Moses (6.31-32), these are not sources of salvation, for that is to be found in Jesus alone: Jn 5.39-40, 45—'You search the Scriptures because you think that in them you have eternal life, and it is they who testify about me; but you do not want to come to me to have life...There is one who accuses you, Moses, in whom you set your hope'—provides the key to this and to our reflection on it. Jesus supersedes the tradition of the patriarchs, or rather shows that in themselves they are void and even deceptive. It is a woman who asks him, 'Are you greater than our father Jacob?' (4.12), to which, the reader knows, there can only be one answer. Jesus brings freedom from a slavery (8.31-33) that those who rely on their descent from Abraham, on the structures from the past as they have understood them, fail to perceive.

Soaked in the language and imagery of Scripture, John denies Scripture any significance except as measured by and defined by Jesus. A feminist exegesis will welcome the emptying of power of the structures of Scripture, the exposure of 'seeking glory from men' (5.41-44), the setting of Jesus as the source of life over against all appeals to Scripture (5.39-47); it will claim as its own particularly a Jesus who freely speaks with a woman and ignores the restrictions men and Jews place on her freedom (4.27, 9), who defends a woman against 'the Law of Moses' (8.5),[1] and who chooses a woman as his first witness against traditional interpretation of the law on valid witness (20.11-18).[2]

But the path is not so simple: it is now a familiar tale that in order to preserve the uniqueness of a Jesus supportive of women, feminists have colluded in the anti-Judaism which has distorted both church and scholarship.[3] It is an anti-Judaism which can claim this Gospel as its nourisher: in emptying past history of its power, and making Jesus the sole meaning and focus of Scripture, John has put a radical question mark by the claim of the Jews to be 'his own' (1.11); they are 'not from God' (8.47), but are of a father who is the devil (8.44).[4] Some feminist exegesis has equally denied God's presence in Jewish or 'Old Testament' experience; does John's path, with all its potential, inevitably lead to such a goal?

All who come to Scripture are addressed by that deep irony of Jn 5.39, 45, 'You search the Scriptures because you think that in them you have eternal life...your accuser is Moses in whom you set your hope'. So too for those who want to maintain for themselves a place within the biblical heritage by seeking in Scripture the resources for understanding and affirming women's experience, John both shares their search and warns that such allegiance to Scripture may prove deceptive and excluding from life.

1. This passage is not part of the original text of John, but may be considered with it from usage and tradition.

2. See B. Witherington, III, *Women in the Ministry of Jesus* (Cambridge: Cambridge University Press, 1984), pp. 9, 118-23, 130.

3. See J. Plaskow, 'Feminist Anti-Judaism and the Christian God', *JFSR* 7 (1991), pp. 99-108.

4. I have explored the anti-Judaic potential of John's attitude to Scripture from a biblical theology perspective in J.M. Lieu, 'The Johannine Literature and Biblical Theology', in S. Pedersen (ed.), *Problems in Biblical Theology* (Leiden: Brill, forthcoming).

A SYMBOLIC LEVEL OF MEANING:
JOHN 2.1-11 (THE MARRIAGE IN CANA)

Lyn M. Bechtel

Many scholars have recognized that the language of the Gospel of John is symbolic in nature.[1] Nevertheless, they are often reluctant to pursue a symbolic level of meaning while reading it. Generally, this relates to the fact that western, individual-oriented thinking communicates its essential truths through a historical narrative mode of communication. In this type of communication 'truth' is conveyed by relating specific events, as experienced by specific individuals and described in their chrono-logical place in time. The emphasis is on the unique and the individual. This type of communication is explicit, with themes and essential truth being presented, primarily, diachronically. People in individual-oriented societies are socialized to assume that this is the only valid mode of communication, and any other mode is inferior or false. It is often assumed that in pursuing a symbolic level of meaning, the literal and historical value of the text is discounted or eliminated and the text turned into allegory.

In contrast to individual-oriented societies, the concern in group-oriented societies is the ability to universalize truth, so that it can continue to speak to and represent the experience of the group, generation after generation. Consequently, group-oriented societies rely heavily on a symbolic mode of commu-nication, in which truth is conveyed through metaphors and symbols set against a historical or quasi-historical background.

1. For example C.K. Barrett, *Essays on John* (Philadelphia: Westminster Press, 1982), and *The Gospel according to St. John* (Philadelphia: Westminster Press, 1978); W. Meeks, 'The Man from Heaven in Johannine Sectarianism', *JBL* 91 (1974), pp. 44-72.

The symbols and metaphors are the main means of communication, the medium for expressing value, the transmitters of culture and regulators of experience,[1] so they are never empty or meaningless.[2] The symbolic mode of communication expresses both the surface, explicit meaning, and the hidden, implicit meaning that gives depth to the literal or surface meaning.[3] Hence, the symbolic mode of communication is ideal as the language of revelation. Themes and essential truth are presented both diachronically (literally) and synchronically (symbolically), with the synchronic level giving depth and complexity to the diachronic level and the diachronic level limiting the range of the synchronic level. Thus, the relationship between the two levels of meaning is similar to that of harmony and melody in music.

According to the social anthropologist Mary Douglas,[4] people in small, well-bonded, group-oriented communities (like the Johannine community) often rely on a 'restricted speech code' or an extensive system of metaphors and symbols,[5] intended to communicate to the group, but not explicitly to outsiders. In this type of communication each symbolic or metaphoric utterance has a double purpose: it conveys literal information and, therefore, functions significantly on a literal level; but it also functions symbolically, shaping the group's social identity by expressing, embellishing or reinforcing the overall social structure. The second function is the dominant one.[6] Such language functions as a bonding mechanism that helps hold the group together. It is this type of language—an extensive, restricted code of symbolic language—that is chosen in John to couch the theology of the community; to convey the life and ministry of Jesus; to express the community's trauma of separation from Judaism; and to formulate a new social identity for it.[7]

---

1. M. Douglas, *Natural Symbols* (New York: Vintage Books, 1973).

2. According to Douglas (*Natural Symbols*), 'Symbols can be rejected; they can be changed, but we cannot do without symbols altogether'.

3. Barrett, *Essays on John; The Gospel according to St. John*.

4. *Natural Symbols*, after Basil Bernstein.

5. Meeks, 'The Man from Heaven'.

6. Douglas, *Natural Symbols*.

7. This is similar to Meeks, 'The Man from Heaven', pp. 44-72.

The literal/historical and symbolic levels of communication are stressed in several of the stories in the Gospel. For example, in the scene with Nicodemus (3.1-14) Jesus speaks symbolically of being born 'from above' (a heavenly origin), yet Nicodemus misunderstands the intended meaning of the phrase and asks, 'How can a person be born when he is old?' Or, in the cleansing of the temple (4.19-22), Jesus says, 'Destroy this temple and in three days I will raise it up'. The Jews reply, 'It has taken forty-six years to build this temple and you will raise it up in three days?' The Jews hear Jesus on a literal level, but Jesus is speaking symbolically of the 'temple of his body' being raised in the resurrection. In both cases the symbolic level is intended for communicating to the Johannine group, but outsiders miss its meaning.

Bible scholars recognize that the Gospel originated in a Jewish-Christian milieu, so it reflects a distinctive Hebraic character.[1] Because ancient Israel was group-oriented, its literature relied on a symbolic mode of communication. Consequently, the same methods of interpretation that are vital to understanding the group-oriented Hebrew Scriptures can also be used to understand the Gospel of John. Therefore, I would like to approach the story of the marriage in Cana as a group-oriented, symbolic communication. Since the literal/historical implications of the story have been well articulated within New Testament scholarship, I will focus primarily on the symbolic level of the story and how it helps create an identity and theology for the Johannine community. I will discuss the historical implications only when they inform and are critical to the symbolic implications.

As a foundation for understanding the story, the historical setting from which the Gospel arises needs to be articulated.

---

1.   R.T. Fortna, *The Fourth Gospel and its Predecessor* (Philadelphia: Fortress Press, 1988); *idem, The Gospel of Signs: A Reconstruction of the Narrative Source Underlying the Fourth Gospel* (Cambridge: Cambridge University Press, 1970); R. Kysar, *The Fourth Evangelist and his Gospel: An Examination of Contemporary Scholarship* (Minneapolis: Augsburg, 1975); *John* (Minneapolis: Augsburg, 1986); H.M. Teeple, *Literary Origin of the Gospel of John* (Evanston, IL: Religion and Ethics Institute, Inc., 1974); and others.

Louis Martyn has carefully demonstrated that John was written
at a time when the Jewish people of the Johannine community
were in the process of 'separating' from Judaism (as seen, for
example, in 9.22, 12.42 and 16.2). Within the synagogue community it was assumed that the beliefs of these Jewish-Christians
'lead people astray' (see for example 7.47), so that the Jewish-
Christians were being 'excommunicated' from the synagogue,
separated from their Jewish roots.[1] This separation creates an
identity crisis for the Johannine community. In the past their
lives and identity have revolved around the traditions, customs
and authority of Judaism, but now they have been separated
from that foundation. Who are they 'now', since they are no
longer a part of the Jewish community? What are they to rely on,
since they can no longer rely on the traditions, stability and
authority of Judaism? It is like the crisis of the maturation
process where, in order to establish individual identity, there
must be separation from the mother, separation from the matrix
of one's being. In character with the identity formation process,
John portrays the community in binary opposition to their
matrix, the Jewish community, thereby shaping and distin-
guishing their new identity. At the formative level the contrast is
essential, so that the differentiation process may commence.[2]
Consequently, Judaism becomes the old religion, tied to the
traditions of the past and espousing knowledge of and orientation toward the human world, that is, 'worldly wisdom'.[3] In
contrast, Jesus is portrayed as a descending/ascending savior
(see for exampe 3.13-14, 31-33; 6.32-38, 41-42; 8.23, 28) with
'heavenly wisdom' who comes into his matrix, the 'world of
Judaism'. But Jesus is rejected (5.43) by the 'world of Judaism',
and is accepted only by the Johannine community. Because they
believe in Jesus, the Johannine community too are rejected by

1.   See J.L. Martyn, *History and Theology in the Fourth Gospel*
(Nashville: Abingdon Press, 1979).

2.   Many mothers can identify with this. As my own daughter was
going through adolescent maturation, I became 'the Wicked Witch of
the North', so that she could differentiate herself and form her separate
identity.

3.   It is interesting to note that the polemic against Judaism is similar
to the polemic against the Canaanites in the Hebrew Bible. It is an
identity formation issue.

the 'world of Judaism'. In 15.18-19 Jesus says,

> If the world hates you, know that it has hated me before it hated you. If you are 'of the world', then the world loves its own. But because you are 'not of the world', but I chose you out of the world, therefore the world hates you.

Now, the community's sense of being 'rejected' parallels that of Jesus. The Johannine community is a community of 'orphans' (14.18) who can 'know' and understand Jesus and 'heavenly wisdom':[1] 'knowing' and 'not knowing' function significantly within the text.

This is a painful period for the Jewish-Christian people, because it entails a radical change and reformulation of their identity. But with the destroying of the old comes the building of the new[2]—in this case, a new covenant community with new communal bonding. Part of the function of John is to formulate a new identity for the community, one that is separated from the Jewish world and united with Jesus Christ, the descending/ascending savior who is not of this world.

John 2.1-11

> 1 On the third day there was a marriage in Cana of Galilee, and the mother of Jesus was there. 2 Invited to the marriage was Jesus with his disciples.[3]

The story begins with the metaphor 'on the third day'. Many commentators have assumed that the phrase functions only on a literal or historical level and has no symbolic value.[4] Some feel that it simply means 'on the third day of the week', the third day after the call of Philip and Nathanael,[5] while others feel it is the

1. See Meeks, 'The Man from Heaven'.
2. See the book of Jeremiah, where this theme is pivotal.
3. The translations are my own.
4. R. Bultmann, *The Gospel of John* (Oxford: Basil Blackwell, 1971); Fortna, *The Fourth Gospel*; Barrett, *The Gospel according to St. John*; R. Schnackenburg, *The Gospel according to St. John*, I (New York: Crossroad, 1989).
5. Fortna (*The Fourth Gospel*) feels that the phrase forms a textual break, added by John to show that the previous events are a period of new creation that culminate in the marriage sign.

third day after the baptismal scene.[1] I will conclude with Brown and others that it is the third day after the baptism of Jesus: then, on the first day there is the calling of Andrew and Peter; on the second day the calling of Philip and Nathanael; and on the third the marriage in Cana. Although this scheme could refer to actual events, it can also tie the story to Jesus' resurrection. In Rom. 6.3-4, Paul connects baptism with being baptized into the death of Jesus:

> Do you not know that all of us who have been baptized into Christ Jesus are baptized into his death? We are buried, therefore, with him by baptism into death, so that as Christ was raised from the dead by the glory of the Father, we too might walk in newness of life.

It could therefore be expected that if being baptized into Jesus Christ signifies a type of death, then the events of the third day should foreshadow resurrection. Finally, in Jn 2.11 the text states that the marriage in Cana on the third day is the first of the signs that point to Jesus' honor or glory (*doxa*). Jesus' *doxa* is his resurrection. Consequently, the possibility that this phrase functions simultaneously on an explicit literal level, indicating the third day of the week after the baptism of Jesus, and on an implicit symbolic level, pointing to Jesus' resurrection, should be entertained.[2] If this is the case, the metaphor 'on the third day' establishes the focus of a story, which adds depth of meaning to Jesus' resurrection for the Johannine community. Since the story comes at the beginning of the Gospel, long before Jesus' actual death, it suggests that resurrection into new life happens during a person's lifetime as well as after physical death (cf. the story of Nicodemus, which espouses the same understanding of resurrection).

The setting for the story is a marriage, the bonding together of

---

1. R.E. Brown *The Gospel according to John* (AB, 29; Garden City, NY: Doubleday, 1966), after Theodore of Mopsuestia.

2. Schnackenburg (*Gospel according to St. John*) feels that on the surface it is a simple miracle story, but the reference to 'hour' and the lavish quantity of wine point to a much deeper meaning. Bultmann (*The Gospel of John*) feels that the story, along with the cleansing of the temple, is symbolic of Jesus' ministry and death and resurrection.

people in a new covenantal relationship.[1] Marriage is a point of transition and change in people's lives, a time of moving from one stage of life to a new one. It is one of life's crisis points; yet it also offers new possibilities, new bonding and new orientation. But in order to begin this new stage people need to separate from the past—from their matrix—and their past ties and orientation.

Next there is a geographical note which frames the story, occurring in vv. 1 and 11. The marriage takes place 'in Cana of Galilee'. Cana seems to have been a Jewish village, indicating that this is a Jewish wedding—though it should not be overlooked that this village is within easy reach of a significant Gentile population (in places like Sepphoris). This new beginning and new bonding happens within Judaism, but within reach of the Gentile world. The new begins in the womb of the old.

The text simply states that the mother of Jesus is 'there' at this Jewish wedding,[2] as if the mother of Jesus is an 'insider'. But Jesus and his disciples are 'invited' to the wedding, as if they are 'outsiders' who require special invitation.[3]

It is interesting that the first character to be mentioned in the story, even before Jesus and his disciples, is 'the mother of Jesus'—although a name is never given. If she is Mary, why is she not named but, instead, consistently called 'the mother of Jesus'? Most scholars feel that the reference to 'the mother of Jesus' is not symbolic, though they can give no convincing reasons why.[4] In a story where symbolism is so central, a

---

1. Fortna (*The Fourth Gospel*) suggests that the wedding feast is the symbol of the messianic age, the new age of revelation. E. Haenchen (*John: A Commentary on the Gospel of John* [Philadelphia: Fortress Press, 1984], I) feels that it is the sign of a coming time of salvation. Brown (*The Gospel according to John*) and Bultmann (*The Gospel of John*) stress that the wedding lasted seven days. Bultmann feels the wedding symbolizes the ministry of Jesus and the messianic importance behind the wedding symbol. The Synoptic tradition uses wedding and banquet symbolism in a messianic context, as does Isa. 62.5.

2. In the Hebrew Scriptures the mother is traditionally associated with arranging and securing marriages.

3. Bultmann (*The Gospel of John*) feels that the disciples are redactional since it is not necessary to have them present.

4. Barrett (*The Gospel according to St. John*), E.C. Hoskyn (*The*

symbolic and metaphorical value for 'the mother of Jesus' should be considered.

In the Hebrew Bible, culture and religion are often referred to as the people's 'mother'—their foundation, their matrix (and the same metaphor obtains in reference to the country, the territory, the community, the group, the nation). Jesus is a Jew; he descends into the world of Judaism, so his 'mother', his matrix, is Judaism.[1] John does not refer to 'the mother of Jesus' as Mary because he is not talking about Jesus' biological mother Mary. He is referring to Judaism, Jesus' matrix; let us note that there is no birth narrative in John, in spite of 'the word became flesh' in 1.14. The metaphor establishes Jesus' tie to Judaism and presents Judaism as the locus of Jesus' identity.

> 3 Lacking wine, the mother of Jesus said to him, 'They have no wine.' 4 And Jesus said to her, 'What with me and with you, Woman (*gunai* [vocative])? My hour has not yet come.' 5 His mother said to the servants, 'Do whatever he says to you.'

At this Jewish wedding wine is lacking. The statement of the mother of Jesus is a simple declaration of fact[2] and, as it stands, contains no request for a miracle,[3] as many scholars have assumed.[4] Although many are preoccupied with why the

---

Fourth Gospel [London: Faber & Faber, 1947]), Brown (*The Gospel according to John*) and Bultmann (*The Gospel of John*) suggest that 'the Mother of Jesus' is Mary who is the church, the 'New Eve'.

1.   Israel is frequently portrayed as a woman in the Hebrew Bible (see for example Jer. 3.1-5; Ezek. 16.1-63; 23.1-49; Amos 5.2; Hosea's 'wife' theme).

2.   M.-E. Boismard, *Du Baptême à Cana* (Paris: Cerf, 1956), pp. 133-159.

3.   As Brown (*The Gospel According to John*) points out, why would the messiah be expected by Judaism to perform miracles? There is no miracle tradition associated with the messiah in the Hebrew Scriptures. Cf. Boismard, *Du Baptême à Cana*.

4.   Many simply assume she is requesting a miracle: for instance Brown, *The Gospel according to John*; Fortna, *The Fourth Gospel*; Schnackenburg, *Gospel according to St. John*; T.J. Korkukch, 'These are Written that You May Believe that Jesus is the Christ, the Son of God' (MA dissertation; Drew University Graduate School, 1991). Bultmann (*The Gospel of John*) suggests that the story teaches us that 'help for all man's perplexity is to be found in the miracle of the revelation'.

shortage occurs,[1] I would rather focus on the significance of the shortage than speculate about its reasons. At a joyful celebration of a new stage in life, wine is used to celebrate and express joy. There is an old Jewish saying, 'Without wine, there is no joy' (*b. Pes.* 109a). The implication for the present occasion is obvious.

In v. 4 Jesus responds to this simple declaration of fact with an abrupt and unexpected reply that undergirds the symbolic quality of the story. Jesus says, 'What with me and with you, woman?' A clue to the meaning of this phrase can be found in its use in the Hebrew Scriptures (Judg. 11.12; 1 Kgs 17.18; Hos. 14.8), where it suggests a lack of relationship or even outright discord or hostility.[2] Here it seems to suggest the breaking of a relationship, namely Jesus' relationship with Judaism, his cultural foundation.

Jesus calls his mother 'woman', which is startling. Although it would *not* be improper or disrespectful to address an ordinary woman in this way (as he often does; see 4.21, 8.10, 20.13, 15), it is inappropriate to call his mother 'woman'.[3] It has a distancing effect that is inappropriate within the family. Although, as Korkukch points out, Jesus is not portrayed in the synoptic Gospels as having 'traditional' family relations (see for instance Mk 3.35),[4] John uses this theme of family relations in a slightly different way. In both his comment, 'what with me and with you', and in his addressing his mother as 'woman', Jesus is distancing himself, separating himself, from his matrix, from Judaism—in the same way that the Jewish folks of the Johannine community have been separated from their matrix, from

1. J.H. Bernard, *A Critical and Exegetical Commentary on the Gospel according to St. John* (Edinburgh: T. & T. Clark, 1928), I; Bultmann, *The Gospel of John*; Haenchen, *John*.

2. It is more of a distancing remark than a clear refusal to act—as Bultmann (*The Gospel of John*), Fortna (*The Fourth Gospel*), and others infer. Brown (*The Gospel according to John*) suggests that it indicates a situation where people are asked to get involved when it is not their business.

3. Fortna (*The Fourth Gospel*) and others. Brown (*The Gospel according to John*) stresses that his address is not a rebuke, nor does it show lack of affection, but it is peculiar for a son to address his mother in such a way.

4. Korkukch, 'These are Written that You May Believe', p. 38.

Judaism, their religious and cultural foundation.

Then Jesus says, 'My hour has not yet come'.[1] The metaphor 'my hour'[2] is a theological concept vital to John. It refers to the 'hour' of Jesus' death (12.27) and, most of all, his resurrection when he will be glorified (12.23; 13.1; 17.1). Jesus' 'hour' is a point of transition and change that also initiates transition and change in the lives of his followers (4.21, 23; 5.25, 28; 16.21, 32). Stating that Jesus' hour is coming but, still, is not *quite* here (2.4; 7.30; 8.20) places the audience in a situation of anticipation.

The Mother of Jesus (Judaism) ignores or, more probably, simply 'does not understand' Jesus' strange statements and his distancing because her vision lies within the realm of Judaism. The dialogue with Nicodemus functions on a similar level. The address 'woman' (not 'Mary'), together with the fact that within Jewish tradition wisdom is personified as a woman, may suggest that Jewish wisdom is incapable of knowing 'the heavenly wisdom' of Jesus. Without this knowledge, the mother of Jesus simply directs the 'servants' to do whatever he tells them.

The 'servants' appear to be servants of Judaism, since they are serving at a Jewish wedding and pay attention to the Mother of Jesus. Yet they also do as Jesus tells them and become witnesses to what occurs. These Jewish servants may symbolize the Jewish folks within the Johannine community who have made the transition from one community to the other.

> 6 Six stone jars for the Jewish rite of purification[3] were standing there, each holding two or three measures. 7 Jesus

---

1.   Brown (*The Gospel according to John*) points out an alternative translation of this phrase supported by Gregory of Nyssa and Theodore of Mopsuestia: 'Has my hour not now come?', although he feels that *oude* is always used in John as a negative.

2.   Fortna (*The Fourth Gospel*) feels that this confrontational dialogue has been added by John to demonstrate that Jesus' greater objective of his 'hour' is more important than wine at a wedding. The request for a miracle is inappropriate but Jesus complies simply because it comes from his mother. Cf. Haenchen, *John*.

3.   It has been suggested that the phrase 'for the Jewish rites of purification' has been added to the Signs-Source material. The phrase is necessary in order to create the contrast between water/the forgiveness of sin and wine/the joy of new life.

said to them, 'Fill the jars with water.' And, they filled them to
the brim. 8 He said to them, 'Now, draw some out and take it
to the steward of the feast,' and they took it.

If the number six has a symbolic/metaphorical value here, that
value is not easy to determine. In light of the Johannine
Prologue and its references to the creation, the number may
relate to the sixth day of creation, the *penultimate* day. Along
the same line, scholars have pointed out that the number six is
symbolic of incompleteness, while the number seven is symbolic
of completeness.[1] The stone jars, which are related to the Jewish
rite of purification, are easier to deal with. Stone is used for
these jars because it is less likely than other materials to break or
be contaminated and made ritually impure.[2] In addition, stone
represents the permanence and stability of Judaism. The rite of
purification is a washing away or forgiveness of sin. When filled
to the brim, these jars provide an abundance of water—each jar
containing approximately twenty gallons. Judaism then provides
an abundance of purification, an abundance of forgiveness of
sins.[3] Yet, despite its purity, stability, permanence and abundance of forgiveness, it is incomplete.

There is scholarly controversy as to whether all the water in
the six jars is turned into wine or only part of it.[4] Yet v. 7
indicates that the six jars, symbolic of Judaism, are filled with
water to the brim, and v. 8 indicates that an undetermined
amount is 'drawn out' and taken to the steward. The 'drawing
out' represents the separation of Jesus and the Johannine
community from Judaism.

1.　See Barrett, *The Gospel according to St. John*; Kysar, *John*; Brown,
The Gospel according to John, though no one is comfortable assigning
symbolic value to the number.

2.　Brown (*The Gospel according to John*) suggests that the Levitical
laws of purity in ch. 11 may give a clue. Cf. Barrett, *The Gospel according
to St. John*.

3.　According to Schnackenburg (*Gospel according to St. John*), in the
Hebrew Scriptures 'abundance' is a sign of salvation (Isa. 29.17; Jer. 31.5;
Hos. 2.24; Joel 4.18; Amos 9.13).

4.　For example Brown, *The Gospel according to John*; Haenchen,
John; Barrett, *The Gospel according to St. John*.

9 When the steward of the feast tasted it, the water now had become wine. And he did not know where it came from, though the servants know who drew the water. The steward of the feast called the bridegroom 10 and said to him, 'Everyone serves the good wine first, and when they have drunk, then the poorer [wine]. But you have kept the good wine until now!'

At this point the 'not yet' of v. 4 and the 'now' of v. 8 collide—the expectation of the future penetrates the present.[1] The change comes when it is least expected and least noticed—like experiences during periods of rapid transition and change, when people are not prepared for what is happening.[2] In the process of being 'drawn out', the separated water is transformed into wine.[3] Water is used to purify, to remove sin from the past. Wine, particularly in the context of a marriage, is used to celebrate new life in the present. This suggests that forgiveness of sin, the separation from the sins of the past, is *incomplete* without transformation and without the celebration and joy of new life. And this transformation of water into wine occurs within the context of a marriage, the bonding together of people in a new covenantal relationship, a point of transition and change, a time of moving from one stage of life to another.

The change from water to wine symbolizes the change in the Johannine community, which has been separated or excommunicated from Judaism.[4] In the process of their separation these Jewish folks have been transformed into a new worshipping

1. Barrett, *Essays on John*.
2. From a suggestion of Professor K. Dey, in private conversation.
3. Bultmann (*The Gospel of John*) posits that the changing of the water into wine comes from traditions related to Dionysus of Syria, pagan epiphany of a god. But Haenchen (*John*) points out that the Dionysus tradition does not transform water into wine, so the transformation is lacking. A. Geyser ('The Semeion at Cana of Galilee', in *Studies in John* [Leiden: Brill, 1970], p. 19) suggests an anti-Baptist polemic, in which the wine of Jesus supersedes the water of purification. See Amos 9.13-14, a post-exilic addition, for the theme of the abundance of wine associated with messianic hope and restoration. R.E. Brown (*The Community of the Beloved Disciple* [New York: Paulist Press, 1979]) suggests a replacement theme in which the wine of Jesus' messiahship replaces the water of purification.
4. Schnackenburg, *Gospel according to St. John*.

community, where 'wine' replaces 'water'.[1] This new community is moving beyond mere removal of sin to the joy and the celebration of the power of 'new life'.[2] They are moving from an orientation to the past to a focus on a point of transition and change in the present.[3]

The steward of the wedding recognizes the change but does not 'know' where the wine comes from, because he does not 'know' Jesus[4] or understand Jesus' power to transform. Like Nicodemus, the 'steward' represents the Jewish world which has experienced Jesus, but does not 'know' him and cannot understand him. The Prologue of John states that 'true light' is coming into the world that was made through him, but that the world will not know him (1.9-10). 'He came to his own home, and his own people received him not' (1.11). In contrast to the steward, the servants do 'know' where the wine comes from because they are involved in the separation. 'Knowing' Jesus is key to the transformation of forgiveness of sins into the joy of new life.

The words of the steward to the bridegroom at the end of the story further clarify the nature of the change. The steward observes that it is the normal, expected social custom to serve the good wine first, when people's palates are sharp, and leave the poorer wine for last, when people are drunk and their palates are dull. Although scholars are unfamiliar with this maxim within the culture at the time, it may simply be a shrewd

---

1. Brown (*The Gospel according to John*) stresses the theme of replacement of worshiping in Jerusalem with Jesus, who is the real temple, as well as the replacement of the water of purification by wine, which is the blood of the grape.

2. Bultmann (*The Gospel of John*) has suggested the influence of the cult of Dionysus on this story. It is interesting to note that at Sepphoris, in the vicinity of Nazareth and Cana, a luxurious third-century CE Roman residence has a Dionysiac mosaic floor which portrays scenes from the life and cult of the god Dionysus, including a marriage in which the passage into a new stage of life is celebrated with wine and great joy. It is not a question of one tradition borrowing from the other, but two traditions dealing with the same theme in a similar way.

3. From a suggestion of Professor K. Dey, in private conversation.

4. Meeks ('The Man from Heaven') stresses that they do not know where Jesus came from, that he came from above.

practice common to human nature.[1] The point is: Jesus breaks with tradition and reverses the expected social conventions. People who understand 'worldly wisdom' are confused by the reversal and cannot understand the change. Only people who can understand 'heavenly wisdom' can understand Jesus' break with tradition.[2]

> 11 Jesus did this, the first of the signs (*semeia*), in Cana of Galilee, and he revealed his honor/glory (*doxa*), and his disciples believed in him.

The story ends by pointing out that this is the first of the signs (*semeia*)[3] that point to the resurrection and the honor/glory (*doxa*) of Jesus. *semeia* are events or actions that point to a deeper meaning and reality and make the origin, identity and significance of Jesus clearer.[4] Because of these signs, people will believe in Jesus (20.31). But how does this story reveal the honor/glory of Jesus? This first sign occurs 'on the third day', so it foreshadows Jesus' resurrection. The story deals with separation, transformation and the celebration of new life with wine— which is similar to the separation of the Johannine community from Judaism and their transformation or resurrection into new life, into a new worshipping community. John expands a traditional view of resurrection to include resurrection into new life now, during one's lifetime.

In Conclusion

Judaism, symbolized by 'the mother of Jesus', is the womb of Christianity. Jesus breaks his tie with Jewish tradition but does *not* reject it outright. At the end of the Gospel the mother of Jesus is standing at the foot of the cross. When Jesus sees his

---

1.   Brown, *The Gospel according to John*; Haenchen, *John*; Bultmann, *The Gospel of John*.

2.   Meeks, 'The Man from Heaven'; Fortna, *The Fourth Gospel*.

3.   John lays out numerous elaborated *semeia* (2.11, the first; 4.46-54, the second; 5.1-9; 6.1-14; 6.16-21; 9.1-16; 11.1-44), which are given so that people may believe 'in' Jesus, along with the mention of his signs (2.23; 3.2; 6.2, 26; 10.47; 12.37). Jesus' signs stand in tension with the people's expectation of signs (2.18; 4.48; 6.30).

4.   Barrett, *The Gospel according to St. John*.

mother and the beloved disciple, he says to his mother, 'Woman, behold, your son' (19.26). He again calls her 'woman', with the same distancing affect. Yet immediately he confirms his continuing bonding to her by saying, 'Behold, your son'. Jesus' mother is always his Mother. Then he says to the beloved disciple, 'Behold, your mother'. 'And from that hour onward the disciple took her into his own home' (19.27). Christianity's Mother is always its Mother. As Jesus confirms his continuing bonding to his Mother, so should Christianity.

Part III
ON THE GENDERING OF THE FEMALE BODY

EVE THROUGH SEVERAL LENSES: TRUTH IN 1 TIMOTHY 2.8-15

Beverly J. Stratton

When I wrote this essay, the church college where I teach was just beginning to develop a sexual violence policy, and the seminary where I am pursuing graduate studies was struggling to deal sensitively and appropriately with a student complaint. Worse, in countless homes and dorm rooms across the nation, men are lifting their hands in anger against their wives or partners. And this will not be the last time. 'I desire, then, that in every place the men should pray, lifting holy hands without anger or argument' (1 Tim. 2.8, NRSV).

A scantily clad woman leans seductively against an automobile in a television advertisement, suggesting to potential car buyers that women like her are part of the package deal. No wonder men think that women 'must have wanted it if they dressed like that', and women feel pressure to binge and purge, trying to make their more lumpy or less perfect bodies match those of the television models. 'Also that the women should dress themselves modestly and decently in suitable clothing, not with their hair braided, or with gold, pearls, or expensive clothes, but with good works, as is proper for women who profess reverence for God' (1 Tim. 2.9).

The American Association of University Women has recently publicized a study describing how the self-esteem of girls in the United States declines dramatically between elementary school and high school.[1] The loss of self-esteem for young women may be related to their absence from the curriculum or to the pattern

1. American Association of University Women, 1992, 'Short-changing Girls, Shortchanging America'. See also S. Daley, *New York Times*, January 9, 1992. Boys' self-esteem also drops, but not so dramatically.

of classroom interactions.[1] Boys do most of the talking in classes, and they receive the majority of comments from teachers. When this situation is pointed out and teachers attempt to change classroom dynamics, if girls talk for what turns out to be slightly more than one third of the time, everyone thinks the girls are getting more than their fair share of attention.[2] 'Let a woman learn in silence with full submission' (1 Tim. 2.11).

A letter from a colleague at a sister college notes that recent program cuts due to the current fiscal situation 'fit rather uncomfortable patterns, mainly having an effect on women faculty, part-time women faculty, etc.'[3] 'I permit no woman to teach or to have authority over a man; she is to keep silent' (1 Tim. 2.12).

It is difficult to find qualified applicants from under-represented groups, even for a faculty position in English or philosophy. No wonder there is only one American woman bishop and no women presidents in colleges of my denomination. The men just have more experience, that's all. 'For Adam was formed first, then Eve' (1 Tim. 2.13).

He: How was I supposed to know she really meant 'No'? Women are always saying 'no' when they really mean 'yes'. She: He said he loved me and we'd get married. I didn't think he'd abandon me once he found out I was pregnant. 'And Adam was not deceived, but the woman was deceived and became a transgressor' (1 Tim. 2.14).

A pregnant HIV-positive woman fights to stop using drugs, and worries that her baby will have AIDS. Another woman faces a difficult situation: her last pregnancy nearly killed her, but abortion is no longer legal in her state, and she cannot afford to travel. A less desperate, but equally tired, supermom returns to suburbia from her 50-hour-a-week job to throw a quick supper on the table, before rushing off to take junior to little league. Across town, an American Indian teen mother

1. C. Gilligan *et al.* (eds.), *Making Connections: The Relational Worlds of Adolescent Girls at Emma Willard School* (Cambridge, MA: Harvard University Press, 1989), pp. 4-5.

2. D. Spender, *Invisible Women: The Schooling Scandal* (London: Writers and Readers, 1982), pp. 56-57.

3. Personal correspondence from Tamara Felden, 12 May 1992.

struggles, with the support of her grandparents, to make ends meet as she finishes high school. 'Yet she will be saved through childbearing, provided they continue in faith and love and holiness, with modesty' (1 Tim. 2.15).

Clearly, contemporary readers confronting 1 Tim. 2.8-15 bring more questions to this text than that of women's authority in ancient or modern churches. Yet if scholars address this most troublesome passage with any interest or agenda at all, the appropriateness of women's leadership is their major concern. Their conclusions are usually either to abandon the text as hopelessly patriarchal and unsuitable for public reading, to explain it away as being addressed to a particular situation long ago, or more often to lift the text as a banner proclaiming an eternal mandate for womanly subordination. If any text merits being labeled 'irredeemable' or even hazardous to one's health, scholarly or otherwise, 1 Timothy 2 seems a prime candidate.

Yet the Bible, even this text, has spoken authoritatively to religious communities for centuries, and it continues to speak faithful words to numerous peoples of faith today. The crux of the difficulty may arise from a faulty starting point: trying to understand what the text 'meant' in its original context.[1] Such interpretation may often lead to interesting results. Our understanding of the social context of early Christianity and of first-century rhetorical methods, to name only two areas, has been greatly enhanced by recent scholarly studies pursuing the goal of figuring out what the text 'meant'. But while the results of this scholarship are valuable and may be intriguing, modern readers are left with a great chasm that must be bridged between the early decades of this era and our own situation nearly two millennia later.

At this point the traditional exegete delivers the original meaning of the text to the modern interpreter, who then is faced with a task that seems something like carrying a collection of ancient manuscripts in a wheelbarrow, while walking a tight-rope over a waterfall. Wanting to preserve the precious treasure in the wheelbarrow, the interpreter may tiptoe carefully across the expanse, preserving the 'meaning' of the text unchanged to hearers on the other side, or she or he may chuck both text and

1. K. Stendahl, 'Biblical Theology, Contempoary', *IDB* , I, pp. 418-32.

wheelbarrow as a mere historical curiosity, in a scramble to get across safely. More likely, though, the interpreter will stand frozen over the chasm, in terror or bewilderment, unable to move, paralyzed by the enormity of the interpretive task and the seeming impossibility of its faithful completion. What hope can be offered to such troubled and terrified interpreters?

Recognizing interpretation as the 'shaping of imaginations' may offer a way for not only confronting, but redeeming, potentially irredeemable texts, and for overcoming the distance between what a text 'meant' and what it 'means'. The phrase 'shaping of imaginations' refers both to what happens when the text is read or performed in communities and to how teachers, preachers and readers interpret texts for their classes, congregations and audiences. How the text works among us when it is read corporately, together with how we choose to prepare our hearers and learners and how we explain and proclaim texts, shapes our imaginations to understand the text's meanings and truth. This approach to interpreting will be applied to the text from 1 Timothy. A variety of perspectives on Eve and women, seen through the history of exegesis of Genesis 3 and 1 Tim., will contribute to a reading of 1 Timothy 2.8-15 that aims not to understand what the text 'meant', but to consider how the text and its truth claims may continue to be understood nearly 2000 years later as an authoritative word of God.

Eve through Several Lenses

A helpful starting point for trying to understand what a text means is a history of exegesis. Whether we are aware of them or not, the centuries of readings of a text have shaped our understandings both of the text and of ourselves. In the case of 1 Timothy 2 we will look at the history of interpretation of Eve in Genesis 2–3. Since we are interested in a contemporary reading of 1 Timothy, we will look both at traditions that might have been available to the author of the Pastoral letters and at later interpretations that may affect our hearing of the letters.

Bible readers may know that Adam and Eve and their stories do not reappear in the Hebrew Bible outside of the first few chapters of Genesis. The intertestamental literature of Hellenistic Judaism, however, includes a variety of perspectives on women and on Eve's role in the garden story. Women as a group are often the subject of misogyny in intertestamental wisdom literature, where they are described as beguiling snares (Sir. 25.21; Sus. 56; also Eccl. 7.26), easily deceived (Philo, *Quaest. in Gen.* 1.33), or as weak in reasoning ability (*Ep. Arist.* 250). Their beauty or adornment is proposed as a proper concern of husbands (*T. Reub.* 5.5), since their deceptive appearances show their natures as scheming and enticing (*T. Reub.* 5.1). Eve is portrayed as being seduced by the serpent (4 *Macc.* 18.8) or by a fallen angel (*Apoc. Abr.* 23.1; *LAE* 9.1, 10.1; *Apoc. Mos.* 29.15), and as a knowing tempter of her husband,[1] bringing death as a result of sin,[2] and as learning from fallen angels to beautify herself (1 *En.* 8.1).

The rabbinic discussions of woman and Eve in the targums, midrash and Talmud parallel those of the intertestamental literature. Women as a group sound something like the young women of 1 Timothy 5, since the rabbis accuse a woman of being swell-headed, a coquette, an eavesdropper, jealous, lightfingered, and a gadabout (*Gen. R.* 18.2). Eve becomes a symbol for all women (*b. Ket.* 61a). Blood and several gynecological concerns (*Gen. R.* 20.6) are discussed and related to various Jewish practices held to be the responsibility of women (*Gen. R.* 17.8). Women are enjoined to modesty and to avoid make-up (*t. Šab.* 95a). Their use of perfume is explained (*Gen. R.* 18.8), and God becomes a divine hairdresser, plaiting Eve's hair before bringing her to Adam (*Gen. R.* 18.1; *b. Ber.* 61a; *b.'Erub.* 18a). Eve is not only seduced by the serpent, but she bears the child of Sammael, the angel of death (*Targ. Ps.-J.* 3.6; 4.1), or is herself identified with the serpent (*Gen. R.* 17.6; 22.2).

Gnostic literature has many things in common with the Jewish literature from which some of it arose. Both literatures associate Eve with the coming of death (*Apoc. Adam* 5.5, 66-7; *Gos. Phil.* 2.3, 68), and in both she has a close connection with the serpent or an evil force (*Hyp. Arch.* II, 4, 89). The relationship of Eve and

---

1. Suggested by *Jub.* 3.21, since Eve covers her shame before offering the fruit to her husband.
2. Sir. 25.24. But see 2 *Esd.* 3.7 and 2 *Apoc. Bar.* 54.15; 56.6, which attribute the onset of death to Adam's sin.

the serpent is sometimes described as explicitly sexual, resulting in the birth of one or more children (*Ap. John* II, 1, 24; and presumably Cain in *Hyp. Arch.* II, 4, 91). Several features, however, distinguish Gnostic literature from the Jewish writings discussed above. The Gnostic creation myth has an androgynous beginning (*Gos. Phil.* II, 3, 68; *Orig. World* II, 5, 113).[1] In Gnostic sources Eve is also strongly associated with bringing life (*Hyp. Arch.* II, 4, 89) and instruction (*Apoc. Adam* V, 5, 64; *Orig. World* II, 5, 113,115). Her violation by the evil beings is explicit and malevolent (*Hyp. Arch.* II, 4, 89; *Orig. World* II, 5, 117). Absent from Gnostic stories about Eve is any mention of beauty, hairdressing, or use of make-up, which were clear concerns of the Jewish writers. In contrast to the Gnostic lack of interest in these matters of appearance, women's adornment and the household as her proper sphere are emphasized by classical philosophers.

Greek philosophers prescribe separate spheres for women and men, with men having the public roles. According to Phintys, 'the things peculiar to a man are, to lead an army, to govern, and to harangue in public. The offices peculiar to a woman are, to be the guardian of a house, to stay at home, and to receive and be ministrant to her husband'.[2] Wives are also to be submissive to their husbands (Xenophon, *Oec.* 7.28), and to limit their speaking.[3] Adornment is limited as well; modesty (σωφροσύνη) is

---

1. While this might also possibly be inferred from the Genesis account, as P. Trible's use of the term 'earth-creature' and insistence on the simultaneous creation of sexuality with the creation of the woman suggest, subsequent Jewish discussions of the creation do not make a point of simultaneous creation. See P. Trible, *God and the Rhetoric of Sexuality* (Philadelphia: Fortress Press, 1978), pp. 80, 98.

2. Phintys, 'On the Temperance of Woman', in T. Taylor (ed.), *Political Fragments of Archytas, Charoudas, Zaleucus and other Ancient Pythagoreans, Preserved by Stobaeus* (Chiswick: C. Whittingham, 1822), p. 70. See also Musonius Rufus, 'That Women Too Should Study Philosophy', in C.E. Lutz (ed.), *Musonius Rufus: The Roman Socrates* (Yale Classical Studies; New Haven: Yale University Press, 1947), p. 41; and Xenophon, *Oec.* 7.22.

3. Plutarch, *Conj. praec.* 142.32. See also H.F. North, 'The Mare, the Vixen and the Bee: Sophrosyne as the Virtue of Women in Antiquity', *Illinois Classical Studies* 2 (1977), p. 35-48.

prescribed, rather than gold, jewels and plaiting of hair.[1] Before looking at how similar prescriptions are the advice of the author of the first letter to Timothy, we turn briefly to the Christian church fathers.

Ambrose and Augustine maintain earlier Greek contrasts between mind and body, reason and senses (Ambrose, *De Paradiso*), identifying women with the inferior flesh (Augustine, *Literal Commentary on Genesis* 11.42). Women are still intrigued with snakes, while cosmetics and extravagant clothing are dismissed as symbols of wickedness or ridiculous things.[2] Like their Greek forefathers, these early church leaders relegate women to the private sphere (Ambrose, *De Paradiso* 11.50), especially with regard to teaching. As in 1 Timothy, woman's adornment is related to the inappropriateness of her teaching. But the fathers were also aware of the competing traditions in the New Testament that recognized women's leadership. To explain why Priscilla was given prominence in Paul's time, Chrysostom notes that women at the time of the apostles

> did not participate in the things women do today, so as to clothe themselves in splendid garments, beautify their faces with paint and eye makeup, urge on their husbands to make them buy more extravagant dresses than their neighbor's wife and their peers have...and all the other ridiculous things you can imagine. Those women of earlier times discarded all these things.[3]

We see in this explanation, again, a linking of women's adornment (or lack thereof) with their teaching authority (or similar lack).

Discussion of Eve over the centuries would be incomplete

1.   Phintys, 'On the Temperance of a Woman', p. 72 and Perictione, 'On the Harmony of a Woman', in Taylor (ed.), *Political Fragments*, p. 59.

2.   B.P. Prusak, 'Woman: Seductive Siren and Source of Sin?', in R.R. Ruether (ed.), *Religion and Sexism: Images of Women in the Jewish and Christian Traditions* (New York: Simon & Schuster, 1974), p. 101, citing Clement of Alexandria, *Paedagogus* 2.12. See also Tertullian, *De Cultu Feminarum*, 2.10; 1.2; 4.

3.   E.A. Clark, *Women in the Eraly Church: Message of the Fathers of the Church* (Wilmington, DE: Michael Glazier, 1983), pp. 158-9, citing Chrysostom's homily, *Greet Priscilla and Aquila*, on Rom. 16.3.

without at least brief mention of the work of feminist scholars of the last hundred years, since it also shapes contemporary hearing of the text. Feminist scholars have summarized and exposed standard interpretations of texts such as Genesis 3 and 1 Timothy 2; they have documented effects of these interpretations on women's lives; and they have re-read these texts in new, often startling ways.

Jean Higgins has succinctly summarized centuries of descriptions of the first woman and her actions.

> We have seen that Eve tempted, beguiled, lured, corrupted, persuaded, taught, counseled, suggested, urged, used wicked persuasion, led into wrongdoing, proved herself an enemy, used guile and cozening, tears and lamentations, to prevail upon Adam, had no rest until she got her husband banished, and thus became 'the first temptress'.[1]

Adrienne Rich, in her book *Of Woman Born*, documents one effect of standardized interpretations; she tells how Gen. 3.16 was understood as mandating woman's pain in childbirth as punishment from God.[2] In the sixteenth century, a midwife was burned at the stake for trying to use opium to relieve the pain, and in the nineteenth century clergy vigorously opposed the use of anesthesia at childbirth.[3] Women's biblically sanctioned pain was not limited to childbirth, however. Joy Bussert describes how battered women understand their abuse as divinely ordained.[4] As Rich and Bussert show, according to many standard interpretations, women's lot in life is not merely described in Genesis; instead, her punishment is prescribed.

Reading the text in new ways, Elizabeth Cady Stanton and her co-authors of *The Woman's Bible* pointed out at the end of the last century that the woman in Genesis 3 was not cursed, nor was she tempted 'by brilliant jewels, rich dresses, worldly luxuries or pleasures, but with the promise of knowledge, with

---

1. J.M. Higgins, 'The Myth of Eve: The Temptress', *JAAR* 44 (1976), p. 641.
2. A. Rich, *Of Woman Born: Motherhood as Experience and Institution* (New York: Norton, 1976), p. 128.
3. Rich, *Of Woman Born*, pp. 128, 168.
4. J.M.K. Bussert (1986).

the wisdom of the Gods'.[1] Nearly a century later, Phyllis Trible expands upon this depatriarchalized interpretation, portraying the woman as an intelligent and perceptive theologian and her mate as 'belly-oriented'.[2]

From the various portraits of Eve, we see that not only do individuals and communities make sense out of their situations through the language of Scripture, but that biblical texts also are read and understood differently in the light of the readers' questions and concerns. The meaning and effect of these narratives do not reside timelessly in the text, but are always created anew in the interaction between text and interpreter. One major question, then, may be who gets to do the interpreting.

Interpreting the Text

The second chapter of 1 Timothy begins by urging that prayers be made for public figures in order that the community 'may lead a quiet (ἡσυχία) and peaceable life in all godliness (εὐσέβεια) and dignity' (1 Tim. 2.2). The men in 2.8 are given the responsibility for offering these public (ἐν παντὶ τόπῳ) prayers, and more detailed instructions are given in the remainder of the chapter for how women, who profess godly piety (θεοσέβαιαν), should behave in the private sphere.

The guidance to the women in 2.9-15 has a concentric structure. Modesty decency or chastity (σωφροσύνη), a standard Greek virtue for women,[3] is recommended for their deportment, which includes both outer adorning in v. 9 and inner function in v. 15. The proper women (γυναιξίν) who do good works, of v. 10, are contrasted with the deceived, transgressing woman (γυνή) from the Genesis garden story, in v. 14. At the center, women are told in v. 11 to learn in a quiet, reserved manner (ἡσυχία), and in v. 12 to adopt this withdrawn mode of living (ἡσυχία) with their husbands, rather than taking up the public teaching of men.

---

1. E.C. Stanton *et al.*, *The Woman's Bible* (repr.; New York: European Publishing Company, 1974 [1898]), p. 24.

2. P. Trible, *Texts of Terror* (Philadelphia: Fortress Press, 1984), pp. 110, 113.

3. See North, 'Virtue of Women'.

In addition to its structural unity, our earlier discussion of Eve through several lenses helps to explain how this variety of topics fits together. Hellenistic readers would recognize the ethical instructions about women's adornment, quiet living and submission to their husbands as standard philosophical *topoi* for proper οἰκονομία (household management). When hearing the discussions of apparel and hairstyles in v. 9, readers familiar with Jewish traditions might call to mind familiar stories about God adorning Eve and braiding her hair, and hence be less surprised when Eve appears directly in v. 13. Contemporary audiences also hear the text, based in part on the traditions about Eve and women and about the use of Scripture with which they are familiar.

How Does the Scriptural Appeal Function?

The allusion to Genesis in 1 Tim. 2.13-15 serves as an example and a warning. The claim that Adam was formed first, then Eve, is an example of the household order (husband before wife) that the author of the Pastorals is promoting. Note that the author of 1 Timothy appeals directly[1] to the women (in vv. 9-12) to adopt the appropriate behavior, rather than citing as a rationale the explicit lordship of the husband over the wife indicated in Gen. 3.16. In addition to indicating the proper ordering of the household, v. 13 may at the same time serve as a subtle refutation of any suggestion of a Gnostic androgynous beginning.[2] Verse 14 also serves a double function. For those who know the Genesis story, 1 Tim. 2.14 gives an example of a woman as a bad teacher, since Adam's listening to his wife led to his sin.[3] At the same time it warns women in the community not

1. While household codes advocating subordinate behavior of wives were prevalent in Greek literature from the time of Aristotle (D.L. Balch, *Let Wives Be Submissive: The Domestic Code of I Peter* [SBLMS, 26; Atlanta: Scholars Press, 1981]), the husbands, not the wives, were addressed.
2. A case is made for the Pastorals being written to combat Gnostic myths in R.C. and C. C. Kroeger, *I Suffer Not a Woman: Rethinking 1 Timothy 2:11-15 in Light of Ancient Evidence* (Grand Rapids: Baker, 1992).
3. The Pastorals are proposed as countering stories from the *Acts of*

to be deceived, as Eve was, by the false teachers that may be sneaking into their gardens. Following the main lines of the Genesis story, the author's advice concludes in v. 15 with an allusion to Eve's sentence. Yet whereas the Genesis story emphasizes pain and toil of childbirth, with only a suggestion of potential victory over the serpent (Gen. 3.15), 1 Timothy openly lauds the saving power of childbearing and only hints at the need for ongoing faithfulness. The author is not proposing here an alternative means of salvation for Christian women. Elsewhere in the letters he states clearly that salvation comes through Jesus Christ. The allusion serves instead to explain how women avoid transgression through the good work of bearing and raising children.[1]

Though we cannot accurately ascertain their availability, given the variety of stories about Eve in Jewish and Gnostic traditions that may have been available to the author, it is striking to note what the author does *not* say. While he portrays the woman as thoroughly deceived, unlike Adam, the author does not portray Eve as a beautified temptress. Missing are the criticisms of Eve as deceiving, scheming or enticing. Neither is her lack of reasoning ability adduced as the reason for her deception. The author sticks to the facts as reported in Genesis, or perhaps even goes beyond them by failing to mention the serpent at all. Eve is not explicitly associated with the serpent in any way in 1 Timothy, nor is she the bringer of death. If anything, 2.15 suggests, with the Gnostic myths but against their often ascetic practices, that woman is lifegiving. Even braids, jewelry and adornment are not rejected as gifts of Satan or fallen angels, but are presented simply as an opportunity to exercise womanly σωφροσύνη (modesty).

If, as interpreters, we begin by asking what the 1 Timothy text

Paul, suggesting that Paul advocated asceticism and encouraged women teachers; see D. MacDonald, *The Legend and the Apostle: The Battle for Paul in Story and Canon* (Philadelphia: Westminster Press, 1983).

1. My colleague, as an untrained reader, and John Chrysostom in his homily on 1 Tim. 2.11-15, may be correct when they read the mysterious 'they' of v. 15 as referring not to women as a group, nor to the husband and wife, but to the children that are to be raised in faith, love and holiness with modesty or self-control.

'meant', it seems that the plain meaning of the text in its original context would be as follows. The passage referred to women as wives in relation to men, their husbands. It prohibited women's teaching because of its public nature and concomitant authority and demanded instead that women live a quiet, reserved life in submission to their husbands. While men were to pray without anger or argument, women were to adorn themselves modestly and to take up their proper domestic role as mothers. As both example and warning, the scriptural story of Adam and Eve was cited.

Truth in 1 Timothy

I hope that during the previous discussions of Eve and of 1 Timothy 2 readers or hearers have been thinking and wondering about the contemporary situations I sketched at the beginning of this paper, and that you are therefore uncomfortable or unsatisfied with the meaning of the text just outlined. If so, then my main point about hermeneutics will have been made: interpretation shapes imaginations.

In this postmodern age, it is common knowledge that pristine objectivity is not a possibility. The interpreter's presuppositions and experiences will necessarily color the reading or hearing of a text. Yet as teachers and preachers of texts, we have both the ability and the responsibility, whether we consciously accept them or not, to shape the way a text is understood. My opening remarks and the discussion of how Eve has been understood or misunderstood over the centuries were designed to shape your imaginations. As interpreters we cannot responsibly read this text today in the same way it was read in the ancient churches, but we also need not remain frozen over the falls afraid to touch it.

The problem with this text and its potential lie not in its past historical context, in the Ephesian congregations it was addressing. Nor does identifying the intent of the author as either laying down timeless laws or combatting a specific error or heresy get at the heart of the matter. The value or irredeemability of this text is determined by our contemporary interpretive engagement with it.

When interpreters begin by looking solely at the original context of a text as historians, trying to reconstruct the original context, or as mind readers, attempting to discern the author's intentions,[1] we are too often tempted either (if we like the picture) to try to reconstruct that context so that the same 'timeless' advice can be applied today or (if we do not like what it suggests) to dismiss the text as irrelevant since our society is so markedly different. While historical reconstructions of the setting of a biblical text may be interesting, these explanations are no more than solutions to an intellectual puzzle. They provide understanding about how a particular text may have been written or used, but the reader may (and often does) remain detached from the text. The Bible and its interpretation loses its 'for you' quality of Scripture.

Recent scholars have suggested alternative approaches to interpretation in general and to biblical interpretation in particular. Stanley Fish[2] reminds us that we are all constrained by interpretive communities who shape the ways we read and understand. With Fish,[3] Elisabeth Schüssler Fiorenza[4] urges us to recognize the rhetorical nature of interpretation and to consider the ethics of our practices. John Barton[5] notes that attitudes about authorial intention and the nature of literature were dramatically different in biblical times from what they are now, so even to be competent biblical historians we may need to adjust our expectations in these areas. David Clines suggests

1. P. Keifert ('Mind Reader and Maestro: Models for Understanding Biblical Interpreters', *WW* 1 [1981], pp. 153-68) suggests the metaphor of the interpreter as maestro, conducting a new performance of the text.

2. S. Fish, *Is There a Text in This Class? The Authority of Interpretive Communities* (Cambridge, MA and London: Harvard University Press, 1980).

3. S. Fish, *Doing What Comes Naturally: Change, Rhetoric, and the Practice of Theory in Literary and legal Studies* (Durham, NC and London: Duke University Press, 1989).

4. E. Schüssler Fiorenza, 'The Ethics of Biblical Interpretation: Decentering Biblical Scholarship', *JBL* 107 (1988), pp. 3-17; and *But She Said: Feminist Practices of Biblical Interpretation* (Boston: Beacon Press, 1992).

5. J. Barton, 'Reading the Bible as Literature: Two Questions for Biblical Critics', *Journal of Literature and Theology* 1 (1987), pp. 135-53.

that using our own strategies and questions is an appropriate alternative to reconstructive approaches.

> [W]e may approach the text with the reading strategies of our own time, not indeed to corrupt the text into saying whatever it is we want it to say but to hear whatever it may have to say on matters we are, out of our own convictions and interests, concerned about.[1]

Paul Hanson's proposal, which he calls a 'hermeneutics of engagement', goes one step beyond the suggestions of these scholars by insisting on the theological dimension of the Bible. God was and continues to be active in the world. So Hanson proposes a communal, dynamic enterprise that recognizes the authority of Scripture by being committed to God's purposes and by critically engaging with both tradition and issues of the contemporary world.[2]

While the purely reconstructive approaches do not treat either the Scripture itself or our contemporary setting with sufficient regard, Hanson's more productive 'hermeneutics of engagement' takes seriously the function of all interpretation as shaping imaginations. By adopting Hanson's proposal, we can agree with the author of the Pastorals that 'all scripture is inspired by God and is useful for teaching, for reproof, for correction, and for training in righteousness' (2 Tim. 3.16), and at the same time acknowledge that our culture requires the words of Scripture to be heard differently.

To begin our 'hermeneutics of engagement', then, we note that 1 Timothy, like all of the New Testament literature, is written to people of faith, to 'insiders', and to a particular group of insiders. If we may, like the author of 1 Timothy, borrow an illustration from another biblical text, the parable most commonly called 'the prodigal son', we could say that the Pastoral

---

1. D.J.A. Clines, 'Reading Esther from Left to Right: Contempoary Strategies for Reading a Biblical Text', in *idem et al.* (eds.), *The Bible in Three Dimensions: Essays in Celebration of Forty Years of Biblical Studies in the University of Sheffield* (JSOTSup, 87; Sheffield: JSOT Press, 1990), p. 32.

2. P. Hanson, *Dynamic Transcendence: The Correlation of Confessional Heritage and Contemporary Experience in a Biblical Model of Divine Activity* (Philadelphia: Fortress Press, 1978), p. 77.

letters are written to the elder brothers, to the responsible children. The meaning and truth of our troublesome passage consist in exhorting the faithful to get their house in order, to manage well the household of God. We need not adopt the particular social practices that are presumed by the instructions to this first-century letter's recipients, but we can turn to Scripture—even to this text—for guidance in understanding our corporate lives as God's family.

First Timothy tells us, as does Paul's letter to the Corinthians, that the unity of the church is important, but it uses a different metaphor. Rather than being the body of Christ, the church in 1 Timothy is the household of God. Just as in 1 Corinthians, each part of the body has a different function and should be satisfied with its usefulness, so in 1 Timothy the household of God requires a variety of functions. First Timothy exhorts all of us to be examples to one another of good conscience and sincere faith, to lead quiet and peaceable lives, to pray for our governmental leaders, to hold our bishops, clergy and leaders to high standards of moral behavior, to maintain monogamous relationships, to honor our elders, and to avoid envy, dissensions, wrangling, slander and craving for controversy. Even the difficult text of 1 Tim. 2.8-15 offers worthy models for Christian communities by holding up prayer, moderation, good works, quiet lives and the loving of children.

What makes this text 'irredeemable' is that too much interpretive attention is paid to silencing women and to locating their worth too exclusively in their childbearing. Perhaps the time has come to consider, like the author of the Pastorals, what the community should do in order to live quiet and peaceable lives. As maestros, then, rather than mind readers or historians, we need to shift the emphasis in our interpretations of this passage and perform a more imaginative reading of the text. Instead of denying women's teaching and mandating their submission, we need men to lift their holy hands in prayer, rather than abusing their partners. Moderation and appreciation of our bodies should be our aim, rather than the display of women as 'trophy wives', or their use as seductive advertising temptresses. The good works, which are of great concern to the author of the Pastorals, should be understood as providing an education for girls and boys of all races that improves their self-images and encourages everyone to speak and think creatively. These good works should also include working to free our lives from the ravages of rape, drug abuse and child abandonment, and from the more slowly eroding, but still damaging, effects of discrimination, harassment and workaholism. We must make quiet lives available to all God's people, regardless of their household or family configuration. As interpreters, we might even hear the τεκνογονία (childbearing) of the women in v. 15 differently. Women, in this most troublesome verse, can be understood not only as bearers of those beloved miracles, children born from our bodies. Rather, like the writer of the Pastoral letters, we are also teachers and examples to beloved and true children (τέκνα) of faith.[1]

1. I would like to thank colleagues at Augsburg College, the Feminist Theological Hermeneutics of the Bible Group of the SBL, and the faculty and students in the Scripture Colloquium at Luther Northwestern Theological Seminary for their helpful comments about earlier versions of this paper.

REFLECTIONS ON VIOLENCE AND PORNOGRAPHY:
MISOGYNY IN THE APOCALYPSE AND ANCIENT
HEBREW PROPHECY*

Marla J. Selvidge

> They will bring her to ruin
> and leave her naked;
> they will eat her flesh
> and burn her with fire (Rev. 17.15 NIV).

A romantic notion concerning the supreme worthiness of Judeo-Christian texts, long held in such high esteem, often dominates interpretation of the books of the New Testament. While some may judge texts to be outdated or even downright immoral by twentieth-century standards, we linger over the text hoping that, in spite of its offensive language and spirit, we can gain something from studying it. The book of Revelation stands in the midst of this embarrassing dilemma. Its enigmatic message, grounded in prophetic epithets also found in Hebrew prophecy, has been lauded and condemned for millennia. Many scholars attempt to rescue the book. They wrestle over the tragic and

---

* Most of the research for this article is taken from my recent article 'Powerful and Powerless Women in the Apocalypse', *Neot* 26.1 (1992), pp. 157-67. This article does not claim to have done an extensive study of Old Testament/Hebrew sources for the book of Revelation. It merely hopes to suggest that similar ideas about violence and women are present within the corpus of the Hebrew prophets. For excellent work on Hebrew sources of the book of Revelation see G.K. Beale, *The Use of Daniel in Jewish Apocalyptic Literature and in the Revelation of St John* (Lanham, MD: University Press of America, 1984); *idem*, 'Revelation', in D.A. Carson and H.G. Williamson (eds.), *It is Written: Scripture Citing Scripture* (New York: Cambridge University Press, 1988), pp. 318-37; F. Jenkins, *The Old Testament in the Book of Revelation* (Marion: Indiana University Press, 1972).

obscure themes of Revelation. Almost every major scholar seeks to find a key, the ultimate answer to unleashing its mysteries. This ambivalent attitude has allowed the violent stories in Revelation to remain in the canons of biblical scholarship. Yet the book of Revelation contains more than a string of violent stories and acts. Similar to passages in Hosea, Ezekiel and Jeremiah, it describes pornographic death threats and scenes against women in order to make its predictions of terror. These scenes portray women either being sadistically brutalized or violently coerced through language that uses their bodies and sexuality as metaphors for activities which threaten the writer of the book of Revelation.

Revelation does more than verbally annihilate its opponents. Its legitimacy may have promoted, even institutionalized, violence against women. It may even perpetuate prejudice, intolerance and injustice. It may also teach tolerance for violence, terrorism and pornography.

The book of Revelation, as well as prophetic writings of ancient Israel, could be positive vehicles serving to protect and enhance the egos of a minority community under seige. Or they could be healthy outlets for feelings of violent revenge.[1] But they do more. The book of Revelation advocates terrorism and, like the ancient prophets, it justifies the complete annihilation of the other in order to bring into existence a new social order. It advocates revolutionary change (religious, social, cultural) not based upon informed rational choice and dissent, but upon the ashes of the other. Revelation advocates the total destruction of a people who are presently in power.

If we are honest with ourselves and our world, we must ask the question. We must wonder about the consequences of reading and meditating on the book of Revelation for the past 2000 years. Has it fostered rather than hindered violence, war and the objectification of the other? How has this book influenced world cultures? Do monotheistic cultures interpret wars, violence and the annihilation of other cultures through the eyes of this seer (the writer of the book of Revelation)? Is pornographic

1. A.Y. Collins, 'The Revelation of John: An Apocalyptic Response to a Social Crisis', *CurTM* 8 (1981), p. 12; and 'Coping with Hostility', *Bible Today* 19 (1981), pp. 367-72.

literature about women an acceptable medium for portraying our enemies?

For at least 400 years people have questioned the wisdom of studying this violent book. Does the book of Revelation idolize violence against the other? Robin Morgan in her book *The Demon Lover: On the Sexuality of Terrorism* traces the history of terrorism back to biblical and pre-biblical times. For her, 'The terrorist has been the subliminal idol of an androcentric cultural heritage from pre-biblical times to the present'.[1] Has the book of Revelation preserved this subliminal idol?

Terrorism and pornography are two very difficult concepts to define, although they often link arms with each other in literature and in life. Paul Wilkinson in *Terrorism: Theory and Practice* defines terrorism as 'a special mode of violence, which may be briefly defined as coercive intimidation. It involves the threat of murder, injury, or destruction in order to terrorize a given target into conceding to the terrorist's will'.[2] T. Drorah Setel attempts to describe features of pornography in her challenging article, 'Prophets and Pornography: Female Sexual Imagery in Hosea':

> The distinguishing features of pornography can be characterized as follows: (1) Female sexuality is depicted as negative in relationship to a positive and neutral male standard; (2) women are degraded and publicly humiliated; and (3) female sexuality is portrayed as an object of male possession and control...[3]

Space will not allow a thorough investigation of every terrorist or pornographic story in Revelation, but it is possible to give two examples of stories or images of woman that seem to display a consistent debauched and violent misogyny that is shrouded in pornographic images.

The seer wishes for a violent end to both a woman he labels Jezebel and a city (or political entity) he calls Babylon the Great.

---

1. R. Morgan, *The Demon Lover: On the Sexuality of Terrorism* (New York: Norton, 1989), p. 24.
2. In Y. Alexander (ed.), *Terrorism: Theory and Practice* (Colorado: Westview Press, 1979), pp. 45-72.
3. In L.M. Russell (ed.), *Feminist Interpretation of the Bible* (Philadelphia: Westminster Press, 1985), p. 87.

Both are images he has appropriated from Old Testament/ Hebrew Bible writings. Both become symbols of a power that he cannot control. They must be destroyed. The prediction of their destruction in pornographic terms reveals the terrorist inclinations of the seer.

Jezebel: The Voice of Satan

> So they threw her down; and some of her blood
> splattered on the wall and on the horses,
> and they trampled on her...
> when they went to bury her,
> they found no more of her than the skull
> and the feet and the palms of her hands (2 Kgs 9.33-35 RSV).

The writer's first portrait of a woman feeds upon a malicious myth about an ancient Sidonian queen. In a voice claiming divine right from the son of God (Rev. 2.18), the writer indicts a popular woman who wields both personal and intellectual power over the people and possibly over the writer. Viciously, he labels his opponent 'Jezebel' (cf. 1 Kgs 16.21),[1] and with that name conjures up loathsome feelings about an ancient powerful woman who challenged the forces of Yahweh (1 Kgs 18.21-46). Here, unlike the ancient Jezebel, wife of a king, she stands alone as a teacher, a prophetess and a leader in the community of Thyatira (Rev. 2.20). The Seer brings charges against her.

> These are the words of the Son of God...You tolerate that woman Jezebel, who calls herself a prophetess. By her teaching she misleads my servants into sexual immorality and the eating of food sacrificed to idols (Rev. 2.20 NIV).

These charges are not new. Hebrew prophets often castigated enemies by using the image of a fallen woman as a symbol for 'fallen' Israel or powerful politico-religious opponents. A 'fallen' woman would be anyone who did not follow ancient patriarchal laws regarding marriage, adultery and other sexual proscriptions. Jeremiah speaks,

---

1. A.Y. Collins ('Women's History and the Book of Revelation', [SBLSP, 26; Atlanta: Scholars Press, 1987], p. 81), says: 'here John is claiming authority of Christ for his own personal point of view'. See also A.S. Peake, *The Revelation of John* (London: Holborn, n.d.), p. 245.

> If a man puts away his wife and she leaves him, and if she then becomes another's may he go back to her again? Is not that woman defiled, a forbidden thing? You have played the harlot with many lovers; can you come back to me? says the Lord (Jer. 3.1).

Jezebel opposed Elijah and the 'prophets of the Lord' and for that crime and others her name became synonymous with evil. Often when women possessed enough courage or power to choose for themselves and against the patriarchal laws they were condemned and castigated in Hebrew society. Their actions or words threatened the balance of powers. A male rarely suffered the stigma of defilement because there were fewer laws governing his sexuality and leadership activities.

The beliefs and teachings of the seer seem to be threatened. He feels the need to attempt to silence the prophetess, but his words are ignored by the majority of the community. Experiencing a loss of confidence he lashes out at a person who is more successful than himself. He aims at conversion and intimidation through the use of terror (Rev. 2.7, 10, 18, 19).[1]

With offensive epithets he characterizes her control in terms of mental, emotional and physical/sexual activities. She uses her superior talents to persuade the people to follow her religious beliefs and practices. The writer labels her dynamic curriculum 'that teaching' (τὴν διδαχήν, Rev. 2.24) which may be the same as 'the deep things of Satan'.[2] Here, Jezebel is in contact with the greatest knowledge one could have of Satan. The writer does not seem to understand the exact content of that knowledge.

Jezebel teaches her followers about cultic prostitution[3] and

---

1. D.E. Aune ('The Social Matrix of the Apocalpse of John', *BR* 26 [1981], p. 27) says that 'John's battle was with the Nicolatians and Jezebel was…a conflict between prophets'.

2. E. Schüssler Fiorenza ('Apocalyptic Gnosis in the Book of Revelation and Paul', *JBL* 92 [1973], pp. 567-69) attributes this teaching to the Christian libertine party the Nicolatians and claims that it was probably Gnostic in origin.

3. A.Y. Collins ('Vilification and Self-Definition in the Book of Revelation', *HTR* 79 [1986], pp. 316-17), says that the problem is a conflict

eating meat offered to idols (Rev. 2.20). Her teachings, apparently, meet the needs of those who listen. People willingly allow her to carry on religious activities. Most do not challenge her although some in Thyatira do not follow her (Rev. 2.24). While she is in control, the writer warns the reader/listener (perhaps the servants; Rev. 2.20), those who will follow her will be severely punished. She will be penalized for her religious activities and her adulteries (Rev. 2.22, τοὺς μοιχεύοντας). The seer claims that she deceives (Rev. 2.20, πλανᾶ) people. She does not need to use 'signs' (τὰ σημεῖα, Rev. 19.20) as the false prophet does or 'magical acts' (τῇ φαρμακείᾳ, Rev. 18.23). She reaches the people through her teaching abilities.

The seer believes that the prophetess deserves punishment for her success, perhaps in the same manner as the ancient queen Jezebel. He threatens her with violence from the son of God 'whose eyes are like blazing fire' (Rev. 2.18). In a powerful visual metaphor he laughs at her accomplishments. He characterizes her church as a bed of seduction which ultimately becomes her prison. (Manuscript A, 02, Alexandrinus uses 'prison', φυλακήν, instead of 'bed'.) Yet she will not repent.[1] She will not change her mind or her ways. But she is not alone. Throughout Revelation, people who oppose John's point of view refuse to repent even when faced with a torturous, scorching death or life in darkness (Rev. 16.9, 11):

> The fourth angel poured his bowl on the sun, it was allowed to scorch men with fire; men were scorched by the fierce heat, and they cursed the name of God who had power over these plagues, and they did not repent... (Rev. 16.8-9).

Since the writer cannot intimidate, change or move Jezebel, he threatens 'her children', τὰ τέκνα: 'I will strike her children dead' (Rev. 2.23).[2] Isaiah writes similar words as he pronounces the doom of Babylon: 'Their infants shall be dashed into pieces before their eyes' (Isa. 13.16). Hosea says, 'Upon her children

of values. She suggests that prostitution is not literal but refers to idolatry in general.

1. Aune, 'The Social Matrix of the Apocalypse of John', p. 27

2. R.H. Charles (*The Revelation of St. John* [Edinburgh: T. & T. Clark, (1920)], p. 72), says that they may be her own literal children or those 'who have absolutely embraced this woman's theology'.

also I will have no pity because they are the children of harlotry' (Hos. 2.4).

This powerless seer may represent a minority opinion in the community. He believes that the power that sent him to prophesy will vindicate him (Rev. 2.26). The portrait of a Jezebel-like woman may be designed to frighten the readers (the community) into assenting to him, or into encouraging them to gloat over their privileged status as those who do not follow her ways.

In any case, while Jezebel may be performing and teaching religious activities condemned by the seer, she remains in power. He is unable to control or change the dynamic leader in any way. He predicts power or authority (Rev. 2.26) for those who do his will or follow his teachings to the end, but the seer can only wish for the woman's demise. He never actually describes or witnesses Jezebel's downfall, although he does, in general, describe the ulimate annihilation of all opposing forces in Rev. 19.

The Mother of Harlots, Ruler over the Kings of the Earth

> The broad wall of Babylon
> shall be leveled to the ground
> and her high gates shall be
> burned with fire (Jer. 51.58).

The annihilation of the 'great city' (Rev. 17.18; also see Dan. 4.30; Jer. 50) was a topic of great joy for the Hebrew prophets and the seer.[1] The seer is taken to the desert where he witnesses the end of the harlot, the great city (Rev. 17.3).[2] Equating it with a great prostitute who, like a queen, sits on many waters, he viciously describes 'her' activities that warrant punishment and painfully details 'her' death by 'rape' (ἠρωμωμένων, Rev. 17.16), 'fire' (ἐν πυρί) and 'cannibalism' (κατακαύσουσιν, Rev. 17.16).

---

1.   J.F. Walvoord ('Revival of Rome', *BSac* 126 [1969], pp. 317-28), suggests that the great city is the Roman Catholic Church or a future worldwide ecumenical church. M.E. Boring (*Revelation* [Louisville, KY: John Knox, 1989], p. 179) lists Babylon, Caesar and the Caesar cult, Nero, the Roman Empire, and the goddess of Rome as possible referents. Other suggestions are Messalina the wife of Claudius and that the harlot only refers to violent times under various Roman emperors.

2.   Could this be the same desert in which the woman clothed with the sun is hiding in Rev. 12.14?

Ezekiel uses similar pornographic images to describe the physical ·humiliation of Israel.

> Wherefore, O harlot, hear the word of the Lord. Thus says the Lord God, because your shame was laid bare and your nakedness uncovered in your harlotries with your lovers, and because of all your idols, and because of the blood of your children that you gave to them, therefore, behold, I will gather all your lovers, with whom you took pleasure, all those you loved and all those you loathed; I will gather them against you from every side, and will uncover your nakedness to them, that they may see all your nakedness...And I will give you into the hand of your lovers, and they shall throw down your vaulted chamber and break down your lofty places; they shall strip you of your clothes and take your fair jewels, and leave you naked and bare. They shall bring up a host against you, and they shall stone you and cut you to pieces with their swords (Ezek. 16.35-40).

This violent description of a 'gang-rape' and 'gang-murder' was predicted for Israel by Ezekiel. Similarily, the writer of the book of Revelation finds pleasure in describing a lecherous scene in which the beasts consume the body of a prostitute.

The seer charges Babylon with using sexual/cultic practices that have a drugging effect upon the kings of the earth. Her sexual power seems to be absolute. It can only be broken by internal strife or revolution. The beast 'will eat her flesh and burn her with fire' (Rev. 17.16). This ability to overthrow the prostitute was given to the beast by God (Rev. 17.17). All of the hosts of heaven and below must align in order to defeat this powerful 'woman':

> She is depicted as a gorgeously arrayed Bacchanal. Her purple and scarlet attire are emblems of luxurious living; the cup from which she drinks and with which she intoxicates the royal partners of her sin is the symbol of her uncleanness.[1]

This scene is reminiscent of Jer. 51.7 (RSV): 'Babylon was a golden cup in the Lord's hand, making all the earth drunken; the nations drank of her wine, therefore the nations went mad'. According to the seer, 'her' crimes are an extravagant lifestyle which involves questionable religious and sexual practices (Rev.

---

1.   Peake, *The Revelation of John*, p. 349.

17.4), and the death of witnesses. 'I saw that the woman was drunk with the blood of the saints, the blood of those who bore testimony to Jesus' (Rev. 17.6). She sits on a beast that has seven heads and ten horns (like the Dragon in Rev. 12.3) and is called the 'mother of prostitutes and of the abominations of the earth' (Rev. 17.5). She is the cause. She is the originator of wantonness.

Unlike the Israelites in Jeremiah 52 who are conquered by Nebuchadnezzar, this woman who is labeled a prostitute is quite effective and successful. Her methodologies have, perhaps, won many over to her way of thinking and living. According to the author, her strength is used to oppress and seduce others in spite of her own intoxicated state (Rev. 17.2, 15). She aligns herself with a supernatural beast (Rev. 17.3). The writer says that she sits on both the many waters and the beast; this is, in graphic sexual terms, a reference to her power and physical prowess (Rev. 17.1, 3).

While he despises the great city/woman, there is also a hint of jealousy. The writer describes her downfall so graphically that there appears to be a hint of joy in relating the gruesome story. If he could not continue to enjoy her 'adulteries' in life, he could be satisfied—even uplifted—by watching her mutilating death. Jeremiah is only one of the prophets who composes poetry about the use of force against an opponent. In predicting the downfall of Babylon, he writes to the Medes:

> You are my hammer and weapon of war:
>> with you I break nations in pieces;
>> with you I destroy kingdoms;
>> with you I break in pieces the horse and his rider;
>> with you I break in pieces the chariot and the charioteer;
>> with you I break in pieces man and woman;
>> with you I break in pieces the old man and the youth;
>> with you I break in pieces the young man and the maiden;
>> with you I break in pieces the shepherd and his flock;
>> with you I break in pieces the farmer and his team;
>> with you I break in pieces the governors and commanders
>> (Jer. 51.20-23).

This terrorist poetry has a sort of 'ring' to it. The writer seems to make a game out of mutilating other people and countries.

A Queen, a Widow and an Alluring Prostitute

Plead with her to forswear those wanton looks,
to banish the lovers from her bosom.
Or I will strip her and expose her naked as the day she was born;
I will make her bare as the wilderness,
parched as the desert,
and leave her to die of thirst (Hos. 2.2-3 NEB).

In grotesque and vividly evocative terms, Babylon the Great's corruption and annihilation is shrouded with conflicting feminine images. Babylon is a widow, a queen (Rev. 18.7), a prostitute (Rev. 18.3), an unclean/menstruous woman (Rev. 18.24), a murderer (Rev. 18.24), and demon-possessed (Rev. 18.2). She is vile and her corruption will be burned (Rev. 18.8). Only here (Rev. 18.5) and in Rev. 1.15 does the writer use the word ἁμαρτία, 'sins', to describe her. Also, only here is she accused of ἀδικήματα, 'misdeeds'. He claims that she is responsible for all those who have been slain or consumed on earth (Rev. 18.24).

Inside her live demons. She provides a φυλακή, 'prison' for every hated and unclean spirit and bird (Rev. 18.2). The writer warns 'my people' to 'come out of her' so that they may not taste of the violence that she will soon experience (Rev. 18.4). Jeremiah writes similar words of warning, 'Get out of the midst of her, my people. Let every man save his life from the fierce anger of the Lord' (Jer. 51.45). The 'woman' has aroused maddening passions, τοῦ θυμοῦ τῆς πορνείας, among the kings and peoples of the earth (Rev. 18.3). The alliance has proved to be a wise investment, for 'the merchants of the earth grew rich from her excessive luxuries...' (Rev. 18.3).

There is a hint of remorse for her grueling, tormenting fate. As the kings and merchants weep and mourn for her (Rev. 18.9, 11), the writer rehearses the material losses they will experience because of her demise (Rev. 18.11-14). But they must also remember that she bought and sold 'the bodies and souls of people' (Rev. 18.13). She has the power over people.

The dragon attempted to consume the child born to the woman clothed with the sun in ch. 12; here Babylon is accused of consuming (ἐσφαγμένων, Rev. 18.24) the prophets and saints and all the people living on the earth. She is nourished by their blood.

There is no forgiveness, no compromise: 'God has judged her

for the way she treated you' (Rev. 18.20). Ironically, what she brought the merchants and kings included things that made them happy. The writer speaks of wealth, music, employment in the trades, light, festivals and public recognition (Rev. 18.19, 22-23).

The emotional tone of Revelation 18 is punctuated with ambivalent views of woman. The writer laments his loss, remembers the seemingly wonderful things that 'she' gave to him (to the world), but continues to pronounce doom upon her. There is an underlying excitement in his description of her presumed sins. He seems to be reliving his life with her.[1] He abhors her independence. She says, 'I sit as queen, I am not a widow, and I will never mourn' (Rev. 18.8). She could never be a widow because she chooses to have many romances among the kings of the earth. She is in control of her own life. The writer has no influence over her. He deplores her values and her lack of commitment to anything but herself. In predicting her fall, he triumphs over her. She has the power to meet the needs of human beings, he does not. He only has the power of revenge.[2]

The stories about Babylon create a truly wretched image of woman who uses her powers to destroy others. She uses her freedom to feed upon people, lulling them into a relationship not only with her richly dressed body, but with the finer things in life that she can offer them. These symbols of the riches, jewels, fine clothing and rare commodities will die with her.[3]

Concluding Remarks

According to Andrea Dworkin,

> Pornography numbs the conscience, makes one increasingly callous to cruelty, to the inflictions of pain, to violence against

---

1.   Collins' ('The Revelation of John': An Apocalyptic Response to a Social Crisis', p. 9) says, 'Revelation produces a catharsis not only by means of individual symbolic narratives, but by the structure of the book as a whole'.

2.   W. Klassen ('Vengeance in the Apocalypse of John', *CBQ* 28 [1966], p. 310), says, 'the wrath of God is central to the Christian Faith'.

3.   Collins, 'Women's History and the Book of Revelation', pp. 80-91.

persons, to the humiliation or degradation of persons, to the abuse of women and children.[1]

It is clear, even for the casual reader, that the writer of the book of Revelation as well as some of the Hebrew prophets objectify woman as the enemy. She is the embodiment of all that is evil. She represents an 'other' who defies all that is good from God. She becomes the scapegoat, hostile image, or projection of the writers' own inabilities to cope with present political circumstances. These graphic and violent images of a female's destruction seem to be both pornographic and designed to produce terror in the minds of the readers.

No one has established a direct causal relationship between violence and pornography in culture and the book of Revelation or ancient Hebrew prophets. But if we read these books carefully and with an open mind, we may find misogynistic, pornographic and violent stories that jolt us out of our comfortable easy chairs. Could the annihilation of the earth in Revelation 20 represent the ultimate and final alienation/annihilation of Mother Earth, of woman? Should we conclude with Tina Pippin that '[the Apocalypse] means death to women...'?[2]

1. A. Dworkin, *Letters from the War Zone* (New York: Harper & Row, 1989), p. 205.
2. T. Pippin, 'Eros and the End: Reading for Gender in the Apocalypse of John', *Semeia* 59 (1992), p. 203.

DISABILITIES AND ILLNESS IN THE BIBLE:
A FEMINIST PERSPECTIVE*

Carole R. Fontaine

In her article 'Women with Disabilities: A Challenge to Feminist Theology',[1] Elly Elshout questioned the way that the experiences of women with disabilities go unobserved in most feminist theological and political discourse. This lacuna has a twofold impact: it continues the ongoing sociocultural marginalization of those who struggle with issues of body and health, and it renders the prevailing discourse incomplete—a serious problem given the ethic of inclusion espoused by feminist theory. Using Mary Daly's analysis of the 'Sado-ritual Syndrome',[2] Elshout examines the experiences of women with disabilities to show how the able-bodied unwittingly participate in patriarchal oppression. This occurs in the adoption of or acquiescence in cultural obsessions with physical purity, the erasure of responsibility and full personhood in those who are viewed as dependent. She also highlights the inherent tendency of the health industry to spread, since it has a self-interest in defining whole groups as 'defective' so that they will then require the services of that same industry. In Elshout's discussion, disabled women become token torturers who must abuse their bodies, forcing them beyond their limits, in order to compete with the 'able'. Likewise, a fixation upon details of one's disability or medical condition ensures that concepts of wholeness are lost.

---

* An earlier version of this article entitled 'Roundtable Discussion: Women with Disabilities—A Challenge to Feminist Theology' appeared in *JFSR* 10.2 (1994), pp. 108-14.

1. *JFSR* 10.2 (1994), pp. 99-104.

2. M. Daly, *Gyn/Ecology: The Metaethics of Radical Feminism* (Boston: Beacon Press, 1978).

From there, it is a short step to finding views of the disabled as 'unwanted' acceptable and normative, so that society easily sanctions the termination of pregnancies where evidence of disability or abnormality is present. All of this is then supported and legitimated by 'objective' scholarship, as the booming field of reproductive technologies amply demonstrates in its promotion of the biases of 'ableism'.[1] Elshout concludes by critiquing the 'victim-thinking' that can be the product of this kind of analysis and afflicts some groups of disabled persons as they attempt to form a counter-culture which re-forms concepts of beauty, health and productivity. She calls for solidarity among differences, such that all the members of the *ekklesia gynaikon* are given an equal place in the formation of a community of discourse which shares a sociopolitical strategy for change. She proposes the new metaphor 'disabled body' as a critical reappropriation of Paul's 'Body of Christ' metaphor, because it speaks authentically of the different realities and conflicts in women's— and, indeed, all people's—experience.[2]

The issues raised for feminist theology by Elshout's examination are ones that are immediately recognizable to any woman who finds herself physically or emotionally 'challenged', as US society has euphemistically chosen to refer to our situation. As a person who has struggled with chronic illness lasting over a decade, I found elements in Elshout's analysis all too familiar. The daily battles that confront a differently abled person in most societies are often so overwhelming and oppressive that their absence from most discussions of the condition of women presents itself to us as yet another disability in talking with others engaged in the feminist enterprise. Whether it is the unquestioning retrieval of the body as the major source of identity and fulfillment, or the barely concealed irritation that so often infuses interactions of the 'normals' with those who have special needs, the invisibility of disabled women in most feminist thought is very real. How are we supposed to enter into conversations about valuing the body and trusting one's intuitions, dearly held points of the feminist doctrine, when

1.   Elshout, 'Women with Disabilities', p. 101.
2.   Elshout, 'Women with Disabilities', p. 103.

giving that status to the body in our own lives can often annihilate the self-esteem we have so carefully built up in opposition to a world that judges us primarily by what we can produce? If we are cynical about the liberation projects going on all around us, if we shake our heads in private over the pitying comments of our sisters about our status as non-mothers (as though essentialist arguments about fulfillment through mother-hood were divine givens!), if we have grown tired of waiting in a world of heavy doors, obstructed ramps and able-bodied persons double-parked in our parking spaces—we have reason.

Anyone with disabilities could easily relate to the stories of the 'clerical abuse' which prompted Elshout to take up these questions. One of the places in which the most potent examples of exclusion can be experienced is the world of the church. It seems to me that the physical organization of churches only reflects that institution's deep ambivalence about the presence of the sick and disabled in its midst. Though the church is tech-nically mandated to act as sanctuary and healing presence to such persons, in fact we are a deep embarrassment to the institution's ideology of healing. How dare we not get well! Haven't we heard that God has come with healing in his wings? Is our faith defective, perhaps, that we so stubbornly resist owning the full promise of healing? Perhaps we have sinned? Have we failed to repent with a contrite enough heart? What-ever the secret explanations the church gives for our presence, we know by its fruits of exclusion that we continue to be a presence of dubious value. I wept when I first attended a baseball game at Boston's Fenway Park and saw the special rows reserved for wheelchairs, as well as the other fine attempts to make us welcome. Were they there only because it was expected that men would be viewing the game, and they had a right to be participating fans? (There were women seated there, too.) Regardless of the reason, I remembered reflecting on the fact that our bodies were made more welcome at a secular sporting event than in the very places where we are taught to seek healing of spirit and flesh.

At least one source of the theological ambivalence about those with disabilities may be located in the tradition's authoritative documents, the Hebrew Bible and New Testament. Surveying both Testaments synchronically,[1] we come away with a coherent view of the way the societies producing those texts understood disability. While synchronic studies are of limited usefulness in such pursuits as historical reconstruction or the fixing of doctrinal 'truth', they provide a useful entry point for discussion by presenting a *gestalt* of folk ideas, literary tropes and cultural values around a given topic. While it is probably the case that views of illness and disability may have changed over time, especially during times of contact with foreign cultures, some of which had concepts of medicine in the late period,[2] there is an underlying unity in the way the Bible views persons so afflicted. Literature on the topic, most often taking a tone which automatically assumes the compassion and goodness of the deity along with the superiority of biblical traditions to those of their neighbors, is extensive.[3]

Illness and Disability as Undesirable Conditions

In medically naive societies, those based on agricultural production, people who cannot participate fully in the common tasks of

1. One may object to treating both Testaments together, since it may lead to a lack of appreciation of the differences between the two, and smack of a Christian triumphal appropriation of the Hebrew Bible. However, the assumption here is *not* that any problems in the Hebrew Bible are automatically 'corrected', subsumed or solved by the New Testament. Rather, since the New Testament flows out of the worldview and concerns of the Hebrew Bible, it cannot be adequately understood without exploration of its antecedents.

2. H.C. Kee, *Medicine, Miracle and Magic in New Testament Times* (Cambridge: Cambridge University Press, 1986), pp. 27-63.

3. For an entry into this literature, see J. Preuss, *Biblical and Talmudic Medicine* (trans. and ed. F. Rosner, MD; New York: Sanhedrin Press, 1978); F. Rosner, MD, *Medicine in the Bible and the Talmud: Selections from Classical Jewish Sources* (New York: Ktav, 1977); K. Seybold and U.B. Mueller, *Sickness and Healing* (trans. D.W. Stott; Biblical Encounter Series: Nashville, TN: Abingdon Press, 1981). Most recently, see H. Avalos, 'Illness and Health Care in Ancient Israel: A Comparative Study of the Role of the Temple' (PhD dissertation, Harvard University, 1991; Ann Arbor, MI: University Microfilms International, 1991).

survival are naturally seen as existing in a more precarious and less desirable state. In a world where 'medical' care is uncertain in its effects, the ill or disabled person presents a potent reminder to observers that woundedness and death are very close indeed. Such persons have the experience of death-in-life, and it is not one envied by others in their society. While these perceptions often lead to injunctions to treat the disabled with special care (Lev. 19.14; Deut. 27.18), the overall view of the disabled is that, as less than whole, they are more at risk (Deut. 28.29; Isa. 59.10; Mt. 15.14; Lk. 6.39; 2 Pet. 1.9; Rev. 3.17). When the literary trope of 'blindness' or 'lameness' appears, it is usually negative in meaning (Prov. 25.19; 26.7; Isa. 29.9; 43.8; 56.10; Mt. 23.16-19; Jn. 9.40-41). Thus, when true believers are told to mutilate themselves—become disabled—if necessary in order to enter the kingdom, the society's extreme repulsion and amazement at such a suggestion serves to highlight the seriousness of the demands being made (Mt. 18.8; Mk 9.45). The notion of casting away one's hand or foot underscores the importance of the requirement for ethical purity over that of 'physical' purity. When the disabled are made the special objects of divine care (Jer. 31.8; Mic. 4.6-7; Zeph. 3.19; Lk. 14.13), this emphasizes primarily the remarkable compassion of the one doing the good deed, not the deserving nature or dignity of the recipient (see below).

Distinctive Problems of Disabled or Ill Women

Because the Bible views women as a group of people who are fulfilled, legitimated, given full membership into their community, and cared for in old age by their children, especially sons,[1] anything which threatens a woman's ability to be a fertile, able sexual partner is considered disastrous indeed. We may think here of the poignant portrayals of the plight of any of the 'special' mothers in Israel. Literarily, at the level of plot, Sarah's infertility is both a stumbling block and an ultimate vindication

---

1.   C.R. Fontaine, 'The Sage in Family and Tribe', in J.G. Gammie and L.G. Perdue (eds.), *The Sage in Israel and the Ancient Near East* (Winona Lake, IN: Eisenbrauns, 1990), pp. 160-63.

of divine plan and power. At the 'personal' level of character-ization, Sarah's knowledge of her precarious social position is enough to turn her into a exigent, conniving would-be mother who later shows no mercy to another, related child when her own son's inheritance is in potential dispute (Gen. 16 and 21). The fertility wars between Rachel and Leah, the shame of Hannah,[1] the literary disappearance of Michal, David's childless royal wife—all of these are eloquent testimonies to the way in which women acquire and retain status and power in the patriarchal world which usually values their breeding bodies more than anything else about them.[2] Any disability or illness which threatens a woman's ability to fulfill her patriarchal purpose[3] strikes at the very heart of her self-esteem, structured as it is by patriarchal expectations, and denies her her 'rightful' place within the fabric of society.

Further, when we add the polluting, almost magical quality of women's functional blood to this mixture of sociocultural and theological attitudes towards women's fertility and its potential diminishment through illness or disability, the situation for the disabled or ill woman becomes even more dire. Not only has she been denied the self-validating act of procreation, and hence full entrance into participation in her society, but any long-term 'female problems' that she might have also render her ritually impure—perpetual outsider to her community, an object of pity and scorn. God's prophet can think of no better reward than to grant a childless woman a son (2 Kgs 4.14-16), and the 'chutzpah' shown by the woman who bled for 12 years as she wrests her salvation from the healer's cloak is as much a measure of her desperation as it is a testimony to her faith (Mt. 9.20-22).

1. M. Falk, 'Reflections on Hannah's Prayer', *Tikkun* 9 (1994), pp. 61-64.
2. See C. Meyers, 'Procreation, Production and Protection: Male–Female Balance in Early Israel', *JAAR* 51 (1983), pp. 569-93, and more recently, *Discovering Eve: Ancient Israelite Women in Context* (New York: Oxford University Press, 1988), pp. 95-121.
3. In the patriarchal view of women's productivity, progeny is our most important product.

Special Origin of Disabilities

While there is some recognition that disabilities may result from accidents (Mephibosheth in 2 Sam. 4.4) or be classified as 'birth defects' (Jn 9.1-3; Acts 14.8), the Bible is clear that, by and large, the meaning of the disability has something to do with the deity or malicious sub-deities.[1] This is by no means a new concept invented by Israel or the New Testament; it is present in some of the earliest myths from Mesopotamia.[2] It is Yahweh who creates the disabled (Exod. 4.11) and who can reverse the disabilities (Ps. 146.8). Sometimes the motive for such actions is punishment for sins (Zeph. 3.19). In later times malicious spirits, sub-deities, are explicitly named as responsible for the brokenness (Mt. 12.22; Lk. 7.21; Acts 8.7). Whatever the reason for the disability, its 'other-worldly' origin sets its bearer apart, marked as specially cursed, protected, or objectified for the sake of divine healing action. Persons bearing such marks of 'otherness' may expect to be treated differently by the 'normal' members of the group. As literary critic Elaine Scarry points out, given the notorious fickleness of divine presence in ordinary circumstances, sometimes the most potent sign of the deity's presence is the human body which has been wounded or impregnated.[3]

Disability and Illness as Forms of Impurity

As Elshout rightly suggests, based on Daly's analysis of the 'Sado-ritual Syndrome', concepts of purity are at work in society's view of the disabled. Those who view us fear becoming what we are; we are a sign in their midst of how fragile and precarious bodily purity really is. Nowhere is this better exemplified than in Levitical passages about access to the sacred precincts:

1.   Kee, *Medicine*, pp. 21-26.
2.   See the myth of Enki and Ninmah, in T. Jacobsen, *The Treasure of Darkness: A History of Mesopotamian Religion* (New Haven: Yale University Press, 1976), pp. 113-14.
3.   E. Scarry, *The Body in Pain: The Making and Unmaking of the World* (Oxford: Oxford University Press, 1985), pp. 181-221.

And the LORD said to Moses, 'Say to Aaron, None of your descendants throughout their generations who has a blemish may approach to offer the bread of his God. For no one who has a blemish shall draw near, a man blind or lame, or one who has a mutilated face or a limb too long, or a man has an injured foot or an injured hand, or a hunchback, or a dwarf, or a man with a defect in his sight or an itching disease or scabs or crushed testicles; no man of the descendants of Aaron the priest who has a blemish shall come near to offer the Lord's offerings by fire; since he has a blemish, he shall not come near to offer the bread of his God. He may eat the bread of his God, both of the most holy and of the holy things, but he shall not come near the veil or approach the altar, because he has a blemish, that he may not profane my sanctuaries; for I am the LORD who sanctifies them' (RSV; Lev. 21.16-22).

This passage refers, of course, to disabled men; women, as non-men, are disabled by nature in this kind of thinking. While disabilities in men cannot totally eradicate their rights as males, they are severely curtailed, at least in matters of holiness. This may be the reason for the reference, in Zephaniah, to God's removing the 'shame' of the disabled and the outcast. In the paradigm of male honor and shame, being less than fully male is certain cause for self-loathing. That the unacceptableness of the disabled before God finds its way into proverbial form in 2 Sam. 5.8, regardless of its sarcastic or metaphorical application to the Jebusites in that text, is significant, because proverbs express the unexamined folk-ideas of a group, commonly held ideas that are felt to be so universally true they no longer require examination or explanation.[1]

The Disabled as Objects of Divine Action

The dignity of the disabled and their status as potentially valued members of their societies is directly challenged by the Bible's continuous portrayal of them as *objects* of divine action. When they are being healed (Isa. 29.18; 35.5-6; 42.16, 18; Mt. 9.27-28;

---

1. See discussion in C. Fontaine, *Traditional Sayings in the Old Testament: A Contextual Study* (Bible and Literature Series, 5; Sheffield: Almond Press, 1982), pp. 28-53.

12.22; 15.30-31; 21.14; Mk 8.22-23; Lk. 4.18; 7.21-22; 13.11, and more), they serve as marvelous plot-devices that show off the power of God or the anointed one. In effect, they form part of the group of God's 'special interests' in the New Testament: like Romans, tax collectors and women, they show how remarkable is Jesus' broad-based concern and willingness to interact with society's 'throw-aways'. The disciples' questions to Jesus over the man born blind are illustrative, as is the messiah's answer; '"Rabbi, who sinned, this man or his parents, that he was born blind?". Jesus answered, "It was not that this man sinned, or his parents, but that the works of God might be made manifest in him"' (Jn 9.2-3). In this divine contract between creator and creature, apparently creatures may be afflicted, willy-nilly, in order to pump up the deity as healer.

While no one could argue about the desirability of such healing being extended to all who suffer, the relentless characterization of the disabled as objectified beneficiaries of divine healing robs them of their true status as courageous, coping, creative persons—persons who are valued just as they are. As objects of healing, the disabled also experience a negative valuation when the healing does *not* materialize: Job's wretched plight serves as a sign to his friends that he must be a very great sinner indeed, or why would he be so afflicted? For those whose physical conditions are not likely to improve, the questions of faith and personal meaning raised by the Bible's continued stress on the disabled/ill person as one in the state of awaiting divine healing can demoralize and disempower rather than providing a means for continued growth.[1]

In summation, the Bible's representation of the sick and disabled reflects the social world out of which it came, a world in which survival depended on individual health or group care for its more disadvantaged members. Concepts of purity, divine origin of disability, and objectification for theological and literary purposes all work together to paint a negative picture of

---

1. The book of Job is of particular help in such cases, since it is clear there that affliction is not a product of sin, or lack of faith: and that howling one's angry questions at heaven is a more wholesome, faithful response than whitewashing the deity with lies.

the possibilities and powers of the disabled. At least one of the challenges faced by such persons is overcoming the burden of this characterization. It is no wonder that churches respond so slowly and ineptly to the special needs of this community, for they are themselves handicapped by their theological legacy. Nowhere is this more potently visible than in the Bible's view of those who are other than physically whole, and feminists who locate themselves within traditions for which the Bible is still normative need to be aware of the content and impact of its outlook on this topic.

A Feminist Re-Reading of the Bible for Disabled Women

As is often the case when direct appropriation is not possible for the critical feminist, situating the voice of the marginalized as *central* rather than peripheral can produce a dramatic re-reading of biblical materials. The New Testament's emphasis on spirit over flesh is usually detrimental when applied to women, since they are viewed primarily as 'flesh makers', ones who induce men to fleshy thoughts which often produce actions issuing in the production of yet more flesh creatures, babies. For disabled women, however, the New Testament's preference for 'spirit' as the defining construct of human anthropology actually *works*. We know better than to identify fully with bodies that are so patently unable to give shape and structure to the yearnings of our spirits. We *know* we are more than the flesh that sometimes seems much more like a trap that ensnares us than the medium that allows us to manifest our inner thoughts. Cast off an offending member to achieve a greater good? No problem: these are the kind of compromises that make up our daily struggle, and the Bible—unlike most of the medical profession— understands that we are more than the physical body, more than our disabilities and limitations.

Similarly, the Bible's view of the disabled as candidates for divine healing can also cut across the medical profession's too-easy dismissal of possibilities and hope for those in our circumstances. The orthopedic specialist who told me to accustom myself to debilitating pain and that I would never walk without a cane again could not imagine that I would ever hike to inaccessible waterfalls or lead dance workshops—but I do. New studios in psychoneuroimmunology (PNI) are confirming that the spiritual practices of many religions offer a real advantage in the management of health problems.[1] Attitude and image can create miracles where western medicine can only shake its collective head. Certainly we must be on guard against purity fetishes, objectification and negative evaluations should 'healing' not be complete or even visible, but the Bible's claim that faith makes a difference ought to be heard and celebrated. The healing stories of the New Testament emphasize over and over again that the faith of the one healed is as much a part of the healing action as the divine compassion that is extended (Mt. 9.22; Mk 5.34; 10.52; Lk. 8.48; 17.19; 18.42; Acts 14.9), thus mitigating somewhat the overall objectification and passivity in the characterization of the disabled or chronically ill. Further, both Testaments show women active and powerful in contexts where fertility—that emblem of women's wholeness and cultural value—is clearly less important than a yearning heart, skillful tongue or firm resolve. These are the kind of characterizations which can empower those existing on the boundaries of normal life. While it is important to us to be seen, heard, included, and valued *as we are* in our brokenness, we must not accept the narrowed choices and silence that society prefers for us. The Bible, in suggesting that our attitudes and expectations shape our experience and ability to receive healing, gives us back the power to imagine ourselves differently and to craft a reality that more accurately reflects our talents as survivors.

Narrative theory in the Hebrew Bible has been in the process of shifting some of its focus from an emphasis on plot structure ('what happens?') to interest in characterization ('who?', 'why?') and its importance as an element which also exerts a powerful influence on the construction and reading of biblical texts.[2] This

---

1.   See, for example, J. Achterberg, *Imagery in Healing: Shamanism and Modern Medicine* (Boston: New Science Library, 1985), as well as works by Deepak Chopra, Herb Benson, W. Brugh Joy and others engaging in the exploration of 'body/mind' medicine.

2.   D.M. Gunn and D.N. Fewell, *Narrative in the Hebrew Bible* (Oxford Bible Series; Oxford: Oxford University Press, 1993), pp. 46-49.

approach includes investigation into the way characters are 'built up' in the minds of readers through weighing the speeches made by and about the character, comparison of such speeches to actions portrayed, inferences drawn based on the narrator's perspectives, and filling in the gaps everywhere in evidence due to biblical authors' particular reticence in filling in details. Applying some of those insights we are able to discover *why* the portrait of Jesus the healer is so very welcoming to the chronically ill and disabled. This healer is notable for many of the things he does *not* do: he performs no painful tests on the one already suffering, he does not indulge in accusing the victim, nor is he particularly interested in apportioning blame. He does not disdain to *touch* the person seeking healing, nor does he exclude those with previously existing conditions. He seeks no payment, except the amendment of life where necessary, and he takes no personal credit for his actions, ascribing to the divine the healing he dispenses. He actually forbids discussion of his deeds, and acknowledges the role of patients in their own recovery, rather than treating them as objects of his care. He seldom delays when presented with a sufferer in need, nor does he require the signing of release forms absolving him of all responsibility for his actions. Indeed, his very willingness to engage in healing acts on behalf of the poor and suffering often lead the reader to wonder about his lack of 'professional detachment' and failure to enforce healthy ego boundaries—such a healer seems almost fated to be consumed by the crowds that throng to him for attention. It is impossible for a reader who is achingly familiar with the faulty health care systems of the United States not to dream longingly of an encounter with such a decidedly un-capitalistic, selfless health care provider. Endlessly available, powerfully efficacious, tenderhearted and understanding—disabled and chronically ill persons necessarily carve out the character of Jesus the healer from the flinty rock of their experiences of the modern medical establishment, and he is seen in high relief. When human doctors fail, a miracle-working rabbi is a blessing indeed.

Unfortunately what is missing from this portrait of the healer is the presence of women who act in a healing capacity, filling roles that were familiar to the sufferer, then as now.[1] Naturally, it was not part of the New Testament writers' agenda to delineate all of the healing options or healers available to their societies, since their main focus is on the remarkable abilities and disposition of Jesus. But the feminist reader of such healing portraits of Jesus misses the midwife, the wise woman, the folk healer, the mothers, wives, sisters and daughters who routinely nurse the ailing members of the traditional household. Typically for the literature of the patriarchal societies who created the Bible, the unseen, unpaid, ordinary work of women in sustaining the everyday life goes largely unrecorded and uncelebrated. In the lived experience of the disabled and chronically ill, however, the touch of women in healing contexts is not one we care to forget.

Examining the tradition of women healers in the Bible, we find the wisdom tradition especially useful in suggesting the shape of women's participation in this socially necessary form of care-giving. Wives, sisters, aunts, mothers and female slaves in the household probably performed routine tasks of health care, such as administering special diets (cf. Tamar in 2 Sam. 13), providing for the patient's basic physical needs, and offering first aid drawn from the rich tradition of folk medicine.[2] Specialized forms of care such as midwifery or 'advanced' herbalism were no doubt particular skills, and the women who practiced them, judging from other ancient Near Eastern evidence, were probably trained by the elder women of their families for such 'medical specialties'. Whether such health care took place within the confines of the extended family, the so-called 'private domain', or in the world of the village and city at large, the 'public domain', women were the ones holding the

---

1. See S.A. Sharp, 'Folk Medicine Practices: Women as Keepers and Carriers of Knowledge', *Women's Studies International* 9 (1986), pp. 243-49; M.J. Hughes, *Women Healers in Medieval Life and Literature* (Salem, NH: Ayer Company Publishers, 1987); and C. Fontaine, 'The Social Roles of Women in the World of Wisdom', in A. Brenner (ed.), *A Feminist Companion to Wisdom Literature* (The Feminist Companion to the Bible, 9; Sheffield: Sheffield Academic Press, 1995).

2. See 'The Social Roles of Women in the World of Wisdom', pp. 32, 40-46, with their corresponding notes.

basin, wiping the brow, and admonishing 'Push!'

In the world of the deities, we find that for goddesses, like their human sisters, healing is a special charge for some: Isis, in her earlier 'trickster' manifestation, with her cures for snakebite and special deeds in recovering the dead; Ḫannaḫannaš, the mother of the Gods, and Kamušepaš, the Ḫattic goddess of magic and healing, from Anatolia; and the many goddesses with healing tasks known to us from Mesopotamian myth all testify for the role of the female in caring for the ill.[1] The latter-day Ptolemaic and Greco-Roman Isis, now a full-scale savior-goddess, must have been a special competitor in appeal to the sick for New Testament audiences. In the mythological tradition which placed her as the savior-sister of Osiris and the loving mother of Horus, their son conceived after Osiris's death by means of Isis's special magical acts, this goddess nicely epitomizes the healing activities of the sister-wife-mother, known to her later followers as 'Queen of Heaven'.[2] Indeed, her enduring attraction must have been a cause for some consternation to New Testament writers, for her powers of transformation and healing were formidable. If we are inclined, out of our own desperation, to admire the picture of all-male healing presented to us in the New Testament, we must remind ourselves continually that it is a portrait that does not include the

1.   For the relevant texts, see *ANET*; for Isis, 'The God and His Unknown Name of Power' (12-13); for Ḫannaḫannaš and Kamušepaš, 'The Telepinuš Myth' (126-28); for Sumerian Ninhursag and those she creates to heal Enki, see 'Enki and Ninhursag: A Paradise Myth' (37-41).

2.   The 'biography' of the later Isis is known to us primarily through late Classical sources: Plutarch, *De Iside et Osiride*; Apuleius, *Metamorphoses: The Oxyrhynchus Papyri*; and Ptolemaic texts ('The Songs of Isis and Nephthys', 'The Lamentations of Isis and Nephthys', and 'The Hour-Watches'). For discussions of these texts and the portrait of the late Isis, see C.J. Bleeker, 'Isis as Savior Goddess', in S.G.F. Brandon (ed.), *The Savior God: Studies in the Concept of Salvation Presented to Edwin Oliver James* (Manchester: Manchester University Press, 1963), pp. 1-17; J. Gwyn Griffiths, *Plutarch's De Iside et Osiride: Edited with an Introduction, Translation and Commentary* (Wales: University of Wales Press, 1970); S.K. Heyob, *The Cult of Isis among Women in the Graeco-Roman World* (Leiden: Brill, 1975); M. Robbins Dexter, *Whence the Goddesses: A Source Book* (New York: Pergamon Press, 1990).

'shadow' of female healers, human and divine, which would have been part of the natural backdrop for the peoples of that time. Indeed, rather than dismissing the healing work of Jesus as a distressing or distasteful Hellenistic 'miracle' element interpolated into our high-minded ethical, historical biblical religion, we might do well to consider that one being promoted as a savior must naturally be shown performing such essential tasks, *especially* if those tasks are often assigned to competing goddess traditions.

If Jesus is indeed the 'Wisdom' (*Sophia*) of God, as claimed in 1 Cor. 1.24, then perhaps we must posit a more 'indigenous' root for the depiction of his work as healer. This is the wisdom tradition of the sages, especially women sages, whose duties included the medicinal arts and tending the sick. Such noted scholars as Rudolf Bultmann and Claus Westermann have taken much care in showing how the sayings of Jesus (whether original to him, adapted by him, or later incorporated into the gospels by the church writers) do nothing if not present this man to us in the guise of the sage.[1] For Westermann, wisdom is the thread which binds the Testaments together.[2] It is not beyond the realm of possibility to think that the healer who is shown justifying his work among the people by using the proverb 'Those who are well have no need of a physician, but those who are sick; I came not to call the righteous, but sinners' (Mk 2.17), might also have understood his work as healer by means of the models offered to him by the wisdom tradition he so frequently quoted. Even when praising this compassionate healer of the first century, it must be the special wisdom of those considering such matters today to recover the buried, authorizing female traditions beneath the brief notices left us in patriarchal sources.

1.   R. Bultmann, *The History of the Synoptic Tradition* (trans. J. Marsh; New York: Harper & Row, rev. edn, 1968), pp. 69-106.

2.   *Wurzeln der Weisheit: Die ältesten Sprüche Israels und anderer Völker* (Göttingen: Vandenhoeck & Ruprecht, 1990), pp. 9, 123-29.

Part IV

ANTI-JUDAISM IN THE NEW TESTAMENT AND ITS
FEMINIST INTERPRETATIONS?

SECOND TEMPLE JUDAISM, JESUS, AND WOMEN:
*YEAST OF EDEN**

Amy-Jill Levine

Contemporary investigations of the historical Jesus, particularly
those which address his cultural setting, are in a state of
ferment. A rising trend in Jesus research has shifted away from
Jesus the eschatological prophet concerned with temple, law,
theology, and the people Israel. Increasingly popular is a
construct derived in good measure from the Q source, which
portrays Jesus as a Mediterranean peasant sage most closely
associated with Cynic social observations. Reconstructions of
second temple Judaism have appropriately moved away from
the constructs of 'normative' or 'catholic'; their replacement,
formative Judaism, was initially developed to convey the lack of
monolithic practice and theology. In some present Jesus
research, however, formative Judaism's diversity has dissolved
into an amorphous ethos virtually indistinguishable from its
Hellenistic gentile neighbors. Yet these various studies have
remained consistent on one issue. Unlike the diverse views of
the man and his cultural matrices, the view of Jewish women in
antiquity has remained as solid as Mrs Lot.

Where feminist analysis had been in the vanguard of
disciplinary rethinking in literature, social theory and cultural
theory, the question of women has remained the handmaiden in
most studies of second temple Judaism and the historical Jesus;
when it does appear in the more recent works, it serves to

*   First published in *Biblical Interpretation* 2.1 (1994); reprinted by
permission.

preserve old dichotomies in new guises.[1] The prevailing hypothesis is that Judaism, however and if ever defined, regarded women as weak-willed, wanton and, in general, worthless. Jeremias, who presents an *appendix* (not surprisingly) on the 'Social Position of Women' in *Jerusalem at the Time of Jesus*, sets the agenda; he speaks of Judaism's

> very low opinion of women, which is usual in the Orient where she is chiefly valued for her fecundity, kept as far as possible shut away from the outer world, submissive to the power of her father or her husband, and where she is inferior to men from a religious point of view... Only against the background of that time can we fully appreciate Jesus' attitude to women.[2]

Similarly, Elisabeth Meier Tetlow depicts a 'Judaism in the first century [that] had emerged from the oriental patriarchal tradition in which women were considered the property of men, with no rights, no role in society except childbearing, and no education'.[3] Such orientalizing of the Jews serves to distinguish them culturally and ethnically from Jesus and his followers.[4] This

1. There are notable exceptions to this observation; see especially Elisabeth Schüssler Fiorenza's sustained comments on the problem of anti-Jewish exegesis in *But She Said: Feminist Practices of Biblical Interpretation* (Boston: Beacon Press, 1992). See also B.J. Brooten, 'Early Christian Women and their Cultural Context: Issues of Method in Historical Reconstruction', in A.Y. Collins (ed.), *Feminist Perspectives on Biblical Literature* (Chico: Scholars Press, 1985), pp. 65-91; *idem*, 'Jewish Women's History in the Roman Period: A Task for Christian Theology', in G.W.E. Nickelsburg and G.W. MacRae (eds.), *Christians among Jews and Gentiles* (Philadelphia: Fortress Press, 1986), pp. 22-30.

2. J. Jeremias, *Jerusalem in the Time of Jesus* (Philadelphia: Fortress Press, 1969), p. 375 (Appendix, pp. 359-76). Jeremias notes, 'there were plenty of disdainful opinions expressed on women. It is striking to see how these opinions outweigh opinions of high esteem, which were by no means lacking' (p. 375). The same comments may also be applied to the Christian canon and patristic corpus, but Jeremias does not make this comparison here.

3. E.M. Tetlow, *Women and Ministry in the New Testament: Called to Serve* (College Theology Society; Lanham, MD: UPA, 1980), p. 6.

4. See, for example, L. Poliakov, *The Aryan Myth: A History of Racist and Nationalist Ideas in Europe* (New York: Basic Books, 1974).

rhetorical move suggests that Palestinian Jews of the second temple period are different not only in attitude but race from those who follow Jesus. The church, in turn, (implicitly) escapes the confines of orientalism for the blessed freedom of Hellenism. The appeal to the Orient is an appeal to an ideological construct that opposes the Christian West to the rest, to the great disadvantage of the latter. Neither the general category of Orient nor the depiction of the Jew is questioned in this move; each categorization reinforces the other, and together they buttress the West's own unreflected self-identity.

In other cases where the tactical use of the rubric 'oriental' is not employed, the strategic orientalist goals remain in place. Judaism as a worldview or a culture is still seen both as distinct from and as regressive compared to both its gentile neighbors and the followers of Jesus in its midst. This portrait is then not infrequently extended to encompass the modern synagogue and community. And indeed, at times the rhetoric draws, consciously or not, on modern stereotypes. For example, Leonard Swidler's *Women in Judaism* finds a 'dominance of a severely inferior status of women and even an intense misogynism in the formative period of Judaism' that is 'in no way weakened or deflected by evidence that there existed at the same time sincere human affection toward wives... or that there were some *domineering* Jewish women' (emphasis mine). In turn, 'since the subordinate position of women, and even misogynism, was so profoundly and intimately bound up with Judaism in this formative period, the inferiority of women and misogynism have also tended to have an overwhelming influence in the subsequent history of Judaism'.[1] This early treatment is groundbreaking in its introduction of the subject matter and is commendable, as are Swidler's other works, in its attempt to eliminate anti-Semitism and sexism from the church and society; nevertheless, it has been criticized for the dependence of its conclusion on select rabbinic citations to define the period of

On (academic) stereotyping of the Orient and its inhabitants see E. Said, *Orientalism* (New York: Pantheon, 1978).

1. L. Swidler, *Women in Judaism: The Status of Women in Formative Judaism* (Metuchen, NJ: Scarecrow Press, 1976), pp. 168-69.

'Formative Judaism'. Swidler, however, has not changed his approach. In his 1988 *Yeshua, A Model for Moderns*, he reasserts that 'Yeshua wanted it to be abundantly clear that his teaching, unlike that of other rabbis, was intended for both men and women' and that 'in Judaism it was considered improper, even "obscene", to teach women the scriptures'.[1]

The scholarship of the 1980s and 1990s appropriates much of this model for moderns. In the entry under 'Women, NT' in the *Anchor Bible Dictionary*, Ben Witherington suggests that 'The Palestinian Jewish culture was one of the most patriarchal in the Mediterranean crescent'.[2] How bad was it? It 'limited women's roles and functions and severely restricted: (1) their rights of inheritance; (2) their choice of relationships; (3) their ability to pursue a religious education or fully participate in the synagogue; and (4) their freedom of movement'.[3] P.W. van der Horst observes that

> [n]ot only Philo and Josephus...but also Ecclesiastes, Ecclesiasticus, Testament of Reuben, the Mishnah, and a great number of other sources present women as creatures who can easily be misled and seduced (and are easily seducing), who need to be protected against themselves, and can best be kept inside the home as much as possible.[4]

---

1. L. Swidler, *Yeshua, A Model for Moderns* (Kansas City: Sheed & Ward, 1988), pp. 93, 84.

2. B. Witherington III, 'Women (NT)', *ABD*, VI, p. 957. This sort of comparison serves only a polemical or apologetic purpose. So R.S. Kraemer: 'Greek and Roman culture can hardly be characterized as inherently less misogynistic than Israelite culture (on what scale would we measure such things, and for what purpose?)...'. See *Her Share of the Blessings: Women's Religions among Pagans, Jews, and Christians in the Greco-Roman World* (New York: Oxford University Press, 1992), pp. 193-94.

3. Witherington, 'Women (NT)', p. 957-57.

4. P.W. van der Horst, 'The Role of Women in the Testament of Job', *Nederlands Theologisch Tijdschrift* 40 (1986), p. 278; reprinted in *idem, Essays on the Jewish World of Early Christianity* (Göttingen: Vandenhoeck & Ruprecht, 1990), p. 99. Van der Horst explicitly follows Swidler's *Women in Judaism* as well as L. Archer, 'The Role of Jewish Women in the Religion, Ritual and Cult of Graeco-Roman Palestine', in A. Cameron and A. Kuhrt (eds.), *Images of Women in Antiquity*

Susanne Heine speaks of the 'strict observance of the precepts of the law expanded casuistically by the Jewish scribes [and] therefore women like Lydia must have found Christian faith even better and more in accord with their hopes'.[1] Similarly, Léonie Archer's *Her Price is Beyond Rubies: The Jewish Woman in Graeco-Roman Palestine*[2] devalues her subject.

Whatever second temple Judaism may have been in terms of theology, politics, economics, or aesthetics, it was, according to this construct, generally bad for women. And, whatever the Jesus movement was, it was good for women. Oppressed, repressed, suppressed, and therefore depressed by patriarchal socio-cultural controls, Jewish women were of course attracted to the 'community of equals' of the Sophia-Christ. The gospel of this 'radically egalitarian [kingdom] ... rendered sexual and social, political and religious distinctions completely irrelevant and anachronistic'.[3] What good news this was! Women were

---

(London: Croom Helm, 1983). Yet van der Horst provides data that contradict his model; cf. his citation from Josephus, *Ant*. 15.29.5: 'Salome sent him [Costobarus] a document dissolving their marriage, which was not in accordance with Jewish law' (p. 121 n. 44).

1. S. Heine, *Women and Early Christianity* (Minneapolis: Augsburg, 1988), p. 84. On Paul, W. Munro, 'Women, Text and the Canon: The Strange Case of 1 Corinthians 14.33-35', *BTB* 18.1 (1988), p. 27, labels 1 Cor. 14.33-35 part of the 'Jewish tradition, savagely anti-feminist'.

2. L. Archer, *Her Price is Beyond Rubies: The Jewish Woman in Graeco-Roman Palestine* (JSOTSup, 60; Sheffield: JSOT Press, 1990). More balanced, but rarely cited, is G. Mayer, *Die jüdische Frau in der hellenistisch-römischen Antike* (Stuttgart: Kohlhammer, 1987).

3. J.D. Crossan, *The Historical Jesus: The Life of a Mediterranean Jewish Peasant* (San Francisco: Harper, 1991), p. 298. See also B. Mack, *Q, The Lost Gospel: The Book of Christian Origins* (San Francisco: Harper, 1993), p. 9, on the 'human community based on fictive kinship without regard to standard taboos against association based on class, status, gender, or ethnicity'. See also E. Schüssler Fiorenza, *In Memory of Her: A Feminist Theological Reconstruction of Christian Origins* (New York: Crossroad, 1984). Although she eloquently and correctly insists that the 'feminist Christian foundation story is that of Jewish women and their vision' (p. 107), she also wonders if 'Jesus' reform of Judaism was so radical that it engendered the articulation of a new ethos' (p. 81). What

the man from his cultural origins smacks not only of theological Docetism but also of sociological anti-Semitism. Further, Jesus and the women among his earliest followers were Jewish both ethnically and culturally. While the views they held of the Jewish people, the temple, sacred Scripture and theology may have differed from those held by others (Pharisees, Sadducees, the Baptist's disciples and so on), such 'Jewish' concerns were not erased.

Secondly, some branches of the Jesus movement, and perhaps Jesus himself, may not have been quite as egalitarian as some have argued. Reformists and revitalizers, sages, prophets, and social critics have not always or even often regarded women as a marginalized group needing liberation or even incorporation; examples of reformers with liberating rhetoric but problematic attitudes to women range from Amos and Hosea to Martin Luther King, Jr, and Mohandas Gandhi. Their words are interpreted by and for women as calling forth a liberationist ethos, but their intent or their focus may not have been on gender-based inequities or women's access to positions of power.

Thirdly, some Jewish women may have joined the Jesus movement without primary regard for their position as women *per se*. They may have been attracted to the message (whatever it was) for the same reasons (whatever they were) that motivated their fathers, brothers, husbands and sons.

And fourthly, a greater methodological awareness of the apologetic effects of comparison is warranted. Too frequently commentators attempt to demonstrate that Judaism, or Christianity, was somehow 'better' for women than other competing movements. The claim that one system is better than the other fails to acknowledge its own essentializing of both women and their traditions. Unacknowledged are its presuppositions: that economic, political and psychological needs are indistinguishable and unimportant; that all women have the same needs and desires; that Christianity and Judaism are ultimately monolithic systems; that those women who chose the less helpful system are misguided, coopted by patriarchalism, or children of the devil. Comparison, especially in case-specific analysis, is a helpful interpretive tool for the historian. Triumphalism is not.

freed from the law (which in these constructs is syno
with oppressive legalism, restricting rituals, and even
based economic exploitation). Witherington again, this
one of his SNTS monographs, states that 'Jewish womer
have seen the new religious roles allowed them in Chr
as being in stark contrast to what had been the case in th
synagogue or at home'.[1]

This essay calls both views—of women in second
Judaism and of women in the Jesus movement—into q
When I look back on the double constructs of the Jewish
who did and did not follow Jesus, I find that the salt of
has lost its taste. Representations of women have t
served as a solvent which separates out the wheat f
chaff, or perhaps better: women are constructed as tl
which ferments the stale domestic beer of Judaism and tl
imported brew of Christianity. The results are intoxica
ultimately both leave a bad taste. New approaches to th
of the second temple and the person of Jesus—extrac
research, Cynic comparisons, cultural anthropology and
continually reinvent both topics. Yet most reconstructi
revisions, by reiterating the traditional construct of first
Jewish women, preserve to some degree the mode
Judaism and liberating Christianity. 'Judaism' remain
guished either implicitly or explicitly from the orient
those Galileans and Judeans who followed Jesus if not
himself.

As alternatives to the constructs just cited, this essa
first, that many second temple Judaisms were muc
welcoming of women's influence and participation
usually acknowledged. Therefore, if Jesus and/or his
followers are seen as offering a liberating worldv
women, then this view should be regarded as represen
critical feminist impulse' already present in Judaism.[2] To

---

then does 'Jewish' or 'Judaism' mean? Much more helpful is
She Said.

1. B. Witherington III, *Women in the Earliest Churches* (
59; Cambridge: Cambridge University Press, 1988), p. 114, cf. p. 7
2. Schüssler Fiorenza, *In Memory of Her*, p. 107.

Diversity in Second Temple Judaism

Neither the reconstruction of Jewish culture nor the search for women's history can remain wedded to the canons of church and synagogue. Our sources must include the pseudepigrapha, archaeology and epigraphy, rabbinic texts, writings by Josephus and Philo, apocryphal, Patristic, Montanist and so-called 'heretical' Christian documents, Hellenistic materials from historians to satirists to oracles to Stoic and Cynic sayings, manuscripts from Elephantine, the Dead Sea, the Cave of Letters, Nag Hammadi, and so on. But casting the net widely is insufficient; the catch itself must be evaluated.

Even when researchers have strayed from their traditional testamentary ties, they have often been selective in their choice of texts. To Witherington's frequent citations of Ben Sira and the *Testaments of the Twelve Patriarchs*, counter-evidence appears in synagogal inscriptions, *Joseph and Aseneth*, the *Testament of Job*, Tobit, Judith, *4 Maccabees, Pseudo-Philo*, Philo on the Therapeutrides, Josephus on gentile women attracted to Judaism (for example, *War* 2.559–61; also Helena of Adiabene) and women in the royal household (Salome Alexandra, Berenice), the *Corpus Papyrorum Judaicarum*, and even the Christian canon. These sources record Jewish women's social influence, educational responsibilities, leadership roles, prophetic vocations, concern for inheritance, prayers, Nazirite vows (Helena, Berenice, etc.), activities in the public sphere, and so on. For example, van der Horst locates the final section of the *Testament of Job* 'in esoteric and mystical circles of early Judaism, of about the beginning of the Common Era, very probably also in a group in which women played a leading role'.[1]

Rather than see restriction as normative, one might take a cue, if not a Q, from studies of early Christian women and argue that their Jewish sisters were not everywhere and at all times confined to the private sphere, religiously marginalized, or socially oppressed. Texts that insist upon such restrictions may

---

1. Van der Horst, 'Testament of Job', pp. 287-88 and 108-109.

represent reactions to women's freedom (such as the Pastoral Epistles compared to the apocryphal Acts) or androcentric idealizations (such as the Mishnah). As Schüssler Fiorenza suggests, 'Could it be that the rabbis' "reality building" and andocentric projection in the Mishnah were the response to the socio-political current within the first and second century that allowed women to question and to undermine the traditional hegemony of the patriarchal social order?'[1] That much data for Jewish women's relative freedom comes from the Hellenistic diaspora is no excuse for dismissing it in an analysis of Jesus' own cultural environment. If Philo is adduced for Jewish misogyny, then Pseudo-Philo can be adduced for women's leadership.[2] Moreover, Hellenism had certainly penetrated Palestine.

Of the various explanations of first-century Jewish women's hypothetically limited roles, levitical purity legislation combined with its later rabbinic elaboration remains the most popular. Recently, this explanation has received some support from the appropriation of both abstract and applied cultural-anthropological models. On the one hand, grid/group modeling has led to the classification of 'Judaism' as entirely patriarchal in practice and rhetoric. On the other, the Jesus movement is then interpreted as a voice against if not a reaction to a Jewish-Hellenistic society operating on the honor/shame model found in (principally Catholic, post-industrial) Mediterranean villages. As Crossan avers,

> It is possible and instructive to take a proposed Mediterranean constant, in this case the politics of sexual honor, and study it across present space and past time and from fieldwork to biblical text. Mediterranean anthropology... can serve as a necessary discipline in situating archaeological artifacts or

---

1. Schüssler Fiorenza, *In Memory of Her*, p. 59.
2. On Pseudo-Philo, see C.A. Brown, *No Longer Be Silent: First Century Portraits of Biblical Women* (Gender and the Biblical Tradition; Louisville, KY: Westminster/John Knox, 1992), and B. Halprin-Amaru, 'Portraits of Women in Pseudo-Philo's *Biblical Antiquities*', in A.-J. Levine (ed.), *'Women Like This': New Perspectives on Jewish Women in the Greco-Roman World* (Early Judaism and its Literature, 1; Atlanta: Scholars Press, 1991), pp. 83-106.

controlling how we imagine the long-ago lives of ordinary people... '.[1]

Jesus' hypothetical rejection of purity legislation becomes then, usually implicitly, a principal motivation for women's affiliation with his new movement.

For example, Witherington speaks of 'the all-consuming interest in purity legislation' which prohibited women 'from taking significant roles in the synagogue due to their monthly period of levitical uncleanness'.[2] But such restriction is not, for Witherington, limited to the synagogue; he also posits that 'Jesus rejected many levitical laws about clean and unclean since he apparently fellowshipped with the unclean, allowed unclean women to touch him... '.[3] The argument that levitical law had such an exclusionary effect on women is not supported by sources either ancient or modern. Women played a role in the public sphere from the mill to the market. Society did not shut down during their menstrual cycles.

Witherington's denial of women's synagogal activities also fails to convince. If the organization of the pre-70 synagogue is unclear, *Qal vaḤomer*, how much more so women's roles within it? Next, he leaves uncited Brooten's pioneering scholarship on women's synagogal associations and leadership titles.[4] Thirdly, since the synagogue was not a site of sacrifice or a locus of priestly matters, Witherington does not explain why purity issues would be of such concern. Even regarding the temple

---

1. Crossan, *Historical Jesus*, pp. 8-9. Crossan's application of anthropological method is by no means unreflective. Perhaps, however, his 'proposed' might be underscored.

2. Witherington, 'Women (NT)', p. 957. See the more extensive commentary in his *Women in the Earliest Churches*, p. 160, and other monographs.

3. Witherington, 'Women (NT)', p. 958.

4. B.J. Brooten, *Women Leaders in the Ancient Synagogue: Inscriptional Evidence and Background Issues* (BJS, 36: Chico: Scholars Press, 1982). Against Brooten are Swidler, *Yeshua*, p. 108 n. 9; and Mayer, *Jüdische Frau*, pp. 90-91. Mayer at least notes that women's place in synagogues is not nearly as clear as their position in the temple cult and that women did visit synagogues and take up endowments for their administration (see pp. 88-89).

there are no comments in the rabbinic literature—a notable absence given the misogyny of some of its contributors—descrying the construction of the Women's Court.[1] Nor does Witherington here distinguish between the concerns of a priest offering a sacrifice and a peasant milking a goat: in the former case, a concern for purity would likely have been greater. Yet even in this comparative situation, the priest is not more 'Jewish' than the goatherd any more than a nun is more Catholic than a layworker; priests and goatherds, Sadducees and tanners fulfill different roles within Jewish society. Finally, this overconcern with purity implies both that Pharisaic practices were normative for all Jews in Palestine if not also in the diaspora and that Pharisaism had a negative view of women. Pharisaic families likely did adhere to certain purity regulations, such that during menstruation either the woman in question did not prepare meals or her family ate in a state of cultic uncleanness. However, it would be incorrect to view such practices uncritically as demeaning or marginalizing to women. Pharisaic women adhered to the same cultic regulations as did Pharisaic men; there was no distinction within the home in terms of cultic practices. Further, as Neusner has demonstrated, 'We do have ample evidence that women as much as men voluntarily undertook the disciplines of santification as the Pharisees understood them'.[2]

Witherington's view shares little in common with the 'common Judaism' recently depicted by E.P. Sanders. According to Sanders, 'purity laws affected daily life relatively little. Their principal function was to regulate access to the Temple... Because impurity was so common, Jews in general were not afraid of it, and they did not behave in strange ways in order to

1.   E.P. Sanders, *Judaism: Practice and Belief, 63 BCE–66 CE* (London: SCM Press; Philadelphia: Trinity Press International, 1992), p. 57. The rites and architecture of the temple were, however, quite androcentric. On women in the synagogue, see, most recently, Kraemer, *Her Share*, p. 106.

2.   J. Neusner, *Judaism in the Beginning of Christianity* (Philadelphia: Fortress Press, 1984), p. 60. Neusner warns, however, that this picture derives from men.

avoid it'.[1] Although perhaps too generous toward his subjects, and perhaps finessing the question of what constitutes 'strange' behavior—what may have seemed quite normal to them may be in fact bizarre to us, as encounters between Reform and 'Ultra-orthodox' demonstrate—Sanders provides a helpful balance to Witherington. And as for Jesus' 'fellowshipping' with menstruants, the claim begs the question. No doubt such a woman's male family members, neighbors and fellow Jews in the marketplace or at the well also did so.

The Cynic construction of Jesus offers a variant of Witherington's view, but it moves even farther from Sanders's 'common Judaism'. The 'Jewishness' of this Jewish-Cynic figure is difficult to locate. John Dominic Crossan asserts:

> It was obviously possible for the first Christian generations to debate whether Jesus was for or against the ritual laws of Judaism. His position must have been, as it were, unclear. I propose... that he did not care enough about such ritual laws either to attack or to acknowledge them. He ignored them, but that, of course, was to subvert them at a most fundamental level.[2]

By the same token, neither to attack nor to acknowledge may translate into taking something 'for granted', which is to accept it at a most fundamental level. Likely always a topic to be debated—the early church shares much in common with modern scholarship—the question of Jesus and the law cannot be so lightly dismissed since the gospel accounts do not suggest that he himself lightly dismissed it. Reinterpretation of the law (for example, logia on divorce, on celebrating the sabbath) testifies not to dismissal but to profound engagement.

Second to issues of purity in discussions of the improved lot of women in the Jesus movement is the debate over their leadership opportunities. Again, the thesis begs the question. Witherington once more summarizes the major view:

> There is no evidence that prior to Jesus' ministry Jewish women were ever allowed to be disciples of a greater teacher, much less travel with such a teacher, or instruct anyone other

---

1. Sanders, *Judaism*, pp. 71, 76.
2. Crossan, *The Historical Jesus*, p. 263.

than children. In such a restrictive context, Jesus' relationship
to women must have seemed radical indeed.[1]

Not necessarily. First, there is no clear evidence that Jewish
women were not so permitted; what body of lawmakers established and enforced this policy? Who were those 'great teachers'
who restricted their fellowship to men? Secondly, that a woman
would follow a 'miracle worker' or 'prophet' would neither be
miraculous nor particularly prophetic. It is unlikely that no
women followed Theudas or the Egyptian or John the Baptist.
Thirdly, the question of women's discipleship roles can be
variously interpreted; would the women around Jesus be any
more 'disciples' than, for instance, the women among the
Hasidim or the Qumran affiliates? Fourthly, non-Jewish women
were attracted to Judaism as they were to Christianity: these
gentile women then became disciples of Judaism.[2] As for
Priscilla, her teaching role may have sprung from her experiences in a non-Christian Jewish context.[3] In turn, her apparent

---

1.   Witherington, 'Women (NT)', p. 957. Witherington swims in the
same stream as Jeremias, *Jerusalem*, pp. 375-76; 'Luke 8.1-3; Mark 15.41
and par. (cf. Matt. 20.20) speak of women following Jesus, and this was
an unprecedented happening in the history of that time. John the
Baptist had already preached to women (Matt. 21.32) and baptized them
(citing Gospel of Nazarenes, in Jerome, *Adv. Pelag.* 3.2); Jesus, too,
knowingly overthrew custom when he allowed women to follow him'.
See also Tetlow, *Women and Ministry*, pp. 56, 93, on Jesus' unprecedented teaching of women. Tetlow goes so far as to suggest that 'if he
had confined his teaching to synagogue and Temple, women would
have been barred altogether from listening to him'.

2.   Cf. Schüssler Fiorenza, *In Memory of Her*, p. 90, on the 'attraction
of women to the oriental cults, among them Judaism and Christianity'.

3.   See Kraemer, *Her Share*, p. 192, following Brooten. This argument
is the converse of the common statement, best expressed by Tetlow
(*Women in Ministry*, pp. 78-79), that Judaism patriarchalized the
church: 'When, at the close of the New Testament period, the Christian
model of servant was replaced by Jewish models of presbyter and bishop,
and in the second century the Old Testament model of levitical
priesthood was applied to ecclesiastical office, women came to be
excluded from the official ministry of the church'. Witherington
(*Earliest Churches*, p. 182) suggests that the gospel writers gave significant attention to women because 'when they wrote there was significant

itinerancy may be traced to the Claudian exile of all Jews from Rome in 49 CE.

While the appropriation of cultural anthropological schema such as an adapted grid/group analysis has some potential for generating insights about or partial understandings of second temple Judaism, it does not offer a framework 'heading off ethnocentrism from the very outset', as one of its principal advocates, Bruce Malina, has argued.[1] Malina locates 'a sense of independence, leadership, task orientation, outward orientation, assertiveness, self-discipline, impassivity, activity, objectivity, analytic-mindedness, courage, unsentimentality, rationality, self-sufficiency, confidence, and emotional control' as 'male ends values'. In turn, the 'corresponding means values such as dependence, non-aggression, non-competitiveness, inner orientation, interpersonal orientation, sensitivity, nurturance, subjectivity, intuitiveness, yieldingness, receptivity, and supportiveness' are seen to shape the 'female side, the underside of Hellenistic society'.[2] The rhetorical essentialism is then applied to Judaism:

> The individual Jewish male could relate to God with female qualities (means values) in both political and kinship institutions and still serve God as male. Judaism thus reveals an embedded religious institution that offers its male adherents a type of social-psychological integration and allows them expression of the total range of human values, male and female. This means that Jewish institutions were largely, if not exclusively, male focussed. The problem for females was: how

resistance to such ideas perhaps especially amongst Jewish Christians'. Liberation appears to begin with Jesus, bypass anything 'Jewish', and reappear among gentile Christians.

1. B. Malina, *Christian Origins and Cultural Anthropology: Practical Models for Biblical Interpretation* (Atlanta: John Knox, 1986), p. iv. See the trenchant review by S.R. Garrett in *JBL* 107.3 (1988), pp. 532-34. Ross Kraemer's *Her Share* also employs Mary Douglas's model, but she recognizes the problems grid/group analysis has for reconstructing women's roles (pp. 18-21), as does A.C. Wire, *The Corinthian Women Prophets: A Reconstruction through Paul's Rhetoric* (Minneapolis: Fortress Press, 1990). For a brief critique of the so-called objectivity of such schema, see Schüssler Fiorenza, *But She Said*, p. 84.

2. Malina, *Christian Origins*, p. 157.

can women as cultural means become ends and still remain female selves? The problem, of course, was simply and selectively unattended to.[1]

Within the 'strong group/low grid' model fall all Christian canonical documents save the gospel of John. The 'radical standpoint' remaining to the rest of the canon's ideology shares with the American, French and Russian revolutions the 'desire to restructure society in order to implement genuine traditional and human values' (surely a good thing from the perspective of his American readers), and questions or even ignores the 'patriarchal and paternalistic modes' of the jural clergy; it also makes these modes 'accessible to females (embodying means values)'.[2] Jesus himself, according to this construct, embodies both the masculine ends values of the deity and the feminine means values accorded in Judaism to the (male) community.

Such a view ignores Jewish impulses toward, *inter alia*, mysticism, healing and wonder-working (ironically, this is precisely the 'Jewish' context in which Crossan locates *his* Jesus[3]). Similarly problematic are Malina's generally vague references to 'Jewish institutions'. Women had roles in temple and synagogue; they also had roles in that other 'institution', the home. The idea that Jewish practice and institutions might be *exclusively* male-focused is one problem; the question of what the 'female self' is—both among those who follow Jesus and for Jewish women—is another still. Beyond the jargon and some actually quite helpful observations, the upshot is the same: early Christianity for the most part provides women greater options than the Judaism out of which it sprang.

1. Malina, *Christian Origins*, pp. 158-59.
2. Malina, *Christian Origins*, pp. 184 (on radical analogies), 163. For Malina, 'at its outset Christianity was a strong group/low grid movement with non-jural standing, providing for male centeredness and male integration' (p. 162).
3. Crossan (*Historical Jesus*, p. 421) insists that 'Jewish' and 'Cynic' be weighted equally, with Jewishness being in general presented in the context of Palestinian peasant turmoil and a magician-type figure.

ITEM CHARGED

P.Barcode:

Due Date: 5/5/2016 10:30 PM

Title: Feminist companion to the
Hebrew Bible in the New
Testament / edited by Athalya
Brenner.

Author:
CallNo.: BS2379 .F450 1996
Enum.:
Chron.:
Copy: 1
I.Barcode:

*Non-reserve items can be renewed by logging
into your library account at www.jkmlibrary.org.
All library materials are subject to recall.*

The Early Jesus Movement

In applying models we also need to consider the exegete's role: what is at stake for us? What confessional, feminist, scholarly baggage do we carry if not unpack? Some Christian feminism speaks of Jesus as liberating women: to their full authenticity as human beings, to a satisfying relationship with God. But liberation 'to' implicitly requires also liberation 'from'. Concerning 'liberation *to*', it is difficult at best to determine what 'authenticity' would have meant to an artisan woman from the Galilee. While some theologians and historians have uncritically and romantically addressed the 'to', they have expended a great deal of energy demonizing the 'from'. And that 'from' is, as Judith Plaskow noted over ten years ago, most often a negatively construed Judaism.[1] The same argument, *mutatis mutandis*, actually appears in Jewish scholarship as well. That is, some Jews proffer positive comparisons of Jewish women to their Near Eastern, Greek and Roman counterparts, which serve the same function as the Christian polemicists. The difference is that there is no one speaking on behalf of 'paganism' here to protest.[2]

1. In her seminal (ovarial?) article, 'Blaming the Jews for Inventing Patriarchy', *Lilith* 7 (1980/5741), Judith Plaskow demonstrated that Christian feminists, seeking to reclaim Jesus from ecclesial doctrine and practices which limited their participation and sense of wholeness, recovered Jesus at the expense of Jewish women's history and of Judaism in general. Her work is generally uncited by those writing on Christian women's history. In some cases it is cited and *then* ignored. Plaskow's point has been echoed by Susannah Heschel, Elisabeth Schüssler Fiorenza, Bernadette Brooten, and others. For a good example of the problem, see Schüssler Fiorenza, *In Memory of Her*, p. 63, in which the author's student presents the following response to Paul: 'He is so taken up with giving a good impression to the pagans that he is reverting to his rabbinic prejudices I think. As if the proper place of woman was in the home bearing children'. The 'reversion' is anachronistic and the viewpoint of the domestic sphere well known from non-Jewish Roman sources.
2. L.H. Feldman, 'Palestinian and Diaspora Judaism in the First Century', in H. Shanks (ed.), *Christianity and Rabbinic Judaism* (Washington, DC: Biblical Archaeological Society, 1992), p. 33, on *War*

I begin with a presupposition different from those who would claim that the culture out of which the Jesus movement emerged epitomized sexism. Yes, Palestinian Judaism, like all other contemporary Mediterranean/Hellenistic cultures, had its patriarchal and androcentric impulses. The question is one of degree. This same society did allow for women's public presence, as not only the (Jewish) sources cited above but also the gospels themselves testify: a woman from the crowd hails Jesus (Lk. 11.27); another seeks his healing powers (Mk 5.24-34 and pars.); a third participates in funerary rites (Lk. 7.11-15); several provide support (Lk. 8.1-3); another frequents the temple (Mk 12.42); one owns a house (Martha), and so on. Several of these examples could be explained as effected by Jesus' message and not as indicating the public presence of Jewish women. Yet the gospel writers themselves do not depict their appearances as remarkable.[1]

Similarly, there is solid evidence for women's participation in Jesus movements. Remaining unclear is, however, the nature, the degree, of this participation.[2] The sayings source, Q, provides one helpful entry into the topic. For all the controversy over its existence as a separate source, its layers and its genres, as least most scholars locate the sayings usually queued under its label as originating with Jesus or his earliest followers. And many locate within these sayings the seeds of an egalitarian ethos.

From the Q materials two tropes concerning women emerge: food and sex. Or, as Luise Schottroff argues, the Jesus movement condemned the 'patriarchal household and its cultural markers: meals and marriage'.[3] But unlike Schottroff, I do not

2.559-61 and the 'relatively more elevated and respected position of women in the Jewish community'. See also L. Schiffman, *From Text to Tradition: A History of Second Temple and Rabbinic Judaism* (Hoboken: Ktav, 1991), pp. 249, 257, on the 'rising status of women' in the Tannaitic period and the unexplored comparison of biblical to ancient Near Eastern marital legislation.

1. See S. Davies, 'Women in the Third Gospel and the New Testament Apocrypha', in Levine (ed.), *'Women Like This'*, pp. 188-90.

2. Kraemer, *Her Share*, p. 131.

3. L. Schottroff, 'Itinerant Prophetesses: A Feminist Analysis of the

think that the sayings indicate a rejection of patriarchal practices. For meals, I propose that in the Q affair the women
catered but that their contribution to the community was either
not recognized or undervalued. For marriage, I do not see the
evidence of household disruption as having led to more leadership opportunities for women. Neither the itinerant mission nor
the likely commendation of celibacy necessarily led to women's
increased status or freedom.

Dining Out

According to Crossan, Jesus transgressed dining conventions
across status lines. He proposes that within ordinary meal
settings, 'taking' and 'blessing' are the prerogatives of the
master, 'breaking' and 'giving' are the tasks of the servant.
Jesus, according to the synoptic gospels, assumed all four roles.
For Crossan, then, 'The male followers would think more
experientially of females as preparers and servers of the family
food. Jesus took on himself the role not only of servant but of
female... long before Jesus was host, he was hostess'.[1]

The first problem is that we cannot pinpoint the background of
the pericopes which depict this supper: were only men present,
as the silence of the Gospels might indicate? What connections
might be drawn to *seder* celebrations (for example, distributing
matzah), or to sacrifices (distributing pieces of meat)? Nor do we
know much about women's actual participation in such areas.
Were women usually seen as 'hostesses' in the first place?
Ironically Witherington, following Swidler, who appeals only to
Strack–Billerbeck, insists that Palestinian Jewish women would
not have served; this was the task of male slaves.[2]

A feminist ideological response would offer a different
perspective on Crossan's historical imaging. The alternative

Sayings Source Q', Institute for Antiquity and Christianity, Claremont
Graduate School *Occasional Papers* 21 (1991).

1. Crossan, *Historical Jesus*, p. 404. See p. 262 on egalitarian meal
practices in Jesus' 'brokerless' kingdom. Malina (*Christian Origins*) offers
helpful observations on the role of fasting in the Jesus community.

2. Witherington, *Earliest Churches*, p. 145. Questions of class/
economics are relevant as well.

way of interpreting his view of meal performance is that Jesus has coopted women's roles. Jesus is the 'Lord of Hosts' and so not a model of egalitarianism.

On the more practical level, Kraemer offers one view that would support Crossan's conclusion on egalitarian meal practices. She proposes that the elimination of dietary laws would have more impact on women's experiences, 'since to the extent that women were involved in the preparation of food and the maintenance of cooking equipment and dishes, they would have borne the major responsibility for the enforcement and observation of such requirements'.[1] But this argument too needs nuancing. Dietary concerns (ensuring the food to be eaten was unpolluted, appropriately tithed and so on) may have been primarily regulated in the market, yet Kraemer does not extend her point to food acquisition. Further, a different spin could be put on the 'burden' of adherence to the laws of *kashrut*: any Jew involved in dietary maintenance could point with honor and pride to such accomplishment. Take away the ritual, and one strips women of a point of honor. Thus Jacob Neusner astutely observes:

> For all of the evidence of this period [the 'age of Jesus'] takes for granted that women prepared meals. Accordingly, women gained a central role in the correct observance of the rules governing cultic cleanness... It follows that women now enjoyed the power to secure sanctification.[2]

It is not clear that this role was positively recognized by the men in their community, nor is it clear that the women themselves appreciated the centrality of their role. But the possibility of both must remain open.

The women of Q appear in the context of food preparation, but they receive no credit for their work. 'There will be two women grinding meal together; one will be taken and the other left' (Q 17.35). The verse is juxtaposed in Luke to 'two in one bed' or 'on one couch' (*klinh*—most likely not a bed but reclining at a meal).[3] In Matthew the logion is paired with a reference to

---

1. Kraemer, *Her Share*, p. 143.
2. Neusner, *Judaism in the Beginning of Christianity*, p. 59.
3. K.M. Corley, *Private Women, Public Meals: Social Conflict in the*

two in the field. Because Q has the tendency to pair men's and women's activities (for example, the mustard seed and the leaven; Q 13.20-21), the reference to the women may well have stood beside one if not both of these two statements. In each case, the point is the same: 'one will be taken and the other left'. The point is not that women's daily work is valued. Rather these passages testify to a sexual division of labor. Luke, or perhaps Q itself, also encodes a second message: women prepare the food; men eat.[1] A similar displacement of women's food preparation appears in Luke's marginalizing of Martha's concern with service (10.38-42).[2]

Q's one explicit description of women's labor exemplifies the negative valuation accorded her food production. The parable of the leaven (Q 13.20) bursts with negative images: yeast, in the symbolic vocabulary of Judaism and the early church, represents moral corruption; the woman's 'hiding' (*krypto*) rather than kneading leaven suggests that her manual labor is under-handed,[3] and the process she cooks up is one of decay.

Synoptic Tradition (Peabody, MA: Hendrickson, 1993), p. 134, on the 'traditional roles of men and women in the context of ancient meal customs'. For a reconstruction of this saying see C.N. Jefford, 'The Dangers of Lying in Bed: Luke 17.34-35 and Parallels', *Foundations and Facets Forum* 5.1 (1989), pp. 106-10.

1. If woman's work underlies the references to spinning and weaving in the parallel saying (Q 12.27), so Schottroff ('Itinerant Prophetesses', p. 5), once again her labor is devalued. She is either in possession of the resources needed by her community (cf. Lk 15.3-10) or she cannot provide for them. If she does so provide, her efforts are not valued: clothes are not to be a concern. On inclusion of Lk. 15.8-10 in Q, see J. Kloppenborg, *Q Parallels, Synopsis, Critical Notes, and Concordance* (Foundations and Facets Reference Series; Sonoma, CA: Polebridge Press, 1988), pp. 176-77.

2. Corley, 'Place at the Table', pp. 162-65: 'The role of women in the context of early itinerant missionary practice is to host the itinerant preachers. They are discouraged from concerning themselves with the diakonia that is the activity of men' (p. 162, in reference to Lk 10.38-42).

3. As Bernard Brandon Scott (*Hear Then the Parable* [Minneapolis: Fortress Press, 1989], p. 236) notes, the figurative use of 'hiding' to describe the process is elsewhere unattested. Following Scott is Crossan (*Historical Jesus*, p. 280). See the alternative but unconvincing

Unfortunately, the parable has become sufficiently domesticated that its negative valences are often overlooked. A helpful modern hermeneutical shift would be to associate yeast with the infection of the same name and thereby regain the connotations of women's dis-ease.

One could argue that the parable revalues both leaven and women by equating women's labor with divine activities.[1] One could read, as Crossan does, with the *Gospel of Thomas*, which compares the woman, rather than the yeast, with the Basileia: 'The Kingdom is like a certain woman. She took a little leaven, concealed it in some dough, and made it into large loaves'.[2] But those negative images keep rising given the context of the saying. For example, Crossan includes among the 'original sayings' yet another pericope from the *Gospel of Thomas*: 'The Kingdom is like a certain woman who was carrying a jar full of meal. While she was walking on the road, still some distance from home, the handle of the jar broke, and the meal emptied out behind her on the road. She did not realize it; she had noticed no accident. When she reached her house, she set the jar down and found it empty'.[3] The woman in this 'Jesus source' is hardly portrayed in a positive manner. Combined, the parables present an image of women's incompetence: the former puts too much yeast into her dough; the latter spills her grain.

Other aspects of food production are coopted by Q's men. Just as Jesus is the good host, so the father exemplifies the good parent who gives his son an egg, fish and/or bread (Q 11.9-13 [Mt. 7.7-11]).[4]

Even the order—as it is usually reconstructed—of the sayings material undermines women's role in food production as well as the value of food production itself. In Q's Temptation, Jesus

discussion in Schottroff, 'Itinerant Prophetesses', pp. 6-7 and n. 17. The attention of the reader is directed less to the woman's hands than to the yeast.

1. Schottroff, 'Itinerant Prophetesses', p. 6.
2. Crossan, *Historical Jesus*, p. xxi.
3. Crossan, *Historical Jesus*, p. xxi.
4. Schottroff, 'Itinerant Prophetesses', p. 5; *idem*, 'Wander-prophetinnen: Eine feministische Analyse der Logienquelle', *EvT* 51 (1991), pp. 332-44.

acknowledges that bread is not the sole requirement of life (Q 4.4//Deut. 8.3: 'Man [*sic*] shall not live by bread alone') Yet his own ability to produce bread—from stone rather than from yeast and flour—is not doubted. If bread is not the staff of life, how much more so is it not the distaff. The structure—bread first from stone, then from flour and yeast—parallels the Genesis creation. The male deity and his surrogate give birth to woman in a pristine, painless manner; she will recreate the originary act, but her reproduction is messy, uncontrolled and accompanied by blood; the blood is analogous to yeast in its association with taboo power and decay. So, in contrast to Jesus, women make bread, but surreptitiously and from decaying elements. Even before we encounter the parable, we are predisposed to dismiss the importance of the woman's work. For Q, the real work is done by the deity, by his son, or by that son's male surrogates. The deity provides the 'daily bread' (Q 11.3).

Woman's marginal representation in turn leads to questions about the economic and social conditions for the production of Q material. Schottroff reconstructs a Palestinian society and Jesus movement in which displaced women found themselves in extreme poverty. Yet Jesus himself is known for wine consumption and enjoying a good meal (Q 7.34), and banquets are a common trope of the source. The ethic of Q is more one of voluntary renunciation of possessions than of famine and poverty.[1]

Gospel references to food and meals do more than signal wishes for the goodies of the eschatological banquet, evoke host–guest relations, or indicate types (such as the upwardly mobile) with whom the Jesus people associated their lord or with whom Jesus actually associated. To provide food is a sign

1. See L. Schottroff and W. Stegemann, *Jesus and the Hope of the Poor* (Maryknoll, NY; Orbis Press, 1986; originally published as *Jesus von Nazareth—Hoffnung der Armen* [Stuttgart: Kohlhammer, 1978], pp. 54-88); ET p. 2. See also Schottroff, 'Wanderprophetinnen', p. 4 on Q 11.3 as indicating a 'land of hunger'. See the brief but helpful commentary in R. Uro, *Sheep among Wolves: A Study on the Mission Instructions of Q* (Annales Academiae Scientiarum Fennicae Dissertationes Humanarum Litterarum; Helsinki: Suomalainen Tiedeakatemia, 1987), p. 134 n. 69.

of honor. And, in Q rhetoric, the honor belongs to men.

Lying In

Moving from meal to marriage, contemporary studies reveal a similar apologetic treatment of women in the Jesus movement. First, most scholars assert that marriage and procreation were obligatory for all Jews. Then, they assert that Jesus' teaching about 'the ability to be single for the sake of the Kingdom opened the door for women to assume roles in the Jesus movement other than the traditional domestic ones ... Herein we see the liberating effect the teaching and life of Jesus had on women... '.[1]

Related to the interest in celibacy is the thesis that the breakdown of the (patriarchal) family among the followers of the Jesus movement permitted, if not forced, women to join the wandering charismatics who proclaimed the good news and lived the life of freedom. Since the gospel evidently splintered families, so this argument goes, mothers-in-law and daughters-in-law, now with no home or at least no welcome within it, took to the road.

Yet the data may be otherwise interpreted. References to women in Q present a domestic picture: grinding meal and baking bread.[2] Women do not accompany the children and Sophia (Q 7.32-35) in the marketplace.[3] Q offers no pictures of

---

1. Witherington, 'Women (NT)', p. 958. In a less strident vein, J.P. Meier, *A Marginal Jew: Rethinking the Historical Jesus*. I. *The Roots of the Problem and the Person* (Anchor Bible Reference Library; Garden City, NY: Doubleday, 1991), pp. 339, 342: 'Celibacy was a most unusual lifestyle, practiced by only a few, including one or two marginal groups. But we should not be totally incredulous if the marginal Jew we pursue, a Jew so unusual in so many ways, should manifest his marginality by celibacy as well... He stood out in his day because of his easy association with female disciples and other women.'

2. See now also Schottroff, 'Wanderprophetinnen', pp. 332-33. 1. So W.J. Cotter, 'Children Sitting in the Agora: Q (Luke) 7.31-35', *Foundations and Facets Forum* 5.2 (1989), p. 79.

3. For a reconstruction of Q 7.31-35, see Cotter, 'Children Sitting', pp. 63-82. Cotter proposes that the referent in 7.31-32 evokes the world not of children at play but of the judicial courts (p. 68). This is the only negative reference to children (p. 70) in Q as well as the general Jesus

women commissioned by Jesus. Nor, outside Q, do accounts of the women at the cross, such as Mk 15.40-41, attest to their roles as itinerant missionaries, as Schottroff suggests.[1]

Evidence for women's itinerant missionary work or itinerant leadership in the Palestinian community may have been suppressed, to be sure, but such evidence may not have existed in the first place. A disciple is not always a leader; a patron does not always set policy.

On the other hand, that Mary Magdalene and others, as Kraemer puts it, 'clearly exercised leadership, in the modern sense, within the earliest movement around Jesus of Nazareth' is possible.[2] Mary may well have been influential in one circle of the Jesus movement, but I see no reason to classify her authority as qualitatively or quantitatively different from that of the various women adduced in Jewish inscriptions and documents. Nor is it clear that she functioned as an itinerant missionary.

Implicitly denying the existence of women missionaries, Meier

tradition. Therefore, it may represent the second stage of Q, when social norms are reinforced (see below). On 7.33-34, see also L.E. Vaage, 'Q1 and the Historical Jesus: Some Peculiar Sayings (7.33-34; 9.57-58, 59-60; 14.26-27)', *Foundations and Facets Forum* 5.2 (1989), pp. 159-76. Corley, 'Place at the Table', notes that 'wailing and piping' were socially coded as women's activities, but the Q text *we have* (as opposed to what may underlie Luke) does connect children, not women, with these activities. On Q 12.42-44 as part of a collection on the theme of 'householder/servant', see A.J. Dewey, 'A Prophetic Pronouncement: Q 12.42-46', *Foundations and Facets Forum* 5.2 (1989), pp. 99-108, following R.A. Edwards, *A Theology of Q* (Philadelphia: Fortress Press, 1976), pp. 65-66. Dewey (p. 100) further proposes that the distinction between male and female servants is a Lukan motif ('Matthew's *sundouloi* is more appropriate').

1. Schottroff ('Itinerant Prophetesses', p. 10 n. 32), arguing against Monika Fander (*Die Stellung der Frau im Markusevangelium* [Altenberge, 1989], pp. 329 onwards), who suggests that the wives of the itinerant missionaries remained at home. And she insists that the 'notion of itinerant prophets, who were economically dependent on a sedentary and patriarchally structured community, is inapplicable' to Q because there were no 'normal' family structures within the movement. See 'Itinerant Prophetesses', p. 9.

2. Kraemer, *Her Share*, p. 174, citing Schüssler Fiorenza, Wire and D'Angelo.

suggests that a follower like Simon Peter had to leave his mother-in-law (Mk 1.30) 'and presumably his wife (1 Cor. 9.5)'.[1] Yet Paul speaks of ministers as being accompanied by 'sister wives', so Meier overstates the case that women were left behind. Conversely, for Crossan the sister-wife is 'a female missionary who travels with a male missionary as if, for the world at large, she were his wife [in order] to furnish the best social protection for a travelling female missionary in a world of male power and violence'.[2] Meier bypasses the women-on-the-road, but Crossan runs over the description of the men: Paul speaks of Peter, and the other apostles. Peter was married; there seems little reason to want in-laws without having a spouse; likely the other Galilean men were married as well. Why then not posit, more simply, that the wives really were wives? Had they a missionary role? The evidence is unclear.

It seems to me likely that Jesus commended an inseparable, Edenic marriage: hence the wives. Just as what has come to be called the sapiential, wisdom, or even Cynic strand of Q pictures a prelapsarian innocence, where shame is eliminated, where the earthly garden provides all needs, and where social pretense is undermined, so too those who inhabit this new Eden would not be divorced. Thus also, the non-Q Mk 10.5-6, summarized in Mt. 19.8: 'For your hardness of heart Moses allowed you to divorce your wives, but from the beginning it was not so'.[3]

What then of the women in the Jesus movement? Some may have gone on the road with their husbands, as 1 Cor. 9.5 but not Q itself suggests. Others may have idealized the mendicant

---

1. Meier, *Marginal Jew*, p. 363 n. 48, and see p. 335.
2. Crossan, *Historical Jesus*, p. 335. The two on the Emmaeus road are therefore 'one named and clearly male, one unnamed and clearly probably female' (p. xiii).
3. Jesus research splits on the authenticity of the divorce legislation. Crossan (*Historical Jesus*, pp. 301-302) posits 'gynecentric' law, with the wife's honor as protected as the husband's. Meier (*Marginal Jew*, p. 132) argues that the earliest form of the divorce legislation 'may have looked something like the Q form behind Luke 16.18/Matt. 5.32, which views divorce completely from the husband's vantage point, since in Jewish law of the time (with rare exceptions) only the husband could effect a divorce'.

lifestyle, but did not themselves participate in it.[1] Still others may have travelled independently or with other women, but once again the evidence is lacking.

Should one accept not only the existence of Q but also the hypothesis that layers can be located, one would find another means of contextualizing women's roles in early Christianity and questioning its alleged egalitarian character. For the second layer of Q, the new social paradigm is one of a settled community rather than mendicant representatives. No longer one of lilies in the field (12.27), the central image is now of houses upon the rock (Q 6.48) and the faithful steward within (Q 12.42b-46). Missionaries who had once wandered from home to home and village to village but who refrained from greeting people on the street are replaced by those (men) who inhabit stable households and who argue their case openly in the agora (3.7; 7.33-34; 11.39-44, 46, 51).[2] Some women then may have lost whatever localized authority they gained when their husbands and fathers returned from preaching the gospel. And, since according to Q the home lacked the status of the open road, women's domestic authority may have gone unrecognized both by the women themselves and by those who controlled community discourse. Still others may have found their houses used by the missionaries and so once again, at best, shared positions of status.

In these cases, marriage was likely preserved. As Horsley states:

> We need not think literalistically that...families were no longer patriarchal. Nor was marriage or the nuclear family rejected or even devalued, as can be seen in the strictures against divorce (particularly by patriarchal prerogative; Mark 10.2-9, 10-12; Luke 16.18; Matt. 5.31-32).

He continues by noting that 'clearly, relations were supposed to be egalitarian in the community',[3] but less clear is how this

1. Uro, *Sheep*, p. 128, following Aune and Kelber.
2. See V. Robbins, 'A Socio-Rhetorical Response: Contexts of Interaction and Forms of Exhortation', *Semeia* 50 (1990), p. 269.
3. R.A. Horsley, *Sociology and the Jesus Movement* (New York: Crossroad, 1989), p. 123.

would function: is egalitarianism practiced within the marriage? Among the families within the movement? Indeed, although absent from the Q source, the various synoptic statements on lust and on divorce would also support such a patriarchally modelled reconstruction of the early Jesus movement. If lust is a problem and remarriage is a temptation, then one result of these concerns might be a sheltering of women.

These observations on the continuity of marriage do not, however, translate into the thesis that members of the early Jesus community engaged in sexual relations. Marriage and celibacy are not mutually exclusive.[1] The thesis that Jesus and/or his immediate, Jewish followers commended the celibate lifestyle does not, however, either distinguish Jesus substantially from others in the Jewish world or necessarily open new avenues of power to women. Celibacy was practiced by a variety of first-century Judaisms, including the Therapeutrides/ Therapeutae (Philo, *Vit. Cont.* 13) and some among the Essenes (Josephus, *War* 2.121; *Ant.* 18.21; Justin Martyr, *Apol.* 14-17). Geza Vermes[2] notes in an excursus entitled 'Prophetic Celibacy' that women were forbidden to soldiers on campaign (1 Sam. 21.5; 2 Sam. 11.11), that participation in the sacrificial cult required abstention from intercourse (Exod. 19.15; cf. 19.9-10); and that temple ministers as well as those taking part in the cult regulated their sexual lives (CD 12.1-2 [on pilgrims]; Josephus, *War* 5.227). Women may have had leadership positions among the Essenes, and Philo observes the cultic activities of the Therapeutrides, but it is not clear that celibacy *per se* led to these positions: celibacy may have been attendant to, rather than the cause of, women's activity.[3]

---

1.   Against Heine, *Women in the Early Church*, who cites 1 Cor. 9.5 as indicating that Jesus and his followers were not celibate. On the possibility of missionary couples' celibacy, see also Schüssler Fiorenza, *In Memory of Her*, p. 169.

2.   G. Vermes, *Jesus the Jew: A Historian's Reading of the Gospels* (Philadelphia: Fortress Press, 1981), citing also, on Moses, *b. Šab.* 87a; *Sifre Num.* 12.1 (from Zipporah's viewpoint), *Vit. Mos.* 2.68-69. See also Jeremias, *Jerusalem*, p. 376.

3.   For the connection of women, asceticism and eschatology, see now Kraemer, *Her Share*, p. 199.

The Q view of procreation and children is metaphorical rather than practical. Images of children are illustrations for adult behavior: 'Truly I say to you, unless you turn and become like children, you will never enter the Kingdom of Heaven' (Mt. 18.3; cf. Lk. 18.7).[1] No mention is made of actual pregnancy and childbirth, and in other early materials procreation is an eschatological problem or is devalued. For example, Paul wishes that all could be as he is: celibate (1 Cor. 7.8-9). Matthew's Jesus speaks of 'eunuchs who have made themselves eunuchs for the sake of the Kingdom of Heaven' (Mt. 19.12). According to Lk. 11.27-28, 'A woman from the crowd raised her voice and said to [Jesus], "Blessed is the womb that bore you, and the breasts that you sucked!". But he said, "Blessed rather are those who listen to the word of God and keep it"'.[2]

Moreover, Q defines motherhood away from the biological, and parental roles are once again coopted by men. The parent is 'Abraham as our father' (Q 3.8), and even his role as progenitor is dismissed: 'God is able from these stones to raise up children to Abraham' (Q 3.8). For the sayings source, seed is from the mustard plant, not the man. The only productive mother is Wisdom (Q [Lk.] 7.35), who replaces the human mother ('woman') of John the Baptist (Q 7.33-35).[3] And even her maternal role is assumed by Jesus, who 'would have gathered your children together as a hen gathers her brood under her wings' (Q 13.34-35). For Q, Wisdom is stripped of her autonomous power. Q 7.35 reverses the presentation of Wisdom in

---

1. What becoming like children actually means is unclear. The traditional view is that a child connotes newness, humility and innocence. Yet Crossan posits that 'to be a child was to be a nobody, with the possibility of becoming a somebody absolutely dependent on parental discretion and parental standing in the community' (Crossan, *Historical Jesus*, p. 269). Support for his view derives implicitly in his text from earlier references to Egyptian, pagan, practices of exposing infants. More helpful is his observation (p. 267) that 'a kingdom of children is a kingdom of celibates'.

2. On this pericope, its parallels and its possible Q origin, see Kloppenborg, *Q Parallels*, pp. 96-97.

3. Luke reads 'Wisdom is vindicated by her children' (Lk. 7.35); Matthew reads 'vindicated by her work' (Mt. 11.19).

Sir. 4.11 as a 'defending mother' and in Wis. 10.14b as 'a powerful patronness/advocate of the unjustly accused'. The roles of dominant and victimized are thereby inverted; Wisdom becomes the mother who must be justified by her children.[1] Wisdom remains fully in the male realm (cf. Q 7.35) as it proceeds from the Father (Q 10.21-22) to the disciple of the teacher (Q 6.40).

These observations on food and sex present a picture of Q far from the theologically and exegetically popular community of equals. If gender egalitarianism was at the heart of Jesus' movement, it is lost to the sayings source. Rather, Q may represent a community externally reviled and internally confused following the shift from mendicancy to settled life, if not earlier by its charismatic leader's death. This group needed order. And it found this order within its own ranks. The Q community defined and maintained itself by controlling the one group within its power: women.

Hermeneutically, the various sayings in Q on serving, on subverting social convention, on conforming attitude to action liberate women today. Historically, the form of liberation they offered may have been otherwise perceived. To the outsider, the life of women in an ultra-orthodox Jewish community is restricted. To many insiders and especially to the convert, life in Williamsburg, just like life under Islamic law or life in a Carmelite convent, is liberating. Such regulated societies provide for all their members order, meaning and sanctification in daily existence; a distance from the outside (profane) world that distracts and detracts from the sanctified life; strong women-based support groups (that is, sisterhoods); and the developed traditions that overcome or at least counterbalance the patriarchalism involved in the community's institution and maintenance. Regulation of clothing, action, relationships is even found by some to counteract the far-too-frequent abuse of and violence against women. Of course the potential for abuse remains, of course in an ideal world women would not be subject to sexism, oppression and violence, and of course many women—socialized into such groups—are dreadfully unhappy.

1.   So Cotter, 'Children Sitting', p. 79.

But one woman's blessed freedom is another's profane if not profanity-filled world.

The women of the Q community may well have been extremely happy, but not, I think, because they were 'liberated' from a purity-obsessed, institutionally restricted, patriarchal Judaism. Nor am I convinced that their celibacy removed them from their traditional roles (since there were children in this early group) or necessarily led to new leadership opportunities.

Did Jesus then offer good news specifically to women? Did women react positively to his pronouncements because they found in his message a freedom denied to them by Judaism? Was the Palestinian Jesus movement egalitarian? Or was it patriarchal Judaism itself that turned Jesus' egalitarian vision into the gendered, marginalizing movement that this particular reading of Q reflects?

If Jesus were an eschatologically inclined prophet who proclaimed the elimination of gendered hierarchies, then he failed on two counts: the end did not come; oppression remained in the communities that proclaimed his name. But just as those words attributed to him inspire the liberation of all peoples—and just as they were spoken to a Jewish audience with the images and insights of Jewish tradition but adapted and adopted by Gentiles—so too today women of various persuasions can unite to reclaim those words of liberation. The past may not be able to reveal the ideal, egalitarian community, but investigation of the texts (if not the texts themselves) offers a means of creating one yet.

THROUGH GERMAN AND FEMINIST EYES:
A LIBERATIONIST READING OF LUKE 7.36-50*

Luise Schottroff

1. The Woman, the Jew and the Man of the Church

On the History of Interpretation of Luke 7.36-50

My observations on the history of the interpretation of Lk. 7.36-50 are based primarily on German scholarly commentaries on the text since 1945, which in turn continue the older tradition of interpretation. In the field of biblical interpretation, neither 1933 nor 1945 makes any difference in the questions of Christian anti-Judaism or sexism. The interpretations all work within a consistent exegetical schema, which I will first present in a simplified form.

In this schema, the woman is a converted prostitute; she has repented of her life as a whore. (I use the word 'whore' because women in the sex workers' movement militantly apply the word to themselves in order to make discrimination visible, and thereby to overcome it.) The erotic aspect of her approach to Jesus (v. 38) is emphasized at length. In the process, the authors create a self-contradiction in their depiction of the woman. Properly, as a repentant whore—as these authors imagine her to be—she ought not to go on acting so 'tarty'. François Bovon helps himself out of the problem by writing: 'Jesus re-interprets the gestures that, in the clichés of the time, were erotic, because the woman's tears indicate the true meaning of her action, even though superficially it is expressed in a manner that is heavily

* This text extends my essay on this subject in L. Schottroff, *Befreiungserfahrungen* (Munich: Chr. Kaiser Verlag, 1990), pp. 310-23 (ET *Let the Oppressed Go Free: Feminist Perspectives on the New Testament* [Louisville, KY: Westminster/John Knox Press, 1993], pp. 138-57).

influenced by her past'.[1] But theologically speaking, the traditional interpretations do not evaluate this repentant whore in the contextual categories of whores, or even women, but in the contextual category of sinners before God. This female figure is generalized into a representative of the *iustificatio impii* and/or the calling of the gentile church.

The Pharisee, in the traditional interpretations, represents the Judaism of the law, which is distinguished from Christianity in this question of unconditional forgiveness. This difference between Pharisaism or Judaism (which are usually equated) and Jesus is often described as 'the surprising element' in the narrative, or 'the new thing' that Jesus brings. The difference between Judaism and Christianity is that between law and gospel, which are understood as alternatives. The Judaism of the law is abolished by Christ.

Jesus is characterized as a brilliant debater and, in particular, as the proclaimer of the new reality, the gospel of God's unconditional grace. It is clear that the figure of Jesus in the narrative becomes a figure of identification for the interpreters. They, too, proclaim the unconditional forgiveness of God. I have asked myself whether these interpreters also identify with the sinners who, in their opinion, the repentant whore represents. But when concrete examples are given to indicate who these sinners might be, the talk tends to run more to drug addicts[2] than to exegetes. We may be permitted to conclude that in this tradition of interpretation Jesus is the prototype of the man of the church, and in two ways: on the one hand, with respect to his magnificent verbal skills, his clever avoidance of embarrassment in what might otherwise be a rather ticklishly erotic situation; and, on the other hand, in his proclamation of the gospel that distinguishes Christianity from Judaism.

Before I mention some individual texts that fall within this schema and inquire into their awareness of the problems contained within the questions of anti-Judaism and sexism, I

1. F. Bovon, *Das Evangelium nach Lukas* (Zürich and Neukirchen: Benziger Verlag, 1989), I, p. 392.
2. E. Schweizer, *Das Evangelium nach Lukas* (Göttingen: Vandenhoeck & Ruprecht, 1982), *ad loc.*

would like to give a brief summary of my own interpretation of the text.

2. The One Who Loved Greatly and Simon the Pharisee

My Interpretation of the Text

I understand the woman as a whore, but not as a repentant whore. When the idea of a whore's repentance is introduced, prostitution is made into a moral problem. Contrary to this understanding, I look at the economic reality of women who have to sell their bodies in order to live. In this text, a whore is presented as a greatly loving human being who, in her life as a whore, has given love in full measure; and yet, her life is so hard that she expresses her powerful desperation in tears. Jesus does not only see the prostitute in her but also the woman who is able to give love. As long as she has no other economic basis for her life, she remains a 'sinner' loaded with cultic and social stigma but, at the same time, she is a greatly loving person with no stigma. I associate the figure of the whore in Lk. 7.36-50 with the discipleship of whores in the Baptizer and Jesus movements (Mt. 21.31-32 par.) and with Jesus' attitude toward 'the least'. Jesus accepts whores as 'the least' among women whose dignity is violated and whose opportunities in life are minimal.

I live in Western Europe, where thousands of Eastern-European women are forced to sell their bodies. We all know the worldwide dimension of the prostitution of women and children. This is the reason for me to fight against the Christian tradition of prostitution as a moral problem, and the Christian idea that prostitution can be overcome by the repentance of the whores.

The Pharisee, Simon, I interpret not as a representative of Judaism or Pharisaism, but as representative of a false attitude toward whores and 'the least' among the people generally. This false attitude can be found in Judaism as well as in Christianity. The text sketches a dialogue between Jesus and this Pharisee in which the Pharisee is criticized as a host (vv. 44-45), and by means of a parable (vv. 40-43) is presented with an opportunity to emulate the magnitude of the woman's works of love. He is to be won over to a new attitude. Nevertheless, we cannot ignore the fact that he is rather reluctantly drawn.

Jesus in this text is a Jewish prophet who confronts other Jews (see also 7.30) with God's will in prophetic speech. The basis of this confrontation is that both of them adhere to the Torah and the God of Israel, the God of merciful love. Conflicts like this one arise out of concrete conclusions about the will of God in a given situation. Mercy and respect in the treatment of whores are at issue, not 'the law', and certainly not the division between law and gospel.

3. Sensitivity to the Problems of Anti-Judaism and Sexism?

Using two examples of interpretation, I want to explore for signs of an awareness of the problems of anti-Judaism and sexism. I will begin with Walter Grundmann's commentary[1]—not because he was an active Nazi, but because he represents the consensus of scholarship. Here we find the type of interpretation I have sketched. Therefore, I need not analyse Grundmann's exegesis in detail now.[2] For Grundmann, the woman is a repentant sinner, grateful and loving toward Jesus; through him she has been saved from 'shame and guilt'. She represents the sinners who are unconditionally forgiven by the gospel of Christ. The concreteness of v. 38 awakens embarrassing emotions in this author: 'This description creates an unpleasant impression'.[3]

Alongside this interpretation, which reveals no consciousness of any problem of anti-Judaism or sexism, I would like to place a

1. W. Grundmann, *Das Evangelium nach Lukas* (Berlin: Evangelische Verlagsanstalt, 5th edn, 1969). The broad circulation of Grundmann's commentaries is partly a consequence of the low price of books in the former East Germany at the time when prices in West Germany were very high.
2. For a detailed analysis of the sexism and anti-Judaism in the interpretation of Lk. 7.36-50, cf. my previous article in *Let the Oppressed Go*, pp. 138-57. In reference to Grundmann on the whole, see L. Siegele-Wenschkewitz, 'Mitverantwortung und Schuld der Christen am Holocaust', *EvT* 42 (1982), pp. 171-80; and S. Heschel, 'Theologen für Hitler: Walter Grundmann und das "Institut zur Erforschung und Beseitigung des jüdischen Einflusses auf das deutsche kirchliche Leben"' in L. Siegele-Wenschkewitz (ed.), *Christlicher Antijudaismus und Antisemitismus: Arnoldshainer Texte* (Frankfurt, 1994), pp. 125-70.
3. Grundmann, *Lukas*, p. 170.

new exegesis that shows some degree of sensitivity to both: that of François Bovon. I shall begin with Bovon's portrait of the woman. That it has been affected by feminist theological discussions is shown by the use of the idea of 'mutuality' of love for God in a theological perspective.[1] However, there is almost no reference to feminist theological publications in the bibliographical notes. Verse 38 is, for him, on the one hand erotic, and then, because of the weeping, on the other hand *not* erotic. The 'hooker' in Luke represents for Bovon the calling of the Gentiles.[2] He does not speak explicitly of the woman's repentance, but understands her tears and gestures as 'both indications of and bases for her forgiveness'.[3] Bovon thereby quite properly dissociates himself from the question whether in this case forgiveness follows repentance, or the other way around— forgiveness first and then repentance; still, he continues to maintain the idea that the woman's sin is overcome by repentance.[4]

The Pharisee is seen in sharp contrast to the woman, whose love is a model. A critique of anti-Judaism is vaguely suggested ('polemic undertones'[5]), but then the anti-Jewish interpretation is carried through. The Pharisee is blind.[6] The overcoming of sin 'does not take place here through a legal control of incapacity and the application of scriptural rules'.[7] Thus the situation is depicted according to the image of a legalistic Judaism, although the open naming of the idea is avoided or, rather, it is named in a remarkably vague footnote about Dupont[8] which avoids giving Bovon's opinion on what Dupont says. The note remains ambiguous, but the substance of the idea of a legalistic Judaism has been introduced into the text. And Jesus is presented primarily as a literary figure drawn by 'Luke', as Lord of the church or similar designations.

1.   Bovon, *Lukas*, p. 395.
2.   Bovon, *Lukas*, p. 389; cf. also p. 25.
3.   Bovon, *Lukas*, p. 395.
4.   Bovon, *Lukas*, p. 396.
5.   Bovon, *Lukas*, p. 389.
6.   Bovon, *Lukas*, p. 393.
7.   Bovon, *Lukas*, p. 396.
8.   Bovon, *Lukas*, p. 396 n. 65: 'Dupont...closes his study with a distinction between ideas of God: that of the Pharisees and that of Jesus'.

Bovon reveals that he knows something of feminist and Jewish–Christian discourse. But in Bovon's work these discourses contribute only to a certain caution in the formulation of anti-Judaism, and not to an open adoption of feminist theological content. The anti-Jewish tradition of interpretation is not criticized. Thus even this new commentary, which in the next twenty years will enjoy very high esteem (as part of the EKK series), stands within the unholy tradition of Christian anti-Judaism as represented by Grundmann. In the description of the woman it also remains attached to the sexist exegetical tradition of moral disqualification of prostitutes.

4. *Feminist Reflections on Anti-Judaism in a German Context*

A difficult problem for the debate on anti-Judaism is the personalizing of anti-Jewish theology. The debate is ostensibly about structural matters (see the homogeneity of Grundmann and Bovon just sketched), but cannot be carried on without citation of textual examples, and thus of particular persons. Have I just denounced François Bovon, taking him as an example, because he has written the newest major German-language commentary on Luke? For years I have taken great care to avoid personalizing conflicts, to the extent that this was at all possible. I prefer to criticize Rudolf Bultmann and Ernst Käsemann because they were and are my respected teachers. I am not interested in leveling moral accusations against them. In their own context, they could not recognize either the problem of anti-Judaism or that of sexism; and, as their student, I also failed to recognize those problems during my period of study. Only through the Jewish–Christian dialogue that has been accessible to the public especially since the beginning of the 1960s have I had my attention drawn to Christian anti-Judaism. It was an essay by Michael Brocke that opened my eyes.[1]

1. M. Brocke, 'Das Judentumsbild neuer Jesusbücher', *Freiburger Rundbrief* 23 (1971), pp. 50-59. In a conversation with Bernadette Brooten in June 1994 I again became painfully aware of the consequences of the murder of millions of Jewish people by Germans. Bernadette Brooten's attention was called to Christian anti-Semitism by a Jewish fellow student, while mine was achieved by reading. The rarity of Jewish

Personalizing the recent discussion is more difficult for me than it is to criticize my teachers, to whom I feel myself attached. On the one hand, as in the case of the examples chosen here, personalization is unavoidable. Still, my interest is not in denunciation but in substantive argument, in promoting the work of a new kind of theology. I understand the uncovering of Christian anti-Semitism to be a long and toilsome process. This holds for my own life too: I have not yet reached the end of the process. The problem seems to me to lie in the fact that, in the German context, a substantive critique is immediately heard as an accusation of moral guilt and a 'killer argument'. However, this only blocks any open discussion or further development toward a new theology. I am attempting, to the extent that it is possible, to make clear to those I criticize that I am not interested in attributing moral guilt to them. On the other hand, such critique is a matter of life and death for Christian theology in a German context. Neo-Nazism shows that even secularized youth who scarcely know the Bible, if at all, have inherited Christian anti-Judaism and Christian sexism; and are turning these as instruments of hate against Jews, foreigners and women.

The German debate over anti-Judaism in feminist theology must be seen in this context. The accusation of anti-Judaism is heard by feminist theologians as moral and personal discrimination. The accusation of anti-Judaism is taken up by representatives of the dominant theology and used to disqualify the whole project of feminist theology, while some scholars fail to subject themselves and their own scholarly and church tradition to a corresponding critique. Andreas Angerstörfer[1] furnishes a published example; I also know of others that are unpublished. The fact is that many feminist theologians in Germany, especially at the beginning, adopted Christian anti-Judaism from the dominant theology without noticing. Today, within the circles of feminist theologians and Christian women, we have active pioneers of a critique of Christian anti-Judaism and together

people among us is a fact that many of us Germans find easy to repress, and we do repress it.

1. A. Angerstörfer, 'Wovon befreite Jesus die jüdische Frau?', *Kirche und Israel* 8 (1993), pp. 161-63.

with representatives of what is, in fact, an anti-Jewish feminist theology. I see two tasks before us concerning the current situation in Germany.

1. Combating theological anti-Judaism and Christian anti-Semitism must be more clearly understood as a task belonging to the content of feminist theology and of Christian identity. The relationship between anti-Semitism, sexism, racism, militarism and the exploitation of nature must be made still more obvious both theoretically (in the concept of patriarchy[1]) and practically in the active work of the women's movement.

2. An effort must be made to achieve sisterly struggle with regard to anti-Judaism in feminist theology. It can only succeed if the discussion is conducted without moral and personal discriminatory (over)tones. Dorothee Sölle[2] has offered some reflections on the preconditions for a sisterly struggle (intersubjectivity, freedom from domination, willingness to risk). The problem here is, how can freedom from domination be achieved as long as anti-Judaism and sexism still, to a large extent, shape the dominant theology in academic contexts? The question of whether a woman hopes to get a job or to achieve some other form of recognition in church or university is always present, though unspoken, in these discussions—and it must be taken seriously. In my context in Germany, an open critique of Christian anti-Semitism or of Christian sexism and the rejection of God's fundamental option for the poor mean exclusion from an academic career.

5. Luke 7.36-50 as a Sign of Hope for a Feminist Theology of Sexuality and Sensuality

The separation of women into honorable 'normal' women and whores, and the discrimination against whores, are instruments of domination. By this means women are forced apart, and they are robbed of their eroticism. Female eroticism appears as something dirty or else as something to be reserved for the marital

---

1. In this respect, I consider the concept of patriarchy enunciated by Elisabeth Schüssler Fiorenza to be a good basis from which to work.

2. D. Sölle, 'Schwesternstreit', in *idem* (ed.), *Für Gerechtigkeit streiten* (Gütersloh, 1994), pp. 112-16.

bedroom. I quote the African American feminist Audre Lorde's[1] classical feminist text on eroticism among women, a text that helps me understand the deeper dimensions of the biblical text.

> The erotic is a resource within each of us that lies in a deeply female and spiritual plane, firmly rooted in the power of our unexpressed or unrecognized feeling...We have been taught to suspect this resource...

Lorde speaks of the erotic as the 'open and fearless underlining of my capacity for joy', as 'self-connection shared'. With Lk. 7.36-50, I would add: eroticism is also the sharing of pain, and the deep union that arises out of the mutuality of this sharing.

It is correct to say that Lk. 7.38 describes an erotic scene. In this narrative, the only actors are the woman and God. The rest is commentary. The woman tells Jesus of her reverence for him, her pain, and her capacity for uncensored love. Jesus accepts this gift in mutuality. By reinterpreting the story to make it the tale of the whore's repentance, it was made to function within the context of the oppression of all women: the separation of whores from 'normal' women and discrimination against female eroticism is thereby perfected. The narrative has always resisted this tradition of interpretation. Jesus, in fact, does not distance himself from the woman's erotic actions or from her real existence as a prostitute. Not only does he not do this, he calls the love of this woman the love of God: 'her many sins have been forgiven her, because she has loved much' (v. 47). Despite a cultural framework in which a whore is qualified as a sinner because she violates the codes of purity, a framework which is not criticized by Jesus, in Jesus' eyes she is a greatly loving person. He does not distinguish between what she shares with him and what she may even have shared with some of her 'johns'—or what she shares with God. For him the woman has loved in the fullest sense of the word—in spite of her being misused. Jesus does not explicitly mention the patriarchal misuse of women and of love. But the story makes it clear that he knows

1. A. Lorde, 'Uses of the Erotic: The Erotic as Power', in A. Lorde, *Sister Outsider: Essays and Speeches* (Trumansburg, NY: Crossing Press, 1984); reprinted in J.B. Nelson and S.P. Longfellow (eds.), *Sexuality and the Sacred: Sources for Theological Reflection* (Louisville, KY: Westminster/John Knox, 1994), pp. 75, 77.

about this misuse and stands up against it. And he supports the woman in her cry for liberation and her power to love. Verse 47 speaks of a love in mutuality and justice, therefore without domination and sexual exploitation. And the subject of this love is a prostitute. Lk. 7.47 is a major challenge to think 'in one breath' of love for God and of women's capacity for love that patriarchal power cannot always succeed in destroying. Even within the conditions of patriarchy there continues to be a resistant and liberating way to love in justice: for wives, whores and men. Therefore, I call this narrative a sign of hope for a feminist theology of sexuality and sensuality.

By way of conclusion, I quote from a poem by a Brazilian prostitute who is involved in the sex workers' movement.

> I am a woman
> I want to be special and precious
> I need love and work
> Sometimes I am small, sad, a child
> Sometimes I am full of power, of dreams and hope.

In the Dangerous Currents of Old Prejudices: How Predominant Thoughts Have Disastrous Effects and What Could Be Done to Counter Them[*]

Leonore Siegele-Wenschkewitz

In the autumn of 1992 Susannah Heschel, the feminist Jewish theologian, came from the United States to Germany as guest professor. During Heschel's stay, neo-Nazi attacks took place in Hoyerswerda, Rostock, Mölln; attacks on former concentration camps and on memorials to Nazi victims became evidence of disdain for foreigners, symbols of an open, developing anti-Semitism in this country. During that time, I held two seminars jointly with Susannah Heschel at the Frankfurt Johann-Wolfgang-Goethe-Institut. The first was on 'The Debate Concerning Anti-Semitism and Sexism in Jewish and Christian Feminist Theology', and the second on 'Jewish–Christian Relationships in Germany from the Enlightenment to the Present'. We recognized our theological cooperation as having a direct relationship to political developments: the stereotype of 'the Jew' shaped by theological tradition is still part of the political debate in Germany. It still functions as part of the 'cultural code' within the concept of 'German uniqueness'. Is there a disastrous relationship in feminist theological interpretation involving the uniqueness of Jews and the identity crisis of a reunited Germany?

Since the end of the 70s, Jewish feminists in the USA have taken notice of anti-Judaism in feminist theory as well as in feminist theology. 'Anti-Judaism', a recently-created term to contrast with 'anti-Semitism', which was created by Wilhelm

[*] Originally published in *Publik-Forum* 12 (June 12, 1993), in German. Translated by Lillian R. Klein.

Marr in 1879, refers to a religiously- and theologically-constituted hatred which incorporates points of view and modes of thought developed predominantly within the Christian tradition. The conceptual differentiation between anti-Semitism and anti-Judaism permits one to trace the multiple and differentiated components of anti-Jewish stereotypes. In our predominantly secular society, anti-Jewish concepts are often no longer perceived as deriving from traditional Christian theology. In this respect, the discussion about anti-Judaism and anti-Semitism in the framework of feminist theology is part of a self-critical negative Christian theology as well as a contribution to research on prejudice.

This issue has been explicitly discussed in Germany since 1986. It engages Jewish as well as Christian feminist theologians. It revolves primarily around two theme-complexes, both of which are tied to anti-Jewish arguments, within feminist theology.

The first cluster of themes concerns Israel's concept of God, the Jewish belief in God. Before Israel developed a monotheistic belief in only one God, it practised goddess worship and goddess belief, affiliated with matriarchal cultures and goddess religions. This goddess worship and goddess belief permitted women to identify the feminine with the divine. According to one feminist theological argument Israel—the Jews—presumably dealt the deathblow to these religions and thereby became guilty of establishing patriarchy. The old stereotype of the Jew as God-killer acquires a new 'feminist' variation and becomes 'goddess-killer'. With regard to the Jewish belief in God, Israel's God is designated a God of revenge, retaliation and anger who, it is assumed, is redeemed and surpassed by the Christian God of love and mercy.

The second complex of themes concerns Christian belief in God and attaches itself especially to Jesus' personality and works. It is argued that Jesus is the first 'new man', the first feminist. Jesus, in distinction from and in conscious opposition to the Jewish milieu of his time, acknowledged and treated women as individuals with equal status to men. Consequently, Christian feminist theology claims more legitimacy than all other religions to demand the emancipation of women. Because the Christian redeemer is presented as a female-freeing God, a decided advantage over Judaism is attributed to Christianity. Again, in this argument, the connection to traditional anti-Jewish patterns of thought cannot be overlooked: Jesus is removed from his Jewish environment. His deeds, beliefs and teachings are interpreted as 'Christian' by reason of their supposed opposition to the religion of the Hebrew Bible, the 'Old' Testament, and to the Jews of his time.

The discussion shows that with such thought patterns and argumentation, feminist authors, without being aware of it, approach the old territory of anti-Judaism. There is a tradition of almost two thousand years' duration of describing the relationship between Christianity and Judaism—especially with regard to the *contrast* between the two religious beliefs. This contrast is perceived as evident in that the Jewish people did not accept Jesus Christ son of God as their messiah and, instead, delivered him to crucifixion. Therefore, God's way with his now chosen people—through Jesus Christ—has been continued by the church. In this view, Judaism does not have its own future as a religion—actually, there is no purpose in its existence at all. After Christ, it was regarded as a surpassed greatness. The relationship between Christians and Jews was characterized by contrast: old/new; encrusted, rigid/liberating; law/gospel; letter/spirit; particular/universal.

This has been the dominant theology in our land; and, in this view, anti-Judaism essentially belongs to Christianity. During the Nazi period, this theology acquired special intensity in the thought of important representatives of Protestant university theology. This segment of academic history, and that of the academic concepts developed during the Nazi period and continued uninterrupted after 1945, are my own research interests. Bible theologians such as New Testament theologian Adolf Schlatte, Gerhard Kittel (both at Tübingen), Walter Grundmann (Jena), Johannes Leopold (Leipzig), the Old Testament theologian Johannes Hempel (Berlin), as well as the famous theological historian from Göttingen, Emmanuel Hirsch, have proposed programmes and models as to how Christianity could be freed from Jews (*entjudet*). In critical debates with Rosenberg's dictum that 'Christianity is Judaism for non-Jews', they wished to show that between Christianity and Judaism there is 'an irreconcilable contrast', that Jesus became 'a repudiator of Judaism' (Schlatter) who had completely separated himself from Judaism. Specifically, the contrast between Christianity and Judaism was described thus: God's revelation to Israel had reproduced itself in Jesus Christ. Since then, the true belief in God flows towards Christianity. Judaism, which had closed itself against Christ, thereby became irreligious. Christians are the true Israel. Such a theology regards Israel as synonymous with the fall from God, with unbelieving, with human ethics and holiness, and denial of God's salvation.

The sharp distinction of the theological opposition between Christianity and Judaism created the conditions for a National Socialist policy toward Jews which was not only available but demanded action. The introduction of the Aryan paragraph or the questionable 'Nürnberg Laws' appeared to this theology as 'measures for a people's politics' in compliance with the Nazi state. If this theology sought, on the one hand, to free Christianity from its Jewish roots, it sought on the other hand to demonstrate close ties between Christianity and Nazism. These goals of a synthesis between Christianity and Nazism were understandably not maintained. The negative view of Judaism, however, the implicit understanding of Christianity as antithetical to Judaism, lived on in the scientific tradition without interruption. The works of known theologians who did not rebel against programmes to eliminate Jews (*Entjudensprogrammen*) were furthered by their students, the clergy and the scientific community. The *Theological Dictionary of the New Testament*, edited from 1933 onwards by Gerhard Kittel, has remained, including its English translation, a standard for exegetical research. The countless biblical commentaries by Walter Grundmann have been the basis for theological literature in Germany for forty years (and a financial basis for the publisher). Schlatter's biblical commentary has had a renaissance since the end of the 70s.

The dominant theology outlived the mass murder in Auschwitz and was maintained, relatively untouched, until the 70s, when it was increasingly questioned in theology and church by critical women and men—first by very few and later by many more. Since the middle of the 60s, through the efforts for dialogue between male and female representatives of Judaism and Christianity, a step-by-step recognition has grown: Christian teaching and preaching is and has been the root of anti-Semitism in that Christianity describes Judaism as its contrast, of lesser value and superseded; and in that Christianity took the place of Israel. Therefore, these critical individuals tied the demand of renewing the relationship between Christianity and Judaism to the goal of advancing a Christian theology without anti-Judaism.

Feminist criticism of anti-Judaism seeks to combine the argument of patriarchy and sexism with that of anti-Semitism and racism. Where is the theological 'place' where criticism can anchor itself on anti-Judaism in concepts of Christian feminist theology? My own position is that such criticism is not only shown to advantage in God's and Christ's teachings but also belongs to the reflection of methods, to the question of the social context/environment, or to the acquisition of writing and tradition. It must be embedded in a 'hermeneutic of suspicion'.

In the concept of 'hermeneutic of suspicion', developed by the American theologian Elisabeth Schüssler Fiorenza, sexism is identified and criticized in biblical tradition as well as in theology. The suspicion does not validate exposed structures of sovereignty manifested in patriarchy, in androcentricity and in sexism. With women pushing at the borders, the structures of sovereignty which rendered them invisible should be tracked down so that they will not be maintained but can be worked against. A hermeneutic of suspicion must—at least in view of German history—equate anti-Judaism and anti-Semitism. Our Christian theological tradition does not only make women invisible and objects of the masculine norm, but it also identifies the 'Other' with Judaism.

It is necessary that this assignment for Christian theology in Germany be thought through once again, and in a special way. One should be aware of a feminist theology developed on German soil as contextual: out of concrete, politically- and culturally-influenced theology; out of our history, culture and religion and thereby also out of our inward anti-Semitism. This should free feminist theological concepts from anti-Semitism by attacking present traces of exacerbation of anti-Judaism and by persisting in this mode. In so doing, our feminist theology faces the task—which has until now been fulfilled separately in society and science—of bringing together Jewish–Christian and feminist discussions. Christian feminist theology has thereby to effect a doubled alteration of paradigm: from an androcentric, patriarchal and sexist theology to a feminist theology; and from enmity with Jews to Jews as bearers of their own identity-values and functioning theology; to an Israel-theology which affirms, to a Christian theology that is indebted to Judaism and at the same time learns respect for the forbidden elements of Jewish belief.

Concretely, this means that various (female) authors—for the sake of the intellectual integrity and political sensitivity of their books, which have collected in them all the antagonistic Jewish stereotypes—must act accordingly, no matter whether this involves a critical revision or removal from the marketplace. It appears to be completely inadequate that whereas feminist theologians recently (February 21, 1988) regarded accusations of anti-Judaism as self-critical—'We, as feminist theologians, also carry the harvest of Christian anti-Judaism with [us] and reproduce it, frequently unreflected, for example, in criticism of the patriarchy of Judaism'—yet such self-criticism remains without consequences.

The German dialogue with Pnina Nave-Levinson (Deja), Susannah Heschel (Cleveland), Judith Plaskow (New York), Eveline Goodman-Thau (Jerusalem), Marianne Wallach-Faller (Zürich), Mirjam Brassloff (Zürich), Cathy Gelbin (Berlin/ Ithaca) and others questions the anti-Jewish stereotype in two ways. Judaism is not a timeless entity, untouched by history or entirely excised from history, Rather, it has changed its greatness during history. The Jewish culture has, like other religions and cultures, developed a feminist movement which demands recognition within the present Jewish quest for identity. Through Jewish feminists, it is becoming increasingly evident that there are traditions for female emancipation in Judaism. The rejection of Judaism as an equally viable and valuable religion and culture, its construction as an Other, has a long tradition in German academic history, a tradition it is necessary to overcome. At present, the abundance of issues related to this problem is reflected in the many initiatives developed for an interdisciplinary research programme. The resolution of the problem will keep us busy for a long time.

Do the Origins Already Contain the Malady?[*]

Edna Brocke

I

Being part of Christian theology as a whole, feminist theology is closely bound up with various, differently-nuanced exegetic traditions. If I, as a Jew, seek to enter the discussion, then it is because I belong to those who would like to make, or at least hope for, a new start within one segment of Christian theology. I have viewed this as a real chance for a beginning, factual and fundamental, of a relational orientation to Judaism as well. This hope was based primarily on the claims advanced by feminists that they wish to read, understand and live the TaNaCh (the Jewish designation for the 'Old Testament', although in a sequence different from the Christian version). A fresh beginning was sought for being open—a new way that would be receptive to other than traditional interpretations. This beginning contained within itself the chance to distance oneself from the anti-Judaism primarily formulated by men.

In retrospect, I ask myself whether my hope was justified. I ask myself, basically, whether there is a branch within Christian theology in which it is possible to overcome the negative Christian relationship to Judaism, and whether one must not conclude that anti-Judaism is fundamental to Christianity. The interesting controversy between the former Bishop of Hamburg Ulrich Wilckens, who backed the thesis that anti-Judaism was basic to the writings of the New Testament and therefore

[*]   Originally published in *Publik-Forum* 13 (July 9, 1993), pp. 14-15, in German. The author is director of the Old Synagogue in Essen; her article is described as 'Jewish observations about a necessary debate'. Translated by Lillian R. Klein.

fundamental for Christianity; and the lively reply by Professor David Flusser of Jerusalem, who attempted to refute this thesis, has unfortunately not been concluded. I think that the issue should be seriously discussed because it touches on the basic question of Christian identity which, since the writings of the New Testament, has been dogmatized rather than discussed. It is possible that expectations, including mine, of new feminist assessments in the contexts of attitudes towards the Jewish people are not to be realized. If this is true, then the resulting dispute is unavoidable.

I I

In addition to basic questions which are not to be directed specifically to feminist theology, there are also those which involve evaluating various texts with regard to their legitimation. Thus Jürgen Moltmann is right when he points out that Jesus, as well as his immediate followers, dealt with an inner-Jewish controversy (in the form of a long process[1])—'differences' which then as now contribute to the life of Judaism. The maintenance of these differences and the constructive association with them is certainly correctly described by the concept of 'pluralism'.

Inner-Jewish pluralism was, however, quickly seized upon by non-Jews who, in a process of differentiation which was not their own, rashly took up their own stances—and here, for the first time, appears the question of legitimation. Many of these stances entered the writings of the New Testament. One can say of them that they were chiefly written by people who themselves knew the inner-Jewish discussions and were affected by them in some way or another. If one bears in mind that the writing-down took place long after the events and was therefore influenced by later points of view, one recognizes problems of interpretation and meaning that could never be structurally solved. This is the case because the writings on Jesus' life in the New Testament have become an article of faith for Christians, as is the case with the TaNaCh for Jews.

1. See *Publik-Forum* 10 (1993).

Because non-Jews two thousand years ago were caught up in a massive, inner-Jewish existential, not philosophic, process, there is the supposition that their position was one of argumentation, hence of confrontation. Since the descendants of these interpreters, that is, the Christians of today, are almost all ex-pagan-Christian, the tradition of interpretation could only develop in this direction.

III

One encounters the same structural problem in world ecumenism. The latter elucidates the same mediation process of existential texts to people whose history is not tied to the story of the text. This occurs, for example, when western Christians want to acquaint Christians in Asia and Africa with themes and questions from their own theological discussion. Included is the difficulty western Christians have in clarifying for their brothers and sisters in Asia and Africa the meaning of discourse with Jews concerning their own Christian theology and existence. Many western Christians have recognized that they cannot understand their own identity as Christians without a parallel, existing Jewish identity. Moreover, they cannot understand the many pictures, parables and examples from the New Testament if they gloss over the Jewish context that has been in existence until today. Western European theology, which was 'exported' through missionary work to Asia and Africa, is and was a theology of baptized ex-pagans in Europe who still knew or suspected the origin of Jesus, the disciples, and the first followers of Jesus—in contrast to baptized ex-pagans in Africa and Asia, all of whom had no knowledge of Jewish themes, and Jews who, then as now, are the living bearers of this tradition. Thus, it is understandable when Christianized people in Asia and Africa understand the exodus from Egypt simply as a model and, as such, interpret it for themselves or see it as they want to. This points us again to the structural question as expressed in Section II.

I V

The TaNaCh is a collection of writings which, before their actual Christian and then Jewish canonization—that is, their official recognition—were open to interpretation and transmission. Judaism held the TaNaCh open, despite its canonization, and developed the tradition of 'Oral Torah'. Emerging Christianity appended the New Testament and after a certain, not very protracted, time, actually 'closed' the process. The relationship between the 'Old' and New Testament was thereby predestined, 'branded'. This rupture within the Christian Bible, which has many facets, should occupy a stronger, more central place in the attempt to clarify Christianity's relationship to Judaism.

For instance: the idea and fantasy of the divinity's multiple appearances is a thoroughly Jewish concept and relevant to the time of the nascent New Testament. As a frame of thought, such multiple appearances cause me no difficulty. They could even have been a bridge of thought between Jews and Christians. However, from the time they became a statement of faith, part of the Christian confession, they could only be divisive. This is so even if the idea itself has not changed but its function has, because the fantasy and the openness are denied further exploration.

As long as this break is not intensively discussed, it appears to me that the TaNaCh, part of the Christian Bible, could be only the first pier of a bridge, of very limited usefulness for this function. A more cautious acquaintance with this break could, on the other hand, contain an opportunity for Christian theologians (female and male). They would stumble upon questions that refer to their own Christian interpretive tradition. Those who have the inner strength to open such questionable formulations will become active in the issue of the relationship to Jews.

V

However, this phenomenon is not only observable in Christian view and interpretation; it also has a structural equivalent in western, post-Enlightenment society at large. Many 'post-Christians' (that is, people who regard their baptism as a distinctive sign of membership, but who nevertheless are not bound to church tradition and do not accept its teachings) disseminate—primarily unconsciously—numerous expressions of anti-Judaism which are of Christian origin. This emanates from centuries of practice, of Christian feelings of superiority vis-à-vis Judaism, of viewing the latter as the 'next highest' level of development. Similarly, believing Christians do not fully realize the continued contract into which the church, with its political power of the past hundreds of years, has made them enter. Structurally, the same phenomenon presents itself again and again. Contextual relationships are no longer comprehensible: they have become so independent that they carry the virulence of their power in themselves.

I ask myself—and other women—if such artificial responses do not also occur with feminists. I also ask if feminists—in their search for a new, altered and independently chosen foundation—do not also fall into similar, structurally-determined snares of meaning, comparable to those which served the similarly unaware post-Christian society.

VI

Jürgen Moltmann was right when he acknowledged that the accusation of anti-Judaism 'must be taken more seriously here in Germany than in other countries because of our past'; but I do not yet see what follows from that. Certainly, the holocaust was planned in Germany, realized by German soldiers, bureaucrats, officials; knowledge of it was denied or repressed by many observers. The holocaust could not have been carried out without the active cooperation—and, above all, without communal and intrinsic Christian self-understanding—of many other governments, groups, parties and individuals. Thus, for example, all extermination camps (not concentration camps) were situated in Polish territory—which was hardly pure coincidence.

The totality of the Christian dimension is decisive: the present division into Eastern and Western churches, Catholic and

Protestant, is merely subsidiary. The expulsion of Jews from Catholic Spain in 1492 was characterized by national or confessional factors no less than the Crusades. Similarly, diverse later manifestations of the same phenomena, within the same parameters, were only secondarily determined by denominational difference.

VII

Could these energetic debates about anti-Judaism be included within a Christian feminist theology, so that feminists recognize the opening and actually subject the debates to self-critical tests in a much wider sense? If this were the case, then feminists would not only take a great step forward in regard to the prevalent 'masculine theology', but also with respect to an infamous eighteen-centuries-old Christian anti-Jewish tradition.

ON 'ANTI-JUDAISM' IN GERMAN FEMINIST THOUGHT:
SOME REFLECTIONS BY WAY OF A RESPONSE

Lillian R. Klein

One factor motivates the two articles by Leonore Siegele-Wenschkewitz and Edna Brocke translated and reprinted here: anti-Semitism has arisen in German feminist theology. Each of the authors deplores it from a different viewpoint.[1] In a short piece not reproduced here, Elizabeth Moltmann-Wendel[2] acknowledges its presence. Indeed, she claims she was 'the first to point out anti-Semitism in goddess theology', and in her response she denies her 'continuing anti-Judaism' (my emphasis).[3] Leonore Siegele-Wenschkewitz traces Christian involvement with anti-Semitism in Germany,[4] and Edna Brocke questions whether 'anti-Judaism is fundamental to Christianity'.[5] It seems that Göttinnenmörder, 'murder of the

1. The authors are theologians, drawing not only from biblical but also from postbiblical interpretive texts written by rabbis and church fathers. In order to minimize any prejudice inherent in my own location as a reader, I am responding to the Publik-Forum articles only on the basis of primary source literature: the Hebrew Bible and the New Testament.

2. In a response entitled 'Malicious and Absurd', published in German in Publik-Forum 12 (25 June, 1993), to being accused of anti-Judaism in her theology. Moltmann-Wendel refused to have her reponse translated and reprinted in this volume.

3. 'Einige Sätze...benützte Susannah Heschel...um meinen fortdauernden Antijudaïsmus zu beweisen. Dieses Buch is jedoch nicht...in der 9. Auflage erschienen, sondern seit 1984 nicht mehr aufgelegt worden...'; Moltmann-Wendel in her comment, 'Malicious and Absurd', p. 24.

4. L. Siegele-Wenschkewitz, 'In the Dangerous Currents of old Prejudices', pp. 342-48 in this volume.

5. E. Brocke, 'Do the Origins Already Contain the Malady?', pp. 349-54 in this volume.

goddess', by Jewish patriarchy provides a new tool to dig up and re-cultivate a worldview made familiar and comfortable by Christianity, a worldview one is reluctant to relinquish in these unstable times. It seems clear that this worldview, this anti-Judaism, is indeed current in Germany. For instance, Susannah Heschel mentions that at a recent meeting, the German author of a paper critical of a German theologian during the Nazi era 'was roundly castigated by a colleague for "defaming" the German Christians'. Understandably, Heschel found the experience amazing, 'like saying you're giving Hitler a bad name'.[1] As a consequence of such convictions, Germany is becoming known in feminist—and theological—circles as narrowly, even blindly, 'German' and Christian. This unfortunately defames the more aware and liberal trends of German feminist scholarship.[2]

Let us have a closer look at the claim of 'goddess murder'. The term 'murder' involves a specific event, a moment in time. However, the evidence for the goddess's demise—biblical and other—points to a process over considerable space and time, a process that was itself the product of multiple forces. 'Murder' requires a body, as in Corpus Christi; but goddesses neither live nor die. Even if the term is understood as figurative or metaphoric, literal objections are belittled by the verbal aggression conveyed by the phrase—directed, as it has been, at Jews. German feminists' self-justification may seem preferable to questioning in the sense of asking *who* really 'murdered' the goddess instead of asking *how, when* and *why*; preferable to the hard work of examining, questioning and evaluating the scholarly premises of such a worldview; preferable to recognizing that when data does not support the conclusions, the reasoning is specious.[3] Furthermore, when such 'reasoning' is

---

1. In E.K. Coughlin, 'The Shock of Anti-Semitism', *The Chronicle of Higher Education* 40.32 (April 13, 1994), p. A10.

2. For instance, Marie-Theres Wacker confronts this issue in her 'Feminist Theology and Anti-Judaism: The Status of the Discussion and the Context of the Problem in the Federal Republic of Germany', *JFSR* 2 (1986), pp. 109-16; L. Siegele-Wenschkewitz addresses 'The Discussion of Anti-Judaism in Feminist Theology—A New Area of Jewish Christian Dialogue' in the same issue of *JFSR*, pp. 95-98.

3. Since the data is literary, multiple valid conclusions may be drawn and different types of reasoning may be employed. Nevertheless,

anti-Jewish in emphasis, the suspicion is aroused that the 'reasoning' is severely biased.

A second, latent factor in these articles is the assumption that Christian egalitarianism 'redresses' Jewish anti-feminism. I will address this latent claim later. First let us turn our attention to the available data—to research in textual and social constructs of the forces which supported and then suppressed the goddess—in order to test the accusation of Jews as perpetrators of 'murder of the goddess', thus those who deny her solace to all females of Western civilization.

We shall proceed from the notion that goddess worship indeed predated god worship. In *The Creation of Patriarchy*, Gerda Lerner discusses the relationship between cultural organization, the role of women and, ultimately, goddess worship.

> Sometime during the agricultural revolution relatively egalitarian societies with a sexual division of labor based on biological necessity gave way to more highly structured societies in which both private property and the exchange of women based on incest taboos and exogamy were common. The earlier societies were often matrilineal and matrilocal, while the latter surviving societies were predominantly patrilineal and patrilocal...The more complex societies featured a division of labor no longer based only on biological distinctions, but also on hierarchy and the power of some men over other men and over all women.[1]

Development of occupations which required physical brawn and enabled males to gain social power inevitably changed kinship and gender relationships. Animal husbandry, hunting and plow agriculture, together with increasing militarism, kingdoms and archaic states, brought modifications in religious beliefs too. According to Lerner,

> The observable pattern is: first, the demotion of the Mother-Goddess figure and the ascendance and later dominance of her male consort/son; then his merging with a storm-god into a male Creator-God, who heads the pantheon of gods and

the conclusions must be based on the data.

1. G. Lerner, *The Creation of Patriarchy* (New York: Oxford University Press, 1986), p. 53.

goddesses. *Wherever* such changes occur, the power of creation and of fertility is transferred from the Goddess to the God [my emphasis].[1]

Point 1: Suppression of the goddess was a regular consequence of masculine-dominated conquest activities.

In related studies, Rosemary Radford Ruether attributes male domination to the introduction of plow agriculture, with the plow 'the tool of male dominance over animals and land. Together with the sword, these tools became the means for male conquest of other men and finally of their own women'.[2] Ruether notes the broad temporal and spatial span in which this gender shift took place, and that it was reflected in legal codes:

> Women of the ruling group which may have shared in earlier stages of aristocratic power, become redefined in law codes of the period from 3000 BCE to 500 BCE. This is reflected in the Babylonian code of Hammurabi, the Hebraic Law codes, and the sixth-century Athenian codes of Solon.[3]

Point 2: Israelite reassignment of women's social roles to inferior positions reflects a broad social trend extending from Mesopotamia to Greece over a span of 2500 years—in which Israel, like other cultural groups, was enmeshed.

In her analysis of 'Women and Culture in Old Europe', Marija Gimbutas provides the term 'Old Europe' for the entire area west of the Pontic steppe in which

> [a] matrifocal society is reflected by the Old European manifestations of the Goddess and Her worship. It is obvious that the Goddess, not the gods, dominated the Old European pantheon...[in which] the male god was an adjunct of the female Goddess, as consort or son.[4]

Gimbutas applies the term 'Old Europe' to this first Mediterranean/European civilization, which was gradually destroyed by repeated incursions of 'Kurgan' Indo-European-

---

1. Lerner, *Patriarchy*, p. 145.
2. R.R. Ruether, *Gaia and God: An Ecofeminist Theology of Earth Healing* (New York: HarperCollins, 1992), p. 164.
3. Ruether, *Gaia*, p. 165.
4. M. Gimbutas, 'Women and Culture in Goddess-Oriented Old Europe', in J. Plaskow and C.P. Christ (eds.), *Weaving the Visions: New Patterns in Feminist Spirituality* (New York: HarperCollins, 1989), p. 65.

speaking pastoralists, also known as Aryans, who brought with them patriarchal values and religions. According to Gimbutas, Indo-Europeans initiated suppression of the goddess.

Point 3: To my knowledge, neither Jews nor Germans are accusing the Aryans of instigating goddess murder.

In his early work *The Hebrew Goddess*, Raphael Patai attests to ample archaeological evidence of household asherahs as household goddesses, 'not matched anywhere by images of male gods'.[1] From inscriptions, Pattai concludes that the goddess was associated with YHWH, and that the 'divine couple' was an integral element of religious life in ancient Israel prior to the reforms introduced by King Josiah in 621 BCE.[2]

In a more recent work, Mark S. Smith suggests that Asherah probably functioned for Israel more as a symbol than as a goddess.[3] At the oldest stages of Israel's religious literature, YHWH suggests a conflation of the imagery of the primary deities, and 'it may be possible to identify in the nature of YHWH elements of Asherah's character, specifically her maternal and nurturing character'.[4] Suppression of anthropomorophic imagery for YHWH may have contributed to the paucity of gender language for Israel's divine being. Nevertheless, Smith refers to Phyllis Trible's identification of specific word contexts to support the male YHWH as having female traits.[5] According to Smith, other influences—'Israel's imageless or aniconic tradition, the influence of the Ten Commandments...polemics against [and] denial of other gods'—were also formative in monolatry in Israel's early history,[6] but Asherah could continue to function symbolically, if not as a goddess. Suggestively, Patai anticipates Smith's conclusions: 'the religion of the Hebrews and the Jews was never without at least a hint of the feminine in its God-concept'.[7]

1. R. Patai, *The Hebrew Goddess* (Detroit: Wayne State University Press, 3rd edn, 1990), p. 39.
2. Patai, *The Hebrew Goddess*, p. 53.
3. M.S. Smith, *The Early History of God: YHWH and the Other Deities in Ancient Israel* (New York: Harper & Row, 1990), p. 16.
4. Smith, *Early History of God*, p. 98.
5. Smith, *Early History of God*, p. 98.
6. Smith, *Early History of God*, pp. 22-23.
7. Patai, *The Hebrew Goddess*, p. 279.

Point 4: If the goddess became a symbol, and if she were already assimilated to the male deity in earlier phases, is it worthwhile to identify the exact culture that 'murdered' her? Or is that consequential only if it can be traced to the Hebrews/ Jews?

And is the Christian church innocent of suppressing goddess worship? Merlin Stone, among others, finds the church complicit:

> But it was upon the last assaults by the Hebrews and eventually by the Christians of the first centuries after Christ that the [goddess] religion was finally suppressed and nearly forgotten.[1]

Furthermore, Tikva Frymer-Kensky reminds us that

> Christianity inherited Hellenistic and Judeo-Hellenistic ideas about women, particularly those expressed in the books of the Apocrypha, which were preserved by the Church as sacred scripture. These ideas were emphasized and magnified by two disparate sources: the philosophic tradition of Plato...and the politico-sociological example of imperial Rome... As the Church became more Greek, it became more patriarchal; as it became Roman, the process intensified. Emerging Christianity incorporated these misogynistic and anti-erotic themes and made them central to its ideas about human existence.[2]

The link between the two biases, anti-Judaism and anti-female (anti-erotic?), is worth noting. Despite the prevalence of Mariolatry, Bible translations during the English Renaissance and German Protestant movements were as anti-female as anti-Jewish.[3] Ilona Rashkow illustrates how textual ambiguities were removed, characters were simplified into 'good' or 'bad' stereotypes, and 'the Hebrew Bible became the Old Testament, a text which...was deciphered and interpreted for the reader'.[4]

---

1. M. Stone, *When God was a Woman* (San Diego: Harcourt Brace Jovanovich, 1976), p. 68.
2. T. Frymer-Kensky, *In the Wake of the Goddesses: Women, Culture and the Biblical Transformation of Pagan Myth* (New York: Macmillan, 1992), p. 214.
3. I. Rashkow, *Upon the Dark Places: Anti-Semitism and Sexism in English Renaissance Biblical Translation* (Bible and Literature Series, 28; Sheffield: Almond Press, 1990), pp. 43-74.
4. Rashkow, *Upon the Dark Places*, p. 17.

Today, many familiar biblical narratives are known only in their interpreted versions which lay guilt and sin on women and glorify men.[1] Christian feminist theologians may be interested in differentiating between the texts of the Hebrew Bible and the New Testament on the one hand, and the directions the church has taken with regard to women on the other hand.

Point 5: Christianity, like other religions, has sufficient stains on its own feminist record to warrant restraint on the part of its theologians in casting blame elsewhere.

In establishing patriarchal monotheism, Judaism necessarily assimilated (or rejected) extraneous male and female gods and their symbols. That contemporary *Christian* feminists bewail the lack of a *goddess* nevertheless remains curious. Despite its trinity, Christianity claims to be monotheistic. Do these feminist Christian theologians *blame* Judaism for creating one of the foundations for their monotheistic church faith?

Point 6: The complaint of German Christian feminists that the Jews killed off the goddess and thereby denied them a Christian goddess is perforce an anti-Christian theology.

These points suggest that some German Christian feminists—perhaps unconsciously—perceive the world through glasses tinted 'anti-Jew' and are—again, perhaps unconsciously—incorporating this worldview into their own academic research. These feminist theologians protect German Christian theology at the cost of textual and theological integrity. In so doing, they both protect and promulgate a familiar paradigm: the Jew as villain.

This leads to a second premise, to which I promised to return: the assumption that Christian egalitarianism 'rectifies' biblical/ Jewish anti-woman tendencies. My remarks in this regard draw upon the work of Amy-Jill Levine entitled 'Second Temple Judaism, Jesus, and Women: *Yeast of Eden'*,[2] which extends the scope of the argument beyond German Christian feminist theology to feminist theology and Western Christian theology in general.

Levine observes that feminist analysis in theological studies 'serves to preserve old dichotomies in new guises. The

1. Rashkow, *Upon the Dark Places*, pp. 95-96.
2. Pp. 302-31 in this volume.

prevailing hypothesis is that Judaism...regarded women as weak-willed, wanton, and, in general, worthless'.[1] And, more pointedly,

> Whatever Second Temple Judaism may have been in terms of theology, politics, economics, or aesthetics, it was, according to this construct, generally bad for women. And, whatever the Jesus movement was, it was good for women.[2]

Levine's arguments, and my own, have certain implications. It is perhaps meet that Christianity abandon defining its own feminist stance by juxtaposition with Judaic attitudes toward women and femininity. Christian feminists—including those in Germany—have ample work to do in discovering Christ's attitudes toward women through fresh interpretations of the New Testament texts, and in exposing the attitudes of the Christian church toward women in the ensuing years through feminist readings of the texts by church fathers. Perhaps German Christian feminists have an opportunity to do the same for the period from the German Reformation to the present. Until these issues—*in themselves, without reference to Judaism*—are addressed, the question will still remain, as voiced by Edna Brocke, whether 'anti-Judaism is fundamental to Christianity'.[3]

In important although perhaps different ways, Jewish and Christian feminists share a purpose. To borrow from Ruether, Gaia and God are within all of us, female and male,[4] and also Jew and Christian. These sources of synergy are misused when directed toward divisiveness. As the world regards the Nazi era with the hindsight of forty-five years, women who use anti-Judaism in an attempt to secure the narrow 'truths' they have assumed from their patriarchal forebears may wish to consider how that will be regarded by future generations. Besides, women have more important things to do with their time, their intelligence and their energy than passively to buy into the patriarchal system of scape-goating.

1. Levine, 'Second Temple Judaism', pp. 302-3.
2. Levine, 'Second Temple Judaism', p. 306.
3. Brocke, 'Origins', p. 349.
4. Ruether, *Gaia*, p. 254. Ruether has valuable practical ideas on how we can realize our potential individually and culturally; cf. pp. 265-68.

BIBLIOGRAPHY

Aberbach, M. and B. Grossfeld, *Targum Onkelos to Genesis: A Critical Analysis Together with an English Translation of the Text* (Based on A. Sperber's Edition; New York: Ktav, 1982).

Alexander, L.C.A., 'Sisters in Adversity: Retelling Martha's Story', in G. J. Brooke (ed.), *Women in the Biblical Tradition* (Lampeter: Edwin Mellen, 1992), pp. 167-86.

Alexander, Y., D. Carlton, and P. Wilkinson, *Terrorism: Theory and Practice* (Colorado: Westview Press, 1979).

Alexandre, M., *Le Commencement du Livre Genèse I—V: La Version grecque de la Septante et sa réception* (Christianisme Antique, 3; Paris: Beauchesne, 1988).

Alter, R., *The Art of Biblical Narrative* (London: George Allen & Unwin, 1981).

—'How Convention Helps us Read: The Case of the Bible's Annunciation-Type Scene', *Prooftexts* 3 (1983), pp. 115-30.

Amerding, C., 'The Marriage in Cana', *BSac* 118 (1961).

American Association of University Women, 'Shortchanging Girls, Shortchanging America', 1992.

Anderson, C.P., 'Who Are the Heirs of the New Age in the letter to the Hebrews?', in J. Marcus and M.L. Soards (eds.), *Apocalyptic and the New Testament* (JSNTSup, 24; Sheffield: JSOT Press, 1987), pp. 255-78.

Anderson, G., 'Celibacy or Consummation in the Garden? Reflections on Early Jewish and Christian Interpretations of the Garden of Eden', *HTR* 82 (1989), pp. 121-48.

Angerstörfer, A., 'Wovon befreite Jesus die jüdische Frau?', *Kirche und Israel* 8 (1993), pp. 161-63.

Ashton, J., 'The Transformation of Wisdom: A Study of the Prologue of John's Gospel', *NTS* 32 (1986), pp. 161-86.

Attridge, H.W., *The Epistle to the Hebrews* (Philadelphia: Fortress Press, 1989).

Aune, D., 'The Apocalypse of John and Greco-Roman Revelatory Magic', *NTS* 33 (1987), pp. 481-501.

—The Social Matrix of the Apocalypse of John', *BR* 26 (1981), pp. 16-32.

Aycock, A., 'Potiphar's Wife: Prelude to a Structural Exegesis', *Man* NS 27 (1992), pp. 479-94.

Bach, A., 'Signs of the Flesh: Observations on Characterization in the Bible', *Semeia* 63 (1993), pp. 61-80.

Bal, M., *Narratology: Introduction to the Theory of Narrative* (Toronto: University of Toronto Press, 1985).

—*Femmes imaginaires: l'ancien testament au risque d'une narratologie critique* (Utrecht: Hes Paris: Nizet, 1986).

—'Heroism and Proper Names, Or the Fruits of Analogy', in M. Bal, *Lethal Love: Feminist Literary Readings of Biblical Love Stories* (Bloomington: Indiana University Press, 1987), pp. 68-88; repr. with an afterword in Brenner (ed.), *Ruth*, pp. 42-69.

—*Death and Dissymmetry: The Politics of Coherence in the Book of Judges* (Chicago: University of Chicago Press, 1988).

—*De theorie van vertellen en verhalen: Inleiding in de narratologie* (Muiderberg: Coutinho, revd 5th edn, 1990 [1978]).

—'Zelf-reflekties: Het bijbelboek Esther en de (on)macht van het geschreven woord' (Lecture at Utrecht University: Women's Studies in Theology, March 15, 1990).

Balch, D.L., *Let Wives be Submissive: The Domestic Code in I Peter* (SBLMS, 26; Atlanta: Scholars Press, 1981).

Balch D.L., E. Ferguson and W.A. Meeks (eds.), *Greeks, Romans and Christians* (Festschrift A.J. Malherbe; Minneapolis: Fortress Press, 1990); repr. in P.W. van der Horst, *Hellenism–Judaism–Christianity: Essays on their Interaction* (Kampen: Kok-Pharos, 1994).

Bardenhewer, O., 'Ist Elisabeth die Sängerin des Magnificat?' *BibS(F)* 6 (1901).

Bardy, G. (ed.), *Eusèbe de Césarée: Histoire Ecclésiastique, I-IV* (SC, 31; Paris: Cerf, 1952).

Barnett, P.W., 'ἀπογπαφή and ἀπογράφεσθαι in Luke 2$^{1-5}$, *ExpTim* 85 (1973–74), pp. 377-80.

Barr, D.L., ' Elephants and Holograms: From Metaphor to Methodology in the Study of John's Apocalypse', SBLSP, 25 (1986), pp. 400-411.

Barrett, C.K., 'The Allegory of Abraham, Sarah and Hagar in the Argument of Galatians', in J. Friedrich, W. Pöhlmann and P. Stuhlmacher (eds.), *Rechtfertigung: Festschrift für Ernst Käsemann zum 70. Geburtstag* (Tübingen: Mohr, 1976), pp. 1-16.

—*The Gospel According to St. John* (Philadelphia: Westminster Press, 1982).

Barthes, R., 'La mort de l'auteur', *Mantéia* V (1968), repr. in *Le bruissement de la langue: Essais critiques, IV* (Paris: Seuil, 1984), pp. 61-67; ET 'The Death of the Author', in R. Barthes, *Image, Music, Text* (trans. S. Heath; New York: Hill & Wang, 1977), pp. 142-48.

Barton, J., 'Reading the Bible as Literature: Two Questions for Biblical Critics', *Journal of Literature and Theology* 1 (1987), pp. 135-53.

Bassler, J.M., 'A Man for All Seasons: David in Rabbinic and New Testament Literature', *Int* 40 (1986), pp. 115-85.

Beale, G.K., *The Use of Daniel in Jewish Apocalyptic Literature and in the Revelaion of St John* (Lanham, MD: University Press of America 1984).

—'Revelation', in Carson, D.A. and H.G.M. Williamson (eds.), *It is Written: Scripture Citing Scripture* (New York: Cambridge Univrsity Press, 1988), pp. 318-37.

Beck, D.R., 'The Narrative Function of Anonymity in Fourth Gospel Characterization', *Semeia* 63 (1993), pp. 143-58.

Beckwith, I.T., *The Apocalypse of John: Studies in Introduction* (Grand Rapids: Baker, 1919).

Bekkenkamp, J., *Canon en Keuze: Het bijbelse Hooglied en de Twenty-One Love Poems van Adrienne Rich als bronnen van theologie* (Kampen: Kok Agora, 1993).

Bibliography 365

Benko, S., 'The Magnificat: A History of the Controversy', *JBL* 86 (1967), pp. 263-75.

Bernard, J.H., *A Critical and Exegetical Commentary on the Gospel According to St. John*, I (Edinburgh: T & T. Clark, 1928).

Beyer, K., *Semitische Syntax im Neuen Testament* (Göttingen: Vandenhoeck & Ruprecht, 1961).

Biggs, R.D., *SA.ZI.GA: Ancient Mesopotamian Potency Incantations* (Locust Valley: Augustin, 1967).

Bird, P.A., 'Images of Women in the Old Testament', in *Religion and Sexism* (ed. R.R. Ruether; New York: Simon & Schuster, 1974), pp. 41-88.

—The Harlot as Heroine: Narrative Art and Social Presupposition in Three Old Testament Texts', *Semeia* 46 (1989), pp. 119-39.

Black, J., 'Ruth in the Dark: Folktale, Law and Creative Ambiguity in the Old Testament', *Journal of Literature and Theology* 5 (1991), pp. 20-36.

Black, M., *An Aramaic Approach to the Gospels and Acts* (Oxford: Brill, 3rd edn, 1967).

—*The Book of Enoch or 1 Enoch* (Leiden: Brill, 1985).

Blomberg, C.L., 'The Liberation of Illegitimacy: Women and Rulers in Matthew 1-2', *BTB* (1992), pp. 145-50.

Boer, M.C. de, 'John 4:27: Women (and Men) in the Gospel and Community of John', in G.J. Brooke (ed.), *Women in the Biblical Tradition* (Lampeter: Edwin Mellen, 1992), pp. 208-30.

Boismard, M.-E., *Du Baptême a Cana* (Paris: Cerf, 1956).

Boring, M.E., *Revelation*: (Interpretation: A Bible Commentary for Teaching and Preaching; Louisville: John Knox, 1989).

Bovon, F., *Das Evangelium nach Lukas*, I (Zürich and Neukirchen, 1989).

Bowker, J., *The Targums & Rabbinic Literature: An Introduction to Jewish Interpretations of Scripture* (Cambridge: Cambridge University Press, 1969).

Boylan, M., 'Galen's Conception Theory', *Journal of the History of Biology* 19 (1986).

Braidotti, R., 'What's wrong with Gender?', in F. van Dijk-Hemmes and A. Brenner (eds.), *Reflections on Theology and Gender* (Kampen: Kok Pharos, 1994), pp. 49-70.

Braun, F.M., *La Mère des Fidèles* (Paris: Casterman, 1953).

Braun, H., *An die Hebräer* (Tübingen: Mohr, 1984).

Brenner, A., 'Naomi and Ruth', *VT* 33.4 (1983), pp. 385-97; repr. in Brenner (ed.), *Ruth*, pp. 70-84.

— 'Female Social Behaviour: Two Descriptive Patterns within the "Birth of the Hero" Paradigm', *VT* 36.3 (1986), pp. 257-73; repr. in Brenner (ed.), *Genesis*, pp. 204-21.

— 'Literary Strategies in the Book of Esther' (Lecture at Leiden: Department of Biblical Studies, September 15, 1989).

— 'Looking at Esther through the Looking Glass', in A. Brenner (ed.), *Esther, Judith and Susanna*, pp. 71-80.

— 'Naomi and Ruth: Further Reflections', in Brenner (ed.), *Ruth*, pp. 140-44.

Brenner, A. (ed.), *A Feminist Companion to Genesis* (The Feminist Companion to the Bible, 2; Sheffield: Sheffield Academic Press, 1993).

— *A Feminist Companion to Ruth* (The Feminist Companion to the Bible, 3; Sheffield, Sheffield Academic Press, 1993).

—*A Feminist Companion to the Latter Prophets* (Sheffield: Sheffield Academic Press, 1995).

—*A Feminist Companion to Esther, Judith and Susanna* (Sheffield: Sheffield Academic Press, 1995).

Brenner, A., and F. van Dijk-Hemmes, *On Gendering Texts: Female and Male Voices in the Hebrew Bible* (Biblical Interpretation, 1; Leiden: Brill, 1993).

Brocke, M., 'Das Judentumsbild neuer Jesusbücher', *Freiburger Rundbrief* 23 (1971), pp. 50-59.

Brooke, G.J. (ed.), *Women in the Biblical Tradition* (Lampeter: Edwin Mellen, 1992).

Brooten, B., *Women Leaders in the Ancient Synagogue: Inscriptional Evidence and Background Issues* (Atlanta: Scholars Press, 1982).

—'Early Christian Women and their Cultural Context: Issues of Method in Historical Reconstruction,' in A.Y. Collins (ed.) *Feminist Perspectives on Biblical Scholarship* (Atlanta: Scholars Press, 1985), pp. 65-91.

Brown, A., *Apology to Women: Christian Images of the Female Sex* (Leicester: Inter-Varsity Press, 1991).

Brown E.R., *et al.* (eds.), *Mary in the New Testament* (New York: Paulist Press, 1978).

Brown, J.C., and C.R. Bohn (eds.), *Christianity, Patriarchy, and Abuse: A Feminist Critique* (New York: Pilgrim Press, 1989).

Brown, R.E., *The Gospel According to John*, I (AB, 29; Garden City, NY: Doubleday, 1966).

—*The Gospel according to John*, II (AB, 29A; Garden City, NY: Doubleday, 1970).

—*The Virginal Conception and Bodily Resurrection of Jesus* (New York, 1973).

—*The Birth of the Messiah: A Commentary on the Infancy Narratives in Matthew and Luke* (Garden City, NY: Doubleday, 1977).

—*The Community of the Beloved Disciple* (New York: Paulist Press, 1979).

—'Roles of Women in the Fourth Gospel', in *idem, The Community of the Beloved Disciple*, pp. 183-98.

—'Rachab in Matthew 1,5 Probably is Rahab of Jericho', *Bib* 63 (1982), pp. 79-80.

—'Gospel Infancy Narrative Research from 1976 to 1986': Part 1 (Matthew), *CBQ* 48 (1986), pp. 468-83.

—'The Annunciation to Joseph (Matthew 1.16-25)', *Worship* 61 (1987), pp. 482-92.

Brown, S., *The Origins of Christianity* (Oxford: Oxford University Press, 1988).

Bruns, J.E., 'The Contrasted Women of Apocalypse 12 and 17', *CBQ* 26 (1964), pp. 459-63.

Bultmann, R., *The Gospel of John* (Oxford: Basil Blackwell, 1971).

Burnett, F.W., 'Characterization and Reader Construction of Characters in the Gospels', *Semeia* 63 (1993), pp. 3-28.

Burrows, E., *The Gospel of the Infancy and Other Biblical Essays* (London: Burns Oates, 1940).

Busse, U., 'Das "Evangelium" des Lukas: Die Funktion der Vorgeschichte im lukanischen Doppelwerk', in C. Bussmann and W. Radl (eds.), *Der Treue Gottes trauen: Beiträge zum Werk des Lukas* (Festschrift G. Schneider; Freiburg, 1991), pp. 161-77.

Cadbury, H.J., 'Four Features of Lukan Style', in L.E. Keck and J.L. Martyn (eds.), *Studies in Luke–Acts* (London: SPCK, 2nd edn, 1976 [1968]).

—'The Ancient Physiological Notions Underlying John I 13 and Hebrews XI 11', *The Expositor* (ser. 9), 2 (1924).

Camp, C.V., *Wisdom and the Feminine in the Book of Proverbs* (Sheffield: Almond Press, 1985).

—'Understanding a Patriarchy: Women in Second-Century Jerusalem through the Eyes of Ben Sira', in A.-J. Levine (ed.), *'Women Like This': New Perspectives on Jewish Women in the Greco-Roman World* (Atlanta: Scholars Press, 1991), pp. 1-40.

Camp, C.V. and C.R. Fontaine (eds.), 'Women, War, and Metaphor: Language and Society in the Study of the Hebrew Bible', *Semeia* 61 (1993), pp. v-184.

Carey, G.L., 'Biblical-Theological Perspectives on War and Peace', *EvQ* 57(1985), pp. 163-78.

Carmichael, C., 'Marriage and the Samaritan Woman', *NTS* 26 (1980), pp. 332-46.

Carson, D.A., 'Current Source Criticism of the Fourth Gospel: Some Methodological Questions', *JBL* 97 (1978).

— 'The Purpose of the Fourth Gospel: John 20.31 Reconsidered', *JBL* 106 (1987).

Carson, D.A., and H.G.M. Williamson (eds.), *It is Written: Scripture Citing Scripture: Essays in Honour of Barnabas Lindars, SSF* (Cambridge: Cambridge University Press, 1988).

Charles, R.H., *The Revelation of St. John* (2 vols; Edinburgh: T & T Clark, 1920).

Charlesworth, J.H.,*The Old Testament Pseudepigrapha* (2 vols; Garden City, NY: Doubleday, 1983).

Charlesworth, J.H. (ed.), *The Old Testament Pseudepigrapha* (Garden City, NY: Doubleday, 1983), I.

Chatman, S., *Story and Discourse: Narrative Structure in Fiction and Film* (Ithaca, NY: Cornell University Press, 1978).

Chester, A., 'Citing the Old Testament', in D.A. Carson and H.G.M. Williamson (eds.), *It is Written: Scripture Citing Scripture*, pp. 141-69.

Clark, E.A., *Women in the Early Church: Message of the Fathers of the Church* (Wilmington, DE: Michael Glazier, 1983).

Clines, D.J.A., 'Reading Esther from Left to Right: Contemporary Strategies for Reading a Biblical Text', in D.J.A. Clines, S.E. Fowl, S.E. Porter (eds.), *The Bible in Three Dimensions: Essays in Celebration of Forty Years of Biblical Studies in the University of Sheffield* (JSOTSup, 87; Sheffield: JSOT Press, 1990), pp. 31-52.

—'Why is There a Song of Songs? And What Does it Do to You if You Read It?', *Jian Dao* 1 (1993), pp. 3-27.

Collins, A.Y., 'Coping with Hostility', *Bible Today* (1981), pp. 367-72.

—'Insiders and Outsiders in the Book of Revelation and its Social Context', in J. Neusner and E.S. Frerichs (eds.), *To See Ourselves as Others See Us: Christians, Jews, Others in Late Antiquity* (Chico, CA: Scholars Press, 1985), pp. 208-218.

—'Oppression from Without: the Symbolisation of Rome as Evil in Early Christianity', in W. Beuken, S. Freyne, and A. Weiler (eds.), *Concilium: Religion in the Eighties* (Edinburgh: T. & T. Clark, 1988), pp. 66-73.

—'The Revelation of John: An Apocalyptic Response to a Social Crisis', *CurTM* 8 (1981), pp. 4-12.

—'Vilification and Self-Definition in the Book of Revelation', *HTR* 79 (1986), pp. 308-20.

—'Women's History and the Book of Revelation', SBLSP, 26 (1987), pp. 80-91.

Collins, A.Y. (ed.), *Feminist Perspectives on Biblical Scholarship* (Atlanta: Scholars Press, 1985).

—*Feminist Perspectives on Biblical Scholarship* (SBL Biblical Scholarship in North America, 10; Chico, CA: Scholars Press, 1985).

Conzelmann, H., *The Theology of St. Luke* (trans. G. Buswell; Philadelphia: Fortress Press, 1961).

Cope, L., 'The Earliest Gospel was the "Signs Gospel"', in *Jesus, the Gospels and the Church: Essays in Honor of William R. Farmer* (Macon, GA: Mercer University Press, 1987).

Corley, K.M., *Private Women, Public Meals: Social Conflict in the Synoptic Tradition* (Peabody, MA: Hendrickson, 1993).

Cornford, F.M., *Plato's Cosmology* (London: Routledge & Kegan Paul, 1937), p. 356.

Cotter, W.J., 'Children Sitting in the Agora: Q (Luke) 7.31-35', *Foundations and Facets Forum* 5.2 (1989).

Coughlin, E.K., 'The Shock of Anti-Semitism', *The Chronicle of Higher Education* 40.32 (13 April 1994), p. A10.

Creed, J.M., *The Gospel according to St. Luke* (London: Macmillan, 1975 [1937]).

Crouzel, H., F. Fournier and P. Périchon (eds.), *Origène: Homélies sur S. Luc. Texte latin et fragments grecs* (SC, 87; Paris: Cerf, 1962).

Culler, J., *On Deconstruction: Theory and Criticism after Structuralism* (London: Routledge & Kegan Paul, 1983).

— *Framing the Sign: Criticism and Its Institutions* (Oklahoma Project for Discourse and Theory; Norma, OK and London: University of Oklahoma Press, 1988), p. xiv.

Culpepper, R.A., *Anatomy of the Fourth Gospel: A Study in Literary Design* (Philadelphia: Fortress Press, 1983).

Daiber, H., *Aetius Arabus: Die Vorsokratiker in arabischer Überlieferung* (Wiesbaden: Otto Harassowitz, 1980).

D'Angelo, M.R., 'Women Partners in the New Testament', *JFSR* 6.1 (1990), pp. 65-86.

— 'Women in Luke–Acts: A Redactional View', *JBL* 109.3 (1990), pp. 441-61.

Darr, K.P., *Far More Precious than Jewels* (Louisville, KY: Westminster/John Knox, 1991).

Daube, D., *The New Testament and Rabbinic Judaism* (School of Oriental and African Studies Jordan Lectures in Comparative Religion, 2; London: Athlone Press, 1956).

Davies, W.D., and Dale, C.A., *A Critical and Exegetical Commentary on the Gospel according to St. Matthew*, I (Edinburgh: T. & T. Clark, 1988).

Derrett, J.D.M., ''Αντιλεγόμενον, φομφαία, διαλογισμοί (Lk 2:34-35): The Hidden Context', *Filología Neotestamentaria* 6.12 (1993), pp. 207-18.

— 'Water into Wine', *BZ* 7 (1963).

Detweiler, R., *Reader Response Approaches to Biblical and Secular Texts* (Atlanta: Scholars Press, 1985).

Dibelius, M., *Die urchristliche Überlieferung von Johannes dem Taüfer* (FRLANT, 15; Göttingen: Vandenhoeck, 1911).

Diels, H., *Doxographi Graeci* (Berlin: de Gruyter, 4th edn, 1965), pp. 417-22.

Dijk-Hemmes, F. van, 'Gezegende onder de vrouwen: een moeder in Israël en een maagd in de kerk', in F. van Dijk-Hemmes (ed.), *'t Is kwaad gerucht, als zij niet binnen blijft: Vrouwen in oude culturen* (Utrecht: HES, 1986), pp. 123-47.

—'Feminist Theology and Anti-Judaism in The Netherlands', *JFSR* 7 (1991), pp. 117-23.

— *Sporen van vrouwenteksten in de Hebreeuwse bijbel* (Utrechtse Theologische Reeks, 16; Utrecht: Theological Faculty, Utrecht University, 1992).

Dijk-Hemmes, F. van, and A. Brenner (eds.), *Reflections on Theology and Gender* (Kampen: Kok Pharos, 1994).

Dillon, R.J., 'Wisdom Tradition and Sacramental Retrospective in the Cana Account (Jn 2,1-11)', *CBQ* 24 (1962).

Dodd, C.H., *The Interpretation of the Fourth Gospel* (Cambridge: Cambridge University Press, 1953).

—*Historical Tradition in the Fourth Gospel* (Cambridge: Cambridge University Press, 1963).

Dollar, S.E., 'The Significance of Women in the Fourth Gospel' (PhD dissertation; New Orleans Theological Seminary, 1983).

Donaldson, L.E., 'Cyborgs, Ciphers and Sexuality: Re-Theorizing Literary and Biblical Character', *Semeia* 63, pp. 81-96.

Donelson, L.R., *Pseudepigraphy and Ethical Argument in the Pastoral Epistles* (Tübingen: Mohr [Paul Siebeck], 1986).

Douglas, M., *Natural Symbols* (New York: Vintage Books, 1973).

Durber, S., 'The Female Reader of the Parables of the Lost', in G.J. Brooke (ed.), *Women in the Biblical Tradition* (Lampeter: Edwin Mellen, 1992), pp. 187-207.

Dworkin, A., *Our Blood: Prophecies and Discourses on Sexual Politics* (New York: Harper and Row, 1976; London: The Women's Press Limited, 1982).

—*Letters from the War Zone 1976-1989* (New York: Dutton, 1989).

Dyer, C.H., 'The Identity of Babylon in Revelation 17–18', *BSac* 98 (1987), pp. 327-31.

Ehrlich, A.B., *Randglossen zur hebräischen Bibel* (repr.; Hildesheim: Olms, 1968[1909]).

Ellingworth, E.P., and E.A. Nida, *Translator's Handbook on the Letter to the Hebrews* (London: United Bible Societies, 1983).

—*Translator's New Testament* (London: British and Foreign Bible Society, 1973), p. 528.

Ellingworth, P., *The Epistle to the Hebrews* (Grand Rapids: Eerdmans, 1993).

Epstein, I. (ed. and trans.), *The Babylonian Talmud* (London: Soncino, 1952).

Eslinger, E., 'The Wooing of the Woman at the Well', *Literature and Theology* 1 (1987), pp. 167—83; reprinted in M. Stibbe (ed.), *The Gospel of John as Literature: An Anthology of Twentieth Century Perspectives* (NTTS, 17; Leiden: Brill, 1993), pp. 165—82.

Exum, J.C., '"Mother in Israel": A Familiar Story Reconsidered', in L.M. Russell (ed.), *Feminist Interpretation of the Bible* (Oxford: Basil Blackwell, 1985), pp. 73-85.

Feldman, D.M., *Birth Control in Jewish Law: Marital Relations, Contraception and Abortion as Set Forth in the Classic Texts of Jewish Law* (Westport: Greenwood Press, 1980).

Feldman, E., *Biblical and Post-Biblical Defilement and Mourning: Law as Theology* (New York: Ktav, 1977).

Feliks, J., 'Biology', *EncJud* IV (1972), pp. 1019-22.

Feuillet, A., 'L'heure de la Femme (Jn 16,21) et l'heure de la mère de Jésus (Jn 19,25-27)', *Bib* 47 (1966), pp. 169-84; 361-80; 557-73.

Fiore, B., *The Function of Personal Example in the Socratic and Pastoral Epistles* (Rome: Biblical Institute Press, 1986).

Fish, S., *Is There a Text in This Class? The Authority of Interpretive Communities* (Cambridge, MA and London: Harvard University Press, 1980).

—*Doing What Comes Naturally: Change, Rhetoric, and the Practice of Theory in Literary and Legal Studies* (Durham and London: Duke University Press, 1989).

Fitzmyer, J.A., 'The Virginal Conception of Jesus in the New Testament', *TS* 34 (1973), pp. 541-75; repr. in *To Advance the Gospel*, pp. 41-78.

— 'Postscript (1980)', in *To Advance the Gospel*, pp. 61-62.

— *To Advance the Gospel: New Testament Studies* (New York: Crossroad, 1981).

—*The Gospel according to Luke I–IX* (AB, 28; Garden City, NY: Doubleday, 1981).

—*The Gospel according to Luke X–XXIV* (AB, 28a; Garden City, NY: Doubleday, 1985).

Fokkelman, J.P., *Narrative Art in Genesis: Specimens of Stylistic and Structural Analysis* (Assen/Amsterdam: Van Gorcum, 1st edn, 1975; Biblical Seminar, 12; Sheffield: Sheffield Academic Press, 2nd edn, 1991).

— *Narrative Art and Poetry in the Books of Samuel. IV: Vow and Desire (1 Sam. 1-12)* (Assen: Van Gorcum, 1993).

Ford, J.M., *Revelation.* (AB, 38; Garden City, NY: Doubleday, 1975).

Forsyth, D.W., 'Sibling Rivalry, Aesthetic Sensibility, and Social Structure in Genesis', *Ethos: Journal of the Society for Psychological Anthropology* 19 (1991), pp. 453-510.

Fortna, R.T., *The Gospel of Signs: A Reconstruction of the Narrative Source Underlying the Fourth Gospel* (Cambridge: Cambridge University Press, 1970).

— 'Source and redaction in the Fourth Gospel's Portrayal of Jesus' Signs', *JBL* 89 (1970), pp. 151-66.

— 'Christology in the Fourth Gospel: Redaction- Critical Perspectives', *NTS* 21 (1974–75).

— *The Fourth Gospel and its Predecessor* (Philadelphia: Fortress Press, 1988).

Foucault, M., 'Qu'est-ce qu'un auteur?', *Bulletin de la Société française de Philosophie*, Séance du 22 Février 1969, 64 (1969), pp. 73-104; ET 'What Is an Author?', in D.F. Bouchard and S. Simon (ed. and trans.), *Language, Counter-Memory, Practice: Selected Essays and Interviews* (Ithaca, NY: Cornell University Press, 1977), pp. 113-38.

France, R.T., *Matthew* (Leicester: Inter-Varsity Press, 1985).

Freed, E.D., 'The Women in Matthew's Genealogy', *JSNT* 29 (1987), pp. 3-19.

—'Who or What Was before Abraham in John 8.58?', *JSNT* 17 (1983), pp. 52-59.

Freedman, H. and M. Simon (eds.), *Midrash Rabbah* (2 vols.; London: Soncino Press, 1939).

Freyne, S., 'Vilifying the Other and Defining the Self', in J. Neusner and E.S. Frerichs (eds.), *To See Ourselves as Others See Us: Christians, Jews, Others in Late Antiquity* (Chico, CA: Scholars Press, l985), pp. 117-143.

Frymer-Kensky, T., *In the Wake of the Goddesses: Women, Culture and the Biblical Transformation of Pagan Myth* (New York: Macmillan, 1992).

Fuchs, E., 'The Literary Characterization of Mothers and Sexual Politics in the Hebrew Bible', in A.Y. Collins (ed.), *Feminist Perspectives on Biblical Scholarship* (Atlanta: Scholars Press, 1985), pp. 117-36.

—'Who Is Hiding the Truth? Deceptive Women and Biblical Androcentrism', in A.Y. Collins (ed.), *Feminist Perspectives on Biblical Scholarship*, pp. 137-44.

Furman, N., 'His Story Versus Her Story: Male Genealogy and Female Strategy in the Jacob Cycle', in A.Y. Collins (ed.), *Feminist Perspectives on Biblical Scholarship*, pp. 107-16.

Gager, J.G., 'Social Description and Social Explanation in the Study of Early Christianity: A Review Essay', in N.K. Gottwald (ed.), *The Bible and Liberation: Political and Social Hermeneutics* (Maryknoll, NY: Orbis Books, 1983).

George, A., 'Le Parallèle entre Jean-Baptiste et Jésus en Lc 1-2', in A. Descamps and A. De Halleux (eds.), *Mélanges Bibliques* (Festschrift B. Rigaux; Gembloux: Duculot, 1970), pp. 147-71; repr. in A. George, *Études sur l'Œuvre de Luc* (SB; Paris: Gabalda, 1978), pp. 43-65.

Gerlach, W., 'Das Problem des "weiblichen Samens" in der antiken und mittelalterlichen Medizin', *(Sudhoffs) Archiv für Geschichte der Medizin* 30 (1937–38).

Geurts, P.M.M., *De erfelijkheid in de oudere Griekse wetenschap* (Nijmegen: Dekker en van de Vesht, 1941).

Geyser, A., 'The Semeion at Cana of Galilee', in *Studies in John* (Leiden: Brill, 1970).

Gilligan, C., N.P. Lyons and J. Hanmer (eds.), *Making Connections: The Relational Worlds of Adolescent Girls at Emma Willard School* (Cambridge, MA: Harvard University Press, 1989).

Gilman, C. P., *Herland: A Lost Feminist Utopian Novel* (introduction by A.J. Lane; New York: Pantheon, 1979). Originally serialized in *The Forerunner*, 6 (1915).

— *His Religion and Hers* (New York: Century, 1923).

— *The Yellow Wallpaper and Other Writings* (L.S. Schwartz [ed. and intro.]; New York: Bantam, 1989).

Gimbutas, M., 'Women and Culture in Goddess-Oriented Old Europe', in J. Plaskow and C.P. Christ (eds.), *Weaving the Visions: New Patterns in Feminist Spirituality* (New York: HarperCollins, 1989).

Glasson, T.F., *Moses in the Fourth Gospel* (SBT, 40; London: SCM Press, 1963).

Goitein, S.D., 'Women as Creators of Biblical Genres', *Prooftexts* 8 (1988), pp. 1-33 (Hebrew original in *Iyyunim Bammiqra* [Tel Aviv: Yavneh, 1957], pp. 248-317).

Goodwin, C., 'How Did John Treat his Sources?', *JBL* 73 (1954).

Gourevitch, D., 'Les études de gynécologie antique de 1975 à aujourd'hui', *Centre Jean Palerne, Université de Saint-Etienne, Informations* 12 (March 1988), pp. 2-12.

Grant, R.M., 'The Origin of the Fourth Gospel', *JBL* 69 (1950), pp. 305-22.

Greimas, A.J. and J. Courtés, *Sémiotique: Dictionnaire raisonné de la théorie du langage*, I, (Paris: Hachette, 1979).

— *Sémiotique: Dictionnaire raisonné de la théorie du langage*, II (Paris: Hachette, 1986).

Groot, M. de, 'Maria en Elisabeth', in C.J.M. Halkes and D. Buddingh (eds.), *Als vrouwen aan het Woord komen: Aspecten van de feministische theologie* (Kampen: Kok, 2nd edn, 1978), pp. 35-41; repr. in *De Vrouw bij de Bron: Fragmenten intuïtieve theologie* (Haarlem: Holland, 1980), pp. 32-40.

Grundmann, W., *Das Evangelium nach Lukas* (THKNT, 3; Berlin: Evangelische Verlagsanstalt, 4th edn, 1966).

Gueuret, A., 'Sur Luc. 1, 46-55: Comment peut-on être amené à penser qu'Elisabeth est "sémiotiquement" celle qui a prononcé le Cantique en Lc 1,46?', *Bulletin du Centre protestant d'études et de documentation: Supplément* (Paris, avril 1977), pp. 3-11.

— *L'Engendrement d'un récit: L'Evangile de l'enfance selon saint Luc* (LD, 113; Paris: Cerf, 1983).

Gundry, R.H., *Matthew: A Commentary on His Literary and Theological Art* (Grand Rapids: Eerdmans, 1982).

Guthrie, D., *The Relevance of John's Apocalypse* (Grand Rapids: Eerdmans, 1987).

Habel, N., 'The Form and Significance of the Call Narratives', *ZAW* 77 (1965), pp. 297-323.

Haenchen, E., *John: A Commentary on the Gospel of John*, I (Philadelphia: Fortress Press, 1984).

Hanson, A.T., 'Rahab the Harlot in Early Christian Tradition', *JSNT* 1 (1978), pp. 53-60.

—'The Use of the Old Testament in the Pastoral Epistles', *IBS* 3 (1981), pp. 203-19.

—'The Domestication of Paul: A Study in the Development of Early Christian Theology', *BJRL* 63 (1981), pp. 402-18.

—'Hebrews', in D.A. Carson and H.G.M. Williamson (eds.), *It is Written: Scripture Citing Scripture: Essays in Honour of Barnabas Lindars, SSF* (Cambridge: Cambridge University Press, 1988), pp. 292-302.

—*The Prophetic Gospel: A Study of John and the Old Testament* (Edinburgh: T. & T. Clark, 1991).

Hanson, P.D., *Dynamic Transcendence: The Correlation of Confessional Heritage and Contemporary Experience in a Biblical Model of Divine Activity* (Philadelphia: Fortress Press, 1978).

Happ, V., *Hyle: Studien zum aristotelischen Materie-Begriff* (Berlin and New York: de Gruyter, 1971), pp. 746-50.

Harnack, A., 'Das Magnificat der Elisabet (Luk. 1, 46-55) nebst einigen Bemerkungen zu Luk. 1 und 2.', *SPAW* 27 (1900), pp. 538-58; repr. in Harnack, *Studien I*, pp. 62-85.

— 'Zu Lc I,34.35.' *ZNW* 2 (1901), pp. 53-57.

—*Lukas der Arzt: Der Verfasser des dritten Evangeliums und der Apostelgeschichte* (Beiträge zur Einleitung in das Neue Testament, I; Leipzig: Hinrichs, 1906).

— 'Über den Spruch "Ehre sei Gott in der Höhe", und das Wort "Eudokia"', *SPA* (1915), pp. 854-75; repr. in Harnack, *Studien I*, pp. 153-79.

—*Studien zur Geschichte des Neuen Testaments und der Alten Kirche, I, Zur neutestamentlichen Textkritik* (AKG, 19; Berlin/Leipzig, 1931).

Harrington, D.J., 'Birth Narratives in Pseudo-Philo's Biblical Antiquities and the Gospels', in M.P. Horgan and P.J. Kobelski (eds.), *To Touch the Text: Biblical and Related Studies in Honor of Joseph A. Fitzmyer, S.J.* (New York: Crossroad, 1989), pp. 316-24.

Hauptman, J., 'Images of Women in the Talmud,' in R.R. Ruether (ed.), *Religion and Sexism: Images of Women in Jewish and Christian Traditions* (New York: Simon & Schuster, 1974), pp. 184-212.

Hayes, J.H. and M. Miller, Jnr (eds.), *Israelite and Judean History* (OTL; London: SCM Press, 1977).

Hays, R.B., '"Have We Found Abraham to Be Our Forefather according to the Flesh?": A Reconsideration of Rom. 4.1?', in *NovT*, 27.1 (1985), pp. 76-98.

Heil, J.P. , 'The Narrative Roles of the Women in Matthew's Gospel', *Bib* 72 (1991), pp. 538-45.

Hengel, M., *The Johannine Question* (London: SCM Press, 1989).

Henten, J.W. van, 'Judith as a Female Moses: Judith 7–13 in the light of Exodus 17; Numbers 20 and Deuteronomy 33:8-11', in van Dijk-Hemmes and Brenner (eds.), *Reflections*, pp. 33-48.

— 'Judith as Alternative Leader: A Rereading of Judith 7–13', in A. Brenner (ed.), *Esther, Judith and Susanna*, pp. 224-52.

Heschel, S., 'Theologen für Hitler: Walter Grundmann und das Institut zur Erforschung und Beseitigung des jüdischen Einflusses auf das deutsche kirchliche Leben', in: L. Siegele-Wenschkewitz (ed.), *Christlicher Antijudaismus und Antisemitismus: Arnoldshainer Texte* (Frankfurt, 1994), pp. 125-70.

Hick, J., 'Sin and the Fall According to the Hellenistic Fathers', in *Evil and the God of Love* (San Francisco: Harper & Row, 1978).

Higgins, J.M., 'The Myth of Eve: The Temptress', *JAAR* 44 (1976), pp. 639-47.

Hilgenfeld, A., 'Die Geburt Jesu aus der Jungfrau in dem Lucas-Evangelium', *ZWT* 44 (1901), pp. 313-17.

Hobart, W.K., *The Medical Language of St. Luke* (Dublin: Hodges, Figgis; London: Longmans, Green, 1882; repr. Grand Rapids: Baker, 1954).

Hooker, M.D., '"What Doest Thou Here, Elijah?" A Look at St Mark's Account of the Transfiguration', in L.D. Hurst and N.T. Wright (eds.), *The Glory of Christ in the New Testament: Studies in Christology in Memory of George Bradford Caird* (Oxford: Clarendon Press, 1987), pp. 59-70.

Hopfner, T., *Das Sexualleben der Griechen und Römer von den Anfängen bis ins 6. Jahrhundert nach Christus*, I.1, (Prague: Calve, 1938).

Hopkins, M., 'The Historical Perspective of Apocalypse 1-11', *CBQ* 27 (1965), pp. 42-47.

Horsley, R.A., '"Like One of the Prophets of Old": Two Types of Popular Prophets at the Time of Jesus', *CBQ* 47 (1985), pp. 435-63.

Horst, P.W. van der, 'Peter's Shadow: The Religio-Historical Background of Acts V.15', *NTS* 23 (1976/77), pp. 204-12; repr. in van der Horst and Mussies (eds.), *Studies*, pp. 153-63.

— 'Der Schatten im hellenistischen Volksglauben', in M.J. Vermaseren (ed.), *Studies in Hellenistic Religions* (EPRO, 78; Leiden: Brill, 1979), pp. 27-36.

—'Seven Months' Children in Jewish and Christian Literature from Antiquity', in *Essays on the Jewish World of Early Christianity* (Fribourg/Göttingen: Universitätsverlag/Vandenhoeck & Ruprecht, 1990).

Horst, P.W. van der, and G. Mussies (eds.), *Studies on the Hellenistic Background of the New Testament* (Utrechtse Theologische Reeks, 10; Utrecht: Theological Faculty Utrecht University, 1990).

Hoskyn, E.C., *The Fourth Gospel* (London: Faber & Faber, 1947).

—'Genesis I–III and St John's Gospel', *JTS* 21 (1920), pp. 210–18.

Hultgren, A.J., *I-II Timothy, Titus* (Augsburg Commentary on the New Testament; Minneapolis: Augsburg, 1984).

Jacobé, Fr. (pseudonym for A. Loisy), 'L'origine du Magnificat', *Revue d'histoire et de littérature religieuses* 2 (1897), pp. 424-32.

Jeansonne, S.P., *The Women of Genesis: From Sarah to Potiphar's Wife* (Minneapolis: Fortress Press, 1990).

Jenkins, F., *The Old Testament in the Book of Revelation* (Marion: Indiana, 1972).

Jeremias, J., *Jesus' Promise to the Nations*, (London: SCM Press, 1958).

Jeske R.L. and D.L. Barr, 'The Study of the Apocalypse Today', *RelSRev* 14 (1988), pp. 337-44.

Joly, R., *Le niveau de la science hippocratique* (Paris: Les Belles Lettres, 1966).

Karris, R.J., 'The Background and Significance of the Polemic of the Pastoral Epistles', *JBL* 92 (1973), pp. 549-64.

Käsemann, E., *The Testament of Jesus: A Study of the Gospel of John in Light of Chapter 17* (Philadelphia: Fortress Press, 1968).

Keifert, P., 'Mind Reader and Maestro: Models for Understanding Biblical Interpreters', *WW* 1 (1981), pp. 153-68.

Kember, O., 'Right and Left in the Sexual Theories of Parmenides', *Journal of Hellenic Studies* 91 (1971), pp. 70-79.

Kent, H.A., *The Epistle to the Hebrews* (Grand Rapids: Baker 1972).

Kilmartin, E.J., 'The Mother of Jesus Was There', *ScEccl* 15 (1963).

Klassen, W. 'Vengeance in the Apocalypse of John', *CBQ* 28 (1966), pp. 300-311.

Klijn, A.F.J., *De brief aan de Hebreeën* (Nijkerk: Callenbach, 1975).

Klostermann, E., *Das Lukas-evangelium* (HNT, 5; Tübingen: Mohr, 3rd edn, 1975).

Knight, G.W., 'AUYENTEV in Reference to Women in 1 Timothy 2.12', *NTS* 30 (1984), pp. 143-57.

Korkukch, T.J., 'These are Written that You May Believe that Jesus is the Christ, the Son of God' (Master's thesis; Drew University Graduate School, 1991).

Kraemer, R.S., 'Women's Authorship of Jewish and Christian Literature in the Greco-Roman Period', in A.-J. Levine, '"Women Like This": New Perspectives on Jewish Women in the Greco-Roman World* (SBL Early Judaism and Its Literature, 1; Atlanta: Scholars Press, 1991), pp. 221-42.

Kroeger, C.C., 'Ancient Heresies and a Strange Greek Verb', *Reformed Journal* 29 (1979), pp. 12-15.

Kroeger, R.C. and C.C. Kroeger, *I Suffer Not a Woman: Rethinking 1 Timothy 2.11-15 in Light of Ancient Evidence* (Grand Rapids: Baker, 1992).

Kudlien, F., 'Zur Erforschung archaisch-griechischer Zeugungslehren', *Medizinhistorisches Journal* 16 (1981), pp. 323-39.

—'Pneumatische Ärzte', PWSup 11 (1968), pp. 1097-108.

Kümmel, W.G., *Introduction to the New Testament* (trans. H.C. Kee; Nashville: Abingdon Press, rev. edn, 1975).

Kysar, R., *The Fourth Evangelist and His Gospel: An Examination of Contemporary Scholarship* (Minneapolis: Augsburg, 1975).

—*John* (Minneapolis: Augsburg, 1986).

Ladas, A.K., B. Whipple and J.D. Perry, *The G-Spot and Other Recent Discoveries about Human Sexuality* (London: Corgi Books, 1983).

Lane, W.L., *The Gospel according to Mark: The English Text with Introduction, Exposition and Notes* (NICNT; Grand Rapids: Eerdmans, 1974).

Laurentin, R., *Structure et théologie de Luc I-II* (Paris: Gabalda, 1957).

—*Les Évangiles de l'Enfance du Christ: Vérité de Noël au-delà des mythes. Exégèse et sémiotique—historicité et théologie* (Paris: Desclée, 1982).

Lerner, G., *The Creation of Patriarchy* (Oxford: Oxford University Press, 1986).

Lesky, E., *Die Zeugungs- und Vererbungslehren der Antike und ihr Nachwirken* (Mainz: Akademie für Wissenschaft und Literatur, 1951).

Lesky, E., and J.H. Waszink, 'Embryologie', *Reallexikon für Antike und Christentum* 4 (1959).

Levine, A.-J., (ed.), *'Women Like This': New Perspectives on Jewish Women in the Greco-Roman World* (Atlanta: Scholars Press, 1991).

Levine, A.-J., 'Matthew', in Newsom, C.A. and Ringe, S.H. (eds.), *The Women's Bible Commentary* (London: SPCK, Louisville, KY: Westminster/John Knox Press, 1992), pp. 252-63.

—'Who's Catering the Q Affair? Feminist Observations on Q Paraenesis', in L. Perdue and J. Gammie (eds.), *Paraenesis: Act and Form* (Semeia, 50; Atlanta: Scholars Press, 1990), pp. 145-62.

Levitas, R., *The Concept of Utopia* (New York: Philip Allan, 1990).

Lieu, J.M., *The Theology of the Johannine Epistles* (Cambridge: Cambridge University Press, 1991).

—'The Women's Resurrection Testimony', in S. Barton and G.N. Stanton (eds.), *Resurrection Essays in Honour of J.L. Houlden* (London: SCM Press, 1994).

—'The Johannine Literature and Biblical Theology', in S. Pedersen (ed.), *Problems in Biblical Theology* (Leiden: Brill, forthcoming).

Lightfoot, R.H., *St. John's Gospel: A Commentary* (Oxford: Clarendon Press, 1956).

Lincoln, A.T., 'Abraham Goes to Rome: Paul's Treatment of Abraham in Romans 4', in M.J. Wilkins and T. Paige (eds.), *Worship, Theology and Ministry in the Early Church: Essays in Honor of Ralph P. Martin* (JSNTSup, 87; Sheffield: JSOT Press, 1992), pp. 163-79.

Lindars, B., *Behind the Fourth Gospel* (London: SPCK, 1971).

Lloyd, G.E.R., *Science, Folklore and Ideology: Studies in the Life Sciences in Ancient Greece* (Cambridge: Cambridge University Press, 1983).

—'Parmenides' Sexual Theories', *Journal of Hellenic Studies* 92 (1972).

Loisy, A., *L'évangile selon Luc* (Paris: Nourry, 1924; repr. Frankfurt: Minerva, 1971).

Loney, I.M., *The Hippocratic Treatises 'On Generation', 'On the Nature of the Child', 'Diseases IV'* (Berlin and New York: de Gruyter, 1981).

Lorde, A., 'Uses of the Erotic: The Erotic as Power', reprinted from J.B. Nelson and S.P. Longfellow (eds.), *Sister Outsider* in *Sexuality and the Sacred: Sources for Theological Reflection* (Louisville, KY: Westminster/John Knox, 1994).

Luz, U., *Matthew 1–7* (Edinburgh: T. & T. Clark, 1989).

Maccoby, H., *Judaism in the First Century* (London: Sheldon Press, 1989).

MacDonald, D.R.,*The Legend and the Apostle: The Battle for Paul in Story and Canon* (Philadelphia: Westminster Press, 1983).

Mackay, W.M., 'Another Look at the Nicolaitans', *EvQ* 45(1973), pp. 111-15.

Maertens, T., *The Advancing Dignity of Woman in the Bible* (trans. S. Dibbs; De Père, WN: St Norbert Abbey Press, 1969).

Majka, F., 'Of Beasts and Christians', *The Bible Today* (1984), pp. 279-84.

Malbon, E.S., and E.V. McKnight (eds.), *The New Literary Criticism and the New Testament* (JSNTSup, 109; Sheffield: Sheffield Academic Press, 1994).

Mansfeld, J., *Parmenides en Zeno: Het leerdicht en de paradoxen* (Kampen: Kok-Agora, 1988), pp. 76-77.

Martyn, J.L., *History and Theology in the Fourth Gospel* (Nashville: Abingdon Press, 2nd edn, 1979).

Mauser, U., 'Paul the Theologian', *HBT*, 11 (1989), pp. 80-106.

McCracken, D., 'Character in the Boundary: Bakhtin's Interdividuality in Biblical Narratives', *Semeia* 63, pp. 29-42.

McKay, H.A., *Sabbath and Synagogue: The Question of Sabbath Worship in Ancient Judaism* (Religions in the Graeco-Roman World, 122; Leiden: Brill, 1994).

—*Good Friday and the Old Testament: A Study Guide for Lent*, forthcoming.

Meeks, W., 'The Man From Heaven in Johannine Sectarianism', *JBL* 91 (1974).

—'The Image of the Androgyne: Some Uses of a Symbol in Earliest Christianity', *HR* 13 (1974), pp. 165-208.

Metzger, B.M., *A Textual Commentary on the Greek New Testament* (London: United Bible Societies, corr. edn, 1975).

Meyer, R., *Hellenistisches in der rabbinischen Anthropologie* (Stuttgart: Kohlhammer, 1937).

Meyers, C., 'Returning Home: Ruth 1.8 and the Gendering of the Book of Ruth', in Brenner (ed.), *Ruth*, pp. 85-114.

Michel, O., *Der Brief an die Hebräer* (Göttingen: Vandenhoeck & Ruprecht, 6th edn, 1966).

Michl, J., 'Der Weibessame (Gen 3,15) in spatjüdischer und frühchristlicher Auffassung', *Bib* 33 (1952), pp. 371-401, 476-505.

Mickelsen, A. (ed.),*Women, Authority and the Bible* (Downer's Grove, IL: IVP, 1986).

Miller, N.K., *Subject to Change: Reading Feminist Writing* (Gender and Culture; New York: Columbia University Press, 1988).

—*Getting Personal: Feminist Occasions and Other Autobiographical Acts* (New York/London: Routledge & Kegan Paul, 1991).

Moessner, D.P., '"The Christ Must Suffer": New Light on the Jesus–Peter, Stephen–Paul Parallels in Luke–Acts', *NovT* 28/3 (1986), pp. 220-56.

Montefiore, H.W., *The Epistle to the Hebrews* (London: A. & C. Black, 1964).

Moore, S.D., *Mark and Luke in Poststructuralist Perspectives: Jesus Begins to Write* (New Haven and London: Yale University Press, 1992).

Morgan, R., *The Demon Lover: On the Sexuality of Terrorism* (New York: Norton, 1989).

Morgen, M., 'La promesse de Jésus à Nathanael (Jn 1.51) éclairée par la haggadah de Jacob-Israel', *RSR* 67.3 (1993), pp. 3-21.

Morsink, J., 'Was Aristotle's Biology Sexist?', *Journal of the History of Biology* 12 (1979), pp. 83-112.

Morton, H.V., *Women of the Bible* (London: Methuen, 1940).

Musonius R., 'That Women Too Should Study Philosophy', in C. E. Lutz (ed.), *Musonius Rufus: 'The Roman Socrates'* (Yale Classical Studies; New Haven: Yale University Press, 1947).

Mussies, G., 'Name giving after relatives in the ancient world: The historical background of Luke I, 59-63 in connection with Matt. I, 16 and XIII, 55', in van der Horst and Mussies (eds.), *Studies*, pp. 65-85.

— 'Variation in the Book of Acts', *FN*, IV.8 (1991), pp. 165-82.

— 'Variation in the Book of Acts (Part II)', *FN* (forthcoming).

Musurillo, H.A., *Symbol and Myth in Ancient Poetry* (New York: Fordham University Press, 1961).

Musvosvi, J.N., 'The Concept of Vengeance in the Book of Revelation and its Old Testament and Near Eastern Context', *Andrews University Seminary Studies* 26 (1988), pp. 83-84.

Needham, J., and A. Hughes, *A History of Embryology* (Cambridge: Cambridge University Press, 2nd edn, 1959).

Neirynck, F., 'Visitatio B.M.V. Bijdrage tot de Quellenkritik van Lc. 1-2', *Collationes Brugenses et Gandavenses* 6 (1960), pp. 387-404.

Neusner, J., *Genesis Rabbah The Judaic Commentary to the Book of Genesis: A New American Translation*, I. *Parashiyyot One through Thirty-three on Genesis 1.1 to 8.14* (Atlanta: Scholars Press, 1985).

Newsom, C.A. and S.H. Ringe, eds.,*The Women's Bible Commentary* (London: SPCK and Louisville, KY: Westminster/John Knox, 1992).

Neyrey, J.H., 'The Jacob Allusions in John 1.51', *CBQ* 44 (1982), pp. 586-605.

—'Jacob Traditions and the Interpretation of John 4:10-26', *CBQ* 41 (1979), pp. 419-37.

Nicol, W., *The Semeia in the Fourth Gospel* (Leiden: Brill, 1972).

Niditch, S., *Chaos to Cosmos: Studies in Biblical Patterns of Creation* (Scholars Press Studies in the Humanities, 6; Chico, CA: Scholars Press, 1985).

Nolan, B.M., *The Royal Son of God: The Christology of Matthew 1–2 in the Setting of the Gospel* (Fribourg Suisse: Editions Universitaires/Gottingen: Vandenhoeck & Ruprecht, 1979).

North, H.F., 'The Mare, the Vixen, and the Bee: *Sophrosyne* as the Virtue of Women in Antiquity', *Illinois Classical Studies* 2 (1977), pp. 35-48.

Onians, R.B., *The Origins of European Thought about the Body, the Mind, the Soul, World, Time, and Fate* (Cambridge: Cambridge University Press, 1988[1951]).

Osiek, C, 'The Feminist and the Bible', in A.Y. Collins (ed.), *Feminist Perspectives on Biblical Scholarship* (Atlanta: Scholars Press, 1985), pp. 93-106.

O'Collins, G., 'Jesus', in M. Eliade (ed), *Encyclopedia of Religion*, VIII (New York: MacMillan, 1987), p. 16.

O'Donovan, O., 'The Political Thought of the Book of Revelation', *TynBul* 37 (1986), pp. 61-91.

O'Fearghail, F., 'Sir 50,5-21: Yom Kippur or The Daily Whole-Offering', *Bib* 59 (1978), pp. 301-16.

O'Toole, R.E., 'The Parallels between Jesus and Moses', *BTB* 20 (1990), pp. 22-29.

Padgett, A., 'Wealthy Women at Ephesus: I Timothy 2.8-15 in Social Context', *Int* 41 (1987), pp. 19-31.

Pagels, E., *Adam, Eve, and the Serpent* (New York: Random House, 1988).

Patai, R., *The Hebrew Goddess* (Detroit: Wayne State University Press, 1967; 3rd edn, 1990).

Peake, A.S., *The Revelation of John* (London: Holborn , n.d.)

Perrin, N., *What is Redaction Criticism?* (Philadelphia: Fortress Press, 1969).

Phintys, 'On the Temperance of a Woman', in T. Taylor (ed.), *Political Fragments of Archytas, Charondas, Zaleucus and other Ancient Pythagoreans, Preserved by Stobaeus* (Chiswick, England: C. Whittingham, 1822).

Pippin, T., 'Eros and the End: Reading for Gender in the Apocalypse of John', *Semeia* 59 (1992), pp. 193-210.

Plaskow, J., 'Feminist Anti-Judaism and the Christian God', *JFSR* 7 (1991), pp. 99-108.

Plummer, A., *A Critical and Exegetical Commentary on the Gospel according to S. Luke* (ICC; Edinburgh: T. & T. Clark, 4th edn, 1901 [1896]).

Plutarch, 'Advice to Bride and Groom', in F.C. Babbitt *et al.* (eds.), *Moralia* (Loeb Classical Library; 16 vols.; Cambridge MA: Harvard University Press, 1927–1969).

Polzin, R., 'Divine and Anonymous Characterization in Biblical Narrative', *Semeia* 63, pp. 205-14

Preuss, A., 'Galen's Criticism of Aristotle's Conception Theory', *Journal of the History of Biology* 10 (1977).

Preuss, J., *Biblisch-talmudische Medizin* (repr.; Wiesbaden: Otto Harassowitz, 1992[1911]) ET *Biblical and Talmudic Medicine* (trans. F. Rosner; New York: Sanhedrin, 1978).

Prusak, B.P., 'Woman: Seductive Siren and Source of Sin?', in R.R. Ruether (ed.), *Religion and Sexism: Images of Women in the Jewish and Christian Traditions* (New York: Simon & Schuster, 1974), pp. 89-116.

Quinn, J.D., 'Is Rachab in Matthew 1.5 Rahab of Jericho?' *Bib* 62 (1982), pp. 225-28.

Rashkow, I., *Upon the Dark Places: Anti-Semitism and Sexism in English Renaissance Biblical Translation* (Bible and Literature Series, 28; Sheffield: Almond Press, 1990).

Rauer, M., *Origenes Werke IX: Die Homilien zu Lukas in der Übersetzung des Hieronymus und die griechischen Reste der Homilien und des Lukas-Kommentars* (GCS, 49.2; Berlin: Akademie Verlag, 2nd edn, 1959).

Reinhartz, A., 'Anonymity and Character in the Books of Samuel', *Semeia* 63 (1993), pp. 117-42.

—'Great Expectations: A Reader-Oriented Approach to Johannine Christology and Eschatology,' *Journal of Literature and Theology* 3 (1989), pp. 61-76.

Rengstorf, K.H., *Das Evangelium nach Lukas* (NTD; Göttingen, 14th edn, 1969 [1937]).

Rensberger, D., *Johannine Faith and Liberating Community* (Philadelphia: Westminster Press, 1988).

Resch, A., *Aussercanonische Paralleltexte zu den Evangelien*. II.3. *Paralleltexte zu Lucas* (TU, X.3; Leipzig: Hinrichs, 1895).

— *Ausserkanonische Paralleltexte zu den Evangelien*. III.5. *Das Kindheitsevangelium nach Lucas und Matthaeus unter Herbeibeziehung der aussercanonischen Paralleltexte quellenkritisch untersucht* (TU, X.5; Leipzig: Hinrichs, 1897).

Reuther, R.R., *Gaia and God: An Ecofeminist Theology of Earth Healing* (New York: HarperCollins, 1992).

Rich, A., 'Notes toward a Politics of Location (1984)', *Blood, Bread, and Poetry: Selected Prose 1979-1985* (New York: Norton, 1986; London: Virago, 1987), pp. 210-31.

—*Of Woman Born: Motherhood as Experience and Institution* (New York: Norton, 1976).

Riches, J.K., 'The Sociology of Matthew: Some Basic Questions Concerning its Relation to the Theology of the New Testament', (SBLSup; Atlanta: Scholars Press, 1983), pp. 259-71.

Robbins, G.A. (ed.), *Genesis 1-3 in the History of Exegesis: Intrigue in the Garden* (Studies in Women and Religion, 27; Lewiston, NY: Edwin Mellen, 1988).

Robbins, V.K., 'Socio-Rhetorical Criticism: Mary, Elizabeth and the Magnificat as a Test Case', in E.S. Malbon and E.V. McKnight (eds.), *The New Literary Criticism and the New Testament* (Sheffield: Sheffield Academic Press, 1994).

Robinson, J. M. (ed.), *The Nag Hammadi Library in English* (San Francisco: Harper & Row, 1981).

—'Miracle Sources in John: An Essay–Review of Robert Towson Fortna, The Gospel of Signs', *JAAR* 39 (1971).

—'Very Goddess and Very Man: Jesus' Better Self', in K.L. King (ed.), *Images of the Feminine in Gnosticism* (Philadelphia: Fortress Press, 1988), pp. 113-27.

Rocca-Serra, R., *Censorinus: Le jour natal* (Paris: Vrin, 1980)

Rosner, F., *Medicine in the Bible and the Talmud* (New York: Ktav, 1977).

Rousseau, A., and L. Doutreleau (eds.), *Irénée de Lyon, Contre les Hérésies*, IV (SC, 100: 1-2; Paris: Cerf, 1965).

— *Irénée de Lyon, Contre les Hérésies*, III (SC, 210-211; Paris: Cerf, 1974).

Rousselle, A., *Porneia: On Desire and the Body in Antiquity* (Oxford: Blackwell, 1988).

—'Observation féminine et idéologie masculine: Le corps de la femme d'après les médecins grecs', *Annales (économies, sociétés, civilisations)* 35 (1980).

Rowland, C., 'Keeping Alive the Dangerous Vision of a World of Peace and Justice', in W. Beuken, S. Freyne and A. Weiler (eds.), *Concilium: Religion in the Eighties* (Edinburgh: T. & T. Clark, l988), pp. 75-85.

Ruether, R.R., 'Feminist Interpretation: A Method of Correlation', in L.M. Russell (ed.), *Feminist Interpretation of the Bible* (Oxford: Basil Blackwell, 1985), pp. 111-24.

Ruether, R.R. (ed.), *Religion and Sexism* (New York: Simon & Schuster, 1974)

Russell, L.M. (ed.), *Feminist Interpretation of the Bible* (Oxford: Basil Blackwell, 1985).

Safrai, C., 'Women in the Temple: The Status and Role of Women in the Second Temple of Jerusalem' (Dissertation, Catholic Theological University of Amsterdam, 1991).

Safrai, S. and M. Stern (eds.), *The Jewish People in the First Century: Historical Geography, Political History, Social, Cultural and Religious Life and Institutions* (CRINT, I.II; Assen/Amsterdam: Van Gorcum, 1976).

Sallmann, N., *Censorini de die natali liber* (Leipzig: Teubner, 1983).

Sanders, E.P. *Jesus and Judaism* (London: SCM Press, 1985).

Sanders, E.P. and M. Davies, *Studying the Synoptic Gospels* (London: SCM Press, 1989).

Sasson, J.M., *Ruth: A New Translation with a Philological Commentary and a Formalist-Folklorist Interpretation* (JHNES; Baltimore: The Johns Hopkins University Press, 1979; *Biblical Seminar*, 8; Sheffield: JSOT Press, 2nd edn, 1989).

Schaberg, J., *The Illegitimacy of Jesus: A Feminist Theological Interpretation of the Infancy Narratives* (San Francisco: Harper & Row, 1987).

—'The Foremothers and the Mother of Jesus', *Concilium* 26 (1989), pp. 112-19. (reprinted in this volume, pp. 149-58).

— 'Luke', in C.A. Newsom and S.H. Ringe (eds.), *The Women's Bible Commentary* (London: SPCK; Louisville, KY: Westminster/John Knox, 1992), pp. 275-92.

Schmidt, K.L., *Der Rahmen der Geschichte Jesu: Literarkritische Untersuchungen zur ältesten Jesusüberlieferung* (Berlin: Trowitzsch, 1919; repr. Darmstadt: Wissenschaftliche Buchgesellschaft, 2nd edn, 1969 [1964]).

Schnachenburg, R., *Gospel According to St. John*, I (New York: Crossroad, 1989).

—*The Johannine letters: Introduction and Commentary* (trans. R. and I. Fuller; Dublin: Burns & Oates, 1992).

Schneiders, S., 'Women in the Fourth Gospel', *BTB* 12 (1982), pp. 35-45.

—*The Revelatory Text. Interpreting the New Testament as Sacred Scripture* (San Fransisco: Harper & Row, 1991).

Schottroff, L., *Der Glaubende und die feindliche Welt* (Neukirchen-Vluyn: Neukirchener Verlag, 1970).

—*Befreiungserfahrungen* (Munich: Chr. Kaiser Verlag, 1990), pp. 310-23 (ET *Let the Oppressed Go Free: Feminist Perspectives on the New Testament* [Louisville: Westminster/John Knox Press, 1993], pp. 138-57).

Schumann, H.-J. von, *Sexualkunde und Sexualmedizin in der klassischen Antike* (Munich, 1975).

Schürer, E., *The History of the Jewish People in the Age of Jesus Christ (175 B.C.–A.D. 135)*, II (ed. G. Vermes, F. Miller and M. Black; Edinburgh: T. & T. Clark, 1979).

Schüssler Fiorenza, E., 'Apocalyptic and Gnosis in the Book of Revelation and Paul', *JBL* 92 (1973), pp. 565-81.

—*The Book of Revelation : Justice and Judgment* (Philadelphia: Fortress Press, 1985).

—'The Followers of the Lamb: Visionary Rhetoric and Social-Political Situation', in *The Book of Revelation*, ch. 7.

—'Remembering the Past and Creating the Future', in A.Y. Collins (ed.), *Feminist Perspectives on Biblical Scholarship* (Atlanta: Scholars Press, 1985), pp. 43-64.

—'The Followers of the Lamb', *Semeia* 36 (1986), pp. 123-46.

—'A Feminist Interpretation for Liberation: Mary and Mary: Lk. 10.38-42', *Religion and Intellectual Life* 3 (1986), pp. 21-36.

—*In Memory of Her: A Feminist Theological Reconstruction of Christian Origins* (New York: Crossroad/London: SCM Press, 1986).

—*Theological Criteria and Historical Reconstruction* (Protocol of the 53rd Colloquy: 10 April, 1986; Berkeley: Center for Hermeneutical Studies in Hellenistic and Modern Culture, 1986).

—'The Ethics of Biblical Interpretation: Decentering Biblical Scholarship', *JBL* 107 (1988), pp. 3-17.

—*But She Said: Feminist Practices of Biblical Interpretation* (Boston: Beacon Press, 1992), pp. 51-76.

Schweizer, E., *The Good News according to Matthew* (trans. D. Green; Atlanta: John Knox Press, 1970).

—*Das Evangelium nach Lukas* (Göttingen, 1982).

Scott, M., *Sophia and the Johannine Jesus* (JSNTSup, 71; Sheffield: JSOT Press, 1992).

Seim, T.K., 'Roles of Women in the Gospel of John', in L. Hartman and B. Olsson (eds.), *Aspects of the Johannine Literature* (CBNTS, 18; Uppsala: Almqvist & Wiksell, 1987), pp. 56-73.

Selvidge, M.J., 'Powerful and Powerless Women in the Apocalypse', *Neot* 26 (1992), pp. 157-67.

Setel, T.D., 'Prophets and Pornography: Female Sexual Imagery in Hosea', in L.M. Russell (ed.), *Feminist Interpretation of the Bible* (Philadelphia: Westminister Press, 1985), pp. 86-95.

—'Feminine Insights and the Question of Method', in A.Y. Collins (ed.), *Feminist Perspectives on Biblical Scholarship* (Atlanta: Scholars Press, 1985), pp. 35-42.

Siegel, R.E., *Galen's System of Physiology and Medicine* (Basel and New York: Karger, 1968).

Siegele-Wenchkewitz, L., 'The Discussion of Anti-Judaism in Feminist Theology— A New Area of Jewish–Christian Dialogue', *JFSR* 7 (1991), pp. 95-98.

—'Mitverantwortung und Schuld der Christen am Holocaust', *EvT* 42 (1982), pp. 171-80.

Sigountos, J.G. and M. Shank, 'Public Roles for Women in the Pauline Church: A Reappraisal of the Evidence', *JETS* 26 (1983), pp. 283-95.

Siker, J.S., *Disinheriting the Jews: Abraham in Early Christian Controversy* (Louisville, KY: Westminster/John Knox Press, 1991).

Simon, I., 'La gynécologie, l'obstétrie, l'embryologie et la puériculture dans la Bible et le Talmud', *Revue d'histoire de la médecine hébraïque* 4 (1949).

Smith, D.M., *Johannine Christianity: Essays on its Setting, Sources, and Theology* (Columbia: University of South Carolina Press, 1984).

— 'The Sources of the Gospel of John: An Assessment of the Present State of the Problem', *NTS* 10 (1963–64).

Smith, M.S., *The Early History of God: Yahweh and the Other Deities in Ancient Israel* (New York: Harper & Row, 1990).

Smothers, T.G., 'A Superior Model: Hebrews 1.1–4.13', *RevExp* 82 (1985), pp. 333-43.

Snyder, J.M., *The Woman and the Lyre: Women Writers in Classical Greece and Rome* (Bristol: Bristol Classical Press, 1989).

Sölle, D., 'Schwesternstreit', in D. Sölle (ed.), *Für Gerechtigkeit streiten* (Gütersloh, 1994), pp. 112-16.

Spender, D., *Invisible Women: The Schooling Scandal* (London: Writers and Readers, 1982).

Spicq, C., *L'épître aux Hébreux* (II; Paris: Gabalda, 1953).

—*L'épître aux Hébreux* (Paris: Gabalda, 1977).

von Staden, H., *Herophilus: The Art of Medicine in Early Alexandria* (Cambridge: Cambridge University Press, 1989).

Stanley, J.E., 'The Apocalypse and Contemporary Sect Analysis' (SBLSP, 25; Atlanta: Scholars Press, 1986), pp. 412-21.

Stanton, E.C., *The Woman's Bible* (New York: European Publishing Company, 1898; reprinted, Seattle: Coalition Task Force on Women and Religion, 1974).

Stanton, G., *The Gospels and Jesus* (The Oxford Bible Series; Oxford: Oxford University Press, 1990).

Stanton, G. (ed.), *The Interpretation of Matthew* (London: SPCK, 1983).

Stendahl, K., 'Biblical Theology, Contemporary', *IDB*, 1.418-32.

Stibbe M., *The Gospel of John as Literature: An Anthology of Twentieth-Century Perspectives* (NTTS, 17; Leiden: Brill, 1993).

Stol, M., *Zwangerschap en geboorte bij de Babyloniërs en in de Bijbel* (Leiden: Ex Oriente Lux, 1983).

Stone, M., *When God Was a Woman* (San Diego: Harcourt Brace Jovanovich, 1976).

Strack, H.L. and J.P. Billerbeck, *Kommentar zum Neuen Testament aus Talmud und Midrash*, II (Munich: Beck, 1924).

Stricker, B.H., *De geboorte van Horus* (5 vols.; Leiden: Ex Oriente Lux, 1963–1989).

Swindell, A.C., 'Abraham and Isaac: An Essay in Biblical Appropriation', *ExpTim* 87 (1975), pp. 50-53.

Szarvas, E., *Les connaissances embryologiques et obstétricales des Hébreux jusqu'à l'époque de clôture du Talmud* (Paris, 1936).

Tallmadge May, M., *Galen on the Usefulness of the Parts of the Body* (Ithaca, NY: Cornell University Press, 1968).

Tannehill, R.C., *The Sword of His Mouth* (Philadelphia: Fortress Press, 1975).

Tavard, G., *Woman in Christian Tradition* (Notre Dame: University of Notre Dame, 1973).

Teeple, H.M., 'Methodology in Source Analysis of the Fourth Gospel', *JBL* 81 (1962).

— *Literary Origin of the Gospel of John* (Evanston, IL: Religion and Ethics Institute, 1974).

Temkin, O., *Soranus' Gynecology* (repr. Baltimore: Johns Hopkins University Press, 1991[1956]).

Temple, S., 'The Two Signs in the Fourth Gospel', *JBL* 81 (1962).

—*The Core of the Fourth Gospel* (London: Mowbrays, 1975).

Tenney, M.C., 'Topics from the Gospel of John: Part II: The Meaning of the Signs', *BSac* 132 (1975).

Ter-Minassiantz, E., 'Hat Irenäus Lc. 1,46 Μαριάμ oder Ελεισάβετ gelesen?', *ZNW* 7 (1906).

Thistelton, A.C., *New Horizons in Hermeneutics: The Theory and Practice of Transforming Biblical Reading* (Grand Rapids: Zondervan, 1992).

Thompson, L.L., *The Book of Revelation: Apocalypse and Empire* (New York: Oxford University Press, 1990).

Thurston, B.B., *The Widows: A Women's Ministry in the Early Church* (Minneapolis: Fortress Press, 1989).

Tolbert, M.A. (ed.),*The Bible and Feminist Hermeneutics* (*Semeia*, 28; Chico, CA: Scholars Press, 1983).

Tompkins, J.P. (ed.), *Reader-Response Criticism: From Formalism to Post-Structuralism* (Baltimore/London: The Johns Hopkins University Press, 1984).

Toussaint, S.D., 'The Significance of the First Sign in John's Gospel', *BSac* 134 (1977).

Towner, P.H., *The Goal of Our Instruction: The Structure of Theology and Ethics in the Pastoral Epistles* (JSNTSup, 34; Sheffield: Sheffield Academic Press, 1989).

Trible, P., *God and the Rhetoric of Sexuality* (Philadelphia: Fortress Press, 5th edn, 1987 [1978]).

Troost, A., 'Als Elisabet en Maria elkaar spreken: over het nemen van het woord', *Schrift* 140 (1992), pp. 60-64.

—'Using the Word in Luke 1–2' (Colloquium Biblicum Lovaniense XLI, The Synoptic Gospels: Source Criticism and the New Literary Criticism; Leuven, 1992).

—'Reading for the Author's Signature: Genesis 21.1-21 and Luke 15.11-32 as Intertexts', in Brenner (ed.), *Genesis*, pp. 251-72.

Tuckett, C.M., 'Feminine Wisdom in Q?', in G. Brooke (ed.), *Women in the Biblical Tradition* (Lewiston, NY: Edwin Mellen, 1992), pp. 112-28.

Turner, C.H., 'Niceta of Remesiana II: Introduction and Text of *de psalmodiae bono.*', *JTS* 24 (1923), pp. 225-52.

Vermes, G., *Jesus the Jew: A Historian's Reading of the Gospels* (London: Collins, 1973).

Verner, D.C., *The Household of God: The Social World of the Pastoral Epistles* (SBLDS, 71; Chico, CA: Scholars Press, 1983).

Vielhauer, P., 'Das Benedictus des Zacharias (Luk. 1,68-79)', *ZTK* 49 (1952), pp. 255-72.

Vorster, W.S., 'Genre and the Revelation of John: A Study in Text, Context, and Intertext', *Neot* 22 (1988), pp. 103-23.

Voss, G., 'Die Christusverkündigung der Kindheitsgeschichte im Rahmen des Lukasevangeliums', *BK* 21 (1966), pp. 112-15.

Wacker, M.-T., 'Feminist Theology and Anti-Judaism: The Status of the Discussion and the Context of the Problem in the Federal Republic of Germany', *JFSR* 7 (1991), pp. 109-16.

—'Feminist Theology and Anti-Judaism: The Status of the Discussion and the Context of the Problem in the Federal Republic of Germany', *JFSR* 2 (1986), pp. 109-16.

Waetjen, H.C., 'The Genealogy as the Key to the Gospel According to Matthew', *JBL* 95 (1976), pp. 205-30.

Wahlde, U.C. von, 'A Redactional Technique in the Fourth Gospel', *Christian Bible Quarterly* 38 (1976).

Wainwright, E.M., *Towards a Feminist Critical Reading of the Gospel According to Matthew* (Berlin: de Gruyter, 1991).

— *The Earliest Version of John's Gospel. Recovering the Gospel of Signs* (Wilmington, DE: Michael Glazier, 1989).

Walvoord, J., 'Revival in Rome', *BSac* 126 (1969), pp. 317-28.

Waszink, *Tertulliani De anima* (Amsterdam: Meulenhoff, 1947).

Weinsheimer, J., 'Theory of Character: Emma', *Poetics Today* 1 (1979), pp. 185-211.

Weiss, H.F.,*Der Brief an die Hebräer* (Göttingen: Vandenhoeck & Ruprecht, 1991).

Westcott, B.F., *The Gospel according to John* (London: John Murray, 1889).

Wettstein J.J., *Novum Testamentum Graecum* (Amsterdam: Dommerian, 1752, II).

Wiesner, J. (ed.), *Aristoteles: Werk und Wirkung* (FS P. Moraux; Berlin: de Gruyter, 1987), pp. 17-26.

Williams, J.G., *Women Recounted: Narrative Thinking and the God of Israel* (Bible and Literature Series, 6; Sheffield: Almond Press, 1982).

Williams, M., 'Variety in Gnostic Perspectives on Gender', in K.L. King (ed.), *Images of the Feminine in Gnosticism* (Philadelphia: Fortress Press, 1988), pp. 2-22.

Wilshire, L.E., 'The TLG Computer and Further Reference to AUYENTEV in 1 Timothy 2.12', *NTS* 34 (1988), pp. 120-34.

Windisch, H., *Der Hebräerbrief* (Tübingen: Mohr, 1913).

Wink, W., *John the Baptist in the Gospel Tradition* (SNTSMS, 7; Cambridge: Cambridge University Press, 1968).

Winston, D., *The Wisdom of Solomon* (Garden City, NY: Doubleday, 1979).

Winter, P., 'Magnificat and Benedictus: Maccabean Psalms?', *BJRL* 37 (1954), pp. 328-47.

Witherington, B., *Women and the Genesis of Christianity* (Cambridge: Cambridge University Press, 1990).

—*Women in the Earliest Churches* (SNTSMS, 59; Cambridge: Cambridge University Press, 1988).

—*Women in the Ministry of Jesus: A Study of Jesus' Attitudes to Women and their Roles as Reflected in his Earthly Life* (Cambridge: Cambridge University Press, 1984).

Wolde, E. van, *Aan de hand van Ruth* (Inaugural lecture, Tilburg; Kampen: Kok, 1993).

— *Ruth en Noömi, twee vreemdgangers* (Baarn: Ten Have, 1993).

Wünsche, A., *Aus Israels Lehrhallen* (repr.; Hildesheim: Olms, 1967[1909]), III.

Wyatt, N., '"Supposing Him to be the Gardener" (John 20, 15): A Study of the Paradise Motif in John', *ZNW* 81 (1990), pp. 21-38.

Xenophon, (trans. C.L. Brownson *et al.*; Loeb Classical Library; 7 vols.; Cambridge, MA: Harvard University Press, 1918–1967).

Yee, G.A., 'Sarah', in ABD, pp. 981-82.

Zahn, Th., *Das Evangelium des Lukas ausgelegt* (KNT, 3; Leipzig: Deichert, 4th edn, 1930 [1913]).